'WITHOUT THE LAW'

ADMINISTRATIVE JUSTICE AND LEGAL PLURALISM IN NINETEENTH-CENTURY ENGLAND

Lawyers, even those concerned with administrative law, think of law as the statutory rules and common law administered by the superior courts. But that view ignores both the evidence of history and the complex pluralism of contemporary socio-legal systems.

Arthurs examines the roots of those systems in nineteenth-century England, where a vast array of specialized courts and private tribunals administered distinctive systems of rules at a distance from, and in competition with, the courts of judges and lawyers. Of special importance were the new administrative jurisdictions that emerged between 1830 and 1870.

Social, economic, political, and professional forces transformed the formal character and institutional expression of law during this period. Arthurs argues that these changes have impoverished our view of what law is and left in their wake a narrow ideology of 'the rule of law' held both by lawyers and by citizens at large.

But a century later we still live with the legacy of a pluralistic legal system – in administrative regimes; in specialized domestic tribunals that operate in exchanges, churches, universities, and trade unions; in commercial and labour arbitration; and in networks of law communities in every circumstance of society. The 'rule of law' is no more description, no less prescription, than it ever was. But the possibilities of a distinctive administrative justice, though fully rehearsed between 1830 and 1870, are still to be realized.

H.W. ARTHURS is president of York University and former dean of Osgoode Hall Law School, York University.

H.W. ARTHURS

'Without the Law'

Administrative Justice and Legal
Pluralism in Nineteenth-Century
England

UNIVERSITY OF TORONTO PRESS
Toronto and Buffalo

© University of Toronto Press 1985
Toronto   Buffalo   London
Printed in Canada
ISBN 0-8020-5654-7

Canadian Cataloguing in Publication Data
Arthurs, H.W. (Harry William), 1935 –
'Without the law'

Bibliography: p.
Includes index.
ISBN 0-8020-5654-7

1. Administrative law – England – History – 19th
century.   2. Judicial review of administrative
acts – England – History – 19th century.   I. Title.

KD4879.A93 1985   342.42'06   C84-099139-8

Publication of this book is made possible by grants from the Social Science
Federation of Canada using funds provided by the Social Sciences and Humanities
Research Council of Canada and from the Publications Fund of the
University of Toronto Press.

'If the Commissioners cannot decide *against* the law, they can decide without it. Their oath binds them to proceed according to good conscience.'

Wm Hutton, Courts of Requests, 1787

Contents

For L.A. and E.H.A.

Preface

Anyone who has ever read or written a preface knows that it serves two purposes. First, it seeks to put the reader at ease and to introduce the major themes of the book. Second, it serves to remind the author at the end of a lengthy enterprise why it was that he began it, and enables him to tot up the credits and debits (mainly the latter) he has accumulated while on leave from the rest of his life. I will try to do both of these things at once.

I suppose I began writing this book in my first weeks as a law student, during a class in contracts. I could not understand why an arbitrator's award should be set aside by a court because it was based on a perfectly practical trade custom rather than on an unworkable rule of contract law. Nor was I much enlightened by a reviewing judge's delphic utterance that 'there can be no Alsatia where the King's writ does not run.' The possibility that people might wish to order their lives by a system of law that judges neither created nor countenanced confronted me next as a graduate student in a seminar on labour arbitration. Judicial review of arbitration awards was inevitable, but would remain problematic, contended my professor, until there appeared 'a new Mansfield' who was willing to come to terms with the modern equivalent of the old law merchant and find a way to incorporate the jurisprudence of labour arbitration into the body of the general law.

This seemed a sensible enough response to the problem of Alsatias, of enclaves with their own law and legal institutions, until I myself became a labour arbitrator. As a newly naturalized Alsatian, I experienced firsthand the infinite range of normative possibilities, the diversity of disputing processes, the intricate connections between everyday behaviour and the living law of industrial relationships – and the mischievousness of having the king's writ meander hither and yon without regard to circumstance or effect.

At the same time, as an academic public lawyer, I had constantly to confront similar fundamental assumptions about the nature of our legal system. The 'rule of law,' for example, posits that everyone is subject to the same law, law that is enacted by parliament and authoritatively expounded (and to an extent created) by the superior courts. There is no place for isolated enclaves of special law in such a legal world. The very fact that lawyers tend to equate 'administrative law' with 'the law of judicial review' shows how deep-rooted is the assumption that law is a thing external to, apart from, even poised against whatever goes on within the administration. Thus, the conceptual structure and the operational vocabulary of lawyers' 'administrative law' both assume that the king's writ must run without let or hindrance through the corridors of public power.

And to what end? As I watched law actually ruling the administration, I became less and less convinced that it ought to do so or indeed that it could do so. To follow an administrative proceeding closely and then to see its denouement in a judicial review proceeding was an exercise in disillusionment. Often, it seemed to me, the judicial review proceeding was brought for tactical advantage – to protract the proceedings, to increase costs, to deny the other party the perishable fruits of an administrative victory. This is not to deny that impressive arguments were mounted – occasionally with deep conviction – by those seeking review. What was surprising, however, was the frequency with which bizarre or spurious challenges proved successful.

Moreover, while the basic justification of judicial review was that it protected citizens against administrative abuse, it appeared that some citizens were more likely to be protected than others. Corporations (or, on occasion, well-organized groups such as trade unions) triumphed over the administration more often than welfare claimants, prisoners, or immigrants. Even worse, when the administration was very much on the side of ordinary citizens, protecting their rights as consumers, workers, or members of victimized minorities, it still managed to lose cases it could as easily have won.

Was this because judges were gullible or guilty of illicit biases against the administration? Occasionally, I concluded, decisions could only be explained on that basis. But as a general rule, judges were simply overcome by the intrinsic difficulty of their assigned task. They were asked to interpret an entire administrative regime – public policy, rules, customs, social dynamic, scientific or technical facts, historical experience, tacit assumptions, argot and all – on the basis of a few hours' exposure to a limited legal issue. As well try to reconstruct the whole of an ancient civilization – or an Alsatia – by glancing at a shard of pottery.

Nor, I came to feel, were judges unaware of their invidious position. The best of them seemed to accept that they would often be making decisions whose implications they could never imagine, and they worked warily and with restraint. Others sought to inform themselves as fully as possible of the administrative context, although their ability to do so was limited by various institutional, procedural, and evidentiary constraints. But too many simply decided that what they could not do, they need not do. If the administration could not be understood in its own terms, it would simply be made to conform to law. The king's writ, after all, recognized no Alsatias.

By the same token, however, it was by no means clear that Alsatia always recognized the king's writ. Sometimes, it is true, administrative regimes devoted to important public purposes were frustrated, inhibited, and intimidated by reviewing courts. But in many instances the effects of judicial review were either dispelled by subsequent amending legislation or obfuscatory manoeuvres or allowed to spend themselves in single instances without affecting the ongoing activity of the administration. The royal writ might occasionally command, but it could not regularly control. I should have thought that its randomness, incoherence, and occasional egregious effects would have persuaded most observers that judicial review was a bad idea, or at best a good one incapable of practical application. Alas, there seemed to be more and more support for Alsatia-bashing.

This support was based on two quite different premises. First, judicial review was said to be required as a matter of constitutional tradition and principle. Second, it was seen as a practical antidote to administrative misbehaviour. When I began this book, it was to test both of these propositions against the evidence of history. If administrative autonomy was indeed accepted at some relatively recent date, we might at least be able to evaluate it on its merits rather than exercising constitutional closure on the subject. And if we were able to view the growth and development of administrative law in a longer perspective, we might be better able to understand its causes and to prescribe appropriate cures for its ills.

This is how I began, then: a lawyer in search of Alsatia, with history as my guide and the rule of law as a landmark looming always over my shoulder. Like the Victorian adventurers who set out to find the headwaters of the Nile and ended up 'discovering' the heart of an unknown continent, I soon realized that I had embarked on a more daunting task than I had imagined. History, of course, was not a guide; it was a series of ill-defined pathways, of hypotheses and explanations, most of which had not been explored previously by someone with my particular objectives. Far from pursuing a straightforward narrative, I found myself scratching for facts, hacking through interpretations, groping toward significance.

I wanted to find the answer to a difficult question. Must administrative law – the characteristic and ubiquitous form of social ordering in modern, industrial societies – indeed be seen as a thing apart from 'law'? If not, what of the other manifestations of law that are also denied that label by lawyers and judges? It soon became clear that I confronted a definitional problem – what would I call this 'non-law'? – and that anthropologists and sociologists would be of more help to me than lawyers in giving form and name to the phenomenon. They, after all, had no vested interest in making 'law' coincide with their own intellectual monopoly and ideological presuppositions. Or so I thought; I later found otherwise.

This is not to say that social scientists are insensitive to either the intellectual structures or the ideology of law. On the contrary, the literature endlessly debates the extent to which and the means by which law is determined by, or determines, social events; it explores the mystifying potential of ideology and its limits; it offers structures that typify and distinguish events, their causes and effects. But lawyers and social scientists apparently inhabit different universes of discourse. The unexplored assumptions of lawyers preoccupy social scientists. Yet the cut and thrust of debates on law's 'superstructure,' on 'semi-autonomous social fields,' on 'transformation' and 'articulation theory,' seldom engages lawyers as participants or attracts them as spectators. Even history, which seems to share with law an affinity for the past as a way of understanding the present, does not address law very often, nor is it addressed by lawyers. Nineteenth-century histories – of local governments, of businesses, of public administration, of social and political movements – by and large ignore both the formal legal system and its administrative, local, or indigenous counterparts. And 'legal' histories only recently have discovered nineteenth-century society.

In short, the historical route may have been the wrong one, given my particular destination. It required me to make an extensive detour through the terra incognita of the 'other' legal systems of Victorian England, and to converse in strange tongues with the inhabitants of another time and place. But in the end the journey proved to be more important than the destination. I have glimpsed Alsatia, I believe, but it was much less memorable than what I saw en route. What follows is a journal of my observations.

Non-legal readers will perhaps smile condescendingly (some already have) at this naïve and atheoretical account of how and why I came to write this book. Legal readers may be too courteous to condescend, but may be equally dubious (some already are) about its thesis. It is asking a lot of lawyers to suggest that they immerse themselves in a legal history that speaks of yesterday – and perhaps a tomorrow – 'without the law.' Readers of every stripe and persuasion are, of course, entitled to their prejudices. I ask only for a suspension of disbelief lasting long enough to give this book a fair read. And I promise in return that the mystery of Alsatia will be revealed in due course.

Acknowledgments

Like most explorations, the writing of a book is necessarily a solitary enterprise. It is therefore surprising to reflect upon the extent of my debt to the many people and organizations who have made its completion possible. The Social Sciences and Humanities Research Council of Canada provided support throughout. The Socio-Legal Centre at Oxford extended its hospitality to me during the critical initial period of my research in 1977–8. That same year Osgoode Hall Law School of York University permitted me to take sabbatical leave, and in 1982 I was given several months of research leave in which to complete this book. Two Osgoode deans, Stanley Beck and John McCamus, successively extended their personal support throughout the long period since I first began my labours.

Numerous research assistants have contributed to the foundation of notes upon which the edifice of the book sits. In the manner of those who laboured on medieval cathedrals (perhaps the metaphor is over-taxed), most of them will remain anonymous, although their work is much appreciated. Three, however, must be mentioned: Heather Leonoff, who initially reconnoitered many of the primary sources; Jess Bush, who undertook most of the work of checking citations; and Lois Gottlieb, who saw the manuscript through its final revision. Susan Gallaugher bore the awful burden of typing and correcting drafts for almost two years.

Various friends commented on earlier versions of the book with intimidating insight and candour: Robert Stevens, Paul Weiler, Paul Craig, Liora Salter, and Doug Hay. Knowingly or otherwise, several others made a difference at crucial moments: Jeffrey Jowell, William Twining, David Sugarman, and Jerry Auerbach, whose fine book *Justice Without Law?* appeared just as I completed my manuscript. And Hans Mohr, who does not recognize any limits to friendship, gave me warm encouragement and thoughtful advice at each step along the way. To all of these I record my thanks while, in the usual way, absolving them of any responsibility for my own sins of omission, commission, or hyperbole.

In recording various debts, I have so far omitted my most obvious creditors: Penny, Joshua, and Gideon Arthurs. In their case, my debt must be calculated in a different currency, for they did not actually help with the book itself. But they did give me what I needed most. First, they provided a bracing scepticism: despite my stated conclusions, they always implied that legal centralism must indeed be my ruling passion. And they made contrapuntal music: the buzz and business of the house reminded me that one does not live by books alone. Above all, they gave me reasons for wanting to write this book: they are my source of love and hope, which make life and work worthwhile.

'WITHOUT THE LAW'

ADMINISTRATIVE JUSTICE AND LEGAL PLURALISM
IN NINETEENTH-CENTURY ENGLAND

1

Paradigms of Law

Nothing just happens. Legal institutions and ideas do not simply emerge, evolve, reshape themselves, deteriorate, or disappear of their own accord. At one time, perhaps, we believed that our legal system was created by a divine hand, or had evolved in the course of the inevitable and unceasing ascent of civilization. Today we generally accept that legal development is the product of many forces – some internal, some external; some intellectual, some socio-economic; some ancient, some recent. The tasks of the historian are to try to identify and assess those forces and to chronicle their effects.

Yet our ability to 'identify' depends upon the categories or labels we have available to apply to events, and our capacity to 'assess' those events depends upon the intellectual tools with which we attempt to do the job. Happily, as Robert Gordon reminds us,[1] history has a way of forcing us to reconsider our paradigms, the assumptions and intellectual structures upon which our analysis and actions are based.

The basic paradigm, the central assumption, the crucial structure that dominates the way most lawyers, judges, law professors – even most people – think about law is this: law is formal; it exists as a thing apart from society, politics, or economics; law has the capacity to achieve, and does achieve, results by encouraging or discouraging behaviour, by attaching specified consequences to behaviour that facilitate it, deter it or undo its harmful effects; law is made and administered by the state; and access to law is provided in courts by legal professionals – lawyers and judges – who invoke a body of authoritative learning in order to argue and decide cases.

To illustrate these notions by commonplace examples, it can be said that law encourages the performance of contracts or protects the sanctity of life by giving damages or imposing severe penalties. Law is made by judges in one case and by the legislature in the other, but in both cases it can only be ascertained, and must be invoked, by those who are learned in the law. When law is invoked, the power of the state is mobilized to accomplish law's purposes: the aggrieved contracting party is made whole, the murderer is sent to prison. Throughout society, contractual obligations and personal security are thus reinforced.

Each step in this analysis, which crudely approximates the way most of us think about law, rests upon the assumption that law lies at the centre of events. Law is neutral – unsullied by close identification with contending interests or classes or political philosophies – yet it engages the power and prestige of the state. Law commands, people obey, and the course of future events is fixed. Law is knowledge, and that knowledge is disseminated by those who understand it best to those who understand it least. Not without reason has this paradigm of law been identified as 'legal centralism.'[2]

If our point of departure were a more general concern to understand society, we would be less likely to place law at the centre of the universe. After all, one of the ambitions of social science is to accommodate all events or phenomena with common characteristics within the same explanatory theory. Indeed, the over- or underreach of a theory can be demonstrated by showing that not all events it purports to explain are explained by it, or that others it does not address are fundamentally similar to those it does. So with 'law.' The formal or centralist paradigm fails to explain why law-like patterns of social behaviour occur even though they lack some of the apparently essential characteristics of formal law. Nor does the paradigm take account of the frequent inability of formal law to achieve the results it is designed to achieve.

Thus, social scientists have not hesitated to propose new definitions of law which at least link it to other apparently similar phenomena. For example, it has been proposed that law consists 'primarily of rules by which persons in society order their conduct, and only secondarily of "norms for decision" developed by the courts and of legislation enacted by the state.'[3] Some of those rules are found in statute books and law reports, to be sure, but others are the often unwritten yet well-understood codes defining standards of behaviour in industrial enterprises and business transactions, among neighbours, and within universities, churches, or public bureaucracies.

If this is what law is, it follows that it must be closely intertwined with the purposes of both the state and the groups or institutions that produce and consume it. Thus, we can no longer ignore its economic function, its political content, or its social effects. Nor can we fail to address the ongoing processes by which different manifestations of law come into existence, shape and are given shape by events, and interact with each other. And finally, we must accept that law is much more diverse in its content, causes, and effects than our original paradigm proposed. This new way of looking at law we may therefore call 'legal pluralism.'

Here, then, we have two paradigms of law, the formal or centralist and the pluralist. But by identifying two different paradigms of 'law' we have created a basic confusion about what we mean when we use the word. Now we confront a problem of translation, as we move back and forth from the language of courts and lawyers to the language of social scientists. It is clear – unless our paradigms are quite misconceived – that the two groups do not inhabit the same universe of discourse.

To the lawyer, the very idea of legal pluralism is a contradiction in terms: there can be no 'law' that the state does not either create or at least formally recognize; whatever law-like rules may be found elsewhere, they must be given some other name – customs, conventions, or understandings, for example – to avoid confusion with real 'law.' But this understandable insistence upon terminological clarity has an important by-product. It preserves for 'law' in the lawyers' sense all of the evocative magic the word has acquired – majesty, mystery, authority, justice, rationality. And it relegates 'law' in the social scientists' sense to a nether world of qualifying adjectives and unnatural synonyms: indigenous, imbricated, or informal law, systems of social control, reglementation, normative systems, or folkways. Law by any other name does not, in our culture, smell half so sweet.

To the social scientist no less than to the lawyer terminological clarity is important. Thus, he will sensibly wish to define 'law,' with its immense wealth of secondary significance, to include the many different phenomena that partake of that significance. Having done so, he will not hesitate to create a subcategory for 'lawyers' law,' whose label emphasizes its limited nature: positive, state, formal, or exogenous law, or some other term that will inevitably grate upon lawyers.

The issue of what is 'law' in turn serves as a proxy for a much more complicated issue. Paradigms are drawn from life and are descriptive (or misdescriptive) of it. But the aspects of life to which lawyers and social scientists respectively refer are very different. In the case of lawyers, one is tempted to say that the boundaries of their own experience define the paradigm of law. Litigants come to judges for adjudication of their disputes, and clients to lawyers for advice, planning, or advocacy on the basis of 'the rules' of common and statute law. Those rules become both the touchstone of lawyers' work and, for them, the organizing theme of 'law.'

There is an irony here, however: often what the litigant or client wants is a result apart from or contrary to the rules; and sometimes his 'problem' will not be the legal rule at all, but the strategy of invoking it, or the choice of the most attractive course of action among the many permitted by the rule. Lawyers (and judges) must surely be aware of the scope of their activities, at least subconsciously, and they must know that there is more to law than 'law.' They themselves are often the authors of corporate structures, contractual regimes, informal understandings between disputing parties, and other private arrangements that operate upon behaviour more immediately than formal codes or case law. Nor are they strangers to aggressiveness, intransigence, negotiation, mediation, arbitration, domestic adjudication, or political devices such as voting or the organizing of consensus, which round out the repertoire of dispute-settling arrangements encountered in organizations, groups, and less formal business or social networks. Nor, to reveal finally the true scope of their knowledge, can they be unaware that few human interactions generate disputes; that most disputes never see the inside of a law office or courtroom; and that parties usually vindicate, compromise, or abandon their claims without reference to 'law' at all.

How, then, does it happen that lawyers, who at some level must know as much as social scientists, resolutely refuse to adopt a definition – and a paradigm – of law that adequately accommodates what they know and what they do? The answer to this question takes us rather far afield. One can understand that lawyers' expertise in the formal rules and their manipulation makes the centralist paradigm particularly attractive to them. It provides a basis for their monopoly over 'legal' services and for the economic and psychic rewards of that monopoly. Moreover, the centralist paradigm has become part of the general culture. Law and lawyers, law and courts, law and legislation – these associations spring immediately to mind and are reflected in school texts, novels, newspaper editorials, and popular speech. These associations reinforce the lawyers' own predictable view of themselves as indispensable actors within the centralist paradigm.

But this paradigm does not exist only in professional self-portraits or as a cultural construct. A concerted effort has been made to ensure that life should imitate art, that the centralist paradigm should be enshrined in the rules of positive law, that pluralism should be suppressed. The general implications of this effort will be addressed in more detail in the concluding chapters of this book. In a preliminary, way, however, consider the case of public law as it discloses how pervasively lawyers' assumptions about law have come to dominate law itself.

At least since Dicey propounded his classic statement of 'the rule of law' a century ago[4] – but in earlier times as well – lawyers have sought to equate the public interest with law, and law with their own particular form of professional knowledge. 'Ordinary' law and 'ordinary' courts, argued Dicey, safeguard the rights of Englishmen against arbitrary official action. As he subsequently contended in *Law and Public Opinion*, arbitrary official action was a particular manifestation of the rise of collectivism which was itself contrary to the earlier individualist tendencies that had made England great.[5]

One need not dwell upon the extent to which Dicey's critics have demolished his logic and falsified his evidence; one need not trace the development of more sophisticated versions of his thesis by successive generations of legal scholars.[6] It is sufficient at this juncture to remind ourselves of the grip his version of the rule of law continues to have upon judges and lawyers. To this very day, prominent jurists explicitly[7] or by inference[8] echo Dicey's views, legislators rely upon them as a blueprint for the design of administrative regimes,[9] professional audiences can safely be expected to applaud them,[10] and legal scholars to derive inspiration from them.[11] Dicey and his rule of law have acquired, within and beyond legal circles, a transcendent, a symbolic significance.

What lies at the heart of Dicey's rule of law is a series of interrelated assumptions that largely reflect the paradigm of legal centralism with which we began. Law is what lawyers and judges do, not what happens elsewhere in society – and especially not what happens in the operations of modern government.[12] Law is both purposeful and benign, and can effectively vindicate both individual rights and contemporary social values. Law is neither immutable nor, at any given moment, free of internal inconsistencies; but it tends toward harmony, with public opinion exercising a magnetic attraction.

None the less, at one point Dicey did acknowledge a fact that is potentially disturbing to the legal centralist paradigm. Noting that parliament was the supreme source of law, he identified the existence of 'cross-currents' of judicial opinion which, as a practical matter, might revise or divert the intended impact of legislation.[13] Although Dicey did not do so, it is possible to extrapolate from his commonplace and uncontroversial observation in order to identify 'cross-currents' emanating from other sources, and other flaws in the cohesion and symmetry of 'the law.' But at least we do see in Dicey some recognition of judicial ideology as a thing apart from law, if not crudely linked to political philosophy or class interest then at least rooted in a distinctive professional world-view.

Consider this world-view in greater detail as it is revealed in the vocabulary and concepts of administrative law. For most lawyers, administrative law is not the law *of* the administration; it is the law directed *against* the administration, the law by which reviewing judges ensure that the administration does not overreach. Indeed, Dicey and his disciple, Lord Hewart, were at some pains to deny the existence of administrative law in the former sense.[14] In the latter sense, what does administrative law seek to accomplish? In essence, it attempts to make the administration conform to the paradigm of legal centralism and to suppress tendencies toward legal pluralism. The administration must observe the principles of 'natural justice' or 'fairness'; the courts are fair and their justice 'natural'; it follows that administrative procedures will be measured by conventions of judicial deportment. The administration must act intra vires, and errors of 'law' will be corrected by reviewing courts; 'law' is of course the law of the courts themselves – the presumptions and interpretative rules by which empowering statutes are construed, the analogies and analytical habits by which decisions are conventionally reached, and the attitudes toward individual, collective, and state action that are immanent in several hundred years of precedent.[15]

Why would reviewing courts insist on substituting their view of law for that of the administration? The answer is again implicit in the vocabulary. Review is the task of 'superior' courts; administrative bodies are 'inferior' tribunals; the two exist in a hierarchical relationship whose ultimate justification can only be to ensure deference by the lower orders to the world-view of the higher.[16] But while the superior / inferior dichotomy may be explained in terms of the origins of judicial review, and especially curial supervision of local justices administering criminal law, it does not necessarily correspond to the relative social importance of the two levels.[17] 'Inferior' administrative tribunals, after all, often have major social responsibilities, such as fixing rate structures, resolving labour disputes affecting thousands of workers, or balancing the economic gains and environmental costs of developmental proposals that would dwarf the ancient wonders of the world. 'Superior' courts, by contrast, are often preoccupied with processing undefended divorces or contract claims or allocating losses as between two automobile insurance companies.

What can be the connection between the law of the courts and the law of the administration? The two do not share personnel, techniques of finding facts and resolving disputes, norms of decision or, often, ultimate socioeconomic or political premises. Yet such is the power of the paradigm that the two are linked in the same structure, and the larger in life becomes the lesser in 'law.'

Nor is this link, this subordination of life to law, easily broken. Legislatures have sometimes attempted to confer upon administrative bodies a considerable degree of autonomy by clauses that are called 'preclusive' or 'privative' – but not 'protective.' The terminology is again instructive: the clauses are pejoratively labelled because they seek to preclude review or deprive courts of the superordinate role they enjoy in accordance with the professional, centralist paradigm of law; they are not portrayed in the jargon of the profession as protecting the distinctiveness of valuable administrative institutions. Nor is the force of the paradigm spent in dismissive labels. It extends to the courts' interpretation and application of such clauses. While the courts' own jurisdiction is implicit, inherent, self-proclaimed, and apparently limitless, the jurisdiction of a body protected by a privative clause is – and will only be presumed to be – explicit, extraordinary, legislatively imposed, and limited. Indeed, lest the legislature be tempted to revise these 'legal' presumptions by language too clear for judicial reconstruction, superior court review of administrative decisions has been accorded virtually constitutional guarantees.[18]

It may be argued that this description of the basic assumptions of administrative law is overdrawn in at least two respects. First, to whatever extent the 'law' enjoys a central and controlling function, it does so not as a result of professional self-aggrandizement but as a consequence of a slow, constitutional evolution toward Dicey's 'rule of law,' an evolution that could have occurred only if it enjoyed the support or acquiescence of a broad spectrum of public and political opinion. Second, and more fundamentally, the example of administrative law does not in fact challenge the legal centralist paradigm, since the administration itself, no less than the courts, is part of the system of state law. Each of these arguments deserves serious consideration.

It would be possible to explore them in the context of a description of our modern legal system, or in the course of adumbrating a general theory of legal pluralism. There is, indeed, a considerable body of recent empirical[19] and theoretical[20] literature that proceeds on this basis. However, history also offers us a way to revise our paradigms, to reinterpret what we 'know'; we will therefore examine certain historical evidence in order to evaluate the special role of legal professionals and the special instance of administrative law in the dialectic between centralism and pluralism. Specifically, we will consider three important episodes in mid-nineteenth-century England – the abolition of courts of local and special jurisdiction, the efforts to create special tribunals for the adjudication of commercial disputes, and the emergence of administrative tribunals and techniques. Both the moment in time and the particular examples of legal change are of special significance.

Why the mid-nineteenth century? As is well known, the industrial revolution wrought profound changes in the fabric of English life – in its economy, demography, social attitudes and behaviour, and, of course, in its politics, law, and government. Lawrence Friedman has suggested that 'in Western societies ... one can isolate one very broad, very important master trend in the development of legal systems over the past two or three centuries. This is the development of a single legal culture out of a pluralistic system.'[21] This development is precisely the one that has given rise to the legal centralist paradigm. If there was a period when it ought to have been visible, it must surely have been when English law was becoming self-consciously 'Western,' using that term, as Friedman does, to connote 'modern,' 'rational,' or 'scientific.' That period, for reasons I hope to explain, extended into the middle decades of the nineteenth century.

And why these particular examples? The reason for looking at administrative innovation and growth is obvious enough: modern administration began with the early Victorian period, and by, say, 1870 all of its important features had become apparent. From an examination of these developments, we will see that administrative law – in the broadest sense – is not derived from the 'law' of the courts and lawyers, but developed at a conscious distance from it and as a reaction to its inadequacies and failures. Moreover, by looking at the active systems of local and special courts and at the ubiquitous experience of commercial adjudication outside the superior courts, we can begin to understand that pluralism, even at that late date, was well entrenched in the English legal system.

Centuries of experience with special jurisdictions, special tribunals, special law, and special procedures for special constituencies provide much compelling evidence for the pluralist paradigm. It must be said, however, that in the debate over the new administrative regimes in the mid-nineteenth century, neither the historical nor the contemporaneous experience of pluralism was often referred to. Yet the parallels cannot have been far from the minds of lawyers. The three episodes to be examined reveal a common pattern of professional hostility, of attempts to suppress or at least capture the 'non-legal' systems, and of subsequent borrowing from them by the lawyers who had opposed them so resolutely.

What does this pattern of professional response tell us about the role of lawyers and judges in shaping the legal system? It is no part of the pluralist hypothesis to deny that legal professionals were highly influential, especially in matters that were perceived to lie within the ambit of their special knowledge and experience. During this period, judges and barristers enjoyed considerable prestige in political and social circles. Solicitors and attorneys performed important facilitating roles as managers, advisers, and lobbyists. Crown law officers and others with legal training found themselves in key roles when called upon to draft, interpret, or administer legislation. In these ways, lawyers had the opportunity to influence general public and political attitudes, to mould subtly the content of the law, and to shape its institutions. We simply cannot assume that legal centralism emerged *consensu omnium* and without the active intervention of its foremost proponents, the lawyers.

And what of our second reservation about the pertinence of the rise of administrative law to the pluralist paradigm? Can we properly argue that the experience of local and special courts and commercial arbitration tribunals during the nineteenth century was related to that of administrative institutions? Obviously, the former operated in the realm of private disputes, the latter in the arena of public policy. But from the perspective of what they tell us about law, there is an important element of continuity and commonality. Weber, for example, recorded the passing of 'étatist or other special courts and procedures' (which would include some of the older and more exotic local and special courts). But in the same breath he insisted that 'neither all special and personal law nor all special jurisdictions have disappeared completely. On the contrary, very recent developments have brought an increasing specialization within the legal system.' Exemplifying these developments, he cites the rise of commercial and administrative tribunals.[22] For Weber, then, the dichotomy between public and private – indeed between the old and the new forms of pluralism – was not for all purposes complete.

At a minimum, all three episodes in the development of the English legal system present for study the concept of specialization, its changing manifestations, and its implications for the centralist or pluralist character of that system. Since specialization is arguably at least one of the indicia of legal pluralism, it is not premature to say that it involves more than nice variations of procedure or even rather different techniques of disposing of disputes. If both the administration and the courts were advancing similar interests and similar policies, their divergent methods of doing so might be a less than cogent basis for distinguishing between them. But the administration and the courts, then as now, often worked at cross-purposes. Where one sought to protect consumers and passengers and workers, the other was at best indifferent and at worst solicitous only of property and its prerogatives. And when the ultimate interests of administrators and legal professionals seemed least likely to collide – neither, after all, had much to lose by draconian interpretation and application of the Poor Laws – they were often locked in factional combat over issues of patronage or pecking order.

When we turn to commercial disputes, we might expect to find a closer affinity between the interests of legal professionals and their potentially most important clients, the expansive and aggressive business interests of the new industrial age. What do we find? As individuals, lawyers no doubt assisted in facilitating the growth and organization of business. But, as Weber remarks, '[I]t may indeed be said that England achieved capitalistic supremacy among the nations not because but rather in spite of its judicial system.'[23] That this view was shared by businessmen of the period is amply evidenced by their tendency to take their legal business elsewhere. The growth of 'elsewheres' is, in the plainest terms, a challenge to Friedman's thesis.

Not so the experience of courts of local and special jurisdiction. By mid-century these had been replaced by a new system of county courts – evidence itself, in Friedman's phrase, of 'a growing tendency for the legal system of the capital ... or its ruling class, to extend its reign deeper down in the population ...'[24] Yet even here the picture is far from clear. As we will see, the 'ruling class' of businessmen who stood to benefit from a more efficient system of local courts sought, in league with Benthamite reformers, to keep those courts effectively free of law and lawyers, of 'the legal system of the capital.' That they did not prevail reminds us again of the power of the legal centralist paradigm.

As our narrative unfolds, then, we must watch for the subtle interplay of influence and ideology among administrators, legal professionals, and business interests, none of which, of course, was a homogeneous group. But although we will see significant changes in each of the areas of our study between, say, 1830 and 1870, we will not be able to detect a change in the direction of legal centralism. Friedman's 'master trend' will, at least at this period, remain more obscure than we might have expected.

Obscurity, in a sense, is inevitable. Paradigms, models, and trends are metaphors: they attempt to capture a complex and contradictory reality in a simple construct or phrase. So too with legal centralism and legal pluralism. These two paradigms – metaphors – offer different ways of describing the legal system; they do not purport to explain how it came about. There is some connection between description and explanation, of course, but the two are not synonymous. The limits of imagination are often fixed by the basic assumptions we make when we approach a subject. For example, if we can conceive of only one 'legitimate' mode of decision-making, we will tend to replicate it in all situations. If we accept that only professionals can cope with 'law,' we will unthinkingly make it impossible for others to do so. However, this is not to claim that our ideas of law alone give shape to legal institutions or define the relationship of laymen to them. On the contrary, it is clear that to the extent that questions of institutional design or professional monopoly are implicated in broader issues of social policy, the power of the paradigm is weakened.

This is an important qualification in the context of administrative law. Our historical account of the growth of administrative law will show how non-curial institutional forms emerged and how non-adjudicative techniques evolved in part because magistrates and courts proved reluctant or undependable agents of new public policies; moral imperatives and political initiatives struggled with traditional legal forms. Similarly, opposition to those public policies frequently was couched in terms of hostility to the institutions chosen to advance them. Specific objection was taken to any attempt to give 'legal' powers to those who were not magistrates or judges. Was this legal centralism asserting itself? Or was the issue of institutional form disingenuously used as to mask the real objective – a desire to render the new public policies as innocuous as possible? Law, we will see, was not merely an ideology that commanded the respect of both professionals and everyone else, an ideal to which all aspired. It was also a means of advancing and legitimating political positions and of mystifying and concealing the very existence of those positions.

Paradoxically, we will also see that the early administrators learned that when a legal system does not exist it may be necessary to invent one. In many of the new regulatory regimes self-generated procedural standards, quasi-legislative techniques ensuring consistent decision-making, and ingenious sanctions began to produce a kind of mimicry of law, a mimicry that often had a greater ring of truth than the 'real' legal system. Law in the larger sense (rather than in the lawyers' sense) seems after all to have had much to contribute to administration. So it did, too, to all manner of business and social relationships, although we must not for that reason romanticize it.

Of course, the law that emerged in administration, in business, and in other contexts was neither intrinsically benign nor intrinsically oppressive, if indeed it is possible to think of such terms apart from the different perspectives of those actually affected. Administrative law as it materialized in the edicts of the Poor Law commissioners was a device for the deliberate infliction of pain upon the needy. Yet had those it abused found themselves aboard an emigrant ship rather than in the workhouse, they would have owed their minimal comforts, their precarious conditions of health, their very lives, to another body of Victorian administrators, the emigration officers. So too with other bodies of 'law' that emerged outside the formal system: the surgeon or the unpaid seaman who used his local court in Bristol as a collection agency may have counted it among the blessings of civic government, while overextended tradesmen pressed for payment by their suppliers may have cursed the same court for its indecorous efficiency. The members of commodity exchanges and other organized industries placed great stress upon the evils of conventional litigation and the irrelevance of common-law doctrine. Did their customers feel the same way when they sought recovery against a broker before a tribunal of his fellow exchange members on the basis of trading rules designed to favour members?

So we cannot ultimately escape the relentless logic of interest, of power, of political perspective – not by taking refuge in the law of the land, not by seeking sanctuary in the enclaves of special law. This much is conceded. But interest may be diluted by the paternalism or professionalism of judges, by power mediated through constraining legal forms, by politics briefly suspended by the temporary equilibriums of legislative compromise. And what is left is law, however we write it and wherever we find it.

Ultimately, then, this book is as much about law as about history. It is, for better or worse, a characteristically lawyerly inquiry – the scrutiny of the title documents, as it were, upon which the claims of a particular (but predominant) view of the legal system rest. This view, the centralist view, claims to describe the way law has 'always' been and to prescribe how it must be now and for the future, or at least until we abandon the values of the rule of law. By offering a new account of how law 'always' was – the pluralist view – I hope to prompt reconsideration of the questions of what law looks like today and what it ought to look like. At the same time, I realize that the use of paradigms or metaphors raises questions of causation, although it does not necessarily bring them into focus. One cannot use terms such as 'centralism' and 'pluralism' without conjuring up opposing visions of the formative forces in law. The one term emphasizes the consolidation and integration of state, economy, law and professionalism; the other emphasizes divergencies and contradictions among and within them.

These formative forces obviously operate within the deep structure of our historical narrative; but, to forewarn the reader, they will not all be recorded with seismographic completeness and precision. Others are already attempting this important enterprise.[25] Our primary concern will be to trace the surface effects of these forces as they become visible in the design and operation of the legal system of mid-Victorian England. This study of effects will tell us something about causes, of course; it will also enable us to view our own legal system in a new and clearer light.

2

Civil Justice in England 1830–1850: The Attack on Pluralism

INTRODUCTION

If we are to use the pluralist paradigm as a way of understanding the legal system of nineteenth-century England – and that of today – some hard questions must be asked and answered. Was the English legal system ever really pluralistic? If so, when and how did it change? Why? And with what significance for our understanding of the development of administrative law in particular and of our legal system in general? We will shortly turn to and pursue at length the first of these questions, which is essentially a factual enquiry. We cannot fail, however, to note the presence of the difficult threshold issue identified in the last chapter: what do we mean by 'law'? This issue presents itself at every turn.

For example, what would we regard as 'evidence' of pluralism, and where would we go to find it? When we seek to describe formal legal institutions and their activities – superior courts deciding cases and legislatures enacting statutes – the task is made somewhat easier by the availability of documentation. However, to the extent that we want to learn about other, more ephemeral or informal legal institutions, the absence of law reports, Hansards, or even rudimentary records make investigation much more difficult.[1] As we shall see, the very fact that a tribunal was considered important enough to be denominated a court of record caused it to be at once assimilated to the central legal system and capable of being historically reconstructed through official archives. However, most manifestations of legal pluralism, including some dealt with in this book, did not involve courts of record; as a result, their activities are extremely difficult to document. Nor has the difficulty been alleviated by studies of businesses or local governments written by historians from a non-legal perspective. Reading such studies – and there are hundreds of them – one can only conclude that law did not exist as a significant presence in social and commercial relationships in nineteenth-century England.

This conclusion may be inconvenient for a specialist researcher and should at least be chastening to adherents of legal centralism. But it seems to have raised few problems in the minds of social or economic historians. Is it possible that, once again, we have encountered a serious problem of translation? On the one side, 'law' spoken in the solemn tones of legal professionals may seldom have intruded upon commercial transactions or neighbourhood affairs. On the other, all social intercourse may be seen to have taken place within and given rise to law that was so familiar to those involved as to be virtually invisible. Law in this broad, pluralist sense bears the same relationship to formal law as conversational speech does to literature. Like speech, it is both ephemeral and pervasive, but it is conventionally and conveniently disregarded by historians. Yet if we could recover speech – and law in the pluralistic sense – we could reconstruct the social history of everyday life in a way that is quite impossible when we are limited to official sources and studies of formal institutions.

These disparities in the availability of historical evidence tend to skew our perception of how things were, and this tendency is exaggerated by a special problem of legal history: it is often written by lawyers. Treating legal history as a history of 'law,' they often seem to accept the legal centralist paradigm implicit in the way lawyers see 'law.' This sometimes results in their deliberate refusal to consider normative and adjudicative systems that did not emanate from the legislature or the courts. Thus, Holdsworth tells us that apart from petty criminal matters, 'practically all the judicial work of the country' was done by the judges of the superior courts in the early nineteenth century.[2] Thus, Atiyah's masterly work on the historical development of contract law[3] does not take into account the work of either arbitrators or local courts, whose extensive activities were almost entirely concerned with the adjudication of contract disputes. If we begin our search for the origins of administrative law believing that Holdsworth's statement and Atiyah's silence accurately portray the English legal system of the period, we might well be travelling in the wrong direction. But if we are prepared to accept, at least tentatively, that civil adjudication in nineteenth-century England was shared among a myriad of special tribunals administering special law for special groups, the emergence of administrative law might be seen as a logical development of the state of the art rather than as a surprising intrusion upon the adjudicative monopoly of the superior courts.[4]

To be sure, we would still have to speculate upon the relative significance of the various influences that prompted this development and gave it specific shape and content; this will be done in later chapters. But a more accurate and less neat picture of the legal system of the period would at least be a beginning, and would help us to revise our notions of 'law' as a preface to understanding the emergence of one particular subsystem, 'administrative law.'

It is convenient to begin our description around 1830. By this time the industrial revolution was well under way. Its pervasive effects were beginning to be understood, and new patterns of political, economic, social, and intellectual life were emerging. But older institutional forms still persisted in local and national governments, in business organizations, in land tenure and agriculture, and of course in law. Over the next forty years or so these older forms were largely displaced by new institutions which from our perspective, one hundred years later, have become so familiar that we (sometimes wrongly) assume they are conventional, traditional, or even consecrated by constitutional custom. Parliamentary democracy, local councils, the limited-liability business corporation, and freehold tenure were all invented long before 1830, but they had acquired new meaning through expansion and reform by 1870.

For the English legal system, particularly, these were years of profound and far-reaching change. In 1828, Lord Brougham, sustained by sucking oranges, made his famous six-hour *tour d'horizon* of law reform. By 1873, the enactment of the Judicature Acts could be seen as but one significant episode in a continuous process of court reform. In 1833, the central government took its first halting steps toward effective administrative adjudication by establishing the factory inspectorate. By 1873, a railway and canal commision had been established with the powers of a superior court; it proved to be the prototype of the modern independent regulatory commission. Most significant for present purposes, the vast armada of local and special courts that largely comprised the English legal system in 1830 was replaced by a new national fleet of county courts in 1846, and was securely anchored within the safe harbour of the common law, at least from the 1850s onward.

The replacement of local and special jurisdictions with a national system of county courts warrants examination for two reasons. First, the existence of such jurisdictions had provided a legitimating precedent, or at least a congenial environment, for the newly emerging administrative tribunals of the 1830s. If towns, occupational groups, and even social classes could have their own special courts and special laws, it is not surprising that the new special-interest functions of regulating factories, public health, and poverty should be dealt with by special laws administered by special tribunals. Second, the suppression of the old special courts and special laws during the mid-nineteenth century presented many of the issues that would come to be debated as the new administrative tribunals struggled to define their relationship with the central, formal legal system. At issue in both cases was pluralism – the tolerance of English law for many forms of dispute settlement, for a multiplicity of normative systems, for the sharing-out of authority beyond the ranks of the legal profession.

So much for significance. Let us now turn to evidence.

LEGAL PLURALISM IN 1830

Reference has been made to Holdsworth's assertion that the superior courts had secured a virtual monopoly of civil adjudication by the early nineteenth century. What did the superior courts look like in 1830, and how had they changed by 1870?

The superior courts – Common Pleas, King's Bench, Equity, and Exchequer – were the product of historical development; no master hand shaped them or defined their obscure boundaries. We know from contemporary criticisms and from literary and other sources that their procedures were regarded as cumbersome, over-technical, and slow.[5] Here is the evidence of a successful litigant, who presumably had no reason to be uncharitable to the superior courts:

At the last Warwick Assizes [1827], I brought an action for £25. It was defended: six witnesses, besides the respective attorneys and parties, attended five days: I obtained a verdict: my costs to the defendant were £66, and probably his own costs due to his attorney would be an additional sum of £50; thus the original debt in dispute was more than quadrupled, besides the time and personal inconvenience lost to all parties![6]

His experience was by no means unusual.[7]

The forms of action, the jury's control over fact-finding, and the law of evidence all helped to make outcomes as problematic as they were expensive. The very rules of positive law were shrouded in the mists of archaic precedents, many of which had yet to be even partially dispelled by clarifying and reforming legislation – codification was imminent, and would remain so – or by systematic exposition and elucidation by scholars and appellate judges. However attractive English justice may have seemed to its proprietors, a dozen judges and a small, élite bar, it seems to have elicited only well-deserved criticism from almost everyone else.

This litany of complaint yielded several decades of reluctant and limited reform, culminating in the Judicature Acts of the 1870s. But what was the impact of the law dispensed by the unreformed superior courts in 1830 upon commerce, the lives of ordinary people, and the affairs of the propertied classes? One can hardly dismiss the law of the superior courts as having no impact at all. About 2,400 cases per year did wend their way into and through the curial maze, and were disposed of by the decisions of superior court judges.[8] Nor can one argue that the impact of the law was merely the sum of those 2,400 decisions. No doubt in certain areas, most likely property, precedents actually had the effect attributed to them by the legal centralist paradigm.

At the same time, the reach of the law of the superior courts should not be overestimated. By 1830, some 90,000 lawsuits were begun annually in those courts.[9] This figure is placed in perspective when we remember that at the same period, over three hundred local and special courts exercised civil jurisdiction as well, and over 300,000 claims were brought in these courts[10] – quite apart from the huge volume of civil disputes dealt with by arbitrators, justices of the peace, domestic tribunals, and administrative functionaries.

Special courts and special law had always been important features of the English legal system, as Holdsworth himself acknowledged.[11] Goebel says that in the seventeenth century 'local custom and courts were still an immensely important part of the law administration in England.'[12] Dawson's work on lay judges provides further evidence.[13] Indeed, the only contentious question is whether by the early nineteenth century they had fallen, in Holdsworth's phrase, into 'decline and decadence.'[14] Judgment on this question will be postponed until an outline of the jurisdiction and functions of these courts has been sketched.

Local and special court systems fell into three categories: decentralized courts of common law (sometimes with special procedural arrangements), courts that applied special customary law rather than common law, and courts with broad discretionary powers and de facto automony exercised in such a way as to establish a local variant of the general law.[15]

Decentralized Courts of Common Law
The courts of the principality of Wales and the palatinates of Lancaster, Chester, and Durham were not emanations of the central courts.[16] Regarded as cognate with rather than inferior to the central courts, each was rooted in a distinct medieval political unit and, at least initially, offered a potential breeding ground for a distinctive local legal system. No doubt as a result of centripedal economic and political forces, however, each had become largely or entirely assimilated into the national legal system by the nine-

teenth century. What was left was a system of specialized judicial appointments, separate tariffs of fees and costs, local procedures (sometimes simpler than those of Westminster), whatever special local legal rules may have been preserved by legislation or custom,[17] and perhaps a special communal courtroom ambiance.[18]

Although such large local systems enjoyed considerable support, the courts of Wales and of Chester were abolished in 1830, following an extensive inquiry.[19] It is difficult to interpret their abolition as an attack on pluralism per se. Those who proposed abolition did so less out of principled opposition to decentralization than because of dissatisfaction concerning the actual operation of the local courts. They were the subject of complaints relating to judicial tenure, competence, and independence.[20] Notwithstanding these complaints, there was considerable opposition (especially in Wales) to merger with the central system of courts. In part this reflected the persistence of local nationalism, a fact recognized by both advocates and opponents of merger.[21] In part it reflected the conviction that locally based justice was cheaper and more accessible than that dispensed by the ordinary courts at Westminster or on assize.[22] This factor was particularly important in the case of Lancaster and Durham,[23] which did not merge with the High Court until 1971.[24]

A second component of the decentralized courts of common law was the old county courts, which had ancient origins as communal courts.[25] Like the palatine courts, however, the county courts had been assimilated into the common-law system as courts of record (although they had, especially in earlier times, also discharged local administrative functions). While several of these county courts were busy as late as 1830,[26] many were by then relatively moribund. The preamble to the County Courts Act of 1846,[27] which recites the link between the old county courts and the new ones established in that year, takes liberties with historical fact.[28]

Finally, several municipal courts of record in Bristol, London, Manchester, and Liverpool were apparently thought to offer such effective service to their local clientele that they not only survived the establishment of the county courts and increased their caseload between 1830 and 1870,[29] but were active until their demise a full century later.[30] Others were the target of sustained and virulent attacks, typically on grounds of cost and inefficiency or because they had fallen into the hands of a small and exploitative group of practitioners.[31] On balance, it appears that the potential advantages of local courts of record were more than offset by their costs, technicalities, and dysfunctional jurisdictional arrangements. As courts of record they were subject to the reviewing jurisdiction of the superior courts, which, however, seem to have been more successful in narrowly confining the scope of operation of even efficient local courts, than they were in reforming those that were notoriously inefficient.[32] Inevitably, the obligation of reform was assumed by the legislature, and just as inevitably, the road to reform seemed to lie in the direction of more professional and more centralized control. In 1835 local councils were empowered to appoint legally trained judges or assessors to all local courts of record, and a year later, all such courts were required to be held by a legally qualified recorder or barrister.[33] In 1835 the jurisdictional boundaries of local courts of record were expanded geographically, to conform to those of the municipal corporation that administered them, and in monetary amount and subject matter.[34] Significantly, in 1839 judges of each local court of record were given power to make rules (subject to the approval of three judges of the superior courts) 'for expediting the business of such Court with most convenience, and at the smallest reasonable expence' [sic].[35] The nexus between the local and superior courts was thus reinforced, as was symbolically illustrated by the requirement that all actions should be commenced in the former, as in the latter, by a writ of summons.[36]

Within a few years, these piecemeal developments were overtaken by the establishment of the new county courts. They are significant in so far as they demonstrate an attempt to accommodate local traditions and institutions within a framework whose standards were established and enforced by the central authorities; in this regard they are reminiscent of contemporary efforts to find similar accommodations in new areas of administrative law. There also is significance in the use of lawyers and judges as the chosen instruments of reform. As will be seen, this development was paralleled by similar legislation, which altered the lay character of the important courts of requests and thus helped to accomplish the triumph of formal law and legalism over older, pluralistic traditions.

Finally, it remains to be noted that when the new county courts were established, parliament was sufficiently sensitive to local opinion – whether based on the self-interest of a small group or on popularly defined civic sentiments – to avoid a clear-cut decision as to whether to continue the old local courts or to convert them into the new county courts.[37] As has been noted, at least a few survived and even flourished.

Distinctive Custom-Based Systems

Unlike the original county courts, which early became involved in the local administration of common law, the courts of some manors, boroughs, and other franchises established by custom, feudal grant, royal charter, or parlimentary legislation were still administering distinctive local systems of special law as late as 1830. As Weber reminds us, the nature of special law changed over time throughout Europe. Beginning as the law of closed kinship groups, it gradually became identified with status-based social or economic 'law communities,' which in turn became more open, fluid, and informal relationships.[38] Although the basis and connotation of group participation changed, it remained true through the mid-nineteenth century that some individuals were governed in important aspects of their life by the internal law of a particular place or trade rather than by the general law of the land.

Milsom, speaking of early English feudal jurisdictions, makes the same point: 'Feudal jurisdiction had started as the power to decide, not just to declare a result reached by applying *external* criteria ... [T]here is a great difference between a lord and his court applying rules within their own control if within anybody's and the same body applying royal rules.'[39] Nor was the distinction between external and internal legal systems confined to the feudal courts described by Milsom. The persistence in English judicature of courts that were entitled and expected to apply 'rules within their own control' rather than common law can be traced over six or seven centuries. Such rules included the law merchant, which was indigenous to the trading community, Jewish religious law in the case of disputes between Jews or between Jews and other persons trading with them,[40] local agricultural custom,[41] and special laws governing miners and mining.[42] The internal legal systems did not quickly dissipate; on the contrary, they continued to flourish at least until the end of the seventeenth century,[43] to exercise Benthamite reformers in the early nineteenth century,[44] and to linger even into the twentieth.[45]

Here we see clear evidence of the broad swath of pluralism that runs through the English legal system. Let us also examine in more detail several of its specific manifestations. Dawson's careful description of the work of one manor court[46] shows that both its caseload and the substantive rules it applied differed markedly from those of a common-law court, as might be expected from a forum in which lawyers neither pleaded nor decided cases.[47] Manor courts, originally divided into courts leet and courts baron – a distinction not always maintained at later periods[48] – were developed in the context of a rural society. They were concerned with a broad spectrum of minor civil and criminal regulatory matters: use-rights in commons, personal behaviour, participation in community work such as the maintenance of watercourses, small debts and promises, and especially protection of copyhold tenure in land. Apparently, proceedings were often not adversarial in form, and disposition was by communal decision.[49] To the extent that a 'legal' system evolved, its vehicle was the presiding officer of the court, ofen the steward of the manor. This official may have had some legal training, or at least often had access to one of the manuals commercially published for the guidance of those holding courts.[50] But the basic source of law was not the manuals, and certainly not the common law itself; rather, it was local custom and bylaws. Indeed, the local law may well have reached results that the common-law courts would not have countenanced, or that they only later adopted – for example, enforcement of informal promises, specific performance, and a primitive form of mortgage of copyhold land.[51]

Involvement in customary rather than common law was not merely the peculiar fate of a few isolated communities. In fact, as Abel-Smith and Stevens remark, until the eighteenth century,

[t]he systems of law administered by the superior courts, together with the appeal courts, were the concern of a very small percentage of the population ... It would be wrong, however, to assume that the poor had no disputes, which today would be expected to give rise to litigation ... While such disputes would be of no interest to the royal judges they might well find their way into one of the two types of local courts – the survivors of the communal courts such as the hundred courts, or the feudal courts such as the manorial courts.[52]

By the nineteenth century, certainly by the 1830s, customary law had become less important both because of the decline in the relative (though not the absolute) size of the rural population, and because of the elimination through enclosure of common lands and the associated use-rights and, more generally, of other customary rights 'prised loose from their sociological and tenurial context.'[53] But the old customary law had by no means disappeared entirely. Brougham's famous speech on law reform, in 1828, referred to customary tenures 'in a thousand manors, all different from the Common-law that regulates freehold estates, most of them different from each other ... Is it right that such varieties of custom should be allowed to have force in particular districts, contrary to the general law of the land?'[54] As late as the 1850s books were being published, and apparently sold, on local customary law and copyhold tenure,[55] and the relatively slow progress toward freehold tenure, even through the late nineteenth century, inevitably left behind pockets of customary land law.[56]

For the most part, however, the manor courts had suffered one of two fates by the mid-nineteenth century. On the one hand, the administrative functions of the court leet had largely passed to new institutions of municipal government, although the survival of the Court Leet of the Manor of Manchester offers us a fascinating late glimpse of the institution at work in a new urban and industrial setting.[57] On the other hand, the adjudication of civil disputes by the court baron apparently came to resemble similar functions performed by courts of requests and other local courts; the Court Baron of the Manor of Sheffield, for example, seems to have operated in this fashion through the 1830s.[58] The Manchester manor court was purchased by a new municipal corporation in 1846 and the Sheffield court was replaced by a new county court in 1847, thus bringing to an end two ancient customary tribunals.

But customary law was not dispensed by manor courts alone. Custom seems to have been frequently used to regulate local economies based on natural resources – agricultural land (as in the manor courts) but also mineral deposits (especially tin) and forests.

The stannary courts, still surviving but hardly vigorous in the 1830s, represented another significant instance of custom-as-law.[59] Rooted in the medieval franchises granted to mining communities, they appear to have survived longest in Devon and especially in Cornwall. The primary function of the stannary courts was to decide disputes affecting mining rights according to customary rules, or enactments of the stannary parliaments; subsequently, they also acquired a concurrent general jurisdiction over all disputes involving tin miners, or arising within the geographical area of the stannaries. In the nineteenth century, however, challenges to the jurisdiction of the stannaries and changes in both the mining economy and the judicial organization of the country led first to the reconstitution of these courts under special legislation and then to their ultimate abolition, despite some local support for their retention.[60]

Similar customary institutions existed elsewhere in the country. For example, in 1831, an attempt was made to revive the ancient miners' court of St Briavels in Gloucestershire,[61] although a royal commission investigating the matter concluded that the court had not actually exercised its mining jurisdiction for many years, 'that the customary mode of working has become altogether inapplicable to the present state of things,' and that the old mine law court 'probably could not be renewed or made available to oust the common law jurisdiction, at least where foreigners [non-residents of the locality] are concerned.'[62] The demise of the mine court did not, however, result in the liquidation of claims based upon customary law. The commission that succeeded to its functions preserved the rights of the 'free miners' – anyone born and abiding in the Hundred of St Briavels who worked in a coal or iron mine for a year plus a day – by awarding them mines and quarries, which they control to the present day.[63]

Other mining courts of the period apparently continued to dispense customary law in relation to mining disputes later than either the stannaries or the Court of St Briavels. Their existence in Flintshire, the Mendips, Cumberland, and Derbyshire has been noted, and they were the subject of books written as late as the 1840s and 1850s.[64]

While some authors of the period advert to the recent or anticipated demise of mining custom, a more accurate view seems to be that customary law, as administered by a special court, was given new force by confirmatory local legislation.[65] This development was attacked as an affront to the pre-eminence of the general legal system: '[I]t cannot be denied that the general liberty of the subject and the protection of the rights of property should always be paramount to local privileges. Now, what does the present [Derbyshire] Act [of 1852] do? Simply this. It institutes many Mining Customs that are in derogation of the Common Law, and therefore repugnant to general public utility.'[66]

Repugnance to 'general public utility' is a theme whose significance was explored in E.P. Thompson's important work on the interaction of forest law and the criminal law in the eighteenth century.[67] The forest courts were organized as a separate system – 'peculiar officers, peculiar courts, peculiar law,' Holdsworth says[68] – at least from the thirteenth century. The lowest level of courts, the Swanimote, comprised the forest steward, four elected lay 'verderers,' and twelve lay 'regarders.' Although it had power to convict and assess fines for breach of the forest laws, sentences of the Swanimote were not legally enforceable until the offender was tried by one of two Chief Justices in Eyre, judges of the royal courts. Since trials at the Eyre were seldom held from the end of the sixteenth century, Holdsworth dates the decline and ultimate collapse of forest law from that time.[69] But Thompson's study demonstrates that forest law effectively operated into the eighteenth century and perhaps beyond; its sanctions were the attachment of offenders, summary confiscation of their guns, dogs, and snares, and power to bind over offenders on punitive recognizances. In effect, these powers provided the forest courts with a quid pro quo, which encouraged offenders to pay a small fine 'in composition.'[70]

Forest law is no more, having been formally abolished only in 1971;[71] even by the 1830s it was generally moribund as an adjudicative system, although it continued to show vital signs in some localities at least until the 1860s.[72] But its persistence well beyond the date when its formal sanctioning system collapsed strongly suggests that customary law must have served some social purpose that the common law could not. Thompson describes this function of forest law in terms that are equally applicable to other systems of customary law. Foresters, he says, in the eighteenth century, 'clung still to the lowest rungs of the hierarchy of use-rights ... [Their] live-lihood depended upon the survival of precapitalist use-rights over the land, and upon some form of social organization (as with the old forest courts and the Verderers and Regarders) by which conflicting claims to use-rights over the same land and timber could be reconciled.'[73]

And on what basis save custom could these conflicting interests be recon-ciled? Customary law 'was often a definition of actual agrarian *practice*, as it had been pursued "time out of mind". How can we distinguish between the activity of farming or of quarrying and the rights to this strip of land or that quarry? The farmer or forester in his daily occupation was moving within visible or invisible structures of law.'[74]

This description of the persistence of customary forest law might be of merely antiquarian interest were it not for its startling similarity to Thomp-son's description, in earlier work, of the role of custom in setting the price of staples[75] and even of wages.[76] As late as 1800, numerous successful prose-cutions were brought for 'forestalling, regrating and monopolizing' (selling above the customary price);[77] here the law was enlisted in aid of custom. And forty years later, populist rhetoric still couched complaints in terms of violations of custom; the distinction between 'the legal code and the unwrit-ten popular code,' says Thompson, was commonplace.[78]

Thompson's analysis of the opposition between these two legal systems – the customary and the formal – is developed in the context of his work on forest law in the eighteenth century but also has apparent relevance to what seems to have been a similar dichotomy persisting into the 1830s and 1840s. Forest law (and, one might say, other customary legal systems) did not mysteriously disappear, nor did it fall into decline because it ceased to serve its special constituency. Rather, forest law was suppressed because it was identified with that constituency. The rise of the Whig gentry, with their resort to common law and lawyers, swept aside local legal systems that had evolved to regulate use-rights in a modest forest economy.

During the eighteenth century one legal decision after another signalled that the laywers had become converted to the notions of absolute property ownership, and that (wherever the least doubt could be found) the law abhorred the messy complexities of coincident use-right ... The rights and claims of the poor, if inquired into at all, received more perfunctory compensation ... Very often they were simply redefined as crimes: poaching, woodtheft, trespass.[79]

The forest law, Thompson insists, did not perish solely because of internal decay:

Utilitarian bureaucrats might later see it as a toothless old relic, but in fact it was the shadowy survival of a concept both more functional and more democratic than any of their own creations ... Research ... might well reveal that the old forest courts died out, not because they were impotent but because they continued to express, however feebly, the interests of the foresters.[80]

It is in the light of this line of argument that one must read attacks on custom as 'repugnant to general public utility.' As to 'repugnance,' Dawson suggested that even the old customary manor courts had constrained feudal and oligarchic power and had attained a reasonable standard of local civil justice.[81] What might a careful study of the remaining manor courts and other surviving customary courts in 1830 reveal? And as to 'public utility,' de Tocqueville observed that '[i]n England there seems to be more liberty in the customs than in the laws of the people.'[82] What is repugnant to one man's utility, it seems, may define another man's liberty. The clash of custom and law may thus be understood in terms of a struggle between competing interests and classes, between competing notions of justice, between competing visions of society.[83] Is this not the true significance of the dichotomy drawn by a lawyer in the 1870s between law and custom, between 'real laws' and 'rabble laws'?[84]

Against this background we can resume our account of pluralism as it existed in England in 1830. We can now see more clearly that several customary legal systems continued to exist side by side with the common law, and that their presence was a fact of social significance. These systems obviously were not widespread, and taken in the aggregate they affected only a diminishing fraction of the population. None the less, they were still more than a mere unevolved judicial species conveniently sequestered in a rural Galapagos. These systems had been of the essence for particular economic interests and local communities. The growing pre-eminence of common law thus not only marked a change in the overall pluralistic character of the legal system, but also signalled shifts in the composition and structure of those interests and communities and in their capacity to sustain a 'communitarian process of dispute resolution.'[85] We will revisit this theme at the end of this chapter.

Local Discretionary Courts

If the older customary systems had considerably receded by 1830, discretion-based local courts had not. The fundamental assumptions of legal centralism were confounded by the presence of a 'court of requests' or 'court of conscience' in most principal cities. Some indication of the significance of such courts can be gleaned from the facts that in 1830, ten of the thirteen busiest local courts (with over 5,000 claims per year) were courts of requests,[86] that the court of requests in one London borough, Tower Hamlets, alone handled almost 30,000 claims in a single year (almost one-third of the entire caseload of all the superior courts),[87] and that by 1840 the claims brought to these courts had increased to an estimated 400,000.[88] It is hardly an overstatement to say that, for most Englishmen of the period, the local court of requests dispensed the only form of civil justice they would ever know.

About 250 courts of requests had been established by 1830,[89] a number that rose to about 400 before they were displaced by the county courts in 1846.[90] Each was created by its own statute upon petition of local inhabitants or municipal institutions. Accordingly, there was some variation in the number, qualifications, and method of appointment of commissioners, the monetary and subject-matter jurisdiction of the court, and the court's procedures. Still, there seems to have been some tendency to conform to a standard statutory model.[91] The jurisdiction of almost all courts of requests was limited in amount, subject-matter, and territory. They were presided over by lay judges (often including local mayors, aldermen, or stewards of the manor), their procedures were extremely simple (usually a single written complaint sufficed to bring a matter on for trial), and the parties themselves testified (as they could not at common law) and presented argument. The mandate of almost all courts of requests was to decide cases according to 'equity and good conscience'[92] which, as will be seen, was a potential source of both strength and weakness.

It might be thought that the relatively limited jurisdiction of the courts of requests trivialized their contribution to the civil justice system. In 1830, some courts could only try claims involving less than forty shillings, but many had jurisdiction up to five pounds, or even higher; over the next decade, higher jurisdictional limits became even more commonplace.[93] However, the significance of even the forty-shilling limit, which also applied to the county courts, should not be overemphasized. In 1800, forty shillings was a considerable amount of money; just over one per cent of the population had a weekly income of at least fifty shillings per week. Even by 1830, forty shillings was considerably more than the weekly wage of almost all manual and clerical workers; anyone receiving, say, sixty or seventy-five shillings might be considered middle-class.[94]

It has been suggested that the court of requests was essentially an oppressive mechanism for securing the payment of debts by the poor, occasionally with the implication that the significance of the court was diminished by its constituency, more often to explain its bad reputation. Support for this view is found in several episodes in which court buildings or officials were the targets of popular agitation or violence,[95] and in some of the evidence given to the Commission on Provincial Courts in 1833.[96] For example, one witness dramatically testified that the availability of courts of requests induced shopkeepers to extend credit to the poor, which had 'a most demoralizing tendency among the working classes' and produced 'the debauchery and wretchedness of the vast population of Manchester.'[97] Leaving hyperbole aside, it does seem that credit was frequently extended to the poor by local shopkeepers, and indeed that numerous claims in courts of requests did involve sales of beer and other alcoholic drinks.[98] What is less clear is the extent to which credit would have been given in the absence of such courts, and the extent to which the courts served other purposes involving different defendants and different types of claims. There is, for example, some evidence that suggests that workers used the court to recover their wages and other benefits.[99] But the only extensive records of a court of requests (that of Bristol) suggest that it was used neither by nor against the poor, but largely for purposes of litigation among the lower-middle and middle classes.[100]

To some extent, these discrepancies in the evidence reflect an ambiguity in the use of the term 'class.' Skilled artisans might enjoy relatively comfortable incomes, while clerks or teachers would earn rather less. But the former might be regarded as workers and the latter as members of the 'middle class' because of the social prestige attached to their respective occupations.[101] To some extent, too, these discrepancies reflect local differences in socio-economic structure, in the structure of local government and local courts, and perhaps in litigious habits. But it is doubtful whether these differences were so profound as to justify the conclusion that patterns of recourse to the Bristol court were radically different from those in other large centres. The relatively small number of working-class litigants therefore blunts the force of the jibe that the court of requests was 'a tribunal of shopkeepers' before whom 'neither the higher nor the lower classes have much chance of obtaining justice.'[102]

Quite apart from any question of class domination, however, it was inevitable that the court of requests would not be regarded with general affection. Whatever other purposes the court served, it was clearly used as a collection agency; large numbers of claims were issued at the same time by a single plaintiff attempting to make good on lines of credit extended to customers.[103] Collection agencies are not likely to be universally popular since they serve, by definition, commercial interests rather than the interests of debtors. Yet even in this regard hostility toward the court does not seem entirely justified. Courts of requests arranged for payment of debts in instalments and established a fixed ratio between the sum owing and the time to be served in prison for non-payment – both, in context, meliorative procedures.[104]

In addition to attracting criticism because of their collection agency function, the courts of requests suffered from various inadequacies in their administration, powers, and facilities, which gave rise to complaints from litigants.[105] A royal commission investigating these and other provincial courts reported in 1833 that many of them suffered from serious weaknesses – limited monetary and geographic jurisdiction, lack of competent staff and judges, impaired powers to issue process, compel attendance, or enforce judgment, and the cost of proceedings.[106] And, in common with many local institutions of the time, their facilities and organization often failed to keep up with the enormous expansion of the urban centres. Many therefore no doubt deserved the epithet 'bear gardens in noise and confusion.'[107]

The royal commission recommended the abolition of the courts of requests, and after several interim measures seeking to remedy specific defects,[108] they were in effect absorbed into the new county courts. A balanced assessment of their contribution – fully consistent with the weight of evidence before the Commission on Provincial Courts – was offered by way of obituary on the eve of their disappearance:

The proceedings were cheap, expeditious, domestic, generally certain, almost always final; much knowledge of local habits and trade bargains was brought to bear upon the adjudication; and remedies were placed within the reach and comprehension of persons whom proceedings more solemn, technical, and therefore more expensive, would have disabled of all redress. On the other hand these courts wanted intrinsic authority; their jurisdiction was limited in point of territory, restricted in amount, often doubtful in respect of matter; though numerous when merely considered as anomalous and exceptional tribunals, they were in fact too few.[109]

Given the appalling nature of the English judicature at the time, this is indeed to praise with faint damning.

In light of this assessment, it might be possible to treat the courts of requests merely as imperfect precursors of the county courts. But to do so would be to ignore their most significant characteristic: although they disposed of most civil suits in England until 1846, they were courts run by and for laymen, and they applied not the fixed rules of common law but the discretionary norms of 'equity and good conscience.' Perhaps the most important and difficult question to be addressed in connection with courts of requests is whether this vague and general language, coupled with the other distinctive characteristics of these courts, actually did produce forms of dispute resolution and substantive results that differed markedly from those that would have emerged in the formal common-law system.

Their only modern chronicler asserts without citation of authority that 'in the course of time it became usual to declare that law should be followed.'[110] However, the available evidence suggests the contrary.

The fullest contemporary account of the work of these courts is that of William Hutton, a Birmingham merchant and civic notable, who served as a commissioner for many years. To the extent that Hutton's description can be taken as typical of his own period (about 1770–1800), let alone of the 1830s, it seems that courts of requests used their wide discretionary powers to resolve disputes amicably and to achieve a genuine blend of communal justice and situation equity. For example, Hutton attempted mediation from the bench, took notice of local employment and commercial customs, and shrewdly used his knowledge of local characters to evaluate their evidence and behaviour.[111]

In all of this, to be sure, there was an element of paternalism: 'I have considered the suitors as my children, and when any of this vast family looked up to me for peace and justice, I have distributed both with pleasure.'[112] But it was a pragmatic paternalism, based not so much on an idealized view of justice – although Hutton was capable of that – as on a robust, practical sense that the decisions of the court had to accord with the exigencies and expectations of life in the community.

Inevitably, the desire to reach results that were 'just' in both a principled and a pragmatic sense forced Hutton to consider the relationship between his court and the law of the land. He self-consciously distanced himself from the common law: 'If the Commissioners cannot decide *against* the law, they can decide without it. Their oath binds them to proceed according to *good conscience*.'[113] And he did not hesitate to make it appear, by well-reasoned arguments, that his decisions were 'without' rather than 'against' the law.[114]

Later direct accounts of the way in which lay judges exercised their jurisdiction are almost entirely lacking. However, evidence given to the 1833 Commission on Provincial Courts by two commissioners of a court of requests suggests, if anything, a more resolute commitment to equity than law:

Q Are [the Commissioners] guided by distinct rules of law, or according to their own notions of equity?

A I should rather say their strict notions of equity, because we are not acquainted with strict rules of law.

Q But occasionally you have to refer to the clerks on points of law?

A Yes, we do.

Q Suppose you thought the law was one way and equity another, what would be done then?

A If it was left to our decision, I think we should give it in favour of equity.[115]

On the other hand, the open-endedness of this commitment to 'equity' should not be overestimated. To some extent, departures from common-law procedures and substantive rules were accomplished not through the use of discretion but by explicit empowering statutes.[116] Even where wide discretion was available, it was not always resorted to. Hutton expressed an instinctive appreciation of the impossibility and undesirability of approaching every dispute tabula rasa: 'The decisions of a Bench should ever be the same. That which is law today should be law forever. If they are founded in equity, they may be adhered to with safety.'[117] This self-imposed limit on discretion, this creation of a special 'law' of the forum, is reminiscent of the emergence of customary law. But it also anticipates and resembles the emergence of administrative law, special law created within the amorphous boundaries of unstructured discretion and apart from rather than in conflict with the formal law of the superior courts and of parliament.

The issue of discretion in administrative law has been treated as an important one by commentators from Dicey to Davis, but it was foreshadowed by a controversy that related squarely to the civil justice system: to what extent did the rules of common law inhibit or promote 'true' justice? To what extent did discretion invite arbitrariness or permit judges to brush aside formalism in order to find truth and do what was right? Atiyah's formidable book sets this controversy in its intellectual context, and seeks to show how, at about this time, there came to be increasing reliance on principle and less reliance on discretion or policy as the basis of judicial decisions.[118] But his data are largely the decisions of the superior courts which may, in any event, not entirely support his thesis.[119] And even if we accept that the dialectic between principle and policy can be detected by an astute observer looking at the formal systems in its own terms, it is more clearly brought into focus by attempting to juxtapose the two systems that exemplified the competing views.

Courts of requests were needed, said Hutton with messianic zeal: 'The straight, the easy, the concise road to justice is blocked up, and the traveller is led through the dark, long, and intricate windings of law.'[120] But the members of the Commission on Provincial Courts, as lawyers are wont to do, clearly preferred law to discretion: 'The suspicion entertained ... by Sir William Blackstone, as to the policy of erecting Courts "with methods of proceeding entirely in derogation of the Common Law, and whose largely discretionary powers make a petty tyranny in a set of standing Commissioners," have not been removed by later experience.'[121]

Were the commissioners justified in ascribing the ills of the courts of requests to their illicit embrace of discretion? The answer to that question involves several separate lines of enquiry. Is it true that the formal system operated with a minimum of discretion, as it professed to do? Were the common-law courts actually more benign, less 'tyrannical,' than the courts of requests? Was the unsatisfactory 'later experience' of those courts, referred to by the commissioners, a reflection of their failure to meet some abstract ideal standard? And did their performance fall below that of the rest of the civil justice system of the period?

In the absence of hard evidence and subject to all the risks of misinterpretation that its absence entails, we may first speculate about the actual presence of discretion in the work of superior courts.

It can be hypothesized that in the formal common-law system there is a tendency toward predictability and uniformity of result. The theoretical commitment to precedent is not the only reason for this. The formal interaction of advocates and judges with a common professional training and informal acquaintanceships, the availability of written records, treatises, and reports, and (at a slightly later date) the hierarchical organization of the courts to facilitate formal appeals – all of these would reinforce the theoretical commitment to make decisions that are predictable and uniform throughout the legal system. Yet we know that even in the superior courts a considerable margin of discretion must exist: the finding of facts, the application of vague standards such as 'fairness' and 'reasonableness,' the identification of gaps in existing rules, the decision to extend them to novel situations, the choice between apparently conflicting authorities, and the interpretation of statutory or common-law rules are some of the formulae through which discretion has always found its way into a system that is ostensibly committed to predictability and certainty.

If discretion was widely exercised in the superior courts, one would not be surprised to find that it was even more frequently encountered in the courts of requests and, indeed, in other local courts. All of the tasks involving the exercise of discretion were undertaken by the local courts as well, but many of the factors that constrain discretion were absent. Lawyers only rarely served as judges, their influence as clerks or assessors was apparently marginal, and they seldom appeared as advocates; the rules and understandings shared among lawyers were therefore absent. There were no written decisions (at least in courts of requests), and hence no reports, no analysis, no refinement of doctrine. [122] Appeals were rare or non-existent, and neither the rationalization of conflicting decisions nor the adumbration of principles and policies was possible. Even informal contact among the part-time members of the large and fluctuating benches of courts of requests probably was sporadic.

Added to these considerations is the important fact that local justice tended to be communal justice. Because the local court was part of the fabric of community life, it was more likely to be responsive to factors that might not impinge on the consciousness of judges of the central system: the personality or reputation of the litigants, the state of the local economy or social climate, local custom, nuances of local speech and behaviour patterns, and the judge's own continuing relationship as a member of the community. [123] Above all, a local judge might be more eager to secure what he imagined to be local social equilibrium and tranquility than to vindicate general rules of law. [124]

To this point, the view of the Commission on Provincial Courts seems to have been justified: local courts exercising broad discretion did, no doubt, decide 'in derogation of the Common Law.' But does it follow that the courts of requests especially were, in Blackstone's phrase, 'a petty tyranny'?

It would be foolish to deny that they had a potential for tyranny. Obviously, discretion can be exercised in ways that are either humane or oppressive, merely idiosyncratic or purposefully responsive to the perceived needs of significant local interests. And how is tyranny to be defined? By what standards are the courts of requests to be judged? One cannot easily compare them with the central courts – themselves no exemplars of justice – because so few of the litigants or causes of action involved in the local courts would ever have found their way into the central courts, let alone stood a chance of final adjudication, because of delays, formalities, and high costs. [125] Indeed, even the potentially important business clientele of the central courts avoided them if at all possible – eloquent testimony to their inadequacies.

It might be appropriate, however, to compare the commissioners of the courts of requests to the justices of the peace and magistrates who administered the criminal law. Both, after all, were lay judges; both exercised local jurisdiction; both were drawn, by the 1830s, from local élites, especially business interests. [126] To the extent that the mandate and functions of the two groups differed, it might be thought that the quality of justice delivered by the magistrates would be superior. The magistrates, after all, were appointed by the lord lieutenant of the county, and the commissioners elected or selected locally; the risk of partiality and parochialism was surely greater in the latter case than in the former. The magistrates were administering the criminal law, laid down over the centuries by parliament and by judicial decisions, reviewed and rationalized by higher courts, and explicated by commentators; the commissioners were exercising a vague jurisdiction of recent invention, usually ignored but occasionally reviled by right-thinking lawyers; the risk of irrationality and egregious error was surely greater in the courts of requests than before the justices of the peace.

But if we take the performance of the magistracy as our measure, the commissioners look decidely untyrannical. Hay's study of criminal justice in eighteenth-century rural England strongly suggests that literal enforcement of the strictures of the criminal law was not the prime concern of the local magistracy.[127] He demonstrates how the great severity of the criminal law was consciously tempered by the frequent exercise of mercy in order to forge a flexible instrument of social control. Even when mercy was an executive rather than a judicial act, its invocation would have come as no surprise to local justices. After all, many of them were on intimate terms with local magnates who secured pardons or other relaxations of harsh penalties, while some were themselves MPs or influential political figures. Conversely, decisions to impose harsh penalties or to convict for more serious rather than less serious crimes were not taken in a political vacuum: 'Benevolence, all patronage, was given meaning by its contingency. It was the obverse of coercion ... When patronage failed, force could be invoked; but when coercion inflamed men's minds, at the crucial moment mercy could calm them.'[128] In the real – as opposed to the formal – administration even of the criminal law, the local exercise of discretion obviously played a crucial role.

Perhaps the activities of the justices in the expanding cities after the 1830s differed somewhat from those of rural areas and earlier times, if only because of changes in the political hierarchy, incipient professionalization of the magistracy, and reform of criminal law and procedure. But the same overt manipulation of the criminal law can be identified at least through the 1820s and the 1830s, and likely even later. It can hardly be denied that local circumstances gave local colour to an apparently neutral, national system of criminal law.[130] And, as will be shown in chapter 5, to the extent that the justices became involved in the enforcement of national adminstrative schemes, such as health and safety legislation affecting mines and factories, that local colour was often vivid and brazen in its self-interest.

No such egregious dereliction or misuse of office was charged against the commissioners of the courts of requests, whose discretion was, if anything, less constrained than that of the justices. Even Winder, who quotes Blackstone's attack on discretionary bodies without disapproval, was prepared to concede that the courts of requests were less tyrannical than the magistrates.[131] Evidence before the Commission on Provincial Courts suggested that these courts were somewhat unpopular, but few specific allegations of partiality were made or substantiated.[132] At worst, the commissioners may have been prone to a 'shopkeepers' bias' and occasionally embarrassed by inevitable conflicts or connections with litigants appearing before them.

Ironically, the most bitter epithets – 'hideous public scourges, inflicting ... monstrous injustice and heart-rendering misery'[133] – were reserved for some local courts which, unlike the courts of requests, were technically courts of record and therefore part of the common-law system. Indeed, in direct comparisons between the discretionary and common-law local courts, the former were regarded even by hostile observers as preferable.[134]

The discretion issue, one may conclude, was essentially symbolic and ideological rather than an authentic concern derived from experience. It is when discretion is juxtaposed to law – rather than exercised within an ostensibly structured system of legal rules – that it attracts the greatest antipathy from judges and lawyers. This issue will be revisited in the context of a discussion of administrative decision-making.

LAYMEN'S VALUES AND PROFESSIONALS' VALUES

During the 1830s, the pluralistic character of the English civil justice system came under frequent attack, and we might be tempted to assume that by 1846, with the creation of the new county courts, it had been erased. Ironically, however, this was the very period during which modern administrative tribunals began to appear, offering a new model of pluralism. The connection between these phenomena did not entirely escape the notice of astute contemporary observers,[135] although it can hardly have been a matter of casual conversation in the inns of court or at meetings of the recently established law society. None the less, recognized or not, at least some of the forces that led to the demise of the old pluralism helped to shape the new.

Industrialization and urbanization were of primary importance. In Felix Frankfurter's phrase, 'Watt and Stephenson were much more responsible for undermining the dominantly feudal legal system expounded by Blackstone, than Bentham and Brougham.'[136] With the new conditions of life, the foundations of local and special justice were swept away in many communities. The relationships of people to each other and to other communities, to authority, and to the means of production and possibilities of consumption were all changed. In the perception of those changes and of the need to resist or accelerate them, to meliorate their effects or take full advantage of them, new social philosophies, intellectual attitudes, and legal values began to develop. What this portended for the development of administrative law will be explored in subsequent chapters.

How, then, did the industrial revolution affect the pluralistic court system? When transportation and communications improved, when a more complex and highly integrated national economy began to emerge, local legal systems became increasingly less relevant and less functional. The interweaving of local life and law postulated by Thompson was characteristic of close-knit agricultural communities and, as he demonstrates, extended to early forms of industrial organization.[137] These quasi-governmental functions of local law did not easily translate into the larger, more diffuse, dynamic, and diversified towns and cities which attracted an increasing proportion of the population. Simple, well-understood rules about the performance of civic tasks or the sharing of communal facilities had little meaning in the context of a society of strangers and an economy of complex and specialized tasks.[138] The old systems could finally survive only where the old forms of social organization lingered.[139]

In a village, for example, maintenance of watercourses might be undertaken by co-operative effort, non-participation in which would be regarded as breach of communal law. Perhaps even in Hutton's Birmingham, a city of some sixty thousand, the judgment of notables could help to ensure that neighbours shared the cost of maintaining the pump that brought them water.[140] But if the needs of a large industrial centre were to be met on a long-term basis, the task could only be performed by a private or public corporate undertaking. Rules and institutions designed for one situation were not easily adapted to another.[141]

Nor were the old local customary courts alone incapable of performing their traditional functions. The dispute-resolving capability even of the new courts of requests was also affected by changing social conditions. This in turn probably contributed to the dubious reputation they had acquired by the 1830s. In a smaller, more stable community – such as Hutton's Birmingham of the 1780s – it is conceivable that sensitivity to local custom, genuine paternalism, or humane behaviour on the bench and in other civic functions might have helped to dissipate the resentment a debt-enforcing agency inevitably attracted.[142] But in the larger industrial towns, with a more mobile, mixed, and miserable population, such civic-minded individuals were less likely to be attracted onto the bench, or once there to be perceived to be dispensing justice or even able to cope with the more difficult and extensive caseload. Even during Hutton's time, the caseload of the Birmingham Court of Requests rose from 50 to 130 per week; by 1830–1, it had risen to about 160; in some other courts, it was two or even three times greater.[143] During Hutton's time, the Birmingham court had seventy-two commissioners, and he could boast of the court 'creating judges in the lower class'; by 1830, amending legislation had considerably increased the property qualifications for commissioners who thereafter were certainly persons of some substance.[144] The narrowing of the base of judicial recruitment, the expansion of the caseload, and the diminished sense of community must all have contributed to the unpopularity of these courts.

We may also speculate about the possibility that changes in the distribution of local political power engendered by social and economic changes affected the nature, function, and symbolic importance of the local courts. In some small and stable places, perhaps, traditions of popular participation lent credibility to ancient communal institutions. In many of the newly industrialized towns and rapidly expanding commercial centres, however, civic government was transformed by the emergence of powerful new interest groups[145] and by the Municipal Corporations Act of 1835.[146] There, courts that had been associated with an *ancien regime* – a lord of the manor, a paternalist like Hutton – naturally attracted the attention of new patrons.[147] This phenomenon has often been noticed in the case of magistrates' benches, which in many places rapidly passed from the control of the gentry to the control of factory owners.[148]

However, although we can hardly deny the growing manifestations of class interest in urban societies that were becoming more and more heterogeneous, we should not too readily assume that the local administration of civil justice was a major theatre of conflict. The increase in property qualifications for commissioners of courts of requests in 1830 hints at a desire by local élites to retain or secure control over local civil courts. However, the short-run gain to them seems more likely to have been in terms of prestige than actual profit or power. In courts of requests, after all, the commissioners were unpaid and overworked, and the court officers were poorly remunerated; neither those courts nor other local civil courts offered significant prospects of valuable patronage. Nor was the civil law as obvious a device of social control as the criminal law. Finally, the local courts, largely preoccupied with the minor disputes of the middle classes, seldom dealt with claims by or against large businesses or their proprietors.[149]

This is not to deny that business had an obvious interest in the availability and efficiency of local courts, as opposed to the more subtle concerns that might be implied from their participation in and control over the bench itself. As urban centres encompassed adjacent villages and towns, and as improved transport permitted goods to flow more freely to customers outside local markets, the jurisdictional logic of local courts was challenged. Businessmen would not be well-served if a debtor could escape the jurisdiction of a local court by moving across an invisible and anachronistic borough boundary,[150] or if an action for goods sold to a purchaser in the next town could only be brought in the superior courts at horrendous cost or in the place where the purchaser lived and according to the special procedures of its ancient manor or borough court (and by paying its occasionally exorbitant fees), or if the purchase of land for a mine or factory became enmeshed in unfamiliar and inhospitable local customary law.

Moreover, businessmen in some places effectively lacked access to any form of local court, either because the ancient communal or manor court had long since been discontinued or was physically distant[151] or because a court of requests had not yet been established.[152] They continued to encounter frustrating local customary law, sometimes given new life by legislation.[153] And they could not be sure that the local courts, where they did exist, would possess the powers, staff, and facilities to deal with their caseload.

Reference to the difficulties encountered by businessmen (especially those who did not operate wholly within a local or neighbourhood market) should not obscure the fact that other users and potential users of some local courts also had serious complaints. Not all of these courts can have operated benignly; it is likely that numbers of them fell under the control of indifferent or oppressive judges, clerks, or practitioners. Moreover, customary laws were the expression of relationships that would last only so long as the boundaries of the universe were the village or manor or hundred, so long as economic rights flowed from traditional patterns of local agriculture, manufacture, or trade, and so long as external social and economic contacts were episodic and ordered. When those relationships were transformed, when the perspectives of local life were altered and its horizons pushed back, much of local customary law became anachronistic and inoperable. Old custom, it is true, was sometimes used to resist this transformation, and occasionally to accomplish it. But more often it '[fell] away through a process of attrition rather than through any frontal assault.'[154] When it did fall away, or was pushed aside, what Dawson called the 'pale abstraction' of the common law perhaps became more vivid and concrete, at least for those who came in contact with its agents or had to cope with its agenda.

The growing interest of business in an efficient system of minor courts and the declining constituency of customary and discretionary systems obviously portended changes in the nature of local justice. In addition, however, by 1830 the local courts were attracting the attention of new interest groups – the Benthamite reformers and the legal profession.

What Goebel said of seventeenth-century local courts may be said from a modern perspective quite objectively, and with equal force, of those of the nineteenth century: 'No one who ventures into the forbidding welter of contemporary [seventeenth-century] charters can fail to be appalled by the multitude and extent of franchises, the tenacity with which they were clung to, and the astounding picture of jurisdictional diversities they disclose.'[155] But to a certain extent such a judgment is both anachronistic and over-influenced by a centralist view of the legal system.[156] Most contemporary participants in these local courts had no occasion to stand back and view the 'astounding picture' from afar; they simply experienced legal pluralism as normal and natural until they had some reason to criticize it.

For those who favoured the 'scientific' reform of government as a good in itself, however, the disparate and idiosyncratic jurisdictions of the local courts were ipso facto a serious weakness. Certainly, neither alone nor in conjunction with the superior courts did the four hundred local courts form a coherent, integrated, efficient and responsive 'system.' What could one expect, after all, from a mélange of institutions assembled over a thousand years and dependent for its capacity to adapt upon the creaky machinery of an unreformed parliament or slow, uncertain, informal evolutionary processes?

The moment for 'scientific' reform of the local courts had clearly arrived by 1830. Since reform would have to be accomplished by national legislation, it would almost certainly result in a loss of local control and local character: how else would courts be created where they did not exist, powers conferred or extended where they were perceived to be lacking, and standards of facilities and administration laid down where they were required? The result would almost certainly be a national system of local courts; Hutton himself had argued that there should be one 'in every manor or district.'[157] But ubiquity does not automatically define function or philosophy. It is fairly clear that there were at least two different possibilities for the new court system – one reflecting its communal history, the other its commercial future.

The attractions of the communal model were less tangible, and its advocates generally less powerful and articulate, than those of the commercial model. What did the communal model offer? It offered the possibility that local justice would continue to be dispensed by laymen, that it would be informal, that adjudication would be leavened by conciliation and compromise, and that cases would be decided according to common sense, situation equity, and custom (where it existed) rather than conventional legal rules. And who would favour such a system of popular, local justice? Most of the working people and small-businessmen who might have been its beneficiaries had neither the motive nor the means to press for it. They were immersed in the daily struggle for existence, were probably made sceptical by their occasional unhappy experiences with lay justices and commissioners of courts of requests, and in any event were without political power. Only the more affluent businessmen and civic officials who already were involved in the old local courts might have supported a new system of community courts, but their commitment was weakened by the obvious problems already referred to.

Still, some voices were heard. A Leeds merchant favoured the appointment of panels of salaried 'arbitrators' in every town.[158] A committee appointed by a public meeting at Newark believed that 'intelligent men may always be found ready to become commissioners, and ... being men of character, education and respectability, and pronouncing their decisions in public, would seldom dare to swerve from strict impartiality and justice.'[159] That opinion was supported by a local attorney, who stressed that such commissioners 'deciding in the midst and in the face of their neighbours, are urged from ... the strongest of all human motives in most minds, to do right.'[160] A gentleman from Lancaster favoured 'first attempting to encourage an adjustment of disputes by the means of domestic tribunals.'[161] Even Lord Brougham, no friend of local customary law, none the less favoured the use of conciliation and arbitration. If litigants could hear 'the calm opinion of able and judicious men,'' he believed, 'their anger would often be cooled.'[162] His original bill to establish 'Local District Courts,' introduced before the report of the Commission on Provincial Courts, would have enabled judges of those courts to function as arbitrators and 'Judges of Reconcilement.'[163]

But other voices spoke with greater authority. Neither commercial interests nor the legal profession were attracted by the possibilities of a genuine communal model. Each, for different reasons, wanted to create a new system of local courts that would be a more effective instrument of law in the conventional sense. These were the voices of the future.

The report of the Commission on Provincial Courts clearly focused on the need to make the courts into a more effective instrument for reinforcing commercial transactions: 'It is a matter of sound moral as well as just legal policy, that no debtor shall be exempted from the legal obligation to pay a just debt, however small.[164] And when the County Courts Act of 1846 was finally enacted, it was captioned, with disarming candour, 'An Act for the more easy Recovery of small Debts and Demands.'[165]

The vindication of the needs of the commercial community – real needs, especially in the changing circumstances of England after the industrial revolution – was hardly surprising. But the old communalism did not fall victim simply to the forces of business. It was under attack as well from lawyers and judges, often marching together with those who bore the banners of science and certainty.

Given the decision to reconstruct the local courts 'upon a simple and uniform model,'[166] especially with the aim of facilitating debt collection, it is understandable that an effort was made to ensure that fixed rules of law would govern their decisions rather than local custom, equity, or discretion. The commissioners of 1833 had been sensitive to the risk of excessive legalism in relation to procedure in litigation over small matters: 'If justice ... is to be administered according to the ordinary rules of evidence, in a court regulated by certain rules of practice, the proceeding ceases to be remedial in its effect. If, on the other hand, all such restraints be dispensed with, the tribunal becomes arbitary, and its decisions too vague and uncertain to be satisfactory.'[167] But they were quite unwilling to apply the same reasoning to substantive rules. In principle, the commissioners were extremely suspicious of discretion, and sought to confine it within narrow limits of law.[168] Judges, they believed, should be experienced barristers with tenure, presumably mandated (and almost inevitably inclined) to dispense 'law.'[169]

Here we see a convergence of economic interest, ideology, and intellectual perspective. The economic interest is clear: a system in which legally trained judges dispense common law is one in which lawyers must almost inevitably be retained as advocates. As we will see in the context of the discussion of commercial disputes, this was a powerful consideration indeed. But it was not the only consideration. As has already been noted, Atiyah detects a shift in judicial discourse in England during the nineteenth century from a pragmatic to a principled style.[170] 'Pragmatism' he identifies closely with equity and discretionary powers; 'principled' adjudication he sees as a manifestation of a familiar Victorian appeal to 'universal' truths, which was characteristic of both the utilitarians and the political economists. This same view may have informed the report on provincial courts, which invoked Blackstone's interdiction against 'largely discretionary powers' as a reason for suppressing the courts of requests. It is certainly discernible in the hostility toward local custom, which was a challenge to the universality of law. But the dichotomy between principle and pragmatism, between law and discretion or custom, was as overstated then as it often is now. For example, custom was sometimes captured in confirmatory statutes or in other written instruments, which made it at least as certain as common-law rules. Nor would it be surprising if busy lay judges had developed guidelines, standard responses, and bodies of precedent, as Hutton had urged.[171] That they may have done so is suggested by a disparaging reference by a legal critic to 'Court of Requests law.'[172] However, even the articulation of a clear 'law of the forum' would not have mollified legal critics; it would not have addressed their concerns about the lay character of most local courts, their estrangement from the control of judges and lawyers, what Hutton saw as one of their prime virtues: 'taking power out of the hands of professional men.'[173]

Those 'professional men,' judges and lawyers, were most concerned about the virtual exclusion of their 'law' from the courts of requests, not simply out of economic self-interest, not simply because of an intellectual commitment to formal, common-law adjudication, but also out of a genuine ideological belief that law, in the formal sense, was and should be the means by which disputes were settled and the affairs of society ordered. This was 'legal centralism' writ large, although perhaps not quite as legibly as it will ultimately appear in our discussion of contemporaneous developments in the fields of commercial and administrative law. In the context of ordinary civil disputes, the role of professional ideology was manifest particularly in the protracted battle, between 1830 and 1846, over the shape of the new county courts which, in a sense, inherited cy pres the business of the courts of requests.

Reference has already been made to the reluctance of lay commissioners to dispense 'law' rather than 'justice.' One obvious riposte by proponents of 'law' was to try to overcome this reluctance by introducing lawyers into the decision-making process. Their case for replacing lay judges with professionals was not always framed in terms of a desire for the application of the rules of law. It had to do with the aura of law as well as its substance, with the tacit assumption that by making the local courts more like the superior courts, the former would assume some of the reputation of the latter. For example, impartiality is central to the enterprise of adjudication, but accusations of incompetence and partiality had been directed at the lay judges. The 1833 report actually vindicated them in relation to the one specific incident charged against them, but it equivocated on the general issue of bias.[174] Moreover, apart from the bias charge, the report noted that problems of consistency were created by the fluctuating composition of the bench and problems of efficiency by the non-attendance of the commissioners. Such problems were perhaps inevitable, given that the commissioners were volunteers whose service on the bench was a sideline to business activities or other civic responsibilities. The report's solution to each of these real or imagined difficulties was the appointment of paid, professionally trained judges who would dispense 'law' and thereby presumably help local justice meet the standards of the superior courts.

Over the next decade, there was increasing reliance on legal professionals as the standard-bearers of formal law and of 'law' as the vehicle of certainty, impartiality, and dignity. During the 1830s, individual courts of requests statutes were enacted or amended to increase the monetary jurisdiction of particular courts (often up to five pounds) and simultaneously to provide for a legally trained judge,[175] although generally the 'equity' or 'conscience' jurisdiction was not explicitly altered.[176] The Bankruptcy Act, 1844, empowered the commissioners of any court of requests to appoint a legally trained assessor subject to cabinet approval,[177] and in 1845 another statute offered to expand to twenty pounds, by order in council, the jurisdiction of any court that appointed a legally qualified judge, who would have power to decide all cases alone when there was an insufficient number of commissioners or in the area of enlarged jurisdiction.[178] On the eve of the introduction of county courts in 1846, then, the camel's nose of lawyers had gone far toward ejecting lay commissioners from their own tent.

Looked at in one way, these developments (and parallel developments in other local courts)[179] can be viewed as a necessary precondition for the enlargement of the monetary jurisdiction of the courts, and their acquisition of extended powers and better facilities.[180] But this interpretation, which proceeds from the premises of legal centralism, begs the question of why only lawyers shoul be permitted to administer law. The answer has always been clear to lawyers. The courts of requests, said one contemporary critic, 'do not, generally, try causes by jury, nor proceed according to the course of the common law, which circumstances are at variance with our national predilections.'[181] The same conclusion was reached with equal facility by a legal author writing one hundred years later.[182] Common law is easily wrapped in the flag of 'national predilection.'

So much for ideology. We must now examine the means by which 'law' was imposed as the new normative basis of local courts. Three conditions had to be met. First, the prevailing method of dispute settlement had to become pure adjudication, purged of elements of mediation, compromise, and communal expectation. Second, lawyers had to secure the right of audience, in both a theoretical and practical sense. Third, the local courts had to be integrated into the central legal system, if not by ensuring common rules of procedure and proof then at least by facilitating review by or appeal to the superior courts. Each of these conditions was achieved by about 1850.

First, the victory of adjudication over other forms of dispute settlement was secured. A judge cannot be everything at once, warned a barrister in an open letter to Lord Brougham in 1831: 'judge, advocate, attorney, arbitrator, referee and pacificator; haranguing, adjudicating, arbitrating, conciliating and reconciling.'[183] Like his own compromise bill of 1833,[184] the County Courts Act of 1846 did not, in the end, adopt Lord Brougham's original proposal that the judges of local courts should be authorized to conduct arbitration and mediation,[185] although adjudicative purity probably was tempered somewhat in practice.[186]

Brougham, however, never abandoned his effort to secure formal recognition of the principle of conciliation. Thirty years after first proposing it, and notwithstanding that 'the profession have an incurable prejudice against every such means ... not unconnected with motives of interest,' he continued to press for the establishment of at least an experimental scheme of conciliation: 'With the profession I will compound; they shall have, so far as I am concerned, no more law amendment to do them injury, no more of costs reduced, no more of litigation prevented. Let them give me this, and I will lay down my head in peace and comfort.'[187] Peace and comfort were not to be his. The profession seems to have been convinced that conciliation would reduce not only social conflict and the cost of legal proceedings, but also the central importance of law and lawyers: 'Lord Brougham ... is always prepared to become the sponsor for any Chimera, provided only that it shall appear to grin at lawyers.'[188]

Of course, it was not merely the departure from adjudicative procedures or rules of common law that presented an obstacle to participation by lawyers in the local courts and threatened to oust them from the new county courts. Although lawyers occasionally did appear in some courts of requests[189] and even dominated a few local franchise courts for their own benefit,[190] some statutes establishing courts of request actually forbade their appearance.[191] And even if they were entitled to appear, they often were deterred from doing so because of the absence of a system of costs and because of the relatively small sums being litigated.[192]

From the point of view of the profession, therefore, it was imperative that the county courts should be established on a basis that would give lawyers access to a lucrative new area of practice. The lawyers' hunger was almost palpable: 'The objections to Local Courts are so many ... The greatest of all is that which is by their supporters esteemed their foremost benefit;

– the absence of legal advisers; – the prosecution of their suits by the parties in person ... Will no member of the House of Commons fight the battle of Law and the Lawyers against the reckless assaults of laymen ...?'[193]

In fact, the County Courts Act of 1846 gave lawyers a monopoly of representation to the exclusion of the 'low attorneys' and other unqualified individuals who often appeared in the old local courts.[194] However, litigants were entitled to appear in person, as in the courts of requests, and many continued to do so[195] because the act established a rather restrictive fee structure.[196] Indeed, far from creating a lucrative source of professional work, the county courts actually siphoned off litigation formerly conducted in the superior courts, and 'threaten[ed] to make almost a revolution in legal economy.'[197] Within a few years, however, the 'revolution' subsided, the fee structure of the county courts was altered,[198] and lawyers were able to exploit the representational monopoly they had been given.

Much of the debate over the new courts also revolved around another financial issue: would the remuneration be sufficient to attract good lawyers to the bench? There were dire predictions about how low salaries would permit the appointment only of 'the travelling drudges of the "Cheap Justice Delivery System" ';[199] there were concerns about the patronage possibilities of the new judicial appointments;[200] there was snide conjecture over the possible apointment of some judges of the courts of requests to the county court bench.[201] But in the end, as one legal editorialist conceded, in the new county courts, 'upon the whole, the standard of judicial competency attained is quite as high as could reasonably be expected.'[202]

It only remained to ensure the integration of the county courts into the formal legal system. Astute observers appreciated that simple and rational rules of pleading and evidence were a strength of the courts of requests and would have to be carried forward into the new county courts. The report of the 1833 commission had said as much, and the point was accepted even within legal circles: 'The public wisely prefers to have their disputes settled by the ancient, dignified, and impartial tribunals of the country ... Wherefore, then, is it that in practice we find suitors going to the County Courts instead of the Superior Courts ...? [The answer is that] ... in the County Courts there is more facility for trying the *merits* of the suit.'[203]

In due course, the superior courts adopted many reforms that originated in the local courts and were introduced into the formal system through the medium of the county courts. There was a price to be paid for the flattery implied by this imitation, however. The courts of requests, and to a significant extent all local courts, had existed in virtual isolation from the superior courts. It is true that the superior courts, in theory at least, exercised supervisory jurisdiction over local and special 'inferior' tribunals. This jurisdiction in some cases rested upon specific statutory provisions, in some upon the exercise of an inherent power to review through the use of the prerogative writs, and in some upon the disposition, in the context of superior court litigation, of collateral issues that might otherwise have been decided elsewhere. But scrutiny of the decisions of the superior courts in 1830 shows how limited was the actual use of the supervisory jurisdiction.[204]

In a number of cases, for example, superior courts decided collateral issues that involved local custom as an evidentiary matter affecting legal or equitable claims.[205] But in only two cases was direct reliance placed upon decisions of local courts – in one case successfully,[206] in the other unsuccessfully.[207] In two other cases, substantive decisions of local or customary courts were directly challenged. In one case the King's Bench refused to decide a question within the jurisdiction of a domestic tribunal,[208] but in the other it overturned the decision of a customary court.[209] A pair of cases involving the judicatures of Chester and Wales disclosed no obvious interventionist impulse in the central courts; rather the contrary.[210] Indeed, another group of decisions relating to forfeiture of costs for failing to resort to the appropriate lower court, based upon statutory provisions, seems to show that the central courts were content to keep their dockets clear of minor cases.[211] Spurious attempts to challenge the jurisdiction of local courts to delay or defeat execution were similarly treated with disdain.[212]

The virtual autonomy of the courts of requests was, indeed, de jure as well as de facto. Typically, local statutes provided that if a writ was issued in the superior courts when a claim might have been brought in a court of requests, the plaintiff forfeited his costs when successful and was liable for double costs when not.[213] Moreover, privative clauses protected decisions of some courts of requests from removal 'into any other Court by *certiorari* or otherwise howsoever.'[214] Notwithstanding these clauses, occasional litigation did occur over the monetary, geographical, and subject-matter jurisdictions of courts of requests.[215] Whatever the technical position, however, it was generally understood that their decisions were not subject to appeal.[216]

The end of this autonomy was foreshadowed by the Small Debts Act, 1845, which permitted superior court review by certiorari in cases involving ten pounds or more.[217] Review implied an insistence on conformity to law, an implication that became explicit when the County Courts Act was passed in 1846. Under that act the decision was to be 'precisely that which a superior court would arrive at'; the old 'equity and good conscience' jurisdiction was abandoned.[218] And, after a brief initial period during which the legal profession protested the failure to provide full rights of appeal,[219] a further amendment of the statute largely rectified this affront to the rights of citizens and the economic interests of lawyers.[220]

The law of the land now governed almost all disputes throughout virtually the entire court system.[221] But to the bemusement of commentators and no doubt to the chagrin of lawyers, litigants simply ignored the new appeal procedures.[222] Was this the sound of one hand clapping?

In due course, the superior courts developed rules and doctrines – 'principles,' in Atiyah's phrase – which helped them to exercise absentee management over adjudication in the lower courts without having to intervene directly to dispose of large numbers of individual cases. Articulation of a standard rule for calculating damages, it has been suggested, was one such instance.[223] These arrangements, in turn, permitted the superior courts to remain small, staffed by a cadre of élite judges, and focused upon the weightier legal problems of a select clientele. What remains unclear is the extent to which the county courts, in contradistinction to the old local courts, actually adhered to 'law.' They were supposed to do so; they could be reversed for not doing so; but it is possible that there was a considerable gap between the ideal and reality, in this as in all else.

What, then, was the ultimate significance of these changes in the English civil justice system between 1830 and 1850? The incorporation of local and special jurisdictions within the formal court structure had apparently ended a tradition of legal pluralism stretching back a thousand years: '[W]herever we find places with any peculiar standing ... or certain industries ... or classes of men differentiated from the general population ... we find historically a special body of law with special courts.'[224]

Lawyers, although ostensibly deferential to tradition, were not much impressed by this tradition of pluralism. On the contrary: 'an isolated or peculiar jurisdiction is in itself an evil of no ordinary magnitude,' said the *Solicitors' Journal*.[225] The attorney-general, himself no legal historian, complained that '[f]or above a century this country has exhibited the anomalous spectacle of distinct tribunals acting upon antagonistic principles, and dispensing different qualities of justice.'[226] The prominent jurists of the National Association for the Promotion of Social Science pointed to 'the necessity of a single comprehensive parent tribunal, and single comprehensive local tribunals, presided over by judges omni-competent in their authority,' although they were prepared to contemplate the appointment of 'assistants or experts in the different ranges of their jurisdiction.'[227] The great legal reformers of the 1872 Judicature Commission sniffed disdainfully at the few vestigial remnants of the old courts: 'We recommend the abolition of all local and inferior Courts of civil jurisdiction. If they did not exist, no one would think of establishing them.'[228] And Dicey, as we know, promoted the 'ordinary courts' and 'ordinary law' to a position of virtual constitutional entrenchment.[229]

So the lawyers appeared to have succeeded in suppressing pluralism. The movement to unify, integrate, and structure hierarchically the English legal system did indeed sweep away most local and special courts. As will be seen, it also swamped the movement for distinctive commercial tribunals and threatened to dilute the idiosyncratic characteristics of private arbitration systems. It reached its high-water mark with the merger of the superior courts and the abolition of their peculiar procedures in 1873.[230] The movement was not one that would likely have developed in the absence of profound socio-economic change or in isolation from general intellectual and political trends favouring 'scientific' solutions. And it probably would not have succeeded if it had not identified and remedied some very real defects in the old system, or if it had been no more than a triumph of legal formalism and self-interest.

As Weber reminds us, however, the scientific or rationalizing tendency of English law did not encompass the substantive law itself, owing to 'the successful resistence of the great centrally organized lawyers' guilds.' It was confined to matters of structure. And here the interests of lawyers and of other influential architects of public institutions more nearly coincided: 'The struggle of the common law lawyers [continues Weber] ... was to a large extent economically caused by their interest in fees ... But their power position ... was a result of political centralization.'[231]

But for all that the English civil justice system seemed to take on a new, unified, and somewhat more 'rational' structure in the period from 1830 to 1870, at precisely the same time, as we will see, new manifestations of pluralism were emerging. From 1830 onward administrative and regulatory experiments proliferated. The very parliament that passed the Judicature Acts of 1873 conceived the prototype of the modern independent regulatory commission, the Railway and Canal Commission. To borrow the language of the judicature commissioners, although administrative tribunals 'did not exist' – or existed only in embryo – someone obviously did 'think of establishing them.' Similarly, although tribunals of commerce 'did not exist' because parliament rebuffed the petitions of business groups to create them, trade associations and chambers of commerce set about 'establishing them' by private arrangements.

To an extent, lawyers did function as the custodians of the central legal system and were often able to vindicate its claims in contests with other regimes. Where lawyers were opposed by influential groups with special legal interests, such as the business communities of the City of London or of Liverpool, they had to accept compromise measures.[232] But where opposing groups lacked economic or political power, as did the Welsh, lawyers were able to inflict considerable inconvenience and hardship on behalf of their clients, their own economic interests, and their legal centralist ideology.[233] And where their claims were uncontested, they were even able to rewrite history, as in the appropriation of the notion of the 'rule of law' for the exclusive use of the central courts and their particular brand of justice.

Ultimately, however, notwithstanding the new meaning they gave to the 'rule of law,' lawyers were unable to inhibit the development of private commercial tribunals or administrative tribunals, although they managed to deprive both of legitimacy. Ironically, the very political strength and principled tenacity with which lawyers rallied around the formal legal system in opposition to various proposed institutional reforms forced practical people to go elsewhere for the solution to their practical problems. As we will see, the same professional opposition that had been mounted against the old pluralism of the local courts was to confront the new pluralism of commercial tribunals, arbitration, and administrative jurisdictions. Nor is this surprising: the economic interests, the intellectual attitudes, the ideology of lawyers were being similarly challenged. But the new pluralism differed in two important respects.

First, in the case of commercial disputes, the legal profession's interests clearly diverged from those of the business community on behalf of which, we must assume, the new county courts had been instituted. This divergence warrants further speculation about the extent to which lawyers and businessmen actually shared common interests in the suppression of the old local courts. On the one hand, the original County Courts Act of 1846 did not give lawyers what they wanted; only with subsequent changes in the tariff of fees and the establishment of clear linkages to the common-law system by way of a right of appeal did the lawyers secure their objectives. On the other hand, neither the legal profession nor the business community was homogeneous. Competition between London and the provinces for legal business, the very different legal requirements and political influence of small local traders and large firms engaged in national and international markets, the dangerous threat to custom-based mining activities from those supported by a more 'modern' legal framework, the uneven penetration of scientific views about government among the various constituencies – all of these complicate any easy assumptions about the identity of interest between law and business in displacing pluralism and in moving toward a centralized and uniform system of civil justice.

Second, when we come to consider contemporaneous events in the development of administrative law, the situation becomes even more complicated. In principle, the rationalizing and centralizing administrators who 'invented' the factory inspectorate, the Poor Law commissioners, and the Board of Health must have been sympathetic to the existence of a comprehensive, standardized national system of minor courts; here their views would have coincided with those of the legal profession. But there was much more at stake than institutional architecture. These new administrative structures were politically controversial, challenging not merely professional interests and ideologies but the prevailing belief in laissez-faire and the rule of local oligarchies of landowners and industrialists.

Again it would be easy to assume that legal and administrative interests must necessarily have been opposed, but the evidence is mixed. Many of those who advocated the policies that engendered the new administrative law were themselves lawyers, as were many of the important new men of the bureaucracy. Moreover, new regulatory legislation created a new market for legal advice and representation. Thus, it is probably true that lawyers' attitudes toward the new administrative regimes were more mixed than they were toward the old local courts, although both the old and the new pluralism presented comparable challenges to professional attitudes and values.

Whether because of a lack of professional cohesion, or because the tasks to be performed were technically more diverse and complex, or because the issues themselves implicated a wider range of political and economic interests, the legal centralist paradigm was not reinforced nearly to the same extent in the design of Victorian government in general as it had been in the design of the local court system. Lawyers might assert pre-emptive claims over the courts – we will see them doing so again in relation to a proposed system of 'tribunals of commerce' – but they could do no more than place the administration within outer boundaries of 'law.' These boundaries shifted from time to time, constrained action on occasion, and defined a pale of settlement within which administrative legitimacy remained somewhat tenuous. But administration was neither reduced to law nor subsumed within the formal legal system as local civil justice had been.

3

Commercial Relationships and Disputes:
The Persistence of Pluralism

INTRODUCTION

The centralizing tendencies of the new industrial economy and of professionalism and of the reformist architects of the legal system combined to transform local civil justice in the mid-nineteenth century. Custom, discretion, accidental procedural distinctions, and local participation, management, and jurisdiction were all consigned to the scrap heap when the county courts were bolted into place as the shiny new components of an integrated national legal system. This transformation largely marked the end of one manifestation of legal pluralism, which had existed 'since the memory of man runneth not.' But pluralism itself persisted and indeed flourished in certain contexts. One of the most important of these contexts was the world of business.

For centuries, businessmen had eluded the welcoming embrace of the central legal system, organized their affairs according to law which was their own, and settled their disputes in forums which they controlled, according to decisional norms and procedures which they consciously contrasted with those of the superior courts.[1] During the nineteenth century, they appeared to have entered at last into a formal union with the respectable law of lawyers and judges and parliament; but, in characteristic Victorian fashion, they also cultivated discreet (and sometimes indiscreet) liaisons in the demi-monde of legal pluralism.

The experience of businessmen is of some significance in the development of our understanding of both history and law. When we contrast the frequent successes of business in maintaining its own legal systems with the suppression of local courts, we may learn something about why changes come about in a legal system and what their effects are likely to be. When we reflect upon the frequent opposition of interest between businessmen and lawyers we may be able to shed new light on the affinity of the two groups, an affinity that is often taken for granted. And as we observe the techniques by which lawyers sought to extend the control of their law over the distinctive institutions of the business community, we will witness a rehearsal of contemporaneous developments in administrative law.

The difficulty we will encounter in reconstructing events that might yield insights into such matters is an exaggerated version of what we have already experienced in our account of local and special courts. Written records of transactions are the stuff of business archives, but such records virtually never betray a conscious awareness of the legal context of business, and seldom tell us much about disputes and how they were resolved. It is true that legal historians in recent years have addressed these latter themes, but their vantage point atop the lofty structures of the central legal system has made it difficult for them to gain an accurate perspective on law from ground level. Yet it is from ground level that law must be viewed if we are to take its true measure. It might be tempting, for example, to assume that the difficulty of establishing limited liability companies before the mid-nineteenth century inhibited capital accumulation and investment; the truth appears to be otherwise.[2] Again, one could easily leap to the conclusion that important commercial statutes in the 1880s and 1890s, such as the Sale of Goods Act, were intended to supply a missing element of certainty and predictability in transactions; this too probably is an error.[3] Or, to take a third example, our knowledge of the businessman's dislike of lawyers, law, and litigation might lead us to ask how business disputes were actually resolved; it is hoped that the account that follows will answer such questions.

In order to avoid being misled in each of these examples, we must first remind ourselves that the rules for buying and selling, lending and borrowing, shipping and carrying are generated primarily by regimes of private ordering – the contract, the course of dealing, the ritual of the exchange. It is extremely doubtful that more than the tiniest fraction of these transactions is made with conscious reference to formal rules and common or statute law. Nor does such law suddenly take over when disputes arise. Private ordering through negotiation tends to yield a variety of non-adjudicated and indeterminate outcomes: satisfaction, acquiesence, renegotiated terms, or compensation. Nor does the failure of negotiation necessarily signal the advent of formal legal intervention. Arbitration and other types of domestic adjudication dispose of a significant number of disputes. Finally, we should not forget that only a small proportion of disputes set down for formal determination actually see the inside of a courtroom: lawyers settle cases too.

All of these observations, recorded in the present tense and based upon facts that are familiar (if undocumented), apply with equal force to the nineteenth century. They help to explain why the connection between formal law and the operative norms of commercial transactions is problematic, and they provide the general context for a discussion focused on formal and informal dispute settlement rather than on the initial creation of transactions or the bilateral adjustment of disputes by the parties themselves.

Although this discussion will be largely based upon the experience of the nineteenth century, we will begin by attempting to locate that experience in a more extended account of the way in which the central legal system of England treated commercial disputes over some six hundred years.

COMMERCIAL DISPUTES AND THE CENTRAL LEGAL SYSTEM

From earliest times to the present, consensual arbitration has been the device to which the business community persistently turned in order to resolve its disputes.[4] Arbitration obviously places considerable distance between its users and the legal system of the state, a distance whose extent and significance we will attempt to measure in the next section of this chapter. A recurring theme of English commercial law has been the attempt to demonstrate that the special needs of the business community can be accommodated within structures established by the state. These included a colourful parade of historical oddities: medieval franchise courts, common-law courts with special juries in the seventeenth and eighteenth centuries, tribunals of commerce in the nineteenth, and the so-called Commercial Court (an emanation of the Queen's Bench Division) from 1896 onward. There is little to be gained from a detailed scrutiny of all of them, especially those that lie outside our period of study. Suffice it to say that their proponents were moved by a variety of economic and political (but seldom jurisprudential) motives, and that the support of commercial 'clients' was generally solicited with the promise of cheap, effective, and knowledgeable adjudication – supported (as arbitration was not) by the enforcing power of the state.[5] As this account will show, implicit in all of these attempts to create or legitimate distinctive forums for the adjudication of commercial disputes was a tacit acceptance of the pluralistic nature of English law.

Franchise Courts[6]

By the fourteenth century, mercantile activity in England had grown to the point where the distinctive legal needs of the commercial community received explicit recognition. The charters establishing or defining the rights of a number of boroughs provided for the adjudication, inter alia, of disputes between merchants by the mayor and other officials. Similarly, merchant guilds commonly were given power to decide a broad range of disputes between members. Franchises establishing or regulating fairs often assigned adjudicative responsibilities to the fair-master or franchise-holder; these were the courts of piepoudre. By a statute of 1353, the so-called staple courts were established in designated centres of various commodity markets. And the Court of Admiralty had extensive jurisdiction in litigation over foreign trade.

Although the jurisdiction and composition of these tribunals varied (and in the case of the borough courts included non-commercial matters) they exhibited certain common characteristics. They afforded merchants at least some role in the actual process of decision (whether as principal decision-makers or as members of a special jury or mixed panel) in order to draw upon their special knowledge of mercantile facts and customs. They explicitly or implicitly relied upon the special rules of the law merchant, rather than upon common law, as the basis of decision, and they employed procedures that were less formal and more expeditious than those of the ordinary courts.

To some extent the emergence of these special commercial tribunals can be attributed to the international character of trade, even at this early period. The domestic courts had no jurisdiction over foreigners or over contracts made abroad, and it was necessary to secure the acquiescence of foreign litigants in the process if it was to be effective; hence, provision was made for their participation. But more than the basis of jurisdiction was at stake. The substantive rules affecting commercial transactions were themselves transnational rather than local in character. Credit transactions or sales by sample entered into at one time or place had to be enforced according to the original understandings of the parties later or elsewhere. This need to project transactions over time and space led to the emergence of well-known substantive rules of obligation, uniformly applied wherever traders met or corresponded.[7] Here again there was a reason for involving the merchant community in the administration of its special justice system: merchants would know the rules and be able to assess conduct in the light of the rules. Finally, the itinerant nature of the merchant community placed a premium on the speedy resolution of disputes. The procedures of the courts administering the law merchant thus tended to be less formal and more easily invoked than those of the common-law courts, a fact that further facilitated (or was caused by) adjudication of disputes by non-lawyers.

No doubt their special transnational quality legitimated the growth of special courts administering the law merchant outside the main body of the common law. However, with the expansion of internal as well as international commerce, the decline of close-knit merchant communities and guilds, and the rise of national consciousness and political power, many of the old medieval tribunals were swept aside, and the common-law courts asserted their primacy. By the end of the sixteenth century, Holdsworth says, 'the internal trade of the country had ... practically ceased to be ruled by a special law and by special courts.'[8]

The processes by which the common law attempted to accommodate and absorb the law merchant will be canvassed below. Suffice it to say at this point that the decline of feudal mercantile jurisdictions is not to be construed as proof that the common law had developed a fully satisfactory alternative.[9]

The Law Merchant in the Common-Law Courts[10]

The law merchant of medieval Europe evolved into the more sophisticated commercial-law doctrines of Italian (and other Mediterranean) trading centres, which were imported into England as its economy developed, particularly from the seventeenth century onward.

The work of assimilating these doctrines and general commercial practice into English law was initially undertaken by the privy council rather than the common-law courts. In the latter part of the sixteenth century, the council had general supervisory power over all courts. Accordingly, it was able to control the processes of commercial litigation by giving directions as to the hearing of commercial cases in the courts, by compelling arbitration and enforcing awards, and by developing new legislation based on information about commercial custom.[11]

The courts of Admiralty and Star Chamber (especially the former) were active in the development of commercial law during this period, particularly in disputes involving foreign merchants; Chancery was also used, especially in matter relating to accounts.[12] But the common-law courts played a less significant part in the process, at least initially. Only in the sixteenth century did they escape the jurisdictional limitations that prevented them from dealing with foreign plaintiffs or transactions, and only in the seventeenth century did commercial litigation acquire any significance.[13]

Whatever constraints were imposed by cumbersome procedures and methods of proof, it was clear that common-law doctrine had first to be reconciled with commercial custom and law. By Coke's time it was accepted that the law merchant was part of the domestic law of England, but as a practical matter it still had to be specially pleaded and proved. Only in this way could English judges be informed of its content. In fact, until the end of the seventeenth century the law merchant was regarded as customary law, and as such was applied only if the judge found it reasonable. This ultimate veto exercised by the common-law judges gave English commercial law a distinctive quality. In effect, while the law merchant was brought within the common-law system, it was not swallowed whole.[14] But neither was commercial law, by the seventeenth century, any longer an autonomous system fed from foreign sources alone.

The final stage in judicial integration of the law merchant with the common law was the work of Lord Mansfield in the late eighteenth century. Later the tasks of invention, reform, and consolidation would pass to public and private legislators; but Mansfield represented the judicial contribution at its highest.[15] Mansfield's accomplishments as a commercial lawyer rested on his familiarity with sources extrinsic to the common law. On the one hand, he was well informed about current commercial practice, and he frequently used special juries of merchants with whom he was personally familiar. On the other hand, his knowledge of Continental legal systems enabled him to draw upon well-developed foreign mercantile codes that reflected internationally accepted practices and principles in the commercial community. With these sources available to him, he was able to take judicial notice of well-established commercial custom, which was deemed to be part of the law, or to seek proof of custom from his special juries and then to settle the law to conform to the newly proved custom. Finally, Mansfield was able to fix the meaning of widely used, standard-form documents by interpreting them authoritatively, albeit liberally and in accordance with the 'true' intent of the parties.[16]

In a sense, Mansfield's work can be construed as the ultimate triumph of the common law over a rival system. If so, it is a triumph of a peculiar sort: the victorious system in effect adopted as its own the form and substance of the vanquished. But subsequent developments put in question even this limited definition of triumph. The special jury, which had been for Mansfield a device for harmonizing commercial expectations and legal outcomes, continued to perform such functions throughout much of the nineteenth century.[17] However, a change in the qualifications of jurors in 1870 led to a decline in its use.[18] And, although from Mansfield's time onward the common law possessed a doctrinal foundation upon which might have been constructed a legal regime acceptable to the commercial community, businessmen continued to seek ways of resolving their disputes without going to the regular courts. As in earlier times, arbitration offered one alternative to common-law litigation. But throughout the nineteenth century, the notion persisted of special tribunals staffed by merchants rather than (or in addition to) judges, and dispensing commercial customary law rather than common law. This notion, in a sense, was the ultimate verdict of business-men on the lawyers and judges who had always been regarded as unusually devoted to commercial interests.

Commercial Tribunals

Throughout the era of active reform of the English legal system, which culminated in the 1870s with the enactment of the Judicature Acts, both lawyers and businessmen seemed to accept that relatively little important commercial litigation found its way into the superior courts. For example, it was estimated in 1846 that only three cases worth £10,000 or more were tried each year in the superior courts.[19] But even though the facts were not disputed, lawyers and businessmen did not necessarily agree upon whether or how such disputes should be brought within the ambit of the central legal system.

At the beginning of the period, at least, lawyers, in language reminiscent of Mansfield,[20] modestly perceived their relationship to the commercial community as essentially facilitative: '[Mercantile Law] merely comes in aid of what is already established. It rarely originates anything; but simply en-forces the obligations of conscience, and sanctions the regulations which, in the course of trade, have been found beneficial.'[21] Later they made more ex-travagant claims. For example, judicial adherence to certain legal principles was said to have improved banking practice: '[T]hose principles for the practical conduct of the business ... have only of late obtained general ac-quiescence, the very opposite notions having, but a few years back, pre-vailed among practical men; whilst the judges, in their decisions on banking questions have never swerved from one line.'[22]

As will be seen, the issue of whether law should shape or be shaped by business practice is central to the issue of how the legal system should deal with commercial disputes. (The same issue will be dealt with in the context of administrative practice.) But a second theme is heard constantly. Even assuming the desire of lawyers and judges to give effect to commercial ex-pectations, the mechanism of the superior courts was woefully inappropri-ate: '[T]he simplest pecuniary right cannot be recovered, or obligation en-forced, except at a cost frequently far *exceeding* the sum at stake, with a delay and harrassment which, in the rapid requirements of business, is often tantamount to a refusal of justice, and with an uncertainty ... which too often induces the abandonment of the most undoubted rights.'[23]

Complaints of technicality, delay, and cost were so commonplace that lawyers were tempted to believe that procedural reforms in the superior courts would induce businessmen to bring their disputes to them. But that was not what businessmen had in mind. In seeking a 'natural' rather than a 'technical' procedure,[24] businessmen were seeking disposition of their disputes entirely outside the framework of the courts and the monopolistic control of the legal profession.[25]

Arbitration, of course, had always been an option for businessmen dissatisfied with curial adjudication; so it remained. But because arbitrators lacked a clear mandate, procedural and remedial powers, and the assurance of finality for their decisions, the alternative of tribunals of commerce gained support in business circles from mid-century onward. As early as 1852, the Liverpool Chamber of Commerce favoured the establishment of local and permanent tribunals, constituted by the state with dispositive powers but with judges who were 'almost exclusively' merchants and traders. Procedures of the tribunal might embrace pre-trial conciliation, but would be summary and informal. Provision was to be made for obtaining the expertise of 'assistant judges cognizant [in the] peculiarity of any particular business,' of accountants, and, on 'difficult points of law,' of higher tribunals, with a possibility of appeal only in large cases.[26]

Soon the idea of establishing tribunals of commerce attracted the support of other major commercial groups – of Bristol, Leeds, Newcastle, and (after some initial vacillation) Manchester, of the Associated Chambers of Commerce, and of 1,500 leading London firms.[27] By 1869, resolutions favouring tribunals of commerce were being passed unanimously and without debate at the annual meeting of the Associated Chambers of Commerce.[28]

But support for tribunals of commerce was not immediate or universal, especially among lawyers. Recognizing that the proposal was '[a] symptom ... of the growing impatience of the public with the present system of law proceedings and law charges,' the *Law Times* none the less dismissed it as '[a]nother hit at the lawyers.'[29] The influential and lawyer-dominated Society for Promoting the Amendment of the Law also rejected it for a variety of practical reasons: opposition to lay judges and the difficulty of obtaining the participation of busy businessmen, problems of jurisdictional boundaries between tribunals in different sectors and between those tribunals and the regular courts, and the multiplication and under-utilization of courts.[30] Other more extreme critics did not hesitate to impugn the proposal because it emanted from foreigners and was based on European experience. Proponents of the tribunals, it was urged, 'want to abolish the juridical section of the British constitution; to cut through the common law of England, of which Englishmen were so justly proud; to abolish trial by jury in all mercantile cases.'[31]

This contest between two powerful groups – lawyers and businessmen – found its way into parliament. Two parliamentary committees, in 1858 and 1871, had explored (and the latter endorsed) the creation of tribunals.[32] A royal commission report in 1874 rejected the idea, however, proposing instead that the proper tribunal for cases involving technical knowledge, or knowledge of commercial practice, would be 'a legal Judge, assisted by two skilled assessors, who could advise the Judge as to any technical or practical matters arising in the course of the inquiry.'[33] The evidence considered by the commission and the reasons proffered for its conclusion deserve scrutiny.

The commission was at pains to point out that there was 'the greatest diversity of opinion' among proponents of tribunals on such important issues as their proposed jurisdiction, the respective roles (if any) of lay and professional judges, 'whether the Tribunals should observe the ordinary rules of evidence ... whether they should be guided by the principles laid down by the Superior Courts of Law ... whether the parties should be allowed to be represented by counsel or solicitors; [and] whether there should be any appeal.'[34] Moreover, the foreign models of tribunals studied by the commission betrayed a similar confounding diversity.

The commission, which had performed the herculean task of reconstructing the entire superior court system,[35] was not deterred by the necessity of selecting features of the new tribunals from among the several schemes favoured by proponents. The real differences of opinion that emerged in evidence seemed to be between the legal community and the commercial community. With some exceptions, trade associations, chambers of commerce, municipal governments, corporate directors, and (to a lesser extent) individual manufacturers and merchants and insurers favoured one form or another of commercial tribunal.[36] Dissenting views within this group came less on any question of principle than from those who favoured adaptation of the new county court system, or who were already involved in the privately established domestic tribunals of trade associations,[37] or who spoke for the commercially underdeveloped areas of the country.

On the legal side, however, the preponderance of opinion was negative.[38] Even those lawyers who favoured tribunals of commerce did so grudgingly.[39] The attachment to the notion of a single, homogeneous, professionaly run legal system seems to have been unshakable. Said the commission:

[I]t is of the utmost importance to the commercial community that the decisions of the Courts of Law should on all questions of principle be, as far as possible, uniform, thus affording precedents for the conduct of those engaged in the ordinary transactions of trade. With this view it is essential that the Judges by whom commercial cases are determined should be guided by the recognised rules of law and by the decisions of the Superior Courts in analogous cases; and only Judges who have been trained in the principles and practice of law can be expected to be so guided. We fear that merchants would be too apt to decide questions that might come before them (as some of the witnesses we examined have suggested that they should do) according to their own views of what was just and proper in the particular case, a course which from the uncertainty attending their decisions would inevitably multiply litigation, and with the vast intricate commercial business of this country would sooner or later lead to great confusion. Commercial questions, we think, ought not to be determined without law, or by men without special legal training.[40]

This desire for legal orthodoxy had led the commission to offer a gratuitous criticism of arbitration in an earlier report.[41] It was the central concern of the majority of the commission. As a later commentator stated, 'The Judicature Acts of 1873 and 1875 were the handiwork of the great Chancery lawyers who undertook the duty of fusing into one harmonious whole the antagonistic systems of common law and equity but they were not designed to promote the economy and speed which the City wanted.'[42] But economy and speed were not the central issues. The reasons of the non-concurring commissioners, no less than the majority report, make this clear.

Action S. Ayrton, a tireless proponent of tribunals of commerce, had already urged that they be adopted as part of the general restructuring of the English courts.[43] He renewed this view in separate reasons underlining the special features of commercial disputes, which distinguished them from ordinary litigation and necessitated decision-making by merchants rather than lawyers:

It appears to me that when a dispute arises in the course of a commercial dealing, the compulsory settlement of it by a Tribunal may be regarded as only a continuance or a conclusion of the transaction, and that it is unreasonable to insist that the parties interested shall, as a condition of having their dispute determined, be required, at an enormous cost and inconvenience to themselves, to create a precedent for the benefit of society, and to add a rule of law to a commercial code.

I consider that the advantages which would result from placing the legal and commercial elements of the Tribunal on an equality, outweigh the objections. The legal Judge could exercise sufficient‚influence over his commercial colleagues to prevent them from acting contrary to settled law, but the sagacity and experience of the commercial men would in general be of more service to the suitors in the decision of their disputes than the legal knowledge of the Judge.[44]

Sir Sidney Waterlow dissented on essentially similar grounds: 'Those who support the present system of trying mercantile disputes seem to regard them all as hostile litigation, and lose sight of the fact that in the majority of cases when differences arise between merchants or traders, both parties would rejoice to obtain a prompt settlement, by a legal tribunal duly constituted, and to continue their friendly commercial relations.'[45] These views hint strongly at a conviction that norms of commercial conduct should prevail over legal norms, a conviction also implicit in 'the well-known fact that in the large majority of commercial disputes the parties avoid the Courts of Law and resort to private arbitration.'[46]

The argument in favour of uniform, professional administration of the legal system was similarly rejected by those who favoured tribunals of commerce:

The argument that the uniform administration of the law would be impaired has, I believe, been usually urged against proposals for withdrawing causes from the Courts at Westminster, and remitting them to inferior Tribunals. It was suggested that this evil would arise from the establishment of County Courts, and from the extension of their jurisdiction, but it is proved by experience that no such evil has arisen, nor does it arise from the exercise of the judicial functions of the Courts of Quarter Sessions or Petty Sessions, or the stipendiary or unpaid magistrates, although their decisions in criminal cases, and in certain civil cases, affect the rights and liabilities of the public in as great a degree as the decisions of Tribunals of Commerce would affect the commercial community.[47]

But it was not to be. Even the limited departure from strict legal control of the process endorsed by the majority of the commissioners – the two expert assessors – was not taken up.[48] Although proposals for tribunals of commerce were brought forward repeatedly for at least another twenty years, they never won official support.[49] The supremacy of legal values was preserved, and commercial disputants continued to take their differences to arbitration and other forums of their own design, which were apparently more congenial than the common-law courts.

The Commercial Court

The search for an arrangement by which businessmen could be persuaded to use the superior courts rather than arbitration did not end with the failure of the effort to establish tribunals of commerce. In the 1890s the continuing disaffection of the commercial community with ordinary legal recourse finally evoked a sympathetic re.ponse from the judges.[50]

Initially, it was thought that if the courts resumed their former practice of sitting in a location convenient for businessmen they would attract commercial litigation. The notion was naïve; although sittings were held in the Guildhall, no sudden upsurge was noted in lawsuits brought by businessmen.[51] A more serious effort to solve the problems of commercial litigation was undertaken between 1892 and 1895.[52] Ultimately, the decision was taken to establish a special list of commercial cases to be tried in the Queen's Bench Division. Cases on the list would be tried by a judge experienced in commercial matters, pursuant to special directions expediting the process, dispensing with or accelerating the exchange of pleadings, limiting the scope of discovery, and requiring the submission of affidavit rather than viva voce evidence.[53]

The so-called Commercial Court, in reality only a special list of cases administratively established pursuant to a resolution of the judges, was in the final analysis a court. On the surface, it seemed to offer expeditious and sympathetic handling of commercial litigation. However, the Commercial Court has always been less successful in attracting commercial litigants than in attracting the praise of judges and lawyers. One recent judicial observer maintained that 'a commercial dispute can be speedily and efficiently determined in the courts as well as by arbitration. The two systems ought indeed to be properly regarded as coordinate rather than rival.'[54] Another legal author contended that the Commercial Court is speedier and cheaper than arbitration, dispenses better justice than that available from non-professional arbitrators, and should be preferred by commercial litigants except in cases where they wish to select an experienced lawyer as an arbitrator and where the 'dispute concerns a straight question of fact involving expert knowledge.'[55]

Despite these claims, the Commercial Court's caseload has never grown to the point where its future was assured, and arbitration and other domestic forums for dispute settlement retain their strong attraction for important elements in the business community.[56] While the fortunes of the Commercial Court ebb and flow, the persistence and vitality of its chief rival, arbitration, is surely a fact of significance. Assuming that there is any truth at all in the claim that the Commercial Court can compete with arbitration in speed, cost, and 'justice,' why would arbitration survive and flourish? Thus framed, the question brings us to the essence of the evidence considered here: 'Legal history presents no more remarkable phenomenon than the increasing and now complete failure in every country of all legal reform, whether embodying simplifications of the law, or expedition of trial procedure or cheapening of cost, to induce commercial men ... willingly to make use of Courts of Law for the settlement of their commercial differences.'[57] It is already clear that the explanation is linked to the limited powers of the legal centralist paradigm. On the one hand, the paradigm fails as description; it does not explain the ongoing attraction of alternative models of adjudication for much of the business community. On the other hand, it fails as prescription; it is unable to impose itself upon events, to force or entice significant elements in that community to bring their disputes to the superior courts, let alone (as we will see) to organize their affairs according to legal rules laid down by the state.

In neither case, of course, is the failure complete. It is important not to overestimate the extent to which business as a whole actively rejected the central legal system or to underestimate the extent to which it passively or unconsciously participated in it. No doubt there was a considerable segment of business that never concerned itself with the problem of adjudicative autonomy. But given the seldom-challenged assumptions of the centralist paradigm, the very existence of some autonomy, of some diversity, of some pluralism is a significant revelation; how significant, we may judge better after examining the phenomenon that represented the greatest challenge to centralism: arbitration.

ARBITRATION IN THE MID-NINETEENTH CENTURY

Consensual arbitration had been known and widely used from earliest times. It remained popular with business disputants despite the various curial alternatives provided from time to time, and described above. However, it is true that the mixed public and private character of the early tribunals dispensing the law merchant somewhat obscured the functional distinctions between consensual arbitration and adjudication in these special courts. It is therefore important to recall that the courts of piepoudre and borough and staple courts 'were part of the English judicial system that heard cases which were not justiciable at common law ... rather than tribunals that merely served as arbitrators of disputes.'[58] When these special jurisdictions declined at the end of the medieval period, it might have been expected that commercial disputes would find a home within the regular court system. This was not to be; the exigencies of commercial litigation apparently could not be accommodated by the common-law courts. As Lord Parker says, '[t]he habit of arbitration' (in the larger sense) 'and the desire for its use persisted' despite the new 'tendency for the institutions of the central government to seek to intervene and control the regulation of trade within the state.'[59]

By the nineteenth century arbitration had ceased to be the exclusive concern of businessmen and was increasingly attracting the attention of judges, who were becoming involved in the enforcement and review of awards, of legislators, who began to use arbitration as a proxy for administrative control, and of lawyers, who saw arbitration either as a competitive threat or as an opportunity for new work. Each of these perceptions will be addressed, but it is necessary first to define and describe the arbitral processes of the period, particularly as they related to commercial disputes.

All forms of arbitration involve the submission of disputes by the parties to the determination of a third person whose decisional authority depends on their consent. Beyond this, generalization is impossible. Consent to arbitration was often authentic, but was sometimes required by court order, legislative instruction, or the rules of powerful private organizations. Disputes were usually determined by adjudication following adversary presentation, but sometimes were resolved by compromise arising out of much less formal procedures. The norms of decision were, on occasion, conventional legal norms, but frequently they were special trade customs or more generalized notions of fairness.

Accepting the diversity of arrangements embraced within the term 'arbitration,' it may be possible at least to offer for descriptive and analytical purposes several models of arbitration commonly found during the period: informal, ad hoc consensual arbitration; arbitration by trade associations; and arbitration under judicial auspices.[60]

Ad Hoc Consensual Arbitration

Of all the models of arbitration, the one that offered the parties the most complete control over all aspects of their dispute was ad hoc consensual arbitration. So long as they were prepared to forgo recourse to the court to enforce the promise to arbitrate, the agreed-upon procedures, or the award, they could choose their own arbitrators, design their own procedures, adopt or accede to any normative standard they might agree upon, or simply confer upon the arbitrator an open-ended mandate to resolve their differences.

There is considerable secondary evidence to suggest that ad hoc consensual arbitration was commonplace; but in a sense its very formlessness has made it retrospectively invisible. Two parties to a transaction, for example, might simply ask a respected individual in the same trade to resolve their differences. This he might do in the privacy of his own business premises or theirs, or in the informal surroundings of a coffee-house or club. He might confine his fact-finding to examination of a sample of goods, the written documents produced by the parties, or their respective recollections proffered in conversation or debate. His award might be pronounced orally or transcribed as a brief note of the result, probably without reasons. Assuming the parties were willing or felt obliged to live by the award, no more would be heard of it.

Ad hoc consensual arbitration may indeed have been as widespread as contemporary lawyers feared and modern scholars imagine it to be; certainly complaints about the state of the superior courts and the relative paucity of commercial litigation suggest that disputes were resolved in some forum other than the courts.[61] However, remarkably little trace of it is found in business histories or records,[62] and the occasional emergence of deviant cases in the context of judicial review or enforcement proceedings offers no measure of the total volume of ad hoc consensual arbitration. But clearly there was some, and certain of its features suggest that it may have been more common than might be supposed on the basis of documentary evidence.

Examination of some twenty awards arising from ad hoc consensual arbitration shows the relatively limited impact of law and lawyers on the arbitration process.[63] Most arbitrators were land agents, surveyors or other experts, or gentlemen; only one was a lawyer. Lawyers appeared as advocates in only one-third of the cases, although they did help the arbitrators to prepare a formal award in an equal number. Sworn evidence was given in only one-third of the cases; informal methods of fact-gathering seem to have been used in the balance. Reasons for decision were seldom given but, when they were, they sometimes contained admonitory language urging the parties to behave equitably and to compose their differences. Most awards extended beyond simple damages to affirmative directions of various sorts – the apportionment of land and other interests, the settlement of cross-claims, the arrangement of ongoing relationships, and the performance of repairs. Costs were more often equally shared than borne by the losing party. In all of these details, there is more than a hint of compromise, of adjustment, which in principle was anathema to curial habits of clear-cut, adversarial decision-making. It is this special quality of arbitration that provides the clue to its possible popularity.

We see in these awards, too, some of the elements that made arbitration ubiquitous in organized sectors of commerce and industry: the existence of ongoing relationships, of intertwined interests, of shared values that transcended a particular transaction or dispute. But if these elements sometimes existed apart from trade organizations or exchanges, as they probably did, why is it so difficult to document the incidence of arbitration that arose simply as a result of the parties' agreement to submit, uncoerced by either the power of an organized group or the order of a court?

Perhaps the answer is that arbitration was not viewed as a thing apart from the ordinary give-and-take of established trading relationships. Here we are reminded of E.P. Thompson's suggestive remarks about the difficulty of distinguishing 'between the activity ... and the rights,' about the farmer or forester 'moving within visible or invisible structures of law.'[64] Informal recourse to arbitration may have been so commonplace an experience that it elicited no more comment than the everyday experience of friendly compromise, to which, indeed, it was related.

Perhaps an equally credible explanation for the non-visibility of ad hoc consensual arbitration is that it did not exist to as great an extent as is generally believed. At least where there were no prospects of renewed dealing, no other perception of common interests or values, no parity of right or power to deter the parties from seeking total victory in the courts – at least in such cases, we might suppose, the parties would not likely go to arbitration. However, that supposition is in turn subject to two important qualifications discussed below. First, the stronger party may have been able to force the weaker to agree to arbitration as a term of the initial unequal bargain. And arbitration might then be conducted in a forum or according to rules that favoured the stronger party over the weaker. Such a situation might well obtain as between, say, members of a trade or professional organization and their one-time clients, or between insurers and insured. In such cases standard-form contracts probably were used to exact the promise to arbitrate.[65] Second, arbitration might prove agreeable to parties who lacked any affinity to each other simply because it promised to be less painful than conventional litigation. This possibility is discussed at length below.

Arbitration by Organized Groups
Optimal conditions for arbitration obviously existed in the context of

organized groups. Here mutuality of interest was high; rules, customs, or traditions – decisional norms – were specifically laid down or tacitly accepted; structures for decision-making were easily developed; and informal sanctioning systems were credibly invoked.[66] Indeed, from one perspective, the fact that conditions so closely resembled those in the public sector helps to explain why these domestic tribunals came to discharge regulatory functions not unlike those of legislatively created administrative bodies. (The affinity between these two kinds of regulatory agencies is explored in the next chapter.)

From another perspective, the function of arbitration by a trade association was (and is) merely to settle disputes between the members in private, according to the rules of the association. Because these disputes often involved major commercial transactions, the 'law' of the association, in effect, often displaced common law and statutes in determining private 'rights' in significant sectors of economic and social life.[67] Take but three examples of this phenomenon. The Liverpool Cotton Brokers Association provided, as the second of the two steps in its arbitration procedure, a right to appeal to its executive committee; in 1872, 882 appeals were heard by that committee.[68] In the same year, 'a sort of arbitration committee ... in Mark Lane,' apparently dealing with marine insurance claims, was reported to 'sit constantly and determine an infinite number of cases.'[69] And, in a quite different context, a boycott of the Irish courts by a group protesting British home rule proposals led to the establishment of a rival arbitration system. Returns from only about one-third of the localities in which the system operated showed that 1,345 cases had been decided in two months, including disputes over wills, title and possession of land, rent, wages, accounts, and assaults.[70]

These examples suggest that the success of any arbitration scheme can be determined by the strength and cohesion of the group it serves. Some negative support for this hypothesis is found in the failure of several chambers of commerce during the 1850s to develop attractive arbitration systems.[71] Unlike schemes established by commodity exchanges or other organized sectors of industry, chambers of commerce attracted a broad range of firms as members and apparently offered arbitration services merely on an ad hoc basis rather than in a continuing, organized fashion. The powerful Liverpool chamber attributed the lack of interest in arbitration to its uncertain legal status – 'unauthoritative tribunals are rarely resorted to' – and launched an ultimately unsuccessful forty-year campaign for the establishment of tribunals of commerce, which 'are constituted by the State and have compulsory powers.'[72] Other chambers, however, elected to persevere in promoting arbitration.[73] By the 1880s their efforts not only were more successful,[74] but apparently even prompted some local lawyers' organizations to establish their own arbitration schemes.[75]

The strength of domestic tribunals in tightly organized industries may have depended to some extent on the intrinsic appeal of decision-making on the basis of customary norms and on the threat of informal sanctions, such as expulsion from the organization. But the more tenuous connections between those who chose to use, for example, the City of London Chamber of Arbitration leads us to seek a different explanation of its attractions. There seems to be considerable force in a contemporary assessment: the establishment of the chamber of arbitration, it was said, 'is the outcome of a long-growing dissatisfaction on the part of the commercial world with our legal system ... and it must be profound and well-grounded dissatisfaction which has led to what is nothing short of a repudiation by business-men of justice as administered in our courts of law.'[76]

In other words, arbitration of this type drew its strength from the fact that the alternative, conventional litigation, was unacceptable. This is a characteristic arbitration shares with administrative law, which evolved not so much to protect the common values of its 'clientele' as to compensate for the patent incapacity of the ordinary courts to respond to the special requirements of regulatory regimes.

Arbitration under Judicial Auspices[77]

Not all arbitration represented a conscious decision to opt for the advantages of private adjudication or to avoid the disadvantages of litigation in the courts. From the 1830s onward, arbitration was the instrument selected by parliament, judges, and, no doubt, lawyers and litigants to make ordinary litigation more efficient.

Although submissions to arbitration by rule (order) of court were contemplated as early as 1698[78] and by the 1820s were recognized as a distinct phenomenon,[79] not until 1833 was arbitration formally identified as a method by which trial of a civil action might be expedited. As part of a larger effort to avoid the necessity of jury trials with their requirement of unanimity, legislation was proposed that would have empowered a judge to refer issues of fact to an arbitrator.[80] This provision was abandoned in the face of opposition, however; it reappeared only in 1854, with the limitation that it applied to 'matters of mere account.'[81]

Much more important than this limited power of compulsory reference was the enactment of statutes that gave increasing legal force to the arbitration process. In 1833, submissions to arbitration, pursuant to a judicial order or to an agreement providing for such an order, were made irrevocable except by consent of the court, and arbitrators so appointed were given power to require the attendance of witnesses and to administer oaths.[82] These arrangements were extended in 1854 by legislation permitting any submission to be made an order of the court, unless the parties had agreed to the contrary,[83] empowering the court to enforce an agreement to arbitrate by staying the action[84] and to appoint or replace an arbitrator when necessary to avoid frustration of the proceedings.[85] Thus, by 1833, or at least by 1854, arbitration had become a credible alternative to litigation. As a result, many disputes were referred to arbitration by order or rule of court, either before or after the commencement of the action. Because referral in this manner was necessary to secure the statutory advantages mentioned above, it is likely that much arbitration that would otherwise have been purely informal and consensual was conducted under court auspices. But it also seems clear that referral to arbitration often was agreed to after litigation was commenced in order to avoid potentially unpleasant consequences – formalism, delay, and inappropriate decisions by juries on matters of commercial or technical fact and by judges administering common law rather than commercial custom. In effect, by facilitating the diversion of litigation into the hands of arbitrators, the law tried to accommodate the needs of the commercial community.

But this was not always how the matter was perceived by lawyers. The number of cases referred annually by judges to arbitrators must be 'very large,' acknowledged the *Law Times* in 1870.[86] But 'we may take it as settled that references to arbitration are mistakes – costly mistakes in all instances.'[87] It was not simply that the parties often selected non-lawyers as their arbitrators. Even when judges made the selection and appointed lawyers, there was dissatisfaction. There were complaints of nepotism in the selection of certain barristers,[88] although salaried masters were available for appointment only in London.[89] There were allegations of partiality and compromise in decision-making, and there were editorial fulminations that by recourse to arbitration, 'the judicial system of England is being undermined, and the functions of a jury are being usurped.'[90]

The Formal Relationship between Arbitration and the Courts
Given the antipathy of lawyers and judges toward arbitration, it is especially important to try to articulate the basis of the relationship between the law of the central legal system and the private regime of law created by the parties and enforced through their own tribunals. In this connection we can concentrate our attention on those critical moments when the central legal

system was called upon to enforce either a promise to arbitrate or an award, or to review and set aside an award. Obviously, so long as the parties abstained from going to court for either enforcement or review, the central legal system had no direct influence on arbitration. But when the courts were asked to intervene in some way, the legal doctrines and judicial attitudes that defined the extent and direction of intervention might ultimately have had a considerable impact upon the arbitration process unless some means were found for minimizing court intervention.

The Achilles' heel of arbitration was the extent to which it depended upon voluntary compliance with both the promise to arbitrate and the award itself. If compliance was not forthcoming, the aggrieved party was faced with the prospect of seeking conventional remedies or resorting to some type of self-help or informal sanction. Moreover, a party who wished to put in question his obligation to arbitrate, the procedures of the arbitrator, or the correctness of the award could do so by revoking his promise to arbitrate or by simply ignoring the proceeding or its outcome, but not by seeking an authoritative legal declaration of his position. Finally, judges and lawyers had independent interests in the arbitration process. The diversion to arbitration of important business litigation represented an economic loss not only to lawyers but also to judges (who became salaried only in the mid-nineteenth century). Arbitral recognition and enforcement of trade custom alongside the common law presented issues analogous to conflicts-of-law problems. And, as has been suggested, legal professionals had an ideological commitment to formal adjudication and the common law, which was affronted by recourse to arbitration and its special normative systems.

For these reasons, it was necessary to clarify the relationship between arbitration and the formal legal system. Would the courts assist arbitration by enforcing promises to arbitrate and awards? Or would they simply allow the parties to live with the inconvenience and uncertainty they bargained for when they forsook the formality of the courts? Would the courts allow (or force) the parties to live with the peculiar procedures or decisional norms adopted by their chosen arbitrator? Or would they insist on conformity to more conventional procedures and rules of law?

In a limited sense, the council and the Star Chamber, Admiralty, and Chancery courts had shown the way during the late sixteenth and early seventeenth centuries by remitting certain disputes to arbitration.[91] The common-law courts were less than supportive, however, and developed a considerable body of technical doctrine, which did not contribute to the attractiveness of the arbitration process.[92]

An important milestone in the evolution of the common law's view of arbitration was Coke's decision in *Vynior*'s case.[93] Although the actual holding in the case is in some doubt, it has been taken to stand for the proposition that either party to a submission may revoke it and thus frustrate the arbitration.[94] Some commentators, perhaps rightly, suggest that no inference can be drawn from *Vynior*'s case that the courts were hostile to, or jealous of, arbitration.[95] But *Vynior*'s case cannot be viewed in isolation. As Holdsworth points out, *Vynior*'s case was but one among many in the seventeenth century exhibiting hostility toward arbitration; as well, the jurisdictional prerogatives of the common-law courts were being jealously guarded against perceived encroachments from other sources.[96] Indeed, Coke believed that the judges were entitled to vindicate the common law and right reason, even against parliament.[97] In the light of this attitude, his disdain for mere consensual arrangements for arbitration becomes entirely credible.

In failing to support arbitration, it must be said, the common-law courts did not intend wholly to deny merchants access to a congenial body of legal doctrine. As has been seen, by the seventeenth century the law merchant to some extent had been assimilated into the general legal system, a process that was ultimately formalized and regularized by Lord Mansfield. But litigation in the regular courts remained a less than satisfactory option for the commercial community. Apart altogether from the often-cited considerations of cost and delay, the hazards of common-law pleading, the possibility that a common-law judge would mistake, misapply, or simply decline to follow commercial practice, the difficulties of proving commercial 'facts' to the uninitiated, and the problem of remedies were all compelling arguments against conventional litigation and in favour of arbitration.

But arbitration did not merely have to compete with the common-law courts, which it could do to some extent. It had ultimately to confront the much more formidable threats of judicial control and enforced legalism. Increasingly, arbitrators were pressed – by both legislation and judicial decisions – to ensure that their awards conformed to legal principles. As Lord Parker notes, 'The process of judicial intervention into arbitration can be seen growing throughout the eighteenth century, as the functions of the law courts and the practice of the mercantile community coalesce into a coherent system.'[98]

How did the courts come to assert control over what were clearly private tribunals? Lord Parker offers a plausible explanation: 'Litigants in arbitration needed the assistance of the courts who in turn exacted a price for such assistance.'[99] The notion that a tacit bargain was struck between the judges and the commercial community has been supported by Horwitz, an American historian who views a similar phenomenon in the United States somewhat more broadly:

[O]ne might loosely describe the process as one of accommodation by which merchants were induced to submit to formal legal regulation in return for a major transformation of substantive legal rules governing commercial disputes. The judges' unwillingness any longer to recognize competing lawmakers is a product of an increasingly instrumental vision of law. Law is no longer merely an agency for resolving disputes; it is an active, dynamic means of social control and change. Under such conditions, there must be one undisputed and authoritative source of rules for regulating commercial life.[100]

The differing courses of economic development and arbitration law in England and the United States perhaps justify the differing emphases in these two views. In the United States, business expansion was more geographically dispersed and less thoroughly organized within the exchanges and trade associations that dominated certain key sectors in England. Moreover, lawyers and courts may have played a somewhat greater role in the United States than in England in organizing business activity.[101] It is therefore not surprising that the suppression of arbitration (which had deep roots in New York, for example)[102] seems to have been more sweeping in the United States than in England.[103]

But the course of development in England, at least, is relatively clear. Arbitration was not so much suppressed by the courts as captured by them. To the extent that this capture succeeded, the nature of the process was fundamentally changed: instead of responding to norms internal to the commercial community, arbitrators had to respect the external norms of the common law. This was an important change indeed:

Traders always thought of the common law as something beyond their experience. It was local, not general, custom and its processes were slow and formal. It is perfectly certain the merchant had a great need of rule and law, but it was rule and law in the market as he and his kind knew and practised it. It was not deduction from cases; it was self-generative from transactions themselves. He ordinarily found it possible to operate his affairs without controversy or aid of lawyers or courts, but should he find himself at odds with someone in the course of trade, he had an all-complete system of law to direct the settlement.[104]

This distinction between the internal norms of the commercial community and the external norms of the common law warrants further exploration. As we have seen, arbitration was on occasion no more than a procedural device to facilitate litigation in the superior courts. In such circumstances, we rightly anticipate that the court that mandated arbitration would wish to ensure that any outcomes were consistent with those the court itself would have produced. But such circumstances were by no means universal. On the contrary, most important arbitration was conducted under the auspices of commodity exchanges or other organized business groups. And these groups did generate a considerable amount of internal 'law' which was highly pertinent to the outcomes of particular disputes. This internal 'law' took various forms. Sometimes it was unwritten custom; sometimes it was custom codified in a set of rules; sometimes it was incorporated *in extenso* or by reference into the very agreement the arbitrator was being called upon to interpret. As Ferguson points out, especially in the latter part of the nineteenth century standard-form agreements tended to substitutes 'trade-made law' for 'state-made law.'[105] The real question about judicial review – raised especially by judges enamoured of universal legal principles – was whether this substitution should be reversed and 'state-made law' made to prevail.

Nor were such questions confined to cases where careful craftsmanship provided a contractual basis for adherence to commercial norms. Even more difficult were cases where no such language clearly invited the arbitrator to disregard 'law.' Would arbitrators decide such cases, as they had always done, on the basis of commercial custom, of 'free decision, compromise or adjustment in terms of moral right and justice,'[106] or would they seek to propitiate reviewing judges by deferring to what they understood to be legal principles? If they did so, would the judges accept the arbitrators' inexpert view of the law, or would they substitute their own authoritative legal conclusions? And questions of substantive law apart, what tolerance would judges show for the less formal procedures of arbitration, and would judicial review itself, however sympathetic, attenuate and frustrate arbitration proceedings? These were all questions implied by the advent of judicial control. Answers were supplied both by judicial pronouncement and by legislation during the nineteenth century.

From 1833 onward, the general tendency of legislation was to seek to strengthen arbitration by enmeshing it more deeply within the apparatus of formal justice. As has been mentioned, the effect of *Vynior*'s case was overcome by the statutes of 1833 and 1854, which had also extended the powers of arbitrators and otherwise strengthened the process. In each instance the touchstone of legal intervention was the requirement that the submission or the award be made a rule of court. Naturally enough, in the context of proceedings to secure the court's imprimatur, an occasion was provided for the court to scrutinize the submission, the proceedings, or the award itself.

But prior to 1854, the parties were entirely free to arbitrate without the court's assistance, and even after 1854 they retained the right to rebut by contract the presumption that they intended their submission to be enforceable by court order.[107] The possibility that arbitration might exist without judicial auspices, whether ad hoc or in the domestic tribunal of some organized group, is important to bear in mind. How would a judge acquire jurisdiction to review the proceedings or awards of arbitrators not linked to the courts by any requirement of a rule or order?

Watson, the author of an early treatise on arbitration, stated in 1825 that '[t]he courts, neither under submissions, by order of nisi-prius, nor by agreement of the parties, will entertain a motion to set aside an award, unless the submission has first been made a rule of court.'[108] The Arbitration Act of 1698, it is true, did empower a judge to set aside any award, whether or not made a rule of court, but only if it had been 'procured by corruption or undue means'.[109] Otherwise, no basis existed for the courts to intervene.

Indeed, the basis of the courts' jurisdiction to review any award on the merits, and especially for error of law, remained relatively ambiguous throughout most of the nineteenth century. Notwithstanding Lord Parker's conclusion that judicial review of arbitration – although 'obscure' in its origins – had become firmly established by the end of the eighteenth century, the picture is not so clear, as he himself admits.[110] Moreover, the scope and extent of the principle of judicial review remained a matter of controversy for some time, particularly in regard to the necessity for arbitrators to adhere to 'law' in reaching their decisions. Successive editions of Russell's classic work on arbitration, from the first in 1849 through the seventh in 1891, reveal a continuing uncertainty on the issues of whether arbitrators were required to decide cases according to law and whether awards could be quashed for legal error.[111] Although the state of the case law is far from clear, some judges throughout the century continued to hold that awards – in general purely consensual, but sometimes under judicial auspices – could not be set aside for mistake of law, at least in the absence of clear illegality or some other egregious error, such as an arithmetical miscalculation obvious on the face of the award.[112] In more general terms, the rather uncertain attitude of the courts was slowly resolved throughout the century by requiring conformity to legal values and consequently by expanding the scope of judicial review.

In the 1830 law reports, for example, only nine cases dealt with arbitration. Six of these cases tended to support the arbitration process. In two, the time for rendering an award was enlarged;[113] in three, attempts to strike down an award on grounds other than substantive error were rejected;[114] and in one, an arbitral opinion was reviewed on substantive grounds and upheld.[115] Of the three decisions hostile to the process, two upheld the long-established right of a party to revoke the submission and terminate proceedings at any time prior to the making of the award,[116] and one quashed an award on the ground of procedural irregularity.[117] The picture is entirely consistent with Watson's assertion that the courts were reluctant to set aside awards for error of law, deferring to the arbitrator's knowledge (and their own ignorance) of the factual context and recognizing the arbitrator's deliberate intention to reach a just result apart from law.[118]

The picture begins to change following the enactment of the 1833 statute, which was intended to give greater legal support to the arbitration system. The law reports of 1840-1 include four cases in which the courts were asked to make procedural rulings relating to the progress of arbitrations. In two cases, the rulings supported arbitration;[119] in two they did not.[120] In addition, review was sought of some twenty-three awards, in seventeen cases without success[121] or with limited success,[122] in six successfully.[123] By 1850, attacks on awards were alleged to be 'frequent,'[124] and courts were accused of setting them aside 'for technical error.'[125] Further facilitating legislation was passed in 1854.[126] The law reports for 1860-1 include ten cases in which the courts were asked to intervene on procedural grounds; success was evenly divided.[127] But of an additional eight cases in which review of an award was sought, it was granted in five cases[128] and refused only in three.[129]

In summary, subject to any distortion introduced by reliance upon reported cases,[130] we see some evidence of two parallel trends: more frequent appeals to the courts to assist the arbitration process, and a greater willingness on the part of judges to overturn arbitral awards.[131] Moreover, these trends acquire some significance when we recall that neither in 1833 nor in 1854 were the courts given a general mandate to review arbitration awards. It seems that review simply followed in the wake of 'assistance.' The Parker / Horwitz thesis therefore appears to be sound.

Reference has already been made to the courts' ability to intervene in submissions after they were made orders of the court.[132] A second technique, ultimately of prime importance, was the stated case procedure. Municipal legislation in 1830 and 1842 had authorized the referral to arbitration of certain controversies.[133] An 1844 statute authorized the arbitrators so appointed to state a case for the opinion of a judge before making an award, or to raise in any award a question for the opinion of the court.[134] Although the parties to commercial contracts could, and apparently sometimes did, confer by contract a similar power on an arbitrator,[135] it is important to note that the courts were doubtful about their ability to respond to these questions. The Common Law Procedure Act of 1854 resolved these doubts, borrowed the stated case procedure first developed in the context of statutory arbitration, and specifically conferred the power to state a case upon all arbitrators acting under judicial auspices.[136]

By 1854, then, arbitrators were invited, but not compelled, to seek instruction from the court. Still, the superior courts lacked the power to set aside awards of purely consensual abitrators. That power was to be conferred only by the Arbitration Act of 1889 which, for the first time, clearly enabled the court to control the arbitrator by compelling him to state a case upon application of one of the parties.[137]

With this power of compulsion, the door was open to broad-gauge judicial intervention to compel conformity to legal rules in the making of awards. This result was perhaps the inevitable outcome of efforts to make submissions irrevocable and awards enforceable: 'There seems to exist an intimate connection between the binding force of the submission and the enforceability of awards on the one hand and on the other the liberty of the arbitrators to apply rules differing from those laid down by the law.'[138]

Yet even by the middle of the nineteenth century, when the courts' powers of intervention were still relatively limited, that connection had emerged in judicial pronouncements. The famous case of *Scott* v *Avery*[139] is regarded as signalling the final acceptance by courts of the right of parties to make a binding promise to arbitrate. In that case, a majority of the House of Lords held that the parties were bound by a contract which stipulated that arbitration was a condition precedent to suit. But both the majority and dissenting judgments agreed that the parties could not preclude ultimate recourse to the courts and thus, implicitly, to legal principles: 'The courts will not enforce or sanction an agreement which deprives the subject of that recourse to their jurisdiction, which has been considered a right inalienable even by the concurrent will of the parties ... Whether this rests on a satisfactory principle or not may well be questioned.'[140]

What was the rationale of a rule that prevented the parties from entirely contracting out of the regime of common law? Only Lord Campbell, of all the judges, attempted an explanation, and he apparently tempered the initial expression of his views. The official report merely records his speculation that the rule 'probably originated in the contests of the different courts in ancient times for extent of jurisdiction, all of them being opposed to anything that would altogether deprive every one of them of jurisdiction.'[141] This speculation was expressed more vividly, however, in the unofficial report:

There was no disguising the fact that, as formerly, the emoluments of the Judges depended mainly, or almost entirely, upon fees, and as they had no fixed salary, there was great competition to get as much as possible of litigation into Westminster Hall, and a great scramble in Westminster Hall for the division of the spoil ... And they had great jealousy of arbitrations whereby Westminster Hall was robbed of those cases which came not into the King's Bench, nor the Common Pleas, nor the Exchequer.[142]

While the unofficial version, whether accurate or otherwise, has a certain ring of plausibility, this explanation obviously does not justify the modern application of the rule.

A more acceptable rationale utlimately emerged seventy years later in *Czarnikow* v *Roth, Schmidt.*[143] Here the parties had unsuccessfully sought to exclude judicial control by a provision in a standard arbitration clause forbidding either one to seek to state a case for the opinion of the court under the Arbitration Act. And here the court's response was explicitly to preserve the primacy of the common law rather than that of the judges themselves. Atkin LJ put the matter most clearly:

The special statutory jurisdiction of the Court to intervene to compel arbitrators to submit a point of law for determination by the Courts ... appears to me to be a provision of paramount importance in the interests of the public. If it did not exist arbitration clauses making an award a condition would leave lay arbitrators at liberty to adopt any principles of law they pleased. In the case of powerful associations such as the present, able to impose their own arbitration clauses upon their members, and, by their uniform contract, conditions upon all non-members contracting with members, the result might be that in time codes of law would come to be administered in various trades differing substantially from the English mercantile law. The policy of the law has given to the High Court large powers over inferior Courts for the very purpose of maintaining a uniform standard of justice and one uniform system of law.[144]

Bankes LJ was also concerned to ensure that '[what] is administered by an arbitrator is in substance the law of the land and not some homemade law of the particular arbitrator or the particular association.'[145] Scrutton LJ was perhaps marginally less dogmatic:

Arbitrators, *unless expressly otherwise authorized*, have to apply the laws of England ... [T]he Courts may require them, even if unwilling, to state cases for the opinion of the Court on the application of a party to the arbitration if the Courts think it proper. This is done in order that the Courts may insure the proper administration of the law by inferior tribunals. In my view to allow English citizens to agree to exclude this safeguard for the administration of the law is contrary to public policy. There must be no Alsatia in England where the King's writ does not run.[146]

But he probably intended that 'arbitrators ... expressly otherwise authorized' were those mandated by statute rather than by contract to depart from legal rules. His allusion to 'Alsatia,' a medieval thieves' sanctuary,[147] impliedly stigmatizes efforts by the parties to escape from the normal legal consequences of their conduct.

This discussion of the techniques and implications of judicial review has carried us well beyond the period of this study. The confrontation between legal centralism and legal pluralism in the 1920s bears no necessary historical relationship to similar confrontations seventy years earlier. Yet it may be argued that the doctrinal seeds of *Czarnikow* were planted in *Scott v Avery*, and that the centralist paradigm that has come to dominate legal thinking in the twentieth century had begun to appear in the middle of the nineteenth. In pursuit of this notion, we now turn to a closer scrutiny of attitudes toward commercial law, especially in the period from 1830 to 1870.

'NOTIONS OF JUSTICE' AND PARADIGMS OF LAW

We have seen that commercial tribunals and arbitration – the latter at one point acknowledged even by the *Law Times* to be 'the natural method of determining a dispute'[148] – attracted considerable professional hostility. This hostility was strong enough to overcome widespread business support for tribunals of commerce. Nonetheless, arbitration, under both curial and private auspices, ultimately came to be accepted as part of the machinery of dispute settlement. In the process, it has been suggested, the nature of arbitration may have been altered at least to the extent that judicial review forced arbitrators to adhere to the norms of the central legal system. In some situations, however, the private power of commercial interests insulated arbitration from any contact with the courts. For those whose economic interests depended upon continuing participation in an exchange or renewal of a course of dealing with the other party, appeals to a court for procedural assistance were as unlikely as a challenge to the award itself.

Moreover, the use of standard-form contracts and other 'private legislation,' such as the rules of various organizations, to define the arbitrator's mandate had the effect of ensuring that arbitrators' decisions would not automatically resemble, and could not be forced to resemble, those of judges, which were based on common-law doctrine.

The situation was not without its ironies. The creation of a special system of law for businessmen, which could not be accomplished de jure by legislation in the case of tribunals of commerce, was accomplished de facto by agreement in the case of arbitration and domestic adjudication. And the autonomy of that system, which would not be countenanced under the Arbitration Act, *Czarnikow*, or other cases, had to a large extent already been achieved by the assertion of economic power or by the perception of participants in private legal systems that appeals to the court would in the long run jeopardize their own interests. In effect, the legal centralist paradigm prevailed in the heavens, while pluralism flourished below.

As Ferguson insightfully remarks, the English legal system 'collaborated in its own circumvention at the points where that was needed.'[149] The relative ease with which that circumvention was accomplished, however, gives rise to a further question. It seems clear that the hostility exhibited by English lawyers to arbitration and tribunals of commerce was not after all founded upon their undiluted devotion to the common law. What was its basis? An obvious economic challenge for lawyers was presented by the prospect of a rival legal system catering for a wealthy business clientele and administered by that clientele without significant professional participation. And this economic challenge coincided with an ideological challenge, as it had in the case of local courts and, as we will see, in the case of administrative law.

Central to any profession's ideology is the notion that its members perform a service indispensable to society. The English legal profession in the mid-nineteenth century was no exception. The antipathy of businessmen for law, as evidenced by their perference for arbitration in all its forms, was taken as an affront to the competence, the self-esteem, the indispensability of the legal profession. According to a legal editorialist, the view of businessmen that legally trained judges 'are incapable of comprehending the technical customs ... by which many commercial contracts are regulated ... arises from a pardonable vanity.'[150] Or perhaps an unpardonable vanity: 'It is far easier for a trained legal mind to master the technicalities of engineering and the like than for an engineer or surveyor to learn the functions of a judge and how to exercise them.'[151] And, of course, economic interest reinforced ideology: '[I]n all cases lawyers will always make the best Judges.'[152]

But beyond this there was an even more fundamental ideological dispute. Legal values and businessmen's values were often opposed to each other. Judges, in referring matters to arbitration (and perhaps even parliament in facilitating arbitration), may have seen that process as a convenient fact-finding device. This view echoed the mea culpa of law reformers who often denounced the notorious procedural shortcomings of English judicature. However, it missed the important point implied in the commercial community's search for its own legal system. That point was captured by an unusually perceptive legal journalist:

The legal and the commercial notion of justice are distinct, and the real complaint of the man of business against the lawyer proceeds upon a sense of this opposition. Justice in the lawyer's sense is adherence to a rule ... Justice in the sense of the man of business is the attainment of a result satisfactory to the feelings of a benevolent bystander who takes an interest in both parties.[153]

This conscious juxtaposition of the 'legal' and the 'commercial' notions of justice seems, at first blush, to provide confirming evidence for Atiyah's well-known thesis.[154] According to Atiyah, important affinities in the thinking of philosophers, political economists, and lawyers can be traced in the formal discourse of law, in legislation and judicial decisions. During the period from 1770 to 1870, he recounts, as a result of a changing intellectual environment, law came to be seen as less pragmatic and facilitative, as more principled and hortatory; thereafter the trend was reversed. One is therefore struck by the fact that 'adherence to a rule' was indeed perceived by a contemporary observer to typify the lawyer's 'notion of justice' at almost the very moment when, according to Atiyah, principled adjudication was at its high-water mark.

But we must also look at the other side of the coin. The businessman's 'notion of justice' was far from principled – indeed, was close to the paternalism which, according to Atiyah, had gone into decline one hundred years earlier.[155] Of course, it is not to be expected that all businessmen under all circumstances strove to ensure that their contractual and other legal relations attained 'a result satisfactory to the feelings of a benevolent bystander who takes an interest in both parties.' Our study in chapter 5 of relations between mine owners and their operatives, for example, will yield little evidence of 'feelings of benevolence,' even as they were understood at the time.

In dealings among businessmen, however – especially those who were well known to each other, or who transacted business together frequently –

pragmatic attitudes toward legal obligations were indeed prevalent. As they had done in earlier times and would continue to do in more modern times, mid-nineteenth-century businessmen consciously declared allegiance to norms of law that originated within their own world of commercial activities: contract, custom, courses of dealing, usual expectations, tacit assumptions, even a sense of what was 'good business practice,' 'reasonable' or 'fair.' And in doing so they were quite aware that they were taking their distance from the regime of legal rules proclaimed by parliament and the judges. This tendency among businessmen was unique neither to the mid-nineteenth century nor to England, as a number of modern scholars have observed. Unger captures the historical point in general terms:

[M]erchant groups in particular would have ... little reason to support the rule of law ... Far better for them to rely as much as possible on rules, tribunals and informal controls set up within the commercial groups themselves. This merchant law has a better chance of being substantively responsive to the needs of trade than principles laid down by remote rules and applied by learned judges. And the outcomes of decisions made by merchant tribunals are more like to be comprehensible to businessmen and predictable by them than any that can be expected from an arcane method of legal analysis or from the balancing of antagonistic social interests by lawyers.[156]

The modern literature of arbitration is replete with similar pronouncements. Isaacs distinguishes the 'legalistic view' that arbitration is simply an informal method of trial from the 'realistic view' that it is a method of reaching results different from those of trial.[157] Sirefman argues for 'the concept of arbitration as an alternative self-sufficient system.'[158] Carlston views arbitration as 'voluntary and consensual in origin ... the judicial organ of systems of law not of univeral application.'[159] Where, then, does a non-universal, self-sufficient system look for its legal sources?

Not all law is formal, found in precedent and statute. Often in mature business systems there will be a strength, for example, in the unilateral oral commitment that is equal to the formal, binding contract in law. One step beyond custom we find contract and agreement as a source of private, less than universal law. It is from these less-than-universal norms of custom and contract that the arbitration process springs. The law merchant brought forth its own tribunals which were superseded as the common law of England absorbed the law merchant. So it is, though to a lesser degree, with arbitration tribunals. It is not the convenience of the arbitration procedure that has caused arbitration to be a familiar feature of a complex system of institutionalized relationships such as are found, for example, in commodity exchanges and boards and in trade associations. Arbitration is more often a product of necessity than of convenience, for it is a necessary part of an emerging system of law internal to two or more business institutions. Commercial arbitration finds its most significant role wherever there is a system of law – either unwritten, informal and customary, or written, formal and contractual in nature – internal to two or more business institutions. The primary source of strength of the arbitration process lies in its relations to such a system of law.[160]

Mentschikoff's writings also explore the tension between arbitral and general legal norms. Echoing Wolaver's estimate of the old courts of pie-poudre – 'their justice was as one human being with another'[161] – Mentschikoff initially believed that in arbitration 'the criteria of decency, whether based on economic, sociological, psychological or business practices have been much more explicitly in the picture both as a matter of argument to the arbitrator and as a matter of statement in the opinions accompanying their awards.'[162] However, subsequent empirical work somewhat tempered her initial views and led her to emphasize the distinctiveness in arbitration of '[f]act finding norms of an informal nature in commercial matters.' There was no intrinsic reason, she concluded, why decisional norms used by arbitrators were to be preferred to those used by courts: each was to be judged in particular instances by criteria such as 'predictability and regularity of result, clarity of articulation and consonance with related norms.'[163]

Predictability is no doubt important in commercial relationships, especially those of a repetitive or ongoing nature. The real question is whether predictability is enhanced by requiring arbitrators to adhere to laws of general application – 'uniform societal norms rather than individualized trade norms.'[164] To the extent that predictability per se is a matter of concern, empirical evidence appears to suggest that 'a nonlegalistic adjudicatory system can be as predictable if not more predictable than a legalistic system would be.'[165]

Mentschikoff also proposed 'clarity of articulation' as a criterion by which the value of awards might be judged. This is natural enough if arbitration is viewed as a purely adjudicative exercise, but 'clarity' may be the last thing that is wanted in certain circumstances. Where the parties' prime concern is the resumption of a mutually profitable relationship, for example, the healing powers of obfuscation might be preferred to a decisive determination of rights and wrongs.

Finally, Mentschikoff has drawn our attention to 'consonance with related norms' as a basis for evaluating arbitral decisions. Among the norms that might be 'related' are the welfare of the trade, exchange, or commercial relationship on the one side and significant considerations of public welfare on the other. If the arbitrator is drawn from within the trade in order to ensure his expertise and acceptability, a danger occurs: 'The arbitrator may be ... inevitably conditioned to believe that the needs of the group are and should be the dominant criteria for decision. He may, indeed, be blind to the needs of the rest of us. This is inherently less likely to occur in our formal legal system.'[166]

How, then, are we to identify 'the needs of the rest of us' upon which a transcendent value should be placed? The issue is in a sense a proxy for the question of whether judicial review of arbitration should be encouraged on the premise that it will vindicate social interests and legal values ignored by arbitrators. The modern literature focuses less on prosaic issues of conformity to contractual doctrine than on the possibility that arbitration will be insensitive, or even hostile, to such public policies as those that maintain competition against monopoly or that hold retailers and manufacturers to certain standards of behaviour in consumer markets.[167] This possibility is enhanced when the very promise to arbitrate may be exacted through the assertion of superordinate economic power. And countervailing arguments based on the unsuitability of the law for deciding commercial disputes may be treated sceptically: 'Commercial men may regard the law as unduly technical and inelastic for their purposes so long as trade is brisk, or at any rate steady: but when markets fluctuate or droop, and they stand to lose more than they can afford, they are more willing to stand on their legal rights.'[168]

On this general view of arbitration, there is little reason to be squeamish about judicial review. None the less, Cohn, speaking from a comparative perspective, notes that '[a] legal system will seldom go so far as to admit frankly that arbitrators are not bound to observe the ordinary rules of law,' but he also concedes that their freedom from such rules often results from the absence of effective controls.[169] Ellenbogen, no friend of arbitral autonomy, begins from the opposite assumption: 'The insistence on the inalienable right of the courts to be invoked on questions of law is peculiar to the English law of arbitration.' However, he too acknowledges the existence of serious discrepancies between commercial and legal notions of 'law.'[170]

At one level, it might seem that this canvass of modern views on arbitration has diverted us from our historical account. In fact, it will serve to sharpen our perception of the issues that are implicit in the views of Victorian businessmen as we turn to their first-hand testimony.

There is ample evidence that during the mid-nineteenth century, many English businessmen thought that the 'law' governing their dealings should reflect the demands of common sense, conscience, and trade custom. '[B]y "law" I mean the custom of the trade,' said a prominent London merchant, 'not the law as it is laid down in the statutory law.'[171] They complained of 'the unsatisfactory decisions which are now so frequently recorded in the large majority of cases.'[172] They were convinced that 'mercantile documents ... are very intelligible to mercantile men, but to lawyers they are full of ambiguities,'[173] and persisted in their attempts to ensure that 'the language of such documents [be given] the meaning which the same would have amongst traders.'[174] And they insisted that in rejecting ordinary law and ordinary courts in favour of special mercantile tribunals they were not seeking 'the substitution of each man's vague idea of justice for the precision of the law, but ... the combination of that precision with the equitable practice of the merchant.'[175]

For their part, lawyers recognized that businessmen did not entirely share their view of law as an integrated body of principles, as an ordered, ptolemaic universe with judges and lawyers at its centre. They were convinced, for example, that merchants were 'very bad law-makers' and 'thoroughly impracticable' because their participation in the enactment of a commercial statute had 'marred the artistic scheme' of its legal draftsmen.[176] The views of businessmen concerning lawyers' abilities to deal with commercial custom were, as we have seen, patronizingly dismissed as 'pardonable vanity,' apparently stemming from a failure to appreciate the omnicompetence of lawyers. Businessmen, explained the *Law Times* patiently, 'would like to see a body instituted which would say to two merchants, "Whatever you may have said in fact, this is what you ought as men of business and probity to have said, and you shall be compelled to act as if you had really said it." ' But such a result was fraught with danger: 'To give anybody whatever the power of exercising such a function would be to introduce uncertainty into all dealings, and to substitute the accidental sympathies of a particular class in a particular case for the settled law of the land.'[177]

The 'settled law of the land' had, after all, two qualities, each of which gave rise during the mid-nineteenth century to controversies between lawyers and other groups. It was, as Atiyah tells us, 'settled' rather than discretionary, and universal rather than a response to the needs of 'a particular class in a particular case.'

As to its settled quality, this is a theme we have already encountered in our discussion of courts of requests, and one that we will revisit when we look at the issue of discretion in the administrative context. As to its universal quality, we have already explored the antipathy of lawyers to local and special jurisdictions in the 1830s. This antipathy also had a long history in commercial law. 'An isolated or peculiar jurisdiction,' said a lawyer inveighing against the proposed tribunals of commerce, 'is in itself an evil of no ordinary magnitude.'[178] In this comment we hear echoes of Mansfield cajoling the law merchant into a liaison with the common law, and of Scrutton defending his right to review arbitrators' awards for fear of licensing a new 'evil.' And we hear Dicey pronouncing anathema upon administrative law.

The issues of law's universality and settled nature, then, recur throughout the period, and in each of the three main contexts we will have explored. But the very vehemence and persistence with which the two points are pressed suggests strongly that they were not universally agreed.

Returning to Atiyah's formidable work, we may accept his conclusion that by about 1870 formalism, the rule of principle, had triumphed in the conceptual thought of lawyers and their intellectual associates. But this conclusion would be overburdened if it were read as denying the existence altogether of pragmatic, instrumental, and facilitative legal behaviour. Within the sphere of private commercial dispute resolution, within the context of the new public administrative regimes, such behaviour did not merely begin to emerge about 1870; it had been there all along. It flourished in situations where practical people had to cope with practical problems, where form was bound to follow function, even where lawyers had to work in partnership with men of affairs or undertake unprecedented public responsibilities.

Nor was this willingness to live 'beyond the law' – in the sense of a universe bounded by legal principles – attributable to businessmen and administrators alone. There was, it seems, a significant gap between the professional ideology of legal formalism on the one hand and the commonplace activities of those lawyers who were administering, advising, drafting, managing, organizing, and planning on the other. Even conveyancing and litigation, the profession's traditional preoccupations, were made to serve instrumental functions on occasion.[179]

Let us rehearse only a few random examples of legal behaviour – some already mentioned, some canvassed below – that cannot be contained within the model of formalism: merchants deciding cases as lay judges in the courts of requests and lawyers acting as factory inspectors in the 1830s; solicitors managing great estates, manipulating railroad charters, and improvising trusts and partnerships to act as quasi-corporate receptacles for capital accumulation in the 1840s; mines, railways, and emigration inspectors learning to use bureaucratic leverage when they were denied formal powers of adjudication in the 1850s, just as businessmen were simultaneously exploring alternatives to formal litigation in the superior courts; cotton brokers and marine insurers constructing and operating their own systems of domestic adjudication in the 1860s; and legislative architects producing the Railway and Canals Commission, the prototype of the modern independent regulatory agency, in the 1870s.

These people were all deeply implicated in law, but their accomplishments represented the triumph of instrumentalism over principle. Whatever may have been the dominating influence of formalism in the superior courts, there apparently remained Alsatias where the writ of principle did not run. It remains only to speculate on the obvious. In these little enclaves (if we may so describe much of society outside the inns of court and their intellectual hinterland) were the roles of legal principles as a blueprint for public and private action and of lawyers as moral tutors to the nation applauded enthusiastically, accepted universally, or even taken quite seriously?

The 'legal notion of justice' and 'the commercial notion' (not to say 'the administrative notion') seem to have been very different, but they did not exist in total isolation. How was each of these actually related to the other, to society, and especially to the economy? David Sugarman, in a provocative essay, asks, 'was law important in the economy' of nineteenth-century England? He responds to his own question: '[I]t is neither clear that industry and trade wanted or needed the law, nor that the law did, or could have provided, the predictability so often asserted ... Yet many of the rich especially ... committed to legal form the arrangements they wished to make, in order to regulate aspects of their social and economic affairs.'[180] This apparent paradox is, as Sugarman suggests, easily resolved: legal forms were adopted not to 'engulf the parties ... in the paraphernalia of the state legal system' but to secure their autonomy from it. In more general terms, Sugarman argues explicitly for recognition of 'the role of the law in the facilitation and legitimation of a plurality of semi-autonomous realms,' and thus implicitly for abandonment of the legal centralist paradigm.

Our study of commercial disputes provides some evidence in support of Sugarman's thesis. But how do we explain the eclipse of local and special courts, which were the most obvious 'semi-autonomous realms' in England until 1846? The answer must surely be that the legal pluralist paradigm no less than the centralist must be analysed to disaggregate its descriptive aspects from those that purport to explain events. The mere identification of its diverse components enables us to say, after the fact, that the English legal system at this time was pluralistic. But this conclusion explains neither why pluralism comprised a particular constellation of elements nor how they changed from time to time.

We are thus driven back one stage to our analysis. Which influential or determinative forces led to the suppression of local and special courts, which stimulated the rise of arbitration, and which tilted the balance against tribunals of commerce at a critical moment in 1873?

One range of theories places primary emphasis on the nature of the formal legal system itself.[181] At one extreme, the legal system as a whole is seen as a representation of the deep power relationships in society, which are determined essentially by economic factors. What appear as discontinuities or contradictions in the system – features that give it its 'pluralistic' character – upon close inspection turn out to be but mystifying symbols, masking an underlying reality in which law inevitably serves power. At the other extreme, the legal system is seen as a vehicle for the promotion of individual autonomy and private ordering. Pluralism is again unproblematic. It is neither subversive nor illusory, but it one of the chief objectives of the system. These approaches might both attribute the rise of arbitration to a supposed global strategy of 'the system' and its proprietors, be they capitalists or legal professionals. The displacement of the local courts in favour of the county courts might be construed by the one viewpoint as a clear-cut move by the creditor class to enhance the efficiency of debt collection, and by the other as a desire to replace the old privilege-ridden, discretion-based local systems with a common-law system that would supposedly facilitate private bargaining and exchange.

By contrast, another type of theory proceeds from the observable tendency of social units with any degree of permanence and cohesion to generate their own internal law or 'reglementation.'[182] These 'semi-autonomous social fields' intercept law emanating from the state, mediate it through their own dynamic processes, and thus alter its intended effects. Obviously, organized commercial communities are quintessential examples of such 'social fields' with sufficient cohesion and power to generate their own internal legal systems.

In some cases, of course, the outcomes, even the procedures, of such systems will bear considerable resemblance to those of the formal legal system. Here we see two reciprocal processes at work. The internal system may consciously or unconsciously imitate the formal system, perhaps because it approves of it, fears it, or is simply anxious to borrow its legitimacy and symbolic strength; conversely, the formal system (as in the case of the Commercial Court), may seek to borrow the practical features and replicate the distinctive atmosphere of a particular domestic system.

On the other hand, the 'social field' may generate influences which, in effect, transform the law of the formal system, leaving it outwardly intact but devoid of practical effect. The parol evidence rule is an example frequently mentioned in the mid-nineteenth century. In certain circles where business was customarily transacted upon a brief memorandum or a handshake, the trader who sought to resist an obligation on the ground that aspects of the transaction were not reduced to writing might find it extremely difficult to do business thereafter. Of course, the extent to which formal law might ultimately penetrate the 'social field' cannot be determined a priori. It is a function of both external and internal forces, which may change over time and which may be implicated in other issues and interests that are simultaneously being resolved.

Finally, there is a range of views concerning the relationship of law to society and the economy that suggests a virtual disjunction between them and, indeed, a lack of internal coherence among legal doctrines. As Alan Watson remarks, there is no 'close, coherent necessary relationship between existing rules of law and the society in which they operate.'[183] This disjunction he ascribes to the fact that '[l]egal rules, once created, live on. They are ... kept in existence by such factors as the absence of effective machinery for radical change, by indifference, by juristic fascination with technicalities, and by lawyers' self-interest.'[184]

There is much in the commercial law of nineteenth-century England to lend credence to this view. An important piece of evidence is provided by an episode we have already considered, the growth of the law of arbitration. For 250 years after *Vynior*'s case was decided, the basic legal rules relating to arbitration were at odds both with the social fact that it was widespread and with its obvious juridical significance. 'Reform' came slowly, in three instalments – 1833, 1854, 1889 – upon terms that were distinctly 'unradical' and respectful of 'lawyers' self-interest.' And, one might add, the explanation for the halting and limited legal recognition of arbitration was to an extent rooted in the 'indifference' of the commercial community, which had been able to make arbitration work largely by 'extra-legal' means.

These crude and brief summaries have not done justice to any of the very different interpretations of law's relationship to the economy and society, but they have at least laid the predicate for several significant observations. First, we cannot accept at face value the legal centralist view that law in the nineteenth century presided over economic relationships and guided them with a purposeful and powerful instinct in aid of the general welfare. We must at least proceed on the basis that the causes and effects of law, even in the formal sense, were too complex to be captured by a simple centralist model and monocausal explanations. Second, if we were to allow ourselves to be confined by the parochial, formalist definition of law, which probably was espoused by most lawyers and many commentators, we would have to strike off our agenda many issues and events that had an obvious and immediate relationship to 'law' even as narrowly defined. Third, we have already identified a number of areas in which the interests of lawyers and those of business diverged (and in which interests within each group varied). This reminds us that we must take account of the special claims and strategic location of the legal profession, and especially of its élite, in any attempt to explain the development of legal ideas, rules, and institutions.[185]

Finally, the study of commercial disputes is in many ways the study of how private values, private groups, and private systems of ordering related or failed to relate to a regime of law generated by state institutions – courts and legislatures. The grouping of these institutions as 'state' institutions might be taken to imply that they acted formally, purposefully, and in concert. What we can now raise in a speculative way, and will later explore in detail, is the possibility that the public sector no less than the private comprises informal, autonomous, and heterodox legal regimes whose influence on events is directly comparable to that which we have glimpsed in our analysis of mid-ninetenth-century English commercial networks.

In an important article, Fuller traces certain affinities between custom, contract, and enacted law, each of which depends heavily upon 'interactional expectancy.'[186] This essentially has been the trajectory of the present argument. We began with a study of local justice, heavily laden with elements of custom. We next considered commercial relationships and disputes; as Fuller says, contract law and customary law are 'near cousins.'[187] Next, we will turn to the most familiar modern example of 'enacted law,' the statute that establishes an administrative regime. We will try to reconstruct within the framework of such statutes in the mid-nineteenth century 'the existence of ... an effectively functioning system [which] depends upon the establishment of stable interactional expectancies between lawgiver and subject.'[188] The exercise will not be as bloodless as Fuller's formulation implies.

4

The New Administrative Technology: Necessity, Invention, and Legal Centralism

INTRODUCTION

We have disinterred the bones of the old local courts and commercial tribunals, which were laid to rest in England a century ago and more, and have conjured up the ephemera of arbitration and domestic adjudication, which persist even today as examples of pluralism. Now we know that the paradigm of legal centralism did not 'always' (if ever) dominate the English legal system. This knowledge will serve as the predicate for a much more difficult inquiry: what is the significance for our understanding of the legal system of the steady growth of administrative institutions and tribunals, the inexorable tendency to rely upon administrative processes for important social business, a tendency that characterized the law of England at least from 1830?

To frame the enquiry in this way is, of course, to postpone for future consideration the critical question posed by legal centralism: does the administrative process indeed generate 'law'? The notion that law and administration exist in juxtaposition has as its most celebrated proponents Dicey and Hewart. We are all familiar with their belief that England (at least as of 1885) knew no counterpart of French administrative law or administrative tribunals, and that the notion of 'special and more or less official bodies' to deal with disputes involving the government was 'utterly unknown to' and 'fundamentally inconsistent with' English law traditions and customs.[1] And we are well aware of the persisting view in respectable legal circles that the administration is to be held on the short leash of legal power by those who are its proper custodians – the judges. Adjudication by the administration is quasi; its legislation is subordinate; and its other activities (to the extent they are visible at all) are either unclassifiable and suspect or political and thus beyond the pale of law. We will not pause to cite Victorian chapter and contemporary verse. This was, and is, the all too typical attitude of judges and lawyers, or at least of those not themselves immersed in administration or otherwise knowledgeable. Nor will we begin by cataloguing the legal qualities of administration in the nineteenth century. This is the business of the following chapters, in which we will consider the implications of administrative 'law' for the paradigms of legal centralism and legal pluralism. What we must first do is provide an account of the emergence of a new administrative technology in England between 1830 and 1870.

Although this dating will surprise few historians (extensive reference to other studies shows how well accepted it is), it may startle some lawyers. No doubt influenced by Dicey's study of law and politics in the nineteenth century[2] as well as by his jurisprudential views, lawyers often seem to feel that the growth of the administrative process occurred only after 1900. It is true that the state intervenes more ubiquitously in social and economic activity today than it did in Dicey's time, and that adjudication by tribunals of various types is, along with other administrative strategies, an increasingly important technique of intervention. But it is wrong to imagine that English law knew no tradition of administrative law or that our century is somehow aberrant.

As Dicey himself once ruefully observed, the sixteenth century was characterized by a high degree of government intervention – 'an evil ... now too well established to need the confirmation of further arguments.'[3] The seventeenth century also witnessed extensive efforts at state regulation and direction.[4] Indeed, until well into the eighteenth century, regulatory legislation addressed many of the matters that naturally concerned a pre-industrial society. Holdsworth, for example, records the great mass of regulatory legislation enacted down to the eighteenth century in relation to commerce and industry, public works, and local government activities,[5] which, he said, were 'interpreted and applied both by the justices of the peace and by the courts of common law ... [and] were thus worked into the technical system of the common law.'[6] Nor did this early regulatory legislation evaporate with the dawn of the industrial revolution.[7] In the result, by the end of the eighteenth century, 'special bodies of public law' had developed.[8] However, there is not a straight line of descent from the administrative law and administrative tribunals of the eighteenth century to those of the present day.

First, as the Webbs' monumental work on municipal government shows, regulation was undertaken in the eighteenth century primarily by local rather than national governmental institutions. The period from 1689 to 1832 was a time of 'extraordinary significance' because of the extent to which the national government acquiesced in local institutional idiosyncracy and regulatory activity.[9] Second, as has already been suggested, the preferred instrument of regulation was typically (but not inevitably[10]) the justice of the peace: 'administrative action was thus undertaken under a judicial form.'[11] This choice was inevitable given the absence of an effective central public administration, quite apart from the relatively passive posture of parliament.[12] But, of course, the third and ultimate cause of the gap between the earlier forms of administrative regulation and those we now employ so widely was the decline of mercantilism and the rise of laissez-faire, especially from the mid-eighteenth century to about 1830. While it is possible to overstate each phenomenon, and accordingly to exaggerate the extent of the change in attitudes toward state regulatory activity, it cannot be doubted that there was a shift in the conventional wisdom.[13] In earlier times, as one writer, perhaps hyperbolically, observed,

everyone had believed in the careful regulation of trade as of the rest of life in the close-knit community of the land. The J.P. had administered a whole collection of mediaeval assizes concerning weights and measures and the price of bread and ale; and the Navigation Acts showed the same instinct to control transferred to the high seas. Adam Smith looked across an ideological gulf at a mediaeval world which feared *engrossing* and *regrating* ... as much as it feared witchcraft; a world in which the 'law of the market' was the obligation to buy 'in market overt', and not to *forestall* the vendor before he got there.[14]

On Smith's side of that ideological gulf lay an England profoundly changed by industrialization, urbanization and, ultimately, by the emergence of new and powerful political and social forces. By the end of the Napoleonic wars, the state had substantially withdrawn from 'interference or surveillance in particular markets.'[15] Withdrawal, some argue, was its major contribution to the 'spontaneous growth' of British industry. This growth was 'responsive primarily to market influences and underlying social institutional forms, not shaped consciously by government design ... In so far as the state was important, its main role was to institutionalize these underlying social and economic forces, to provide security ... It was concerned more with the context than with the process.'[16]

Yet by 1830 the tide was turning. The national government, which had sublimated its legislative impulses in the enactment of local and private acts, began to reassert itselft in the articulation of national policies.[17] The justices of the peace were substantially divested of their administrative functions.[18] New institutional arrangements began to emerge at both the national and local levels, and currents of change began to flow through all aspects of English life – change that would, it was hoped, cleanse away the worst effects of the industrial revolution.[19]

The industrial revolution significantly altered all aspects of English life: on this fact there is substantial agreement even among those whose views on its causes and effects differ.[20] By 1830, the new technology had helped to bring about changes in patterns of trade and transport, in the distribution of urban and rural populations, in social organization and living conditions, and in political power and ideology. Conceding that for some life was better – though for how many and whom is a matter of great controversy – by 1830, the social consequences of industrialization had begun to attract considerable concern.

Although it might not be strictly true to say that the industrial revolution created abuses that were previously unknown,[21] there can be no doubt that their extent and intensity could only be measured on a new scale. So, too, the reaction to them: from the 1830s, an increasing antipathy toward these abuses coalesced with the conviction that they could be cured through rational diagnosis and the application of scientific solutions. In the beginning, no doubt, there was some ambivalence over the issue of whether the cure lay within the sphere of individual or state responsibility. By the 1830s, however, the possibilities of state action had begun to attract adherents.[22] These adherents were by no means an organized political movement, believers in a single coherent ideology, or even united by their debt to Bentham.[23] 'It is not ... in the political theories of the time, not in any party platform or philosopher's dreams, that the reasons for the growth of England's central government can be found ...'[24] If in none of these, then where?

Some observers explain the growth of the new administrative regimes as an attempt to draw the teeth of regulation, to 'conventionalize' it,[25] to manage its impact so that it would advance the interests of one powerful group at the expense of others who were less able to influence its growth and direction,[26] or to pacify the population and maintain a 'strong tutelary grasp' over it.[27] In contrast, many seem persuaded that administrative growth should be taken at face value, as the straightforward result of public concerns about particular newly perceived social 'evils' and of the learning process of the administrators who tried to deal with them.[28] But no one argues that proponents of these new regimes were seeking a general transformation of society, the state, or the law.

On the contrary, it seems clear that administrative growth was generated by transitory coalitions of supporters, some of whom responded to one crisis, some to another.[29] They differed on the nature of the appropriate response even when the need for some response was clear, and were divided by degrees of doubt over the relative claims of national and local authority, the need for extreme parsimony or merely modest thrift in public expenditures, the contributions of science, the exemplary effects of punishment, the deference owed to old property and new money, and the precise boundary between those who could and should care for themselves and those who were incapable, vulnerable, and worthy of protection. Thus, they accepted the necessity of state intervention and its expression in administrative form with differing degrees of reluctance and more often in the social than in the economic sphere.[30] But once they accepted it at all, the die was cast and fundamental changes in the organization and powers of government were set in motion.

English government, as organized in 1830, was incapable of accepting the important responsibilities to be assigned to it by the reforming movements of the following decades. Each new legislative scheme thus articulated not only new standards of behaviour in the marketplace or of health in the community, for example, but also portended new developments in the shape and technique of the central administration: 'Such administration as existed was local, uncoordinated and centrifugal. What was needed was executive power, centralised, directed and centripetal, through the agency of which these extentions of legislative activity could find their consummation.'[31]

In 1830, the central administration was '[b]y Continental standards ... absurdly small ... rarely touched the life of the ordinary individual and showed little concern for his well-being.'[32] But local government was overgrown and chaotic, comprising some 15,500 parishes governed by 5,000 justices of the peace, 200 chartered boroughs with mayors and other officers possessed of various degrees of democratic mandate, honesty, and effectiveness, and 1,800 special authorities to remedy the failures of parishes, justices of the peace, and boroughs to perform their tasks.[33] These special authorities were not an adequate substitute for a well-organized central administration: '[They] could not meet the challenge of an industrial society; created to remedy a single evil, their scope and powers were too narrow; representing rate-payers who prized economy over improvement, they were held back by lack of money; diverse and anomalous, they became enmeshed in jurisdictional conflicts.'[34]

A portrait of the national government as it existed in 1830 is hardly more flattering. Parliament itself had not yet initiated the fundamental changes that would slowly democratize the franchise, define the conventions of cabinet responsibility, and reduce the power of the Lords. The administration was an uncoordinated melange of departments, offices, boards, and commissions,[35] staffed often – but not always[36] – by incompetents and sinecureholders, some functioning virtually without ministerial direction, some with ministerial participation extending to the most trivial and routine tasks.[37]

Implementation and enforcement of legislation was left substantially to the courts, especially to the local justices of the peace who functioned so unsatisfactorily as a local administration in much of the country.[38] Nominated by the lord lieutenant of the county, they were almost inevitably drawn from local élites, initially from the traditional gentry and later from the new, assertive class of merchants and manufacturers.[39] Unpaid and frequently preoccupied with other matters, including some that must have raised doubts about their impartiality, they often failed to demonstrate a sympathetic and conscientious attitude to their administrative responsibilities. Usually untrained in law or other relevant disciplines and unaided by a supporting bureaucracy, they lacked the intellectual and physical apparatus for systematic and consistent enforcement of national policies, even when they were anxious to conform to them.

Ostensibly presiding over this vast, amorphous, and amateur cadre of local justices and other special authorities were the professional judges of the central courts. In theory, they were to move the underzealous to action and restrain the overzealous. But they cannot have maintained particularly intensive or effective surveillance,[40] and in any event are unlikely to have been the avant-garde of an interventionist government that did not yet exist.

New definitions of government's responsibilities, therefore, evoked new ideas about government organization. The Factories Act of 1833 was a pivotal event in the process of rethinking government organization.[41] Previous factories legislation had failed because it was dependent on enforcement by local justices. Acting under the influence of Benthamite reformers – principally Edwin Chadwick, who was active in many similar enterprises[42] – the royal commission of 1833 recommended the appointment of factory inspectors by the national government with a mandate, and extensive powers, to enforce the proposed new legislation. Adoption of these recommendations by parliament and their refinement in the crucible of legislative and administrative experimentation ultimately transformed the machinery of English government, both local and national. Similar issues were raised in even more dramatic form in 1834 with the passage of the new Poor Law.[43] Acting again under the considerable influence of Chadwick and his fellow

Benthamites, a royal commission recommended, and parliament enacted, a new method of administering poor relief. This involved an even more sweeping displacement of local autonomy in a matter of considerable local concern, and an even greater enhancement of the power (though not particularly the size) of the central bureaucracy. It also helped to stimulate fundamental reform of English local government in the following year.[44]

The reorganization of administration thus involved a considerable shift of power from local to national government and a dramatic restructuring at both levels. As will be seen, the displacement of local élites and the loss of local autonomy gave rise to considerable protest and reinforced the opposition of those whose real concern was to forestall the development of state intervention at any level.[45] But Dicey to the contrary notwithstanding, such intervention did occur throughout the period and it did find expression through administrative tribunals and other instrumentalities. By about 1870, the state of the art of administration had achieved a sophistication and complexity which is quite recognizable a century later.

The present study does not purport to encompass the entire history of administrative development in the nineteenth century. Rather, examples will be offered of the increasing use throughout the century of various administrative institutions to handle the increasingly complex business of modern government. This pattern spoke both to an evolving appreciation of administrative potential and to a declining willingness to rely upon the courts as instruments of public policy, either as an original choice or for purposes of appeal or review. And this nineteenth-century growth of administrative activity brings into question the very historical assumptions of Dicey's rule of law.[46]

Should we linger over Dicey's many and manifest misunderstandings of the phenomena we are about to explore? Now that his influence has, in a sense, transcended his work, fed and been absorbed into the culture of public law and its predominant centralist paradigm, detailed revision of his historical views may be of limited value. However, it is at least worth noting two important lines of criticism of Dicey's work as a salutory reminder of the perils of legal historiography.

First, Dicey's almost wilful ignorance of nineteenth-century administrative developments has been attributed to his own considerable antipathy on ideological grounds to state intervention in the economy.[47] One might pursue the point by documenting Dicey's political views, by explicating the links between ideology and administrative innovation, or by rehearsing the debate over state intervention with its familiar rhetoric. But the reader is forewarned that here the point will simply be noted rather than pursued. My purpose is primarily to describe what happened to the legal system rather than to identify political causes or effects.

In thus stating the objective of this historical account, we immediately confront a second important insight offered in the context of a recent assessment of Dicey's work and influence: Dicey, it has been proposed, must be understood not in terms of his own limitations, but by locating him within the larger context of nineteenth-century intellectual discourse in law, history, and politics.[48] Accepting the cogency of this proposal, the following account contextualizes administrative growth and development only to a limited extent. This reflects no insensitivity to the claims of social or intellectual history; rather, it responds to the logic of this study, which, to repeat, is as much about law as about history. In assessing the extent to which the legal centralist or the pluralist paradigm generally captures the English legal system in the nineteenth century, it is not possible to do full justice to all of the perspectives that may be encountered in crossing the same terrain. Our preoccupations will be technological – with the institutions and processes of administration – rather than ideological or intellectual.

We will see how new norms of conduct were generated often at the very margins of legislation and beyond those of common-law doctrine, how those norms were made effective by means not familiar to the courts or specifically mandated by parliament, and how these developments sometimes took place without the assistance of (and even in direct opposition to) the superior courts, the magistracy, and the legal profession. Four contexts are presented in which such developments occurred. The first two – self-regulation by the domestic tribunals of enterprises, trade organizations, and professions, and statutory arbitration – we may regard as transitional arrangements. We will then examine the two enduring innovations in the technology of administration, the inspectorates and the independent commissions. As we examine all of these, and especially the latter two in detail, we may gain some useful insight into the nature of the English legal system as a whole.

SELF-REGULATION BY DOMESTIC TRIBUNALS

From several points of view, self-regulation might have been expected to emerge as a leading response to the new sensibilities and reformist tendencies of the 1830s. First, it had one undeniable attraction to both politicians and businessmen of the period: state intervention with its unpalatable ideological implications, its potential bureaucratic costs, and its unpredictable demands for new standards of behaviour was rendered unnecessary. Second, organization for self-regulation was consistent with a more general tendency to secure both status and tangible benefits through private organization.[49] Finally, and perhaps most important, self-regulation tended to induce behaviour in the marketplace that would yield maximum benefit for those who controlled the machinery of regulation.

Self-regulation is unlikely to occur spontaneously, however. At a minimum, those participating in the self-regulating regime must share a common perception of the mutual advantage to be derived from participation. Such a perception might result from commercial interdependence or cooperation, from antipathy toward competing groups or possible state intervention, from a desire to gain for all participants the rewards of greater public esteem, political influence, or market power, from altruistic concerns to advance science or to provide a better public service, or simply from a tradition of solidarity. Moreover, to be effective, a self-regulating group has to be able both to take effective disciplinary measures vis-à-vis its members and to secure acceptance by the public of self-regulation as an adequate substitute for external controls.

Needless to say, neither the possible advantages nor the necessary preconditions of self-regulation were universally appreciated or objectively present in all industries or occupations. None the less, by the 1830s self-regulation was a familiar phenomenon, and it flourished throughout the following decades, although sometimes as an unsuccessful rehearsal for subsequent state intervention, sometimes under specific and limited legislative mandate.

An early illustration of an elaborate system of domestic decision-making was the Crowley Iron Works.[50] Throughout the eighteenth century, the iron works and its associated community were ruled by a council that promulgated and amended a code of laws – 'the ancient constitution' – enforcement of which was in the hands of an arbitral court whose principal sanction was outlawry and expulsion from the Crowley 'kingdom.'

More typical, however, was the emergence of self-regulation in industries dominated by powerful trade associations. The stock exchange and the Lloyd's sector of the insurance industry, for example, both provided elaborate machinery for the resolution of disputes between members and between members and their clients.

At least as early as 1850, but almost certainly from its establishment fifty years earlier, the rules of the London Stock Exchange provided that members were subject to the disciplinary jurisdiction of the exchange's committee.[51] Similar arrangements prevailed in the important provincial exchanges.[52] However, the availability of arbitration apparently did not attract disgruntled clients sufficiently to inhibit entirely their recourse to the courts.[53]

It is clear that arbitration of disputes between brokers and between brokers and clients suffered from certain institutional weaknesses. Brokers who were not members of the exchange were obviously not bound by its rules or subject to the control of its committee. The committee's only real sanction against its members for refusal to arbitrate was expulsion for breach of the rules.[54] As against client-claimants, the jurisdiction of the committee depended (after 1854) upon their willingness to execute a binding submission to arbitration under the Common Law Procedure Act, 1854, and to forswear further civil or criminal proceedings.[55] Nor were the courts entirely prepared to abandon jurisdiction over such disputes,[56] even though they were sometimes willing to define the rights of litigants according to the rules and customs of the exchange.[57]

To what extent recourse to the courts reflected a lack of confidence in the impartiality of the committee rather than its jurisdictional defects is unclear. At a minimum, civil litigation must have been a temptation for clients confronted with substantial losses as a result of what they perceived as sharp practice, bad advice, or negligence by members of the same 'club' as the committee that would sit in judgment. None the less, self-regulation by the securities industry apparently was considered preferable to earlier legislative attempts to license brokers,[58] an attitude that has influenced the shape of regulation down to the present.[59] The history of Lloyds insurers followed a roughly similar pattern,[60] and a number of important industries also developed mechanisms of self-regulation.[61]

The experience of the cotton trade was perhaps typical.[62] From the end of the eighteenth century, increased international trade in raw and processed cotton led to the development of new and more sophisticated marketing arrangements. Crucial to these arrangements was the dissemination of information about the movement of goods and prices; the task was undertaken first by individual entrepreneurs, then by collective effort. That effort led, in turn, to regular but informal meetings of brokers and to the establishment in 1841 of the Liverpool Cotton Brokers' Association. Regulation of the market was initially conducted 'on the lines of an unwritten code, which clearly defined the functions, and plainly set forth the rights and duties, of both merchants and brokers, in their individual capacities and in their conduct towards each other.'[63] This arrangement, it is claimed, worked well: 'There was universal trustfulness; all transactions were plain, honest, and above-board ... [T]here was no wrangling between merchants and brokers on the one hand, nor between spinners and brokers on the other.'[64] In 1863, however, market dislocations caused by the American civil war created problems that apparently could not be resolved through the informal processes of the association, and formal rules were adopted. These rules provided for recourse to arbitration and, following 'several palpably incorrect decisions,' to an appellate tribunal composed of the association's president and committee.[65]

Although self-regulation in the cotton industry was apparently satisfactory to those involved, and concern for the public interest was claimed by Lloyds and the stock exchange, it is also true that such schemes could be used, and were used, in aid of arrangements that were highly injurious to the public. For example, price-fixing and market-sharing rules in the coal industry were codified, promulgated by the industry association, and enforced through a domestic tribunal.[66]

If political sensibilities had not yet hardened against private collusive arrangements to restrain competition, they had none the less progressed to the point where 'artificial' market restraints were generally under attack. An earlier attack on the medieval guilds was paralleled by a move, between 1800 and 1830, to strip the great concessionary companies of their monopolies and regulatory powers.[67]

Still, the attractions of self-regulation were not easily resisted, especially when those claiming the privilege professed a desire to advance knowledge and to improve the quality of their goods or services and possessed sufficient political and economic power to sit in judgment on their own claims. Thus, the 1830s and the surrounding decades were the period in which the self-governing professions and occupational monopolies began to emerge.[68] Generally established at first as voluntary associations, they rapidly claimed and received legislative sanction and statutory powers.[69]

Whether, like some purely private bodies, these statutorily established trades and professions abused their position is beyond the scope of this study. No doubt they had some success in raising standards, but there is also reason to believe that for this advantage the public paid a considerable price in terms of the cost and availability of various services. On balance, it may be that only the prospect of external control displacing self-regulation motivated these domestic regulatory systems to maintain a reasonable standard of concern for the public interest.[70]

STATUTORY ARBITRATION

The distinguishing characteristic of self-regulation – its domesticity, its dependence on group norms and internal institutions – is also a serious weakness. Non-members of the group may be suspicious of its sincerity and unwilling to bring complaints against members to its domestic tribunal. Moreover, the group's view of appropriate conduct may differ significantly from that of a complainant or the general public, or it may fail to provide access to its domestic tribunals for non-members. Finally, even where the complainant and the regulated group are agreed about both the relevant norms and the desirability of recourse to domestic adjudication, it may be difficult to devise effective remedies. In the absence of empowering legislation, a domestic tribunal may be unable to do more than expel the offender from the group. It may be unable to secure redress for the complainant or to prevent the offender from conducting his affairs independently of the group. Of course, some of these shortcomings may be cured by legislation, and others by the realpolitik of particular markets. But it is sometimes not possible to persuade non-member complainants that anything short of independent third-party adjudication is appropriate.

The question of neutrality and effectiveness in adjudication is not the only problem for self-regulation. Another important weakness is that self-regulation presumes the existence of a cohesive group and of a sufficient volume of disputes to sustain the development of norms of conduct and regulatory machinery. Occasional disputes between individuals who enjoy only random or sporadic contact, or who perceive themselves to be diametrically opposed in interest, are unlikely to be amenable to domestic adjudication.

Against this background, the frequent provision in regulatory legislation for arbitration of unresolved differences may be seen as a transitional device. It was a partly private solution in so far as it somewhat resembled self-regulation and, of course, was a familiar arrangement for resolution of commercial disputes. Under some statutes, the parties were permitted to select their own arbitrator and, presumably, to bind or persuade him to apply norms of decision appropriate to their paticular circumstances. However, arbitration was also sometimes used as a primitive tool of state intervention. As will be seen, many of the statutes in question either required or invited the disputants to submit to arbitration by a justice or a state functionary or board, with the implicit or explicit expectation that the norms of decision would derive from public policies. Arbitration that is statutorily compelled thus stands partway along a spectrum from purely private to purely public regulation.

Statutory arbitration is transitional in another sense. Particularly as it was used in the early decades of the nineteenth century, it seems to have represented a desire by the state to avoid conventional adjudication by the courts at a time when no realistic public-sector alternative was available. As has been suggested, the machinery of government prior to the 1830s (and even thereafter) could not cope with substantial burdens of administration. Direct state regulation was perceived to be wrong in principle, prohibitively expensive, and fraught with the danger of a self-aggrandizing bureaucracy. Arbitration posed no such problems. On the other hand, the courts – both the central courts and the local magistracy – were unsuited to the tasks of administration for reasons already mentioned. From the fact that lay justices of the peace, for example, were specifically designated as arbitrators, it can be inferred that (at least in the view of parliament) what was to be avoided was the technicality and formality of the court proceedings. Otherwise, adjudicative functions could simply have been imposed on them in their magisterial capacity. A similar inference can be drawn from the later assignment to various boards and commissions of arbitral functions in addition to the activities clearly identified as falling within their core jurisdiction.

It also seems likely that the considerable respect of businessmen for commercial arbitrators, based in part upon their ability to respond to custom, to deal with technical, trade, or accounting terms, and to introduce a mediative element into their decisions, produced similar expectations of statutory arbitrators. These expectations were ultimately transferred to administrative tribunals.

Statutory arbitration, then, was available across a broad spectrum of social and economic concerns: safety at work,[71] industrial disputes,[72] tithes,[73] differences between corporate shareholders,[74] compensation for the compulsory taking of lands for public purposes[75] and their taking or injurious affection by railways[76] or waterworks,[77] disputes involving the conveyance of mail,[78] and disputes between railway companies, presumably involving shared facilities, the forwarding of traffic, and improper rate preferences.[79] Indeed, in the movement in the 1840s to relieve parliament of the burden of private legislation by providing standard clauses to be included in all situations requiring sanction by statutory instrument, arbitration was almost routinely prescribed.[80]

In some of these cases, arbitration was merely authorized as an alternative to litigation in the courts or before a special administrative tribunal; in others it was the only specified method of resolving disputes. In either case, it appears that matters ultimately decided by a public tribunal were often initially committed to arbitration.

It is not clear to what extent these statutory provisions were actually invoked, in part because the triggering mechanisms were often included in private acts of incorporation, in deeds, or in contracts. However, while such arbitration was by no means unknown,[81] it did not actually offer an alternative to permanent state machinery for the implementation of public policies. Where the underlying conditions for arbitration were absent, such as a shared perception of mutual advantage, there may have been considerable reluctance to use the process or accept its outcome.[82]

A clearly inappropriate use of the device was the requirement that disputes between mine owners and safety inspectors over operating rules be submitted to arbitration. In what may have been either a naïve or a cynical attempt to win the co-operation of the owners, the governing statute required that the secretary of state select an arbitrator from among three persons nominated by the owner.[83] Predictably, the owners either refused to nominate anyone or nominated 'most prejudiced persons' (including themselves) who either declined to hear the case at all or, if they did hear it, rendered decisions against the inspectors.[84] Provisions for the use of arbitration to resolve similar disputes relating to the safety of factory machinery and emigrant ships were similarly abused.[85]

Beyond revealing the obvious potential for abuse of the process, these provisions also give us a more general insight into attitudes toward the administration. By identifying inspectors and other officials as parties to a 'difference' or dispute, the legislation seemed in a curious way to treat public policy as their responsibility rather than that of government itself. This impression is fortified by arrangements authorizing the secretary of state to select an arbitrator, presumably on the basis that he himself was no more closely identified with his officials than with the other party to the dispute, the recalcitrant owner of a mine, factory, or ship.

If the arbitrator's functions were regarded as purely technical – say, determination of whether equipment met a stipulated standard – this arrangement might be understandable. However, close connections almost surely existed (and in the case of mines were explicitly mandated) between the expert arbitrator and the firm whose conduct was called in question. Was parliament prepared not only to distance itself from the very policies it had enacted, but indeed to connive in subverting them? Or was this particular use of statutory arbitration simply the inept adaptation of a familiar device in order to escape from a conundrum: how to secure quick, expert, and impartial adjudication when the superior courts were not quick or expert, the magistracy was not impartial (as we will see), and the administration itself was cast in a partisan role?

Even where the statutory scheme was more sensibly constructed, arbitration had only limited potential. It was ultimately too remote from the increasingly self-conscious, integrated, and politically accountable executive branch of government. What began to become clear after 1830 was the relationship between the formation of public policy and its implementation. Governments were not in the end prepared to see their policies subverted or redefined by autonomous decision-makers such as arbitrators (or for that matter commissioners or even judges). Statutory arbitration therefore tended to be useful primarily in relation to matters involving few questions of public policy, such as the quantum of compensation for the compulsory taking of land, or injurious affection in the building of public works, or the commutation of tithes. Responsibility for the serious business of regulating social and economic affairs rested elsewhere.

THE INSPECTORATE

Statutory arbitration presented in exaggerated form a problem with which Victorian legislators and administrators had to grapple in many contexts: how to achieve effective and consistent local implementation of national policies? The intensity of their response was largely determined by the degree of commitment to those policies exhibited by all concerned: the public, politically powerful interests, the courts, and of course, the legislators and administrators themselves.[86] However, the response was also determined by the state of the art of public administration; what was needed was not only will but way. Of course, the two were closely related: a minimal will to enforce legislation might well lead to reliance upon inappropriate, even dysfunctional, ways. In the present context, the focus will be upon the development of enforcement techniques and the evolution of the idea that special 'administrative law' was implied by the very decision of the state to intervene.

Working conditions in factories early attracted such intervention. Child labour and harsh conditions of work for women and young persons were the initial concern. Industrial safety and maximum hours of work later came into prominence. The Factory Act of 1833[87] was not the first to seek to reduce these social costs of industrialization. Legislation to protect the 'health and morals of apprentices' and other workers had been enacted in 1802, and other statutes followed.[88] But, says Holdsworth, they failed because '[n]o machinery was provided for enforcing these Acts,'[89] a verdict echoed throughout the voluminous literature.[90] What was not missing in the pre-1833 legislation was a system of sanctions. From the beginning the legislation had contained criminal penalties, albeit of a derisory amount.[91] Amending statutes had sought to improve the effectiveness of the criminal sanctions by increasing penalties, disqualifying biased magistrates, easing the procedural and evidentiary burdens of the prosecution, and depriving offenders of various technical defences.[92] But some of these measures were quickly abandoned, and none was sufficient to compensate for the fatally inadequate administrative structure upon which enforcement of the legislation rested.

The 1802 act had assigned responsibility for administration to two honorary 'visitors' appointed by the local justices;[93] no legal or technical credentials were required: one was to be a clergyman, the other a lay magistrate. They had the right to inspect premises, but the success of their visit depended upon the accuracy of a register of apprentices. The register was provided by the employer and almost certain to be defective.[94] Their entire arsenal of administrative weapons consisted of the power to secure medical intervention, in certain extreme circumstances, at the employer's expense.[95] Subsequent legislation, far from improving these woefully inadequate arrangements, actually abandoned them altogether.[96]

Objectively, therefore, the reforms most needed in 1833 were in the administration of factories legislation rather than in the system of sanctions. As experience within the general system of criminal justice was demonstrating contemporaneously, even the most extreme penalties did not deter crime, nor would they have deterred violations of industrial standards, given the improbability of complaint by insecure employees, the intrinsic difficulties of detection and proof, and the intimate identification of the local magistracy with factory owners. Any system that ultimately depended upon criminal sanctions would not have succeeded.

None the less, it has been suggested that the decision of the royal commission of 1833 and of parliament – to turn to strengthened administrative controls rather than adopt the much harsher criminal penalties proposed by reformers – represented a symbolic victory for employers seeking to avoid the taint of criminality, and there is certainly evidence that the employers' views prevailed on the matter of sanctions.[97] If so, with the wisdom of hindsight it is clear that the employers made a serious strategic error. The lessons learned from experience under the Factories Act, 1833, were to be highly influential in the subsequent design of regulatory legislation. The early pioneers of this administration, suggests one author, 'wrought a great work ... and ... prepared the way for vast extensions of administrative control.'[98]

The key innovation of the 1833 act was the national government's acceptance of continuing and primary responsibility for the act's enforcement. This implied a posture of initiative rather than passivity, central rather than local administration, and directive and persuasive rather than purely coercive strategies.

The act provided for the appointment by the central government of four inspectors with power 'to make all such Rules, Regulations, and Orders' needed to implement the act,[99] breaches of which were punishable by fine or imprisonment upon conviction by a justice or by the inspector himself.[100] The inspectors were given all necessary powers in support of their criminal jurisdiction,[101] and were protected from legal challenge by either appeal or prerogative writ proceedings.[102]

These arrangements represented a shift from the former reliance upon the criminal law to primary reliance upon administrative regulation; criminal sanctions were relegated to an ancillary role. The shift was underlined by a subsequent ministerial direction to the inspectors to refrain from acting as magistrates,[103] and by legislation in 1844 depriving them of their power to do so.[104] Moreover, experience with prosecutions before local justices was extremely disappointing, especially prior to 1844. The former statutory disqualification of biased justices had been omitted from the 1833 act, so that offenders could be tried not merely by a sympathetic bench but by their business associates, by close relatives, or even by themselves.[105] To the various inevitable deficiencies of statutory drafting were added restrictive legal interpretations, especially those of the government's law officers.[106] Evidence of violations was difficult to procure because of the inability of a few inspectors to make frequent and unanticipated visits to thousands of factories in hundreds of communities.[107] And if all of these obstacles were overcome, convicting magistrates exercised a discretion to reduce even modest minimum penalties to virtual invisibility.[108]

Yet the record of the first factory inspectors is not entirely bleak. As was clear from the outset, the requirements of the law would only be met if most employers could be persuaded to co-operate in enforcement. Early efforts to secure such co-operation were interpreted (perhaps rightly) as a sign of weakness, and the employers failed to respond to polite exhortation.[109] The inspectors soon developed regulations that both defined the required standard of conduct and provided prima facie evidence of breach. In 1836 these regulations were consolidated into a code and promulgated by the home secretary, and in 1844 were incorporated in legislation.[110] As the inspectorate grew in size, acquired a supporting echelon of local superintendents (albeit with limited powers), and developed greater administrative and technical skills, and as the objectives of the legislation came to be more widely understood and accepted, the regulations provided the basis for a more efficient and professional administration.[111] But the process of evolution was lengthy and halting.

By the new legislation of 1844 the subordinate position of the inspectorate vis-à-vis the Home Office was further emphasized. Not only did they lose (as they had already lost in fact) power to impose penalties, they were also deprived of their power to make regulations.[112] However, the general administrative arrangements under the act were considerably clarified and strengthened, and the inspectors acquired for the first time responsibility for safety standards[113] as well as a more clearly articulated mandate regarding children and female workers.[114]

This new responsibility brought a new approach to sanctions. Instead of relying solely upon criminal prosecution, even though this was now made a marginally more promising prospect,[115] the inspectors were given power to make remedial orders; if an employer declined to implement the safety measures required by the inspector, recourse to arbitration was provided.[116] However unsatisfactory arbitration may have been as a remedy, the principle was at least established that inspectors were to make their intervention more effective by making it more explicit.[117] Until the end of the century, arbitration remained the method by which contests over remedial orders were to be waged,[118] although it was supplemented from 1878 by the power of a court, convicting for violation of the act, to order compliance with the act's requirements.[119]

Finally, the 1844 act also introduced the important notion that fines would be increased in situations in which death or injury resulted from the statutory violation.[120] Provision was made for payment of the fine to the injured worker (but, bizarrely, not to the survivors of a deceased worker).[121]

From the point of view of institutional history, it is technically true that enforcement of the legislation continued to depend upon criminal prosecution. Inspectors' orders, arbitration awards, and court orders for compliance were not self-enforcing; fines were provided in each case for disobedience. This was the Achilles' heel of the legislation: its penalties were modest, magistrates were loath to impose even these to the maximum permitted,[122] and at least one vigorous campaign of enforcement was countered by the formation of a 'National Association of Factory Occupiers' to pay fines for convicted employers.[123]

As Paulus's study of pure-food legislation has shown, even when the superior courts (somewhat atypically) interpreted the regulatory statute with some sympathy for its objectives,[124] the lower courts were able to frustrate attempts to secure compliance through prosecution.[125] To the extent that obedience to the legislation took hold, credit must thus be given primarily to administrative intervention. Through formal regulations and orders, through increased surveillance and informal discussion, through more accurate reporting and more effective publicity, manufacturers were gradually brought into compliance.[126] What Paulus describes as 'antagonistic cooperation' slowly gave way, under pressure of public opinion rather than threat of legal sanctions, to an attitude of accommodation between the manufacturers and the inspectorate.[127] Similarly, the slow and grudging acceptance by employers of the factories acts (especially in matters of industrial safety) was largely attributable to the increasingly professional administrative skills of the inspectors.[128]

The mines inspectorate trod the same difficult path as the factory inspectorate. If anything, its travails were made more poignant by the appalling circumstances of mine labour and by the apparent inevitability of having to reinvent the wobbly wheel of its precursor.

In the mines, as in the factories, politically powerful interests managed to fend off state interference.[129] Attempts to use the ordinary civil and criminal law to reduce the toll of human misery and make good the losses of workers injured and killed in the mines came to nothing.[130] The first regulatory legislation, in 1842, sought to prevent the underground employment of women and to regulate the employment of boys; like the early factories acts, its enforcement provisions were inadequate.[131] Attempts to use moral preachment and paternalism to promote compliance provided predictably unavailing.[132] In due course, an attempt was made to expand and strengthen the mines inspectorate by the enactment of the Coal Mines Inspection Act, 1850.[133] Like the Factory Act, 1844, the new act added a concern for safety to the initial concern for exploitation of women and children, and it also provided for inspection of mines, authorized the inspectors to issue remedial orders, and provided that fines imposed for violations of the obligation to report accidents should be paid to the families of those killed in accidents.[134] However, these primitive arrangements were ultimately dependent upon enforcement by magistrates and other judicial officers who declined, for illicit reasons explored below, to enforce the law. It was upon this rock of judicial subversion that enforcement of the act of 1850 foundered, just as attempts to use the general law had done and continued to do.

Coroners' juries were reluctant – indeed, they virtually refused – to bring in verdicts upon which subsequent criminal or civil proceedings might be based. Jurors were identified with and sometimes even closely related to mine owners or managers, or were simply dependent upon them for employment.[135] They were sometimes directly tampered with,[136] but often needed no overt instruction to reach perverse conclusions of fact or law,[137] to render 'the usual ... verdict of "Accidental death" without remonstrance or comment.'[138] When, atpyically, a matter found its way into the criminal courts, '[a] verdict of manslaughter so seldom occurs that it scarcely operates as a check. Indeed from the result of such verdicts, manslaughter does not appear to apply to colliery accidents.'[139] Occasional convictions, mostly of workers or lower-level supervisors,[140] were accompanied by jury recommendations for mercy.[141] But owners were seldom, if ever, held criminally accountable for unsafe working conditions.

Nor did civil proceedings provide the recourse that was denied in the criminal courts. Even the enactment of Lord Campbell's Act (which gave a right of action to the survivors of persons tortiously killed) failed to improve matters. Widows could not afford the cost of letters of administration or of litigation, were reluctant to alienate the employer (who might permit them to occupy a company-owned house, award them a small gratuity, or offer employment to other family members), and sometimes could not even find local lawyers to take their cases,[142] let alone to match the distinguished counsel and expert witnesses marshalled by the employer.[143] In one instance, indeed, the Home Office provided almost £200 to enable a widow to sue the Moss Hall Company, Wigan, 'for wrongful act, neglect or default' leading to the death of her husband. But the presiding judge made a highly prejudicial remark about the notorious carelessness of miners, and the jury found for the defendant.[144]

In short, Dicey's 'ordinary courts' and 'ordinary law' had nothing to do with miners, a fact eloquently observed by Inspector Mackworth in his semi-annual report for June 1854:

The most striking fact which arises in the experience of the inspection is the practical immunity from all responsibility, criminal or civil, of the managers of mines. During [the inspectorate's] three years' existence, there has not been a single conviction obtained, although about 3,000 lives were sacrificed. In no instance I believe in England, were the widows and children of the sufferers able to recover compensation, however great the neglect or default which caused the death of those on whom they depended for subsistence.[145]

Mackworth set his legal observations in their social context. Working in conditions he explicitly compared to the Black Hole of Calcutta, miners were shown to have a life expectancy considerably less than that of agricultural labourers.[146] More than ten years after a minimum age for underground workers had been established, children of ten and eleven, of six and seven, even of four, were contributing to the mortality statistics.[147] Fifteen years after the enactment of legislation prohibiting the practice, miners were sometimes still paid their wages in a beer-house.[148] Mutual benefit societies could not adequately replace wages lost through death, injury, or illness.[149] Miners and generations of miners were 'condemned to work ... in a foul and poisonous atmosphere,' concluded Mackworth: 'I say condemned because starvation or the parish [workhouse] are often the alternatives.'[150]

No more dramatic illustration can be found of the moral and institutional imperatives that gave force and shape to the growth of administrative law. People were being maimed, killed, and degraded; the law – the formal legal system – had nothing to say about the matter; a new normative system and new techniques of enforcement were desperately needed. Only the administration could respond to that need. Characteristically, the inspectorate itself helped both to create political pressure for those new norms and techniques and to design them, despite a very limited formal mandate to do so.

Throughout the early 1850s, the inspectors' reports were replete with urgent demands for changes in the law and its administration.[151] No doubt in part because of public pressures generated by these reports, a conference was convened in 1854 in which the six inspectors participated, along with forty-nine owners and four workers. Each participant was given a single vote, and 'important inaccuracies' were allegedly introduced into the minutes by the owners.[152] It is hardly surprising, therefore, that the ensuing legislation of 1855 was labelled 'a masters' measure,' as indeed it was in many respects.[153]

The 1855 act, however (itself superseded in 1860), did improve administrative technology in several significant aspects. Following the pattern of the factories acts, there was a shift in emphasis away from requiring compliance with general safety standards and toward the adoption and enforcement of 'special rules' governing practices in each mine. The content of these rules was subject to government approval, and in the event of disapproval (again following the precedent of the factories acts) to binding arbitration.[154] Arbitration as an alternative to prosecution was provided in the event of non-compliance; potentially more important, employees were given a statutory right to refuse to perform work proscribed by an inspector without liability for misconduct, but this self-help remedy was not carried forward into the 1860 act.[155] Experience under the 1855 act again revealed the relatively limited contribution of formal law and legal institutions, and the creative potential of non-coercive administrative intervention.

As has been mentioned, the procedures for appointing arbitrators were so totally controlled by the owners that they were virtually unusable as an enforcement device. Some inspectors were able to secure criminal convictions for violation of the special rules or other provisions of the legislation, [156] and even to use prosecution as a lever to exact modest compensation for the families of deceased workers. [157] But the magnitude of these legal victories should not be exaggerated. For example, one inspector reported that during one year in his district, there were fifty-two accidents involving ninety-nine deaths; thirteen prosecutions resulted in eleven convictions and fines totalling £23 10s. [158] Others reported similarly high rates of conviction but a relatively low incidence of prosecution, and modest (though increasing) levels of fines. [159] Some slight success was recorded on the civil side, but survivors were denied compensation even in cases involving undoubted negligence and illegal conduct on the apparent grounds that the deceased workers had accepted the risks of their employment, that the owner was unaware of conditions, and that the negligent act causing death was that of the workers themselves. [160]

Against these extremely modest advances must be set a number of notorious defeats. Several major disasters involving scores of deaths resulted in exoneration of the mine owners. [161] In some areas of the country, the local magistracy was completely dominated by mining interests. Mackworth records an acquittal, despite one of the most 'gross violations of the commonest rules of prudence and safety,' by a bench of magistrates that included three mine owners against whom similar charges were pending, and in whose mines fully one-third of all accidents in his district had occurred. In another case, the entire bench (except for clergymen) was made up of mine owners. Mackworth had to secure a writ of mandamus to compel the magistrates even to hear his charges, several of which were adjourned, others of which were dismissed on technical grounds, and one of which resulted in the imposition of a derisory fine of fifty shillings. Compelled to do so by further mandamus proceedings and a judicial threat of punishment, the bench heard one of the adjourned cases, and again imposed a fine of fifty shillings. Bolstering his often-voiced views concerning 'the acts of oppression and injustice engendered by the arbitrary rule which exists in the ironworks valleys,' Mackworth forwarded to the home secretary the opinion of the prosecuting attorney, Bruges Fry, who concluded that 'the colliers may scarcely be considered to have the power to call their souls their own.' [162]

Yet Mackworth and his colleagues do not seem to have been entirely dispirited during the period following the enactment of the 1855 legislation: the new device of 'special rules' gave them some sense that progress could be made.

These rules or codes were drawn up by owners or associations of owners and, in most cases, acquiesced in by the inspectors.[163] Where no rules or inadequate rules were proposed, the inspectors' primary recourse was to persuasion rather than prosecution. Great emphasis was placed upon drafting the rules 'in a style which an ordinary work-person can easily understand' and upon frequent reiteration of the rules to workers.[164] Perhaps because they themselves had drafted the rules, many owners became more interested in enforcing them. Moreover, the inspectors frequently brought new safety devices to the attention of mine owners and secured their adoption. The inspectors themselves, while continuing to protest against the absence of effective methods of enforcement, did acknowledge that advances had been made by 'the more agreeable medium of friendly negotiation.'[165]

In any system based upon negotiation, however, compliance was bound to be purchased at a price. In the case of the 'special rules' system, that price was the abuse by some employers of their power to make and enforce rules. Most special rules seem to have permitted the employer, at his option, to discipline or fine offending employees by means of a wage deduction, or to prosecute them in the ordinary manner.[166] But this sanctioning system was sometimes illicitly used to impose on workers onerous hours of work, wages, and work standards in order to increase production and decrease labour costs.[167] In protest, workers threatened to strike and did strike, and on at least one occasion successfully appealed to an arbitrator to obtain modifications in the special rules.[168] The inspectors were sometimes drawn into these labour-management disputes as mediators.[169]

But it was ultimately as mediators in the larger sense, between the harsh realities of local political and economic power and the declared public policy of safe working conditions, that the inspectors continued to function. Prosecution remained a peripheral technique for harassing egregious offenders,[170] and civil suit a virtual irrelevancy. The moral compulsion of on-the-spot inspection was diluted by its infrequency.[171] Even the coercive effects of adverse publicity were reduced by a government decision to curtail free distribution of inspectors' reports.[172] The only real hope for compliance remained the ability of the inspectors to persuade employers to accept responsibility for the workers' safety.

Mackworth himself never abandoned his pursuit of effective sanctions. Unless criminal conviction were to become a realistic possibility, he said, 'it is useless to expect that the same attention will be paid to the safety of workmen as to that of passengers on a railway.'[173] Ironically, as will be seen, railway safety no more depended upon the prospect of prosecution than did mine safety.

The subsequent administration of mine safety legislation will not be traced in detail, but it must be said that prosecution was not the way of the future. The 1860 act[174] carried forward most of the provisions of the 1855 act, clarified and strengthened them, and further expanded the functions and powers of the inspectors. And it belatedly adopted the provisions of the Factories Act, 1844, disqualifying biased magistrates. The emphasis shifted somewhat in an amending statute of 1862, which required that parallel escape shafts be provided in all mines and, for the first time, provided the purely civil remedy of an injunction, at the suit of the attorney-general, to prohibit the operation of nonconforming mines.[175]

From 1850, and particularly after 1860, inspection and administrative enforcement were repeatedly strengthened: mine owners were required to produce accurate plans of their mines and to report the opening and closing of mines;[176] inspectors were to be notified of all serious accidents and invited to all inquests resulting from mine fatalities;[177] rules were to be posted prominently for the information of employees;[178] and penalties for obstruction of the inspectors were increased.[179]

Ultimately, safety in the mines improved; between 1851 and 1861 the death rate fell by almost one-half;[180] the inspectors made their greatest impact by helping to identify causes of accidents and promoting the introduction of safer working procedures and new technical devices. But these prophylactic measures could not be introduced without the co-operation of employers, and co-operation was secured but slowly.[181] It has been suggested, with respect to the analogous field of pure-food legislation, that the reluctance, especially of magistrates, to stigmatize manufacturers as criminals retarded general obedience to legislated standards.[182] This observation underlines the special contribution of the inspectorate, and explains why, ironically, it rather than the ordinary courts was the authentic agent of the rule of law. What could not be gained by adjudication had to be secured by informal discussion, guidance, compromise, publicity, exhortation, bluff, and co-operation.

The inspectorate was not merely an effective engine of enforcement. There is ample evidence of its contribution to the development of new legislation and improved administrative arrangements. The inspectors had the facts and experiences to create feedback, to provide information upon which further developments might be based.[183] As well, they often undertook deliberate campaigns to generate public pressure for reforms.[184] Opponents of reform often characterized these initiatives as mere self-aggrandizement by power-hungry bureaucrats.[185] But a fairer judgment is that the inspectors were highly motivated by moral imperatives and a desire to deploy their professional skills in the public interest.[186] Here again we turn to Mackworth:

In reporting the causes of the death of 200 persons annually and the means of arresting them, I feel the duty I owe is of too sacred a character to allow any personal considerations, however powerful they may be, to disguise or palliate the truth ... I have felt it my duty ... to bring forward some of the most serious cases of neglect ... in the hope that it may conduce to increased attention to the position of working colliers at large ...[187]

And not only Mackworth; his much less outspoken colleague Higson makes a similar plea:

Although I am no advocate for shackling the hands of proper persons, and thereby retarding the energy of capitalists by stringent legislation, inasmuch as I believe that any incautious interference with the expenditure of capital will prevent the natural expansion of trade, yet I cannot disguise the fact that the Statute for the regulation of coal mines requires considerable amendment[188]

Inevitably, the self-assertiveness of the inspectorate raised questions about its relationship to the legislature it served and to the executive of which it was a part. Specifically, what was to be the connection between those who actually executed policies and those who were politically accountable for them? This is a point of particular sensitivity when it is seen against the background of a shift in the primary burden of enforcement from the magistracy to the inspectorate. The local justices had been awarded both by some contemporary writers and by some historians a derivative legitimacy based upon their theoretical constitutional position as part of the judicial system,[189] if not on their social and political importance as the (often oligarchic) proprietors of local power and authority. No similar legitimacy accrued to the inspectors. In some situations they were answerable only to parliament, although they lacked direct access to it and were unable to respond to criticism. In other situations, they were responsible to ministers, but the absence of a developed law of administration left unanswered important questions concerning control over formulation of enforcement strategies, the adequate deployment of administrative resources, and even the source of authoritative interpretations of the statute itself.

Administrative technique thus evolved at the same time that the need for administrative organization came to be understood. As Mitchell suggests, '[O]ur grandfathers learnt in the nineteenth century that government cannot be put out to arbitration. The evolution of the regulatory powers under the Factories Acts marks both the stages of their learning, and also the steady evolution of ministerial responsibility.'[190] His reference to arbitration is not, of course, to be taken literally. He was referring to all non-departmental arrangements for administrative decision making.

In this regard, it must be noted that a serious structural weakness of the early factory inspectorate was its lack of a politically responsible central authority. The four original inspectors were coequals and were initially disinclined to pursue common methods or policies. This situation was exacerbated by the reluctance of the Home Office to facilitate any co-ordinating activities by the inspectors, or even to permit them common offices and staff.[191] However, from the inception of the inspectorate in 1883, and especially after the passage of the 1844 act, the Home Office increasingly asserted ultimate control and accepted political responsibility for the execution of statutory policies.[192] By the end of the decade the inspectors had surrendered all collective responsibilities and had become clearly subordinate to the Home Office.[193] Other inspectorates followed a similar course.[194]

In attempting a summary assessment of the inspectorates, it is important not to overestimate the extent to which they were actually able to transform conditions of life and work for their 'clients.' At the same time, we must not underestimate their significance as a major innovation in the technology of administration.

The inspectorates laboured under two handicaps which were both extrinsic to their formal structure and powers. The first of these was the state of scientific and technical knowledge. Although the emigration officers, for example, were asked to evaluate the safety of the vessels they were clearing for embarkation, there were (at least initially) no sure and accepted standards by which various aspects of the ships' construction, equipment, and cargo stowage could be judged.[195] Similar controversies existed in relation to mining practices, sanitary sewers, and railway equipment.[196] Thus, the inspectors could move no faster toward eradication of the 'evil' they sought to contest than the pace of scientific discovery and technological change would permit. Conversely, however, they could and did use these new developments as an important tactical weapon in securing compliance with legislative objectives.[197]

The second handicap was the extremely modest scale of Victorian government owing, even in a period of relative growth, to a passionate parsimony.[198] While we may accept the extreme reluctance to spend money for public purposes as evidence of the political values of the predominant interests[199] rather than of psychopathology, it extended well beyond those aspects of government activity that impinged directly upon business activity. For example, although the Poor Law (as we shall see) was itself inspired by a desire to inhibit public expenditure on relief, the commissioners charged with implementing its policies were as meagrely financed and understaffed as the inspectorates we have been examining. Victorians, it seems, were loath to spend a little to save a lot. Thus, although the inspectorates and other new administrative institutions accomplished a great deal considering how small they were, their accomplishments were less than they might have been.

Beyond their specific achievements, however, the inspectorates made their mark on both government and law. Working without historical precedent, without adequate powers, and without proper political support or judicial co-operation in areas fraught with conflicts of interest, ideology, and legal interpretation, this remarkable group of pioneers did no less than lay the practical foundations of modern administration and social policy.[200] In doing so they made law: they drafted statutes which parliament enacted; they interpreted legislation and adumbrated it in advice, rulings, and bulletins; above all, they secured, through all the formal and informal activities recounted here, adherence to law's purposes and policies. Their experience illustrates the inaccuracy of any notion that the central courts, exercising original or reviewing jurisdiction, alone articulated, interpreted, or applied law in nineteenth-century England.

THE INDEPENDENT REGULATORY COMMISSIONS

We have examined the work of one distinctive Victorian administrative institution – the inspectorate. Now firmly embedded within departmental structures and accountable through ministers to parliament, the inspectorates remain a familiar feature of British government. Not so that other important Victorian regulatory device, the independent commission.

As we shall see, a number of new governmental initiatives were confided to autonomous, special-purpose commissions that were ultimately responsibile only to parliament. This arrangement, which allowed the commissioners to operate without ministerial control, gained them independence, and in principle contemplated that professional judgments would prevail over 'mere' politics. Such commissions were not so readily perceived to increase the size and cost of the central government – a further attraction given the parsimonious attitudes already referred to. But the absence of ministerial accountability also made them vulnerable to political attack, and their proliferation may have appeared to diminish the coherence and efficiency of government generally. In any event, independent regulatory commissions fell under a political cloud from which, in the United Kingdom, they have never really emerged; they flourish elsewhere.

An account of the rise and fall of the regulatory commissions in the mid-nineteenth century illustrates the difficulty of any attempt to deal with administrative technology and law without a close analysis of its context. Commissions per se, after all, were by no means a Victorian invention, although they acquired new sophistication after 1834.[201] Commissions to undertake and operate public works such as canals and turnpikes were ubiquitous; some central government departments were headed by boards or commissions presided over by a minister; and commissions of inquiry were well known.[202] Even independent regulatory commissions had a relatively long pedigree. The commissioners of sewers, since the sixteenth century, at least, had possessed powers to order the undertaking of drainage works and the removal of obstructions, to levy and enforce the payment of taxes, and to fine and imprison; the 'law' they administered was customary rather than common law, and was explicitly drafted to maximize discretion.[203] Needless to say, these extensive powers led to frequent clashes within which the premises of judicial review of administrative action first seem to have been articulated.[204]

The nineteenth-century independent commissions, then, were located within a long, if controversial, tradition. This fact makes it rather difficult to accept that they were unpopular because they were constitutionally novel or anomalous. But if we understand more clearly what work they did, what interests they served and opposed, we may come closer to explaining why the commissions, unlike the inspectorate, did not become a permanent feature of public administration.

Before attempting this analysis it is useful to sketch the formal structure and powers of a reasonably typical and (at this period at least) noncontroversial commission, the Inclosure Commission. If the work of the sewer commissioners radically altered the physical features of many parts of England, the concern of the Inclosure Commission was with a phenomenon hardly less significant. Dramatic changes in farming methods and in the structure of agricultural communities were implied by the movement to 'enclose' land for private ownership after centuries of communal use. This movement resulted in considerable dislocation, especially for small holders and commoners; parliament throughout the eighteenth century had consistently adopted procedures that ignored or suppressed their interests. Neither the requirement of local consensus nor the enactment of individual enclosure statutes provided them with real protection, the former because it was too difficult to secure, the latter because they were too easy.[205]

The rural enclosure movement was virtually complete by the end of the eighteenth century.[206] However, new administrative arrangements were adopted in 1836 to deal with its last chapters and with the now more important problems of common lands in cities and towns. Under the 1836 statute, responsibility for enclosure of common lands was assigned to commissioners locally appointed by interested landowners.[207] The local appointees were apparently vulnerable to manipulation, despite provisions for an umpire to resolve differences between them.[208] By 1845, responsibility was therefore transferred to nationally appointed commissioners with more elaborately defined powers, procedures and staff resources.[209] The commissioners were authorized to delegate to assistant commissioners their extensive powers of investigation and to act upon their reports. Provision was made for local hearings both as an initial matter and as a form of recourse against proposed orders for enclosure.[210]

The mandate of the commissioners was indeed broad: 'having regard as well to the Health, Comfort and Convenience' of local inhabitants, to determine whether the proposed enclosure would be 'expendient,' to recommend enclosures for parliamentary approval, to make provision, inter alia, for allotments for exercise and recreation and for gardens for 'the labouring poor', and to establish the valuation of affected interests.[211] However, their decisions, while immune from appeal or prerogative writ review,[212] did not ultimately dispose of the rights of parties. Parliamentary approval was still required for the enclosure. Moreover, anyone dissatisfied with a decision of the commissioners could bring an action, triable at the assizes, against the recipient of a favourable decision or against the commissioners themselves.[213] In lieu of such action, the parties were invited to arbitrate their differences, but in either event the decision was binding.[214]

Certain common features of the independent commission – and of the modern administrative agency – can be perceived in the Inclosure Commission: the identification of a complex socio-economic issue; a determination to resolve it by procedures in addition to formal adjudication on the adversary model, including investigation and report, negotiation, and rule-making; a willingness to entrust adjudicative tasks to persons other than judges; a reliance upon standards of decision-making other than vindication of common-law rights, including such vague concepts as 'expedient'; and an ultimate ambivalence concerning the residual functions of parliament and the courts vis-à-vis the special new machinery.

The significance of these features was not lost on astute contemporary observers. Identifying the social and political changes that produced the reform and regulatory legislation of the 1830s and 1840s, a perceptive editorial in the *Law Magazine* of 1853 argued that '[t]he duties attendant on those important enactments were so various and laborious, that it became necessary to form a kind of government in miniature ... a commission, for the purpose of forming rules and regulations for the due performance of those duties, and to direct and superintend their execution.'[215] A 'government in miniature' – the phrase tells all; it explains both the strength of the independent commissions and the intensity of opposition to them.

It was the Poor Law Commission rather than, for example, the Inclosure Commission that came to be viewed as the archetypal independent commission. And it was the experience of the Poor Law Commission that seems ultimately to have turned British parliamentarians and scholars against the notion of administrative autonomy.[216]

The Poor Law Amendment Act, 1834, provoked intense political controversy.[217] It imposed draconian measures on the poor and was attacked by both Tory paternalists and radical and working-class critics.[218] Moreover, the Poor Law, apart from the social policy it embodied, engendered political opposition because it challenged the centuries-old arrangements for local control over poor relief, and because it was part of a general assault on the contemporary morass of local government. It therefore attracted the hostility of traditional, locally based élites.[219]

Presumably, however, if the Poor Law commissioners had been as ineffectual in discharging their mandate as many other instruments of both the national and local governments were, all of this opposition would have been contained within tolerable limits. But their administrative success gave special cogency to complaints against them and thus against the very notion of independent commissions.

Neither the impassioned attack upon nor the stonewall defence of indoor relief – the workhouse system – bears directly on our understanding of the institutional innovations introduced by the legislation. They do serve, however, to remind us that we cannot explain the evolution of legal institutions in crude Darwinian terms – the survival of the fittest – without asking at the same time 'fittest for what?' If the 'what' is repudiated politically, the means for accomplishing it may similarly come to be viewed as illicit.

In the context of the present analysis, an effort will be made none the less to focus on administrative means rather than political ends. In aid of this effort comparisons will be made of several independent commissions, and examples will be given of the way in which each dealt daily with the grist consigned to its particular mill. It is hoped that this approach will permit us to discern the true technological nature of the independent commission apart from its transitory incarnation as the vehicle of policies and the object of passions.

The Poor Law Amendment Act, like the Factories Act, sought to combine central authority with local enforcement. This it did by creating a board of commissioners empowered to promulgate regulations and to audit and compel their implementation by the newly created Poor Law guardians, who were responsible for administration in local areas especially established for the purpose. [220] In a similar fashion, the General Board of Health, established in the wake of the cholera epidemic of 1848, functioned primarily through arrangements with existing local authorities while reserving power to itself to create special structures if confronted by deteriorating health conditions and an intransigent local administration. [221] In theory, these arrangements meant that the commissioners would not have to attempt directly to enforce the law throughout the whole country, as the overextended factories and mines inspectorates had to do. In practice, however, local cooperation was not easily won or effectively maintained.

The Poor Law commissioners in particular waged an aggressive campaign to secure the establishment of local boards of guardians. These boards were to be locally elected, but the commissioners had the power to unite existing poor-law districts. [222] On occasion they tried to create more rational and unified structures by direct correspondence with local authorities, [223] on occasion by appeals at local meetings, and, on occasion, by recourse to coercive legal measures. [224] The Board of Health, however, generally responded to local initiatives, met with deputations, and maintained a watching-brief over areas in which conditions seemed to be deteriorating.

Given the existence of local bodies, the next task was to persuade them to act in conformity with national policies. The Poor Law commissioners maintained a steady barrage of circular letters to local boards of guardians, for example, to rally them against the 'evils' of outdoor relief: 'The Commissioners had confidently hoped that sound principles of Poor Law Administration had been so extensively disseminated as to render it unnecessary at this time under particular circumstances to explain the advantages of the Workhouse System.' [225] The Board of Health circulated an extensive essay on the interpretation of its statutory powers and the relative merits of various types of sewers, urging that 'by a judicious exercise of the powers given by the Act ... much good may be effected ...' [226]

The Poor Law commissioners had power to promulgate regulations, and thus the ability to lay down detailed instructions that would have to be followed. [227] However, its 'general rules' were subject to parliamentary scrutiny and criticism, and it therefore often preferred to issue individual directives, or 'special rules', to each local board. [228] The Board of Health and the Railway Commission possessed no such power to enact general regulations.

Both were concerned with major public works projects, however, and were able to secure some uniformity and general standards through the co-operation of parliament as it enacted the usual special statutes authorizing such works.[229]

The Railway Commission was particularly ingenious in overcoming its lack of regulation-making power. The commission was required to certify that a railway was 'complete' before it could commence operations, and it had the power to attach conditions to its certificate. From the outset of its operations, railways were put on notice that a certain minimum frequency of service to third-class passengers would be required, 'with a discretionary power ... of allowing alternative arrangements,' and that railways failing to comply with 'requisitions' concerning equipment and construction standards would be denied the required certificate on the ground that they would not be considered to be 'in a fit state for receiving the public traffic with safety.'[230]

In effect, this announcement enabled the Railway Commission to define with some specificity the basis upon which it would grant or withhold the required certificates. Using its explicit statutory power to ensure the provision of daily round-trip third-class service (for working-class commuters), it laid down requirements of minimum speeds (twelve miles per hour), amenities (seats, protection from weather) and maximum fares (one penny per mile).[231] Similarly, a detailed code of construction requirements was developed, which ultimately led to the widespread adoption by the railways of important safety measures.[232]

The task of ensuring compliance with the directives of the commissions fell in the first instance to local officials or to the field staff of the commission itself. Under the Poor Law, the local guardians were required to make detailed and frequent reports of their activities; their reports were closely monitored, their accounts audited, and their premises inspected by Assistant Commissioners.[233] The Board of Health lacked the field staff of the Poor Law Commission and was forced to retain the services of engineers and other personnel, on a part-time basis, to conduct inspections on its behalf.[234] The Railway Commission, on the other hand, employed engineers (some, at least, on secondment from the army) and used them as well as its secretaries and other officials to conduct enquiries.[235] While it might have been thought expedient to make available to those being inspected the instructions given to inspectors, they were kept confidential.[236] In at least some circumstances, however, the commissions indicated a willingness to treat information provided them as a matter of public record, and they generally were eager to publish the inspectors' reports themselves.[237]

When confronted with a complaint or some unusual occurrence – an increase in local mortality rates, a railway accident, the untoward death of a pauper – the commissions relied upon the investigations of coroners' juries and occasionally judicial findings as well as upon those of their own officials.[238] They seldom received oral testimony or argument from those directly involved. From the absence of direct contact with 'litigants,' it might be inferred that the commissions did not actually perform adjudicative functions. Indeed, the Poor Law Commission was explicitly forbidden to determine cases of individual entitlement.[239] This inference is strengthened by the absence of any authority to impose conventional remedial sanctions such as fines or damages, and by the commission's tendency to frame its orders as 'suggestions' or 'requests.'[240] But any such conclusion would misperceive the true strength of administrative determinations.

Much of the business of the commissions appears to have consisted of responding to inquiries from the public, local officials, and other governmental bodies who were generally content to act in the manner laid down by the commission. Within the space of just a few typical weeks, the Poor Law Commission was consulted by magistrates as to the appropriate orders to be made against local guardians; by guardians as to the use of funds for prosecution of a local newspaper for libel against them, of rioters who had vandalized a workhouse, of an absconding paterfamilias who had left his family in their charge, and of a suspected murderer whose crime was 'wholly unconnected' with parish business; by guardians defending civil claims for past debts and for dilapidations by the owner of the local workhouse property; by a labourer denied relief; and by a medical officer seeking to recover from a third party the cost of treating an injured pauper.[241] The commissioners responded quickly and authoritatively: the magistrates were told their decision (ordering guardians to pay relief they had refused) was 'illegal'; the use of parish funds for various purposes was or was not authorized; the labourer's complaint was investigated; the medical officer was told he had no claim. The business was disposed of, and there was seldom reason for the commissioners to deal with the matters further.

The activities of the Board of Health were not dissimilar. A magistrates' decision was sent forward for consideration; a coroner's jury requested a consultation; and a local authority sought assistance in obtaining a loan to enable it to undertake sanitary works. The board fended off the coroner's jury until its deliberations were completed; it promised to 'do everything in its power' to arrange the loan from the commissioners of public works, who promptly indicated that they had no funds available; and it sought a legal opinion on the magistrate's decision.[242]

Public expectations of the board sometimes exceeded its capacity to respond. It was invited to investigate a mine explosion, to suppress a varnish-works considered a local nuisance, and to prevent the establishment of a paupers' burial-ground.[243] In each case, it pointed out its lack of jurisdiction and declined to act, although it hinted on the last occasion that it would reconsider the matter if the complaint was restated 'on purely sanitary grounds.'

This ambivalence – a recognition of limited competence straining against the desire to respond to serious complaints – is also seen in the work of the Railway Commission. Many complaints against railways clearly lay beyond its purview: the refusal of a railway to carry the goods of one customer and the private carriage of another, discriminatory rate structures, the exclusion of all save a few favoured hackney cabs from the station forecourt, the placement of first-class carriages next to the engine, and, repeatedly, the failure of trains to arrive and depart on schedule.[244]

However, the absence of any legal power to act did not always deter the commission from responding to public expectations, especially when the public was personified by the Duke of Wellington and his close friend Arbuthnot. When they complained of being kept waiting by the South Eastern Railway, the commission wrote the railway, acknowledging that the commissioners 'have no authority by which they can compel the performance by Railway Companies of the services which, in their advertisements, they bind themselves to perform for the public and no power by which they can punish the breach of the promises which are therein virtually held out ... [However] they cannot refrain from expressing the deepest regret ... [at the serious complaint of the Duke].' The railway was requested 'without delay [to] take such steps as may be necessary to prevent the repetition of the evil ...' that had been the subject of numerous previous complaints and would injure the railway's reputation and interests.[245] One can only speculate as to whether the railway did respond either to the ire of the Iron Duke or to this toothless admonition.

Yet for all that the commission lacked 'authority' in the formal legal sense, it was often willing to play a facilitative role. For example, the commission frequently received requests from inventors either to provide a trial for some new safety device or to compel its adoption. As the commission advised Captain Shrapnel, the inventor of a communications device, it had no power 'to undertake the trial of inventions' or, as it told another inventor, 'to compel Railway Companies to adopt any particular break.'[246] Yet it referred a request that it stipulate the type of roof required on third-class carriages to the inspector-general for his opinion and discussed the matter with several companies, referred suggestions from the public on the possible causes of accidents to inspectors for investigation, and invited inspectors to examine new inventions 'with a view to their own information.'[247]

While disavowing any claim to 'power to interfere with the internal arrangements of the Railway Companies except in matters by which the safety of the public is affected,' the commission declared illegal contracts that purported to exculpate the railway for injury suffered by passengers' carriages, circulated the opinions of 'Eminent Engineers and Managers of Railways' cautioning against unduly long excursion trains, and 'requested' railways to adopt improved lighting devices, greater intervals between trains, and other safety features.[248] And the commissioners, to cite a final example, declined to 'express in their official capacity any opinion as to the legal construction of any Provisions of Acts of Parliament which have no relation to the public duties which they have to discharge.'[249] Accordingly, they refused to respond to requests for their views concerning the financial requirements of an act incorporating a railway, the failure of a railway to provide certain promised facilities, and a railway's disclaimer of liability for horses injured in transit.[250] But they did refer such inquiries to the appropriate parliamentary committee.

In sum, the picture emerges of bodies busily performing a great range of informal but none the less important tasks whose cumulative effect was to shape with some precision emerging regulatory policies and the behaviour of administrators and of persons affected by the policies. And all of this, it seems, was accomplished essentially without a formal system of sanctions, aggressive overreaching, or jurisdictional excess.

How were the commissions able to accomplish so much with so little? In part, the explanation resides in the willingness of most people to acquiesce in both formal law and official instructions. In part, too, acquiescence was promoted by the cordial and co-operative attitude of the commissioners (who obviously realized that they were thereby facilitating their own task).[251] But it is also true that the commissions secured compliance in part by their power to coerce, albeit by means seldom encountered in the courts.

Typically, of course, the commissions could institute prosecutions before magistrates for disobedience of their orders or other violations of the legislation.[252] This they did, or threatened to do, on occasion,[253] but with a lack of enthusiasm engendered by inconclusive and unhappy results. The Board of Health, for example, early on instructed one of its inspectors 'not to occupy his time at present in prosecutions, as the Board will postpone the consideration of the Penalties for neglect for the present ...'[254]

But prosecution was not really the preferred or the most effective method

of securing compliance. When violations of their regulations were un-
covered by the Poor Law commissioners, they sometimes chose to exercise
their prosecutorial discretion against bringing charges in exchange for
assurances of future compliance.[255] They also resorted to such devices as the
removal from office of offending local guardians.[256] And compliance with
their regulations was further promoted by statutory provisions making void
and illegal all payments that contravened the regulations, 'any Law,
Custom or Usage to the contrary notwithstanding.'[257]

It was the Railway Commission, however, that offered the most elaborate alternative sanctioning system. Reference has already been made to
the use of a discretionary power to certify that railways were 'complete' as a
means of securing compliance with standards laid down by the commission.[258] Where compliance was absent, certificates were withheld pending
corrective action or granted on negotiated terms.[259] Where there was a failure to abide by the conditions attached to the certificate, it was revoked.[260]
In essence, it seems that the commission opted for the carrot rather than the
stick. This technique was used with great imagination in connection with the
commission's scrutiny of applications for the undertaking of major
schemes, such as the completion of a rail network between England and
Scotland. The commission published notice of the criteria by which such applications would be judged: the bona fides and ability of the promoters to
secure parliamentary approval, the national and local advantages of the
proposal, its engineering feasibility, and estimates of costs and traffic 'so
far as may be necessary to judge of the probability of the Line being completed and efficiently worked.'[261]

The commission was prepared to undertake a preliminary technical
assessment of proposals[262] and, in one significant case, actually released a
preliminary 'judgment' deciding which of two rival railways would be permitted to build a particular line. The commission specifically acknowledged
that this judgment was 'to a certain extent provisional' and was subject to
modification or reversal if new or altered facts were adduced, either by the
losing party or by a new party, or upon application to parliament.[263]

This combination of devices – discretion structured by the announced
decisional criteria, early involvement at a technical level, and preliminary
judgment – tended to produce results more closely conforming to the commission's goals of safe and dependable service than results that might have
been produced by a simpler win–lose formal adjudicative model of decision-
making. Applicants tried to meet the criteria, were shown how to do so during the preliminary technical consultations, and were afforded the opportunity to respond to the provisional judgment by counter-argument or an
offer of improved performance.

The characteristic and most effective form of administrative 'coercion,' therefore, was not the power to punish but the power to give or withhold. Its most attractive formulation, moreover, was neither open-ended discretion nor legal rules of self-defeating precision, but a flexible structure capable of adaptation to particular circumstances. And its chosen mode of expression was less often the definitive statement of a final decree than the explanatory or hortatory circular, the inquiry or request, the admonition, threat, or tentative indication of outcomes.

To the modern eye, these methods of operation seem entirely familiar. Indeed, as has been suggested, certain features closely parallel aspects of the systems of civil and criminal justice of the period. But neither efficacy nor even tradition could ultimately confer legitimacy upon the 'government in miniature,' the commission, when it was considered as a technique of administration apart from the policies it embodied.

For some critics, its flaw was that it purported to exercise legal powers but not look like a court. The Railway Commission, for example, did not include a lawyer, its powers were not clearly defined, and there was no right of appeal.[264] It was not enough to create a 'tribunal of impartial men,' complained one legal writer; what was needed was 'men separated, like the Judges of the land, from all professional ties and placed above all political influences.'[265]

For others, a commission's original sin was precisely that it was 'placed above all political influences,' that it exercised administrative and delegated legislative functions but was not politically accountable. As the Webbs were later to argue, 'The case of the Poor Law Commission between 1834 and 1847 has become a classic example of the absolute necessity of definite ministerial responsibility in Parliament for every executive Department without exception.[266]

It is impossible to disaggregate the effects of political attacks on the commissions from those attributable to legal or constitutional objections. It is clear, however, that the combined effects were fatal. Initially, the Poor Law commissioners operated under what is now known as a sunset law, and were given a five-year mandate.[267] This was extended, with difficulty, until 1847. In that year, the Poor Law Board Act transformed the body of independent commissioners into one presided over by a senior cabinet minister.[268] The Board of Health, whose five-year mandate likewise made it vulnerable to attack, suffered a similar fate.[269]

The history of the Railway Commission was rather more complicated. Rapid expansion and extensive speculation in railways had produced a host of problems by the 1840s – a deluge of individual incorporating acts, financial manipulation and instability, and questions of safety and convenience, rates and routes – that cried out for state intervention.[270] From 1840, as has been seen, increasingly significant responsibilities were conferred on the railway department of the Board of Trade.[271] However, its most determined attempt to exercise its powers, in 1844–5, resulted in a serious political set-back.[272] Growing concern, particularly about railway speculation, then led to the establishment of a strong, independent Railway Commission in 1846.[273] However, by 1851 the speculative boom with which it had been designed to cope had collapsed, the commission was dissolved, and its functions were reassigned to the Board of Trade.[274]

With the abolition of the autonomous Poor Law Board, the Board of Health, and, finally, the Railway Commission, it seemed that the notion of independent regulatory agencies had run its course after a relatively brief period of experimentation in the 1830s and 1840s.[275] Moreover, the opponents of the independent commissions who had emphasized the need for political accountability appeared to have won out over those seeking a more pristine judicial structure. Extensive adjudicative functions thus came to be encapsulated within the executive departments of government in ironic imitation of the anachronistic mixed adjudicative–administrative functions of the old local magistracy. In obedience to one constitutional principle, that of cabinet responsibility, another putative principle, the separation of executive and judicial powers, was (to the extent that it ever existed) laid to rest. Or so it seemed.

Not surprisingly, within a very few years an attempt was made to resurrect the principle of the separation of powers and to assign to the courts important adjudicative responsibilities in relation to railways. In what can only be described as an impressive victory of murky legal ideology over the clear lessons of administrative experience, much of the revived jurisdiction of the Board of Trade over railway routes and rates was exiled, in 1854, into the wilderness of a reluctant and inept Court of Common Pleas.[276] There it languished for almost twenty years, hostage to the notion that all adjudication is properly the business of the courts.

And, again not surprisingly, the experiment of judicial involvement proved a dismal failure because of 'the difficulty ... of a court of law interfering with good effect in railway management.'[277] The solution was an obvious one: a new, independent Railway and Canal Commission was established in 1873 to retrieve responsibility for the administration of the Railway and Canal Traffic Act, 1854, from the Court of Common Pleas.[278] The wheel had, not for the first time in this narrative, been reinvented.

The primary concern of the 1854 (and 1873) statutes was to ensure that railways and canals would receive and forward all traffic '[without] undue or unreasonable preference or advantage' to anyone 'so that no obstruction may be offered to the public desirous of using such railways or canals ... as a continuous line of communication, and so that all reasonable accommodation may ... be at all times afforded to the public in that behalf.'[279] Additional functions assigned by the later statute to the commission included arbitration, where provided by statute or on consent of the parties, of 'any difference to which a railway company or a canal company is a party'; approval of certain agreements affecting railways and canals; resolution of any dispute concerning carriage of mail (at the option of the carrier); and the fixing of through tolls, rates, fares, and routes.[280]

These complex functions, now regarded as typical of the work of administrative agencies, had been poorly and fitfully performed by the Court of Common Pleas. The court apparently had decided about forty cases in the twenty years it exercised jurisdiction; the new Railway Commission decided fifty-four cases in the first two years of its operation.[281] The relative triviality of the court's contribution is further illustrated when it is contrasted with the work of the railway department and its inspectorate in relation to safety matters during this period. That a court with plenary powers should have been able to accomplish so little in comparison with the relative success of an aggressive, but lightly armed, administration helps to explain why the future of regulatory intervention was not entrusted to judges.

A partial explanation of the court's record is found in the passivity of the government, which failed to undertake regulatory initiatives: 'Laissez faire was now far more than at any other period the prevailing attitude of Ministers towards railway questions.'[282] But the only two proceedings brought to enforce the 'through traffic' provisions of the 1854 act were both dismissed.[283] Other explanations are only speculative – perhaps the court was slow, formal, expensive or inexpert; perhaps litigants had no confidence in it; perhaps the new legislation expressed a new determination to regulate more strictly. But it is at least clear that the commission was expected to accomplish what the court had not. In introducing the 1873 legislation, the views of its framers on the court's performance were made explicit:

Experience since the passing of the [1854] Act had very conclusively shown ... that a Court of Law was not an authority fitted for giving effect to an Act so peculiar and special as the Railway and Canal Traffic Act. Upon certain points ... good and valuable decisions had been obtained; but with respect to a great part of it the Court of Law, to which the carrying of the Act had been confided, had not been able or at all events certainly had not succeeded in giving effect to the intentions of Parliament in passing the measure. The difficulty was felt at the time the Act was passed ... But, after all, it turned out, as many expected, that a Court of Law would be a cumbrous and unfitting body for putting such an Act in force; that, from the very fact of its being a Court of Law, it deterred many from coming to it who would otherwise be most anxious to avail themselves of the powers and protection of the Act; and it was of itself most reluctant to undertake the duties imposed upon it by Parliament.[284]

Their expectations of the new commission were equally clear:

[T]his tribunal would be superior for this particular purpose to the Court of Common Pleas. That Court was not well suited for the administration of the laws of railway and canal traffic, nor did [Mr Fortescue] think the habits of the legal mind were best fitted to decide questions which were not questions of strict law, but of discretion, of administration, and of special knowledge directed to a special subject. He did not think that these questions should be submitted to a purely legal tribunal, although the presence of an eminent lawyer upon it would be of the greatest advantage. They were all aware of the difficulties and fears which surrounded an entrance into a court of law, and thus parties had been prevented from making use of rights which had been conferred upon them by the Canal Act of 1854. This tribunal would, he believed ... be well adapted for the duties which it had to perform, and would decide the questions which came before it promptly, efficiently, and cheaply.[285]

In lieu of judges, three full-time, independent commissioners were to be appointed, 'of whom one shall be of experience in the law and one of experience in railway business.'[286] And in lieu of the traditionally passive posture of judges, the commissioners were invited to inform themselves of facts by inspecting property, requiring the production of documents and the giving of testimony, conducting inquiries through assistant commissioners, and utilizing assessors with engineering or other technical knowledge;[287] they were to 'conduct their proceedings in such manner as may seem to them most convenient for the speedy despatch of business.'[288] Legal regularity, a value apparently so significant that it had led to the disastrous experience with the court twenty years earlier, was distilled into a controversy over the commission's amenability to judicial review.

In its functions, internal organization, and administrative autonomy, as well as in its controversial relationship to the legal system, the Railway Commission represented the resumption of the earlier period of experimentation in administrative design. Ironically, in its functions and organization it proved to be the prototype of the independent regulatory commission which is now more typical of North American than British administrative tribunals.[289] But it also presented afresh the issue with which the Franks Committee was still grappling a century later: how to reconcile effective administration with the conflicting principles of ministerial responsibility and judicial autonomy. This issue continues to defy resolution.

It is true that on balance the Railway Commission of 1873 was not judged a success. A contemporary critic observed that it had 'the power enough to annoy the railroads, and not power enough to help the public efficiently.'[290] But from the point of view of institutional development, the Railway Commission of 1873 clearly advanced the state of the art beyond what it had been in mid-century. Its appearance, especially after the earlier controversial experiments with independent commissions, testifies yet again to the consistency with which 'ordinary courts' and 'ordinary law' were judged inappropriate for the handling of important public and private business.

CONCLUSION

It has been possible in this chapter to sketch in only a few of the many techniques of law-making, decision-making, and enforcement with which government responded to its newly perceived responsibilities in the mid-nineteenth century. In a way, the most surprising aspect of this account is that it is so unsurprising to the twentieth-century reader. If we were to ask ourselves when administrative law emerged, we would have to see when its distinctive characteristics and institutions became identifiable: 'The problem is ... to indicate the period when such administrative tools as delegated legislation, administrative tribunals, inspection, and exchequer grants, came into general use. That period was the 1830's.'[291] Those characteristics gave rise to controversies that have persisted to the present. Carr, writing in 1941, makes this point:

There they were, in full view, a century ago – central government replacing a loose local administration, the paid professional official superseding the unpaid amateur, the delegation of legislative power, the possibility of appeal from administrative decision, the strictness of judicial interpretation, the well-intentioned bureaucrat's outpacing of public opinion, and so on. Most of the modern criticisms of bureaucratic encroachment were ... audible in the eighteen-thirties. How modern it all is![292]

So the new administrative technology was largely in operation in the 1830s, or at least by the 1870s, emitting the very legal and political controversies we recognize today as its inescapable by-products.

But despite our general familiarity with the techniques and problems of Victorian administrators, we can have only a limited sense of their world. The context in which the new technology emerged is barely hinted at by our few fleeting and commonplace references; its actual impact upon the real problems of individual people can hardly be measured by accounts of a few incidents randomly selected over the span of a few weeks, months, or years. In a sense, the evidence presented here hardly supports the generalizations we must next attempt to make. Yet, in another sense, some generalizations almost demand our attention. It is clear that extraordinary developments were occurring during the nineteenth century in the technology of administration as in all other spheres of intellectual activity. A genuine effort was being made to translate public policies – whether later judged wise or foolish, benign or oppressive – into social reality. This effort engaged the talents, energies, and moral commitments of what must be acknowledged to be an extremely able and serious group of administrators. It produced a massive outpouring of legislation and, it will now be suggested, of 'law' in the large sense in which that term is used by almost everyone except lawyers. And it was an effort which was, in significant measure, conducted outside the traditional institutions of law if not in direct opposition to them.

The next chapter will describe the relationship between law and administration during this critical period of the mid-nineteenth century in order to lay a foundation for better understanding both what people then conceived law to be and how administrative law can today be accommodated within a legal system that continues to deny it legitimacy. This chapter concludes with a brief reminder of what was added to English law in the forty-year period from the enactment of the Factories Act to the establishment of the Railway and Canal Commission.

Here is what became commonplace between 1833 and 1873: new regulatory statutes that created their own special administrative structures; a new armoury of administrative weapons intended to secure close and continuing compliance with standards of social and economic behaviour; a new class of administrators whose formal and informal influence on law (even as conventionally defined) rivalled that of legal professionals; and above all a new sensitivity to the limited capacities of the superior courts, to the vested interests of the magistracy, and to the need to define the relationship of each to the administration and of the administration to law and politics.

In short, we have seen that as Victorians confronted the practical problems of government in the new industrial age, they made a series of individual, although not unrelated, administrative inventions and refinements of extraordinary breadth and diversity. Taken individually, each of these inventions can be explained by – and can help to explain – the context of social, political, and economic events within which it occurred. Taken as a whole, however, can we recognize in them something more than the sum of their separate parts? And, to paraphrase, that 'something' may have been magnificent, but was it 'law'?

5

The Emergence of Administrative Law: The New Pluralism

INTRODUCTION

What, if anything, do the developments in administrative technology just described tell us about the nature of law in Victorian England? If we approach them within the analytical framework of legal centralism, these developments hold little interest. Parliament has enacted a statute; officials have been instructed to act in compliance with it; courts have authoritatively construed it in the exercise of their original or reviewing jurisdiction; officials do as they are bid; public compliance follows as a matter of course. Nothing untoward has happened.

But suppose we choose to describe events differently. A new regime of rules has emerged, in part because of legislation, in part because of independent, unanticipated, and creative initiatives taken by administrators; officials perceive statutes not as a limitation on action but as a licence to act; judges misinterpret and obstruct as often as they read fairly and facilitate; compliance is not always a reflexive response to the law's command, but often a deliberate and delayed reaction to the stimulus of administration. This interpretation of events, which indeed seems far more consistent with the evidence, requires radical revision of the centralist paradigm of law.

Such an interpretation, and revision, will be attempted in this chapter. It will be suggested that bodies of law were created, interpreted, and applied by and within the administration. This 'administrative law' differed from the law of parliament and the courts in so far as the roles of legislators and judges were played by administrators; the rules themselves differed in form and content; methods of fact-finding, law-finding and decision-making often departed from the styles familiar to legal professionals; compliance was seldom secured by recourse to damages, fines, or imprisonment, but rather by admonition, negotiation or – as a last resort – the giving or with-holding of benefits. Yet, it will be argued, for all that administrative law was distinctive, it was none the less law.

To be sure, we will have to be alert to Weber's 'imperceptible transitions' as we move from the articulation of general standards to the patterned exercise of discretion, from formal adjudication by courts, magistrates, and tribunals to the routine assertion of official judgment, from the exercise of state coercive power to the application of informal pressure. But we should not be over-concerned to mark with precision the point at which 'law' leaves off and some other form of social ordering begins. That point is, as Weber reminds us, 'entirely a question of terminology and convenience.'[1] Rather, we should devote ourselves to the difficult task of comprehending how administrative law both differed from and resembled the law of parliament and the superior courts.

This exercise requires us to explore the relationship between the administration on the one hand and legislation, adjudication, and what may be called legal values on the other. Each of these terms requires definition. For purposes of this discussion, 'the administration' is used generically to refer to boards, commissions, inspectorates, and ministries. 'Legislation' and 'adjudication' also are used in a generic sense. The former encompasses the processes by which prospective rules of general application are made, including the enactment of statutes by parliament. The latter embraces decision-making, which involves the finding of facts and the application to them of a predetermined standard, including the activities of the superior courts. In neither case is the conventional example – statute or judicial decision – exhaustive. Finally, 'legal values' is used to conjure up such notions as predictability, participation, and fairness, which are said to be of the essence of 'legislation' and 'adjudication.'

LEGISLATION AND ADMINISTRATION

Since the 1830s, modern administrative law has been almost entirely statute-based. This is not to deny the persistence of domestic regulatory arrangements, often (though not always) sanctioned by legislation, or to overlook the frequent formal or informal administrative adumbration of rules or making of decisions without direct reference to or reliance upon the very words of a statute. But at least in a broad sense, administration came to be regarded as the projection and implementation of legislative policy. From the 1830s on, 'it came to be assumed as easily as it had previously been rejected that legal change would often imply administrative machinery for the purpose of enforcement.'[2] The linkage between legislation and administration was essential because statutes that in the eighteenth century were generally 'private, local and facilitative,' had become 'public, national and obligatory.'[3] Now the implementation of policy was the state's concern as well as that of its potential beneficiaries. Now a general standard of social and economic behaviour was to prevail (and not just in administrative law) over custom, local law, and the realities of political power within local élites. And, above all, legislation now was no longer merely declaratory of the common law or the source of new private rights. Making due allowance for the imperfect state of parliamentary democracy, after the 1830s legislation became, at least in theory, 'the ordinary day-by-day machinery of State interference designed to bring the greatest happiness to the greatest number.'[4] Such machinery, which more and more functioned systematically and continuously, had to be tended by an appropriate complement of overseers and operatives – 'commissioners, inspectorates, and executive officers.'[5]

It would be naïve to imagine that these functionaries were the mere millhands of government with no relationship to legislation other than their mechanical responsibilities. They often helped to bring legislation into existence, to revise and strengthen it, and to defend it against attack. Chadwick's initiatives in promoting factory, poor-law, police, sanitary, and local government legislation were unusually pervasive, but not unique.[6] But the administration did not possess a monopoly on moral entrepreneurship. Since the executive did not yet enjoy complete control over the legislative process, many important bills originated from individual or pressure-group initiatives.[7] Moreover, the weight of political sentiment by no means always favoured either state intervention or a stronger administration, and administrative proposals were often rebuffed.[8]

Indeed, antipathy to state intervention was often disguised as a practical or principled objection to the administrative mechanism necessary to give it effect. The Poor Law commissioners, perhaps understandably stigmatized as a 'tyranny ... extensive and ... uncontrolled' for their powers in relation to poor relief,[9] were also condemned for asking for general powers to abate public-health nuisances. These powers were stigmatized as over broad and thus unconstitutional: '[T]o confer the powers asked for ... though statute might legalize it, is contrary to law.'[10] Establishment of a railway commission was attacked on the grounds, inter alia, that its members were not judges and that there were no appeals from its decisions.[11] When the General Board of Health was established in 1848, it was condemned as an example of unwarranted interference with local autonomy and of the growth of central government, despite its modest mandate and minuscule staff.[12] In general, there was ample evidence to support the hypothesis that '[t]hose who dislike the statutory delegation of legislative power or the statutory creation of a non-judicial tribunal will often be those who dislike the policy behind the statute and seek to fight it at every stage.'[13] The prerogatives of parliament and of unsavoury vested interests sometimes refuted the logic of administration. For example, parliament persisted in its cumbersome procedure for incorporating railroads by means of private bills rather than by assigning responsibility to a department or commission.[14] It is difficult to discount the possibility that those earning huge fees by appearing for or against applications for incorporation were instrumental in ensuring retention of the procedure[15] or that other illicit considerations prompted members of parliament to accede to their pressure.[16]

Finally, at a purely technical level, control by legislative counsel over the drafting of statutes was resented by administrators who were more sensitive to the implications of proposed language. Chadwick, for example, argued that specialist administrators in particular areas should draft their own bills because they were 'more conversant with the particular class of subjects than any set of gentlemen suddenly assembled, and giving only a part of their time to it.' He even praised a statute 'drawn without the advantage of a "Legislative Counsel" ... by plain people, locally acquainted with the subject ...' which he described as 'one of the few statutes which the framers have written in the English tongue, with an endeavour not to mystify, but to explain its provisions.'[17]

In part, Chadwick was addressing a problem in communication, a matter of concern to any administrator seeking to secure compliance by non-specialist readers of a statute or regulations.[18] In part, however, he may have been seeking to avoid the unhelpful intervention of lawyers who might be less enthusiastic about the policy of the legislation than its administrators.[14]

Yet there was more to legislation than the policies it embodied, the institutional arrangements selected to advance those policies, and the language used to express them. In such matters, the influence of the administrators, while often significant, did not always prevail. But once legislation was enacted, someone had to translate it into practical measures and, in order to do so, had to give specificity to often vague language and apply either the original words or their detailed reformulation in particular instances. These two processes were sometimes consecutive, sometimes contemporaneous, but they were processes in which the administration usually played a key role.

First, there was the general problem of translating open-textured language into detailed commands so that those bound by a statute would know in advance precisely what was expected of them. On occasion, such supplementary legislative activity was explicitly authorized, and power to make or approve rules was given to an administrative body such as the Poor Law Board, the original factory inspectors, or the home secretary.[20] Sometimes, however, without recourse to such explicit authority and even in its absence, administrative bodies simply proceeded to 'legislate.' They laid down detailed codes of behaviour or performance which, for operational purposes, took precedence over the words of the statute itself.

Three examples may be cited. The emigration officers worked out fixed ratios of cargo to ship tonnage, on the basis of which they made judgments concerning the ships' seaworthiness.[21] The factory inspectors and the Board of Health both circulated information bulletins advising those affected of the proper interpretation of legislation and of the standard of conduct expected of them.[22] And the inspectors of the Railway Department of the Board of Trade developed, without express statutory authority, an elaborate code of requirements setting safety and amenity standards for railways.[23] Technical standards, advisory bulletins, codified discretion: whatever the legal status of these administrative arrangements (and it was often dubious), they operated with quasi-legislative effect to secure conforming conduct.

Several important constraints on subordinate or quasi-legislation must be mentioned. First, many statutes required that rules or regulations be approved by a cabinet minister or laid before parliament.[24] These requirements were sometimes less than inhibiting. The Poor Law commissioners, fearing parliamentary scrutiny of their 'general orders,' instead issued thousands of pro forma 'special orders' to local guardians. These 'special orders' did not require approval, although, like 'general orders,' they had the effect of requiring uniform behaviour.[25] Second, as has already been indicated, clarification of the principle of ministerial responsibility reduced the ability of administrators to act autonomously. Increasingly, the right to make rules and regulations was reserved to those charged with political responsibility.[26] Third, the legislative functions of administrators were to some extent inhibited by external legal controls in the form of the opinions of the government's law officers,[27] refusals by magistrates to accept administrative interpretations in enforcement proceedings,[28] or intervention by a higher court in prerogative writ or appeal proceedings.[29]

There was also the problem of applying the legislation – original, subordinate, or 'quasi' – in particular instances. This process was obviously adjudicative in part, but it was legislative as well. A pattern of individual decisions or even a single test case that interpreted vague language in a particular way, pressed it to or past its limits, or treated it as incapable of practical application could effectively rewrite a statute. For example, extended legislative controversy arose over the issue of whether the 'seaworthiness' of emigrant ships should be judged by predetermined standards laid down in the governing statute, or on the basis of essentially unstructured, on-the-spot discretionary decisions by emigration officers. Although parliament finally opted for the latter formula, the emigration commissioners soon issued detailed technical manuals to the officers. These manuals in effect structured and confined the commissioners' discretion, which parliament had explicitly declined to do.[30] In another episode, parliament rejected the prolonged and vocal objections of the factory inspectors and established a procedure by which manufacturers could seek arbitration of orders to fence machinery. The inspectors 'repealed' the provision by announcing that they would refuse to exercise their discretion to invoke the arbitration process.[31] In both cases the crucial element was the existence of a broad discretion as to how or whether to invoke a statute in particular circumstances. This invites a brief detour to consider more generally the significance of 'discretion' in the development of administrative law.

Reference was made in previous chapters to the growing antipathy of Victorian lawyers to the notion of discretion. However much that antipathy may have been reflected, as Atiyah suggests, in changing styles of formal legal discourse, it could hardly be expected to dictate the language of the new, regulatory statutes.[32] As the experience of the Emigration Acts shows,[33] the conferring of broad discretionary powers upon officials was made necessary by a combination of factors: the absence of experience with administrative intervention per se and with the particular field of activity; an inadequate scientific base coupled with the experience of rapid technical innovation; and the unpredictable problems posed by the application of the legislation to ships with idiosyncratic engineering features. Legislative draftsmen could avoid addressing these difficult issues by passing them forward to administrators, who would have to deal with them on a daily basis. Discretion was the vehicle by which this transfer of responsibility was accomplished.

However, the conferring of discretionary powers set in motion other forces. By avoiding statutory specification of standards of seaworthiness, levels of support for the indigent, or safety measures in mines or factories, statutory draftsmen and parliamentary proponents may have sought to convey the impression that these were technical rather than political issues.

They may have dampened debate, or at least truncated it, by avoiding controversy over the soundness and practicality of specific measures. Moreover, they may also have provided the administrators who received discretionary powers with at least a thin cloak of presumptive expertise to protect them from political criticism and deflect judicial review.[34]

Sometimes, however, the conferring of discretionary powers produced precisely the opposite results. The very technical nature of the matters that were consigned to administrative discretion also made the administration vulnerable to attack. Whatever expertise administrators actually possessed – and it was occasionally negligible[35] – it was often disparaged as being less than that of the practical men of affairs who had ongoing responsibility for the conduct of an enterprise.[36] Moreover, given the uncertain state of scientific and technical knowledge, administrators could be drawn into controversies resulting from changes in the conventional wisdom[37] or attacked for their own failure to achieve results.[38] When administrative discretion was directed to non-technical matters, as it often was, it proved to be a lightning rod for criticism. The well-known jibe that the Poor Law commissioners conducted themselves like a 'pacha of three tails' hinted not only at their presumed cruelty, but also at their allegedly unbounded discretion.[39]

None the less, it is easy to see that any centrally directed regime of poor laws, public health, or accident prevention must have relied upon the assignment to administrators of virtually unlimited discretion. What is less obvious is that they used that discretion not so much as a mandate for arbitrary and unpredictable decision-making but as a framework for their own legislative activities.

Ultimately, too, this supplementary legislative activity by the administration influenced the formal amendment of statutes by parliament.[40] Thus, although administrators were never entitled to enact, amend, or ignore statutes, they seem often to have come close to doing all of those things. Certainly, they played a variety of vital roles in the legislative process. The limits of those roles came to be defined by parliament, by the courts, and by administrative practice itself. This process of definition can fairly be described as an important development in the emergence of modern administrative law.

ADJUDICATION AND ADMINISTRATION

The legislative activities of Victorian administrators dealt with problems, as it were, at wholesale; adjudication disposed of them at retail. Here was the potential for real controversy, since adjudication touched not merely general aggregations of hostile interests but specific individuals and enterprises, and not merely those who were its primary subjects but the judges, lawyers, and magistrates whose interests and ideology were affronted by any trespass upon their claimed monopoly over adjudication.

This concern was not new. Adjudication by emanations of the executive was a bête noire of English constitutionalists long before the 1830s. The suppression of the conciliar courts, including Star Chamber, in the seventeenth century was part of the struggle between the king and parliament, with which the common-law courts were allied.[41] And if the king could no longer create special courts, neither they nor he could tamper with the independence and function of the regular courts.[42] On the contrary, the regular courts asserted and gained a controlling jurisdiction over the functioning of all inferior tribunals.[43] This in crude terms, was the theoretical constitutional framework out of which modern administrative law was to emerge.

The reality was otherwise, however. As control of the executive passed from the crown to parliament, the logic of the alliance against administrative adjudication evaporated. Although parliament could not directly interfere with the superior courts or the local justices, it was increasingly prepared to order them to do its bidding through legislation. When, during the early and middle years of the nineteenth century, judges, and especially magistrates, demonstrated antipathy or indifference to parliament's wishes, parliament had no alternative but to entrust adjudicative tasks increasingly to the administration, which it now more or less controlled. After 1851, especially,

the central departments sat as judicial boards, much as did regular courts of law. But the line between the judicial and administrative was never clear ... Gradually, and for the most part unnoticed, [the central administration was] gaining judicial powers as well as legislative powers, thus laying the basis of the modern administrative state, with its characteristic and wholly necessary extension of wide discretionary powers.[44]

This strong current of development in administrative law between 1830 and 1870 did not flow unimpeded through all channels of constitutional and legislative thought. Adjudication was one thing, enforcement another. Except for a brief experiment under the Factories Act,[45] judges retained the sole power to impose penal sanctions. According to Roberts, 'Parliament displayed a scrupulous economy in the granting of general powers of compulsion.'[46] Although, as has been seen, a variety of non-penal sanctions was available, administrative decision-makers were often denied power to make directly enforceable remedial orders.[47] When the administration did acquire new sanctions and remedies, these were sometimes dependent for their enforcement on arbitrators or courts.[48] And although the administration was often shielded by statute from the superintending jurisdiction of the superior courts, some attempts to exclude appeals or judicial review were lost in parliament or, if successful there, were overturned or ignored by subsequent judicial decisions.[49]

This cross-current, to borrow Dicey's phrase, in the direction of a judicial monopoly of adjudication may appear to justify his insistence that administrative law is incompatible with the English legal tradition. To the extent that it predominates, the cross-current certainly tends to feed the paradigm of legal centralism. However, closer examination of the facts shows that Dicey, and the generations of lawyers influenced by him, have overestimated the extent to which adjudication was and is reserved to judges.

In the first place, it is by no means clear that the survival of the courts' primary jurisdiction in penal matters and of their reviewing jurisdiction over administrative decision-making was attributable to constitutional considerations. On the contrary, it is inconceivable that opponents of state intervention (including Dicey himself[50]) failed to realize that any derogation from administrative adjudication was sure to impair effective regulation. Magistrates were notoriously unwilling to convict their reputable fellow members of the upper middle class, let alone their close associates.[51] When conviction was inevitable as a result of prosecutions conducted by inspectors, they were equally unwilling to impose even the modest maximum fines provided.[52] What opponent of state intervention could be anything but a supporter of the magistrates' monopoly over penal sanctions?

Once the administration began to acquire the right to seek injunctions against the operation of unsafe mines or factories, or to prohibit the opening of 'incomplete' – actually unsafe – railways, or to prevent the sailing of unfit vessels, the issue of penal sanctions became less important.[53] To the extent that disobedience of an administrative order carried only a small fine, it is true, the situation was not much changed. However, the consequences of non-compliance gradually became more serious: miners declined to work in mines that had been declared unsafe by an inspector, customs officers refused to clear unseaworthy vessels, decisions of the Railway Commission were made a rule of court and enforced 'in like manner as any rule or order of such court,' and failure to fence factory machinery following an inspector's notice to do so involved considerably increased liability for any ensuing injury.[54] Thus, although prosecution generally remained the ultimate, if often unavailing, technique of enforcement, the administration slowly gained greater control over other sanctioning systems.

But administrative adjudication was under attack on other fronts. The very notion that the procedure and evidentiary rules of administrative decision-makers did not replicate those of the courts was thought to be an evil per se. Confronted by advice from the law officers that they were to hear all matters in person and in each other's presence, the Poor Law commissioners protested. Such requirements they rejected as '[not] applicable to any administrative Board.' Such a board, the commissioners continued, 'is not bound by the same restrictions or placed in the same circumstances as a Court of Justice ... [I]t may initiate enquiries and its members may form a judgment upon any facts which may be accessible to them. The arguments derived from Courts of Justice ... seem to us inapplicable to most of the business transacted by an administrative Board.[55] What seemed to the administration a positive procedural advantage was, to its critics, the very basis of objection.[56] One is reminded of lawyers' concerns about local courts, which did not 'proceed according to the course of the common law,' and about proposals for tribunals of commerce, which would, a legal critic feared, 'abolish the juridical section of the British constitution.'

Turning from procedure to substance, it is difficult to form a clear view as to whether administrative decision-makers construed and applied the operative provisions of their statutes differently from conventional courts. While interpretative styles varied from one administrative context to another, we can at least hypothesize that interpretations were purposive, in the sense that they reflected the administration's own view of what would best advance its strategy of regulation. On occasion this may have led to an understatement of the full potential of statutory language when the prevailing strategy was to secure co-operation and avoid confrontation.[57] Often enough, however, administrative interpretations were expansive. The emigration commissioners, says their foremost chronicler, rejected narrow interpretations of their governing statute; they 'spoke the language of *salus populi suprema lex.*'[58]

But there is reason to believe that elsewhere, especially in professional legal circles, more restrictive interpretations prevailed. Inferences to this effect can be drawn from the use and threatened use of collateral civil proceedings to forestall administrative initiatives,[59] from the willingness of local justices and reviewing courts to brush aside administrative interpretations and substitute their own,[60] and from the precautions taken by legislative draftsmen to restrict or prevent judicial review, especially in the superior courts, a topic dealt with below. These inferences are strengthened by perusal of the opinions of those rather conservative lawyers, the law officers, which presumably were based on sound judgments about how legislation would be interpreted by courts.

Although the law officers thought it 'safest to adhere to the literal meaning of the words,'[61] it is difficult to document a directly contradictory posture on the part of the inspectorate, which appears only occasionally to have overtly resisted or protested the opinions of the law officers. But the general attitude of the early administrators, as evidenced by their daily behaviour, was that they sought to advance the basic objectives of the legislation by any means available and without particular regard for either formal adjudication or authoritative interpretation. Even the railway commissioners, who frequently declined to be lured into controversies not clearly assigned to them by their statute, seemed to have treated the legislation as no more than an outer boundary for the regulatory activity they did undertake.

In short, the administration seems to have been divided from other formal legal institutions and actors less by conscious differences over the substantive outcomes of adjudication than by unconscious assumptions about the nature and importance of adjudication itself. For lawyers (including the law officers) and for judges, adjudication was an event of high significance, invested with symbolic importance by formal and informal rituals, fraught with implications not merely for the immediate parties but for the law itself. For administrators, adjudication as an intellectual activity was familiar enough, but it existed as one of the repertoire of possible responses to practical problems – and not necessarily the most useful. Adjudication was unlikely therefore either to be wrapped in ritual or to be undertaken with special concern for how the outcome would reflect, and affect, the general law.

This difference in attitude toward adjudication may explain the struggle to deny the administration control over the process, or even access to it. Objections to administrative adjudication were couched in quite different terms, however. The administrators, it was urged, must as a matter of constitutional principle not be given adjudicative powers with which to judge their own cause. This proposition seemed so self-evident that it attracted, for example, the support of both those who were opposed to the whole principle of factory legislation and those who felt the legislation of 1833 did not go far enough.[62] Indeed, after only a few years, the law officers, speaking for all who subscribed to this 'constitutional' principle, were able to prevail upon the home secretary to require the factory inspectors to cease using their statutory power to act as magistrates.[63]

But if inspectors and other administrators were not to have adjudicative powers, who would? As we have seen in our studies of the enforcement of safety standards in factories and mines, a number of other recipients of such powers were apparently thought to be more appropriate. For example, in controversies over fencing for unsafe factory equipment or the content of special rules for mine operations, engineer arbitrators were deemed preferable even though their sympathies were predictable, and the list of eligible arbitrators was established by the employer whose interests were affected.[64] In the assignment of blame for fatal accidents at work, coroners' juries, an ancient and honourable institution, were deemed preferable – even though witnesses and jurors alike were local residents who, if not directly suborned or intimidated by the employer, were at least very much in awe of him. And, of course, violation of this legislation was subject to prosecution before that stern and sturdy seat of British justice, the local magistrates' bench, even though its members were frequently related to the accused by blood or marriage or financial interest.

Upon each of these bodies, in preference to the administration, parliament conferred formal adjudicative powers. Why? Was it because the administrators, many of whom were not lawyers, lacked the skill or knowledge to make legal rulings? Surely not: even fewer of the magistrates were lawyers, legal issues seldom arose, and the law officers, legal clerks, and other legal advisers were as available to the administration as they were to the magistracy. Was it because the magistrates were part of the established legal hierarchy within which appeals and prerogative writ procedures operated to ensure that the new regulatory legislation would be 'worked into the technical system of the common law' by the superior courts?[65] Surely not: few people could afford to seek review of the decisions of magistrates; the superior courts tended to show the decisions some deference on review; and in any event their decisions were to a significant degree protected by privative clauses that limited or excluded review.[66] Was it because administrators were prone to forms of misconduct to which judges – and especially magistrates – were immune? Again, surely not: even a priori judgments to that effect must have given way before any objective assessment of actual experience.

The contrasts between what legal theory claimed and what legal reality offered were too strong to be ignored. By mid-century even utterly conventional legal publications were prepared to recognize the need for 'the establishment of sundry special courts of a special nature,'[67] for commissions that amounted to 'government in miniature,' combining legislative, executive and adjudicative functions, and for members with the 'requisite qualifications' in situations 'when the subject-matter of a commission necessarily requires knowledge and experience of a specific description to deal with it efficiently and properly.'[68]

Yet parliament moved, if at all, only in the direction of more firmly excluding the administration from the tasks of formal adjudication. In 1854, for example, the Court of Common Pleas was given potentially important new jurisdiction to regulate railways.[69] It is difficult to avoid the cynical conclusion that this and similar attempts to exclude the administration from formal adjudication were part of a deliberate strategy to undermine the regulatory enterprise altogether. This strategy served not only the immediate interests of those who owned railways, mines, and factories, but also the long-term interests of all who wished to resist, for their own reasons, a shift in power from the periphery to the centre, from the old oligarchies to the emerging technocracy of government, and from the old intellectual forms of law and politics to their new manifestation in administration. To what extent these apparent conflicts among Victorian élites were real and to what extent illusory or mystificatory is a matter of continuing controversy.[70] But understood as a strategy, the resistance to formal administrative adjudication had important consequences at two levels.

First, it allowed businessmen, confronted with new regulatory initiatives, to appear to acquiesce in the new standards demanded of them, while in fact insisting upon institutional arrangements that would largely shelter them from the effects of regulation. Moreover, it allowed them to resist proposals that involved more effective administrative intervention, not on the basis of embarrassing claims of self-interest but on grounds of constitutional principle.

Second, it taught administrators certain lessons that endeared them neither to lawyers nor to businessmen. Although some examples of formal adjudication persisted or (as in the case of the Railway and Canal Commission) reappeared, administrators were shown that the game usually was not worth the candle. Since they were to be denied formal adjudicative powers or, if granted them, frustrated in their exercise, administrators had to find other ways of accomplishing their goals.

The power to give or withhold benefits was one such way, and the process of investigation, report, and recommendation was another. Both were quintessential activities of Victorian commissions and inspectorates. And both activities, we must now appreciate, were closely allied with, or even identical to, adjudication. When they decided to deny an emigrant ship permission to sail, to issue a notice that factory machinery was unsafe, to permit the construction of a railway bridge or forbid the payment of legal expenses by Poor Law guardians, administrators were adjudicating. Such adjudication lacked many of the outward manifestations of decision-making by courts, but it did involve strikingly similar intellectual processes – the ascertainment of facts and the application to them of a standard announced in, or at least derived from, a statute.

It is true that even such informal adjudication was avoided whenever possible. The characteristic procedure was not the tendering of evidence, cross-examination, advocacy, and formal pronouncement of a decision, but rather on-the-spot inspection, periodic questionnaires, written interrogation and reply, suggestion, admonition, persuasion, and negotiation. It is precisely in this idiom, as we have seen, that Victorian administrators were most fluent. And so they had to be: even informal adjudication of large numbers of cases soon would have swamped their modest complement.[71] But lest we be tempted to over-stress the difference between formal and informal adjudication, we must remember that most civil lawsuits, and much of the administration of criminal justice, was and is conducted in similar fashion.[72] Reference has already been made to Brougham's futile attempts to institutionalize such procedures as a formal step in the resolution of civil disputes; we can well imagine that they would be no more enthusiastically inscribed in the lexicon of administrative techniques. None the less, whether by conviction or under compulsion of circumstances, non-adjudicative procedures predominated.

This, then, is the eddy caused by Dicey's 'cross-current' of formal legalism: an exaggerated, frothy commitment to formal adjudication swirling on the surface and, far below, administrative behaviour tending away from such adjudication whenever possible.

We have not, so far, closely considered another form of adjudication – that associated with appeals from or judicial review of administrative proceedings. The putative role of the courts as guarantors of administrative legality was not confined to reviewing adjudicative decisions. In theory, and subject to the procedural whimsicality of the old prerogative writs, it extended to ensuring that all administrative acts were authorized by law. Judicial review was, therefore, potentially important at both a symbolic and a practical level.

The significance of judicial review did not escape those responsible for drafting and administering Victorian regulatory statutes. In general, their reaction was to reject it rather than to facilitate it. In so doing, they implicitly recognized the distinctiveness and the autonomy of administrative law, although their concerns were typically framed in practical rather than jurisprudential terms.

Bentham had warned against 'the licentiousness of interpretation' of legislation by judges.[73] His disciple, Chadwick, had been concerned about the same problem from the outset of his work on the Factories Act. Having urged the royal commission considering that legislation not to rely upon local magistrates for enforcement,[74] he later sought to preclude judicial review of the factory inspectors and other administrative bodies.[75] Attempts to permit appeals from emigration officers to justices of the peace were rebuffed on the grounds that such appeals would likely lead to further prerogative writ proceedings 'upon such a simple question as whether a cask of biscuits was good or bad,' and that the emigration officers were in any event as impartial as the justices.[76] During the drafting of the Poor Law in 1834, Lord Althorp rejected as 'absurd' the notion that there should be an appeal from the commissioners to either the courts or the cabinet; ultimately, however, they were made amenable to review by certiorari in the King's Bench.[77] And, to cite one more example, the earliest income tax legislation permitted only administrative, not judicial, review of tax assessments.[78]

On balance, early administrative legislation showed sensitivity to the debilitating prospect of endless appeals against the decisions of either commissioners or justices of the peace. The Factory Act, 1825, had introduced a clause precluding appeals against decisions of the justices, a provision carried forward in 1831, in the important act of 1833, and extended to the inspectors, and supplemented by a further privative clause forbidding certiorari proceedings in the act of 1844.[79] The mines labour legislation of 1842 permitted one appeal to quarter sessions, but foreclosed further review proceedings.[80] The Poor Law of 1834, which conferred unusually broad powers on the commissioners, did provide for certiorari against them, but confined appeals against conviction by the justices of either quarter or general sessions.[81] The Inclosure Act of 1846 permitted anyone dissatisfied with a decision of the commissioners to bring an action at assizes 'on a feigned issue' against either the commissioners or the person favoured by their decision or, by consent, to submit the claim to binding arbitration; prerogative writ review, however, was expressly foreclosed.[82]

Implicit in all of these measures limiting review and appeal was the assumption, confirmed by experience, that it would be used to delay and frustrate the enforcement of legislation. But the conventional legal wisdom of the period did not accept that review would necessarily have such an effect:

Few know how much courts of inferior or special jurisdiction are paralysed by the delays of the court of Queen's Bench ... [but] the taking away of certiorari in so many statutes is the oddest sort of mending of the blunders of inferior tribunals. In the hope of preventing delay and litigation, it has substituted oppression and injustice. Better quicken the tribunal of appeal than deprive the public of its protection.[83]

This position ultimately carried the day. Judical review and appeal were to become potential if not actually common features of administrative adjudi-cation and adjudication by the local justices. In an extended series of judg-ments, it was decided that the various privative clauses in the Factories Acts did not protect decisions made without jurisdiction.[84] Moreover, from 1857, the Summary Proceedings Act provided for an appeal by way of stated case to the superior courts against errors of law by justices of the peace, al-though this does not appear to have produced any immediate flood of ap-peals under regulatory legislation.[85] In any event, the pattern of privative clauses had not, except in a few instances such as the Emigration Act, pro-tected administrative decisions per se.[86] And even in those few instances the administration was still exposed to civil suits for damages.[87]

In the context of a system in which the administration lacked formal ad-judicative power and in which those who possessed it – the magistrates – were often hostile to the new legislation, it is not surprising that judicial review was sometimes sought as a means of enforcing such legislation rather than challenging it. Reference has already been made to mandamus pro-ceedings brought by the Poor Law commissioners to compel local guardians to perform their statutory duties.[88] Relatively rarely, and rather unsatisfac-torily, mandamus was also used by the mines inspectors to compel magis-trates to hear and determine charges against mine owners.[89] And in one unusual episode, the law officers advised the factory inspectors on means of contriving a test case to secure the interpretation of a controversial section of the legislation by a higher court. Since the order of a magistrate 'cannot be appealed against or removed by certiorari, there is no means of raising the question hostilely, but if the parties can so arrange it that a Magistrate shall refuse to convict, the question may be raised by an application to the Court of Q.B. for a mandamus.'[90]

On balance, while judicial review did assist various administrative actors from time to time, it tended to be a negative influence. Decisions were often unsympathetic, even hostile, to the new interventionist philosophy; some-times they were insensitive to the procedural, evidentiary, and institutional qualities that distinguished regulatory legislation from criminal law; and, proposals for quicker appeals notwithstanding, they were almost always time-consuming and obstructive.

Yet, by the 1850s, there seems to have been a decided swing in favour of judicial decision-making, not only at first instance but also by way of review. For example, the Coal Mines Inspection Act of 1850 (and its amending statutes in 1855, 1860, and 1862) did not carry forward the privative clause of the 1842 act.[91] And the assumption of railway jurisdiction by the Court of Common Pleas opened up the possibility of appeals from that court up through the entire judicial hierarchy.[92] Only in 1873, when the new Railway Commission reclaimed jurisdiction from that court, was the issue of judicial review of administrative decisions joined clearly and in modern terms. The ghost of judicature was not to be laid. At the committee stage of the 1873 legislation, the issue of judicial review was confronted, and its supporters carried the day. A government amendment was proposed to enable the commissioners in their discretion to state a case for the opinion of any superior court 'upon any question which in the opinion of the Commissioners is a question of Law.'[93] This discretionary power was thought insufficient by the opposition:

Mr. Denison said, it was perfectly impossible for the Railway Companies to accept the Amendment of the right hon. Gentleman the President of the Board of Trade, and they were united and determined upon that point. Nobody knew who were to be the Commissioners, and he would not trust any three men in the kingdom with despotic powers of interpretation without any appeal unless they choose to grant it. He could not make any compromise in this matter.[94]

And in a similar vein:

Mr. Leeman contended that the clause, by taking away the right of appeal, deprived the Companies of the right, which belonged to every subject of this realm. ['No, no.'] It was said that there was to be only a right of appeal if the tribunal should think fit. But the Chief Commissioner and another of the Commissioners were not to be lawyers, and while this was so there was to be no right to appeal from their decision, even on points of law. An appeal as a question of fact was not asked at all. He would appeal to the House on a matter of justice not to deprive Companies of a right of appeal.[95]

Despite the admonition that 'the individual trader had to deal with powerful Companies, holding very long purses, and that unneccessary liberty of appeal might thus place the trader practically at the mercy of the Carrier ...'[96] and the solicitor-general's reminder that there were many cases where the right of appeal depended on the leave of the Court, and there was a very large number of cases in which no right of appeal existed at all. In very many instances the amount involved would be very small, and it would be very oppressive to give a right of appeal merely because one of the parties was a great and wealthy corporation. Again, in many cases the law was perfectly well settled. There was no occasion for distrusting the proposed tribunal so far as to suppose that it would prevent the opinion of a Court of Law being taken on any question, the decision of which might be requisite for the future guidance of the tribunal itself ...[97]

and despite the offer to 'make an appeal absolute in those cases in which the Commissioners were not unanimous,'[98] nothing less than a complete right of appeal on questions of law would apparently satisfy the opposition. In its final form, the act required the commissioners to state a case upon the request of either party on questions which, in its opinion, were questions of law.[99]

While adumbrating the issue of judicial review, which continues to haunt the design of administrative agencies, the debate and its outcome were overtaken by events. Despite a provision that 'save as aforesaid, every decision and order of the Commission shall be final,'[100] the commission was soon successfully attacked in prerogative writ proceedings.[101] Thereafter, appeals and motions for prohibition became a regular feature of important cases before the commission.[102] Fifteen years later, a general right of appeal from decisions of the commission was created on all issues save questions of fact and of locus standi, qualified by expanded, but now gratuitous, safeguards against prerogative writ review.[103] To further enhance legal regularity, an ex officio judicial commissioner was substituted for the former member 'of experience in the law.'[104]

The actual effects of formal adjudication by the superior courts and local magistrates in original and review proceedings are difficult to estimate throughout the period and across the spectrum of administrative activity. It is clear that much of the effective work of social and economic regulation was undertaken by the administration without recourse to either formal or informal adjudication. In many fields – factory safety, pure food, poor relief, railway safety, and enclosure, for example – the administration laid down standards of conduct by subordinate or quasi-legislation, and secured adherence by persuasion, education, compromise, and other informal processes.[105] As even legal observers realized, this placed a great premium on abilities different from those expected of a conventional adjudicator: 'Upon [the administrators'] ... tact and aptitude for the delicate business, must, in a great measure, have depended all the operative part of the measure, and much of its ultimate success.'[106] Such activities were largely immune from judicial scrutiny, although they resulted in the development of norms no less effective in practice than those formally announced by the courts or parliament.

Even where adjudication was the preferred method of securing compliance, or perhaps the method of last resort, it almost always remained at the lower levels of the judiciary, the local justices. As has been seen, the unifying element of adjudication at this level appears to have been only the unstated reluctance of most magistrates to criminalize most entrepreneurial activity. The magistrates were largely shielded from review. When the higher courts did become involved in the new law of administration, they too often exhibited little sympathy for, or even comprehension of, statutory policies. And, on the relatively few occasions when the higher courts gave a large and liberal interpretation of regulatory legislation, their decisions apparently were ignored by the lower courts.[107]

Finally, it is impossible to trace the emergence by the 1870s – or perhaps even by the 1980s – of a coherent body of judge-made rules of administrative law.[108] Some basic notions, such as natural justice and ultra vires, had emerged long before the nineteenth century.[109] However, even today these remain imprecise concepts, designed to remedy abuses of administrative jurisdiction rather than to rationalize substantive administrative doctrines or to enhance prospectively the quality of administrative decision-making. Holdsworth's claim that 'new bodies of public law' emerged from the supervision by the courts of the decisions of justices and commissioners is overstated.[110] But this is not to deny that 'new bodies of public law' came into existence; only that it was the courts, rather than the administration itself, that created them.

LEGAL VALUES WITHIN THE ADMINISTRATION

Why does it matter whether administrative law was or was not 'law' in a fundamental sense? The answer to this question has been understood from Bentham's day to the present. It is because, in Weber's cogent phrase, '[t]oday the most common form of legitimacy is the belief in legality, i.e. the acquiescence in enactments which are formally correct and which have been made in the accustomed manner.'[111] The legal qualities of administration can thus be seen as a proxy for the issue of legitimacy. And legitimacy is worth fighting over: it is a measure of the extent to which various institutions and systems can command obedience, elicit participation or co-operation, and manage social behaviour without coercion.

Administrative law has long laboured under the disability that it lacks legitimacy because it is not really 'law.' Dicey, who has obligingly played counterpoint to the themes of this enquiry, may once again be heard from. He juxtaposed decisions of the 'ordinary courts of law' concerning 'distinct breach[es] of law' with the activities of 'persons in authority' who exercised 'wide, arbitrary or discretionary powers of constraint.'[112] The pejoratives can be heard in every note. 'Courts of law' are revered institutions; 'persons in authority' are men with mortal failings. 'Distinct breaches of law' signals a limited intrusion on freedom, an intrusion made possible, in Weber's phrase, only by 'enactments which are formally correct and ... made in the accustomed manner.' 'Wide, arbitrary or discretionary powers' by definition threaten unlimited intrusions, intrusions (in Dicey's view of history, at least) made other than in 'the accustomed manner,' and all too likely not to be 'formally correct.'[113]

Setting aside Dicey's chronology, as we now must, in view of the evidence we have considered, his characterizations of both law and administration remain. To what extent did these reflect nineteenth-century realities? It is indeed true that social control and economic regulation in the mid-nineteenth century were tasks largely undertaken by two distinct groups: the local magistrates, closely identified with the ordinary courts on the one hand, and the administrators, inspectors, and commissioners, 'persons in authority,' on the other.[114] But while the former group no doubt purported to act 'in the accustomed manner' – that, after all was their patent of authority – it was by no means obvious that they exhibited due regard for legal values. Nor can one say that, in general, 'persons in authority' acted 'arbitrarily.'

If it is important for the rule of law (as Dicey claimed) that people should be penalized only for 'distinct breaches of law' – and that they should not commit such breaches with impunity – administrative behaviour generally deserves praise rather than abuse. The whole thrust of administrative regulation from 1830 onward was to lend specificity, predictability, uniformity, and rationality to the law. General statutory standards were translated into detailed codes[115] as the administration willingly traded away its large discretion in order to provide better guidance to those it sought to regulate.[116] Information about the law and the administrative codes was widely disseminated and advice was given, both in general terms and in response to inquiries, as to the legality of conduct actually being undertaken or in contemplation.[117] Uniform national standards were pursued, often in defiance of fierce local opposition and special interests, sometimes with needless single-mindedness,[118] sometimes with politically expedient deference to local sensibilities.[119] And the formal and informal participation of those being regulated in the process of defining new rules of conduct at least gave such rules the ring of rationality, even if it did sometimes also subvert their ultimate effect.[120]

It would be foolish to pretend that these tendencies always came to rest at their proper destination. Sometimes they were prematurely abandoned because of misconceived administrative arrangements, inadequate staff and budgets, or lack of scientific or technical knowledge.[121] Sometimes, too, they were carried to excess.[122] And sometimes they were deflected by external realities; Benthamite administrative technique, after all, 'depended upon men behaving rationally and was faced everywhere by their patent irrationality.'[123] But there is no mistaking the basic aim of administrative developments during this period. It was to establish legitimately and enforce consistently new and generalizable standards of behaviour – new 'law.' Equally, there is no mistaking the fundamental inconsistency of 'arbitrariness' or unfettered discretion with this aim. Departure from the new administrative legality would not only be impolitic, inviting political resistance and judicial review.[124] It would also be inefficient, requiring constant redecision of similar cases instead of the mere application of firm, pre-established standards or their widespread voluntary adoption by law-abiding local officials and businessmen.

To place these comments in perspective, we must remind ourselves of the behaviour of the other group involved in regulatory activities, the local justices. Their regime was arbitrary indeed. By the early nineteenth century, when they were not exercising unfettered discretion as the extralegal government of the country,[125] they were acting under local and private statutes that were often obscure and, almost by definition, the antithesis of what Dicey called 'the ordinary law of the realm.'[126] They virtually declined to enforce not only the earliest national regulatory legislation, but also the general criminal law to the extent that it impinged upon powerful local interests.[127] When confronted with prosecutions by the new inspectorate after 1833, they took refuge in procedural technicalities, provoking legislative rebuke, adopted questionable interpretations of the legislation, and vitiated inescapable convictions by imposing trivial penalties.[128] Predictability and uniformity were undermined as the justices declined to accept administrative codes and rulings and even ignored the authoritative pronouncements of higher courts.[129]

Nor do the developing standards of administrative propriety suffer by comparison with those of local justices. In the early days of the inspectorate, it is true, several episodes called into question its impartiality and professional standards. Attempts to secure voluntary compliance with the factory acts, or perhaps merely social affinity, involved some inspectors in compromisingly close association with employers; fear of working-class agitation led to an ill-advised government attempt to use inspectors to monitor political sentiment; and officials occasionally sought to extract licit or illicit advantages from firms they were meant to be regulating.[130] But each of these episodes led to the development of rules of administrative behaviour, which ensured greater impartiality and professionalism.

In contrast with rather exceptional lapses by the administrators, abuses were apparently widespread among the local justices. No virtue of adjudication, it might be thought, exceeds that of impartiality. Yet so often did justices sit in judgment on cases involving their own pecuniary interests or the interests of close relatives or associates that special disqualifying legislation had to be enacted and then strengthened to stop deliberate avoidance.[131] And even where no presumption of bias disqualified justices from hearing cases, their behaviour on the bench often showed a marked lack of impartiality.[132]

It has sometimes been said that some of the pioneering administrators had grandiose visions of social order or moral obligation which transcended the perspective of their charter statutes and had a powerful directing influence on their work.[133] Chadwick is the example most often given, but it can fairly be said that many others were so deeply involved with the formulation of policy that their enforcement of it was influenced by 'political' considerations.[134]

Circumstances already canvassed did generate pressures for such political activity. At least in the early Victorian period, no significant establishment of civil servants (apart from the military) existed from which might be drawn new cadres of inspectors and commissioners. Persons who had been active in securing enactment of the regulatory schemes were obvious candidates for such appointments. Not only did they approach their work with well-developed and well-known views, but they retained connections with a constituency of patrons and supporters.

Moreover, the original enactment of a new scheme was almost sure to be only the first verse in a long legislative saga. An initial attempt at regulatory activity in any field was likely to be flawed by confused and compromised parliamentary intentions, by a lack of technical knowledge, by sheer inexperience in draftsmanship and regulation. Even if the statute was well conceived in its own terms, those terms were almost sure to be revised by new political circumstances, new scientific discoveries, new revelations of evil and possible good, and new judicial interpretations.[135] In fact, some of the early regulatory statutes were not meant to last; they were enacted to have effect only for a fixed period of years.[136]

Thus, subsequent legislative battles were likely to occur, and administrators were likely to be drawn into them, if they did not actually provoke them. When debates over amendment or re-enactment took place, the administration naturally wished to recite the lessons of experience; other protagonists, perhaps with more extreme intentions, battled over total repeal or radical transformation of the scheme. Since such debates were always imminent, the administrators were in effect committed, willingly or unwillingly, to continuing political controversy. The fact that many of them participated in it extensively and, by modern standards, indiscreetly, is not the worst that can be said of Chadwick and his contemporaries: 'What do ... the technicalities of political responsibility matter, if the people perish ... We do well to be thankful to some of these men for their improprieties. This is the heroic age of the civil servant who was also a social reformer.'[137] That role was not one that could be played indefinitely, however.

In part, the political–legislative activities of administrators gave way before a clearer articulation and functional division of responsibilities. The factory inspectors were stripped of their controversial adjudicative powers, first by ministerial directive and then by statute. Soon they declined even to give interpretative rulings on the legislation.[138] Although they remained relatively minor political players in subsequent dramas, they were no longer at centre stage.[139] The 'heroic age' subsided into the smugness and conservatism of the later Victorian period. From the 1850s onward, reform was less spectacular and the role of civil servants in it less public. Moral entrepreneurship began to be replaced by a new ideal – that of the civil service as permanent, professional, meritocratic, and non-political. The Northcote-Trevelyan reforms did not speak directly to political activity,[140] but by changing the basis of recruitment and advancement they may have helped to support tendencies toward diminished political activity that had been in train since the 1830s. In any event, direct and outspoken advocacy of legislation by civil servants was muted by new rules and conventions that demanded anonymity.[141] And the experiment of autonomous administrative agencies with responsibility for both the development and the execution of policy was largely abandoned in favour of departmental organization and ministerial responsibility for policy.[142]

While 'persons in authority' were groping toward professionalism and neutrality, many local justices continued to be deeply enmeshed in politics, both local and national.[143] Moreover, unlike that of their overzealous official counterparts, the political behaviour of magistrates sometimes took the form of defying or subverting legislative policy in their own interest rather than seeking its more effective implementation in the national interest.[144]

There is no intention in any of these comparisons to idealize all administrators or to asperse the entire magistracy.[145] However, it must be understood that the emergence of coherent bodies of administrative law and of standards of administrative propriety were largely attributable to internal forces rather than to imitation of the 'ordinary' justices of the peace, or even of the 'ordinary' superior courts.[146] To explain why this was so, it is important to turn to a description of the 'persons in authority' of whom Dicey speaks disparagingly.

As Parris's helpful study of the Victorian bureaucracy shows, a significant number of the senior officials responsible for the development and enforcement of the new regulatory policies had legal training.[147] For example, twenty-one of the fifty-eight men who held office as permanent secretaries during the period from 1830 to 1870 were barristers.[148] Roberts's study of the inspectorate shows that of sixty-four inspectors (of a total of 140) for whom biographical data are available, during the period from 1833 to 1854 twelve were practising lawyers and one a professor of jurisprudence.[149] The ubiquitous Chadwick was a lawyer,[150] as was his mentor and preceptor of so many Victorian administrators, Jeremy Bentham. Keeping in mind that the technical nature of their tasks demanded that a substantial number of inspectors be doctors, scientists, engineers, or mining experts, the relative significance of the lawyers' presence becomes even greater.

No doubt some of those listed as barristers had obtained only a professional qualification (as many gentlemen of the time did), with little intellectual training in law and no practical experience. However, Roberts is at pains to describe the lawyers–inspectors as coming 'directly ... from the practice of law'; he records that several commissioners were 'barristers of no little account,' and observes that in addition to those who were legally trained, eight were magistrates and deputy lieutenants.[151] Indeed, it is clear that by mid-century the legal profession had begun to recognize the career possibilities for its members as assistant commissioners or inspectors while expressing concern about inadequate remuneration and the difficulties that might be encountered when they resumed private practice.[152] In short, it is clear that men of law were a formidable presence in the new administrative class. The emergence of lawyers in those ranks is, in a way, hardly surprising. On the one hand, the inspectorate 'was a new career for the well-educated, and generally speaking the sons of gentlemen';[153] restricted opportunities in private practice at this time naturally led some lawyers to seek out new careers. On the other, 'the ideal of professional commitment' in nineteenth-century England 'inherits a large part of the moral prestige of the ideal of the gentleman.'[154] As we have seen, the new work of the administration was conceived very much in moral terms.

Thus, those lawyers who, for a variety of reasons, responded to the challenge and opportunity of the new administrative roles may well have acted as carriers of legal values. They were not the only ones, of course, to recognize and promote predictability through published rules or to strive for effective implementation of policy through purposive interpretations. Administrative rationality as well as legality was served by such techniques, as would have been understood by some of the engineers, ex-military officers, and others who experienced the discipline of the new industrial enterprises. And even though legal values may have been promoted by lawyer–administrators, among others, these values were seldom manifest in recognizable legal forms. The Benthamite passion for rationality, order, and effectiveness, after all, had not transformed the central legal system itself.[155] Still, there was a significant legal presence within the new bureaucracy, and its special attitude toward law helps to explain the tension between the administration and the other important legal influence within government, the law officers.

The law officers were the government's professional legal advisers, and their opinions in principle controlled the interpretation of legislation by the administration. But their legal attitudes were more conventional. They continued, after all, to advise private clients, and almost inevitably '[they] shared in part the conservatism of the courts.'[156] Perhaps it was their ongoing association as members of a conservative profession closely identified with business interests; perhaps it was their professional posture of detachment from their administrative 'clients'; perhaps it was simply the intellectual and analytical style – 'a contractualist view of society and a professional hostility to statute'[157] – which they shared with judges and other lawyers. Whatever the explanation, the law officers' views of the legislation they were called upon to interpret often had the effect of inhibiting rather than facilitating its administration.

Several examples related to the Factories Acts illustrate the point. Penalties under the act were to be increased if non-compliance resulted in 'bodily injury'; the law officers advised that the phrase did not extend to a case where the victim had died instantly.[158] The word 'night' was not defined in the act, and the law officers advised that it must 'be interpreted by the Common Law as it was in the case of Burglary' before the enactment of a statute

enlarging the common-law definition of 'night' for criminal-law purposes.[159] Since not all rope-works used power to operate machinery, enforcement of the act against those that did – although 'unavoidable,' since
the use of power brought them within its terms – was none the less to be
avoided: '[T]his ... construction cannot be what the legislation intended and
... it may be productive of much inconvenience and injustice ...'[160]

The law officers were not simply purveyors of legal advice which the administrators were free to accept, reject, or forestall by their own independent interpretations. The law officers, with increasing success, pre-empted
the administration as the authoritative interpreters of legislation.

For example, until 1837 the factory inspectors exercised power to issue
instructions to manufacturers; this power was virtually nullified by orders
from the Home Office making its exercise subject to the prior approval of
the law officers. Similarly, the elucidation of difficult points of interpretation of the Factory Act for the guidance of local justices was taken from the
inspectors and given to the Home Office, which relied on the advice of the
law officers.[161] By 1844, the law officers' control over the interpretation of
the legislation was so well accepted that the inspectors were even reluctant
to discharge their statutory mandate (and the direction of the home secretary) to draw up a summary of the new Factory Act for purposes of display
in factories.[162] A few years later, when the inspectors sought reconsideration
of an unhelpful opinion concerning required mealtimes, they were rebuffed
with a single terse statement: 'The Law Officers adhere to their former
opinion.'[163] It is clear that at least in the view of the law officers, the 'law'
belonged to the lawyers.

This view did not prevail at all times and in relation to all of the new
commissions and inspectorates, some of which continued to offer interpretations of their legislation for the guidance of magistrates, local officials,
and the public.[164] Nor could it have prevailed. Interpretation did not arise
only in discrete, formal episodes; it was a daily activity implicit in each act
of each official and in the cumulative effect of those daily acts as they hardened into intellectual perspectives and administrative routines. Ultimately,
therefore, it was the analytical approach and substantive outcome of the
law officers' opinions, even more than their claimed monopoly over interpretation, that most seriously affected the administration.[165] There is little
contemporary evidence to support the conjecture, but recent studies suggest
that the penumbral effect of 'law' upon the administration may be even
greater than the direct effect. Initial tendencies to see law as purposive and
facilitative are quickly suppressed as restrictive rulings rein in particular administrative initiatives. Legal constraints, once experienced, may thereafter

be anticipated, so that administrators no longer seek to use their powers to the full.[166]

It would be wrong to lay at the feet of the law officers full responsibility for the diminished pace of administrative innovation after the initial excitement of the 1830s and 1840s. They did, after all, give support to administrative views on occasion, and certainly performed the necessary function of suppressing inconsistent views so that the administration could speak with a single and definitive voice.[167] What appears, with the wisdom of hindsight, to be a limited and unhelpful view of legislation must be understood in its context. The law officers were, after all, working with legislation that was often poorly drafted,[168] and with interpretative rules and a legal tradition that were tending toward increasing formalism.[169] Most important, they increasingly had to perform their functions in an atmosphere of political, professional, and judicial hostility toward the administration.[170] Yet on balance it does seem that the law officers, for better or worse, promoted conventional legality within the administration and to that extent inhibited the development of distinctive traditions of administrative legality.

The position of the superior courts vis-à-vis the administration was not dissimilar. As has been pointed out, the lower courts had ultimate responsibility for punishing violations of the new regulatory statutes, and they were often protected from appeal or prerogative writ review. The superior courts thus had only limited opportunity to affect the emerging administration and to shape its attitude toward law. Anything other than their virtual immersion in the administrative process would have left the administrators (and local justices) free in a practical sense to develop their own distinctive approaches. But when review in the higher courts did impinge on the development of administrative law, its impact was, on balance, negative.

There were, of course, several instances of judicial decisions which, in some crucial way, lent legitimacy to administrative initiatives, although the effect even of these decisions was diminished by the failure of local justices to follow them.[171] But the preponderant trend of decisions was hostile to the administration. An important example of this judicial attitude was *Ryder* v *Mills*, in which the Court of Exchequer held that the Factory Act did not prevent employers from working children in relays throughout the day, thereby evading what the inspectors believed to be the maximum daily period of employment.[172] Because the Factory Act contained penalties, said the court, it was to be strictly construed; and strict construction favoured the employer. The court explicitly acknowledged that the inspectors' contrary interpretation 'would have the effect of securing to the children ... the more effectual superintendance and care of the inspectors ... [and] would advance the intended remedy. But then this result could only have been obtained by a larger sacrifice of the interest of the owners of factories, and we cannot assume that Parliament would disregard so important a consideration.'[173] One need not embark upon extravagant accusations of class bias to bolster the conclusion that the court consciously chose one of two possible interpretations ostensibly based on an 'ordinary construction,' with the full knowledge that it was departing from the administrative interpretation that would 'better promote the supposed object of the Legislature.'[174]

Ryder v *Mills* was not unique, but it did validate Chadwick's prophecy that judicial review would be damaging to the administration because judges would be sympathetic to individual litigants and insensitive to the impact of their decisions on 'large classes of cases and general and often remote effects, which cannot be brought to the knowledge of judges.' In the event, the decision in the case substantially undermined the enforcement of the legislation and triggered an involved and frustrating attempt at revision.[175] Similar decisions relating to the early Railway Commission and the Lunacy Commission 'paralyzed administrative actions at crucial points.'[176] The later Railway Commission was likewise confounded by frequent judicial review.[177]

When the administrators sought the aid of the court, the results were much the same: 'The threat of court action gave force to ... [administrative] investigations and suggestions. Unfortunately, the old historic courts of law acted slowly, and with great care not to allow the agencies to exceed the narrow and occasionaly ambiguous limits to their powers set forth in statutes. There was always apt to be a flaw.'[178] The Poor Law commissioners encountered debilitating delays whenever they sought mandamus to compel compliance by local officials; the Board of Health 'did not consider common law prosecutions of nuisances worth the time or expense.'[179] The Board of Trade's few attempts to enforce by lawsuit compliance with through-traffic requirements were rebuffed, and its protracted and earnest prosecution of a recalcitrant railway for breach of safety standards was similarly fruitless.[180]

In Factory Act enforcement, too, prosecution often proved unavailing, both because of the commercial affiliation of magistrates and, more frustratingly, because 'in defining the limits of the government's power the courts usually took a narrow, technical and conservative view. Their common-law bias went against the ideal of a benevolent, active state, as did their respect for the rights of local government and private property.'[181] And occasional attempts to sponsor civil test cases on behalf of injured workers came to naught.[182]

To some extent, therefore, the opposition between judicial and administrative notions of legality made frequent recourse to parliament inevitable. Paulus records what appears to be an atypical instance of judicial intervention in the legislative process to preserve statutory language which a court had earlier construed in a manner favourable to the administration.[183] For the most part, however, administrators found themselves in the position of drafting new or amending statutes to repair the damage of hostile judicial interpretations and to make effective policies that parliament had already adopted, or thought it had adopted, often at their own instigation.[184]

Recourse to parliamentary legislation as a method of vindicating the administrative view of legality involved serious risks. Such legislation was politically sensitive and liable to attract considerable resistance in both government and opposition ranks;[185] in a parliament not yet dominated by party, whip, and cabinet, the outcome of legislative proposals was by no means certain. Moreover, the differences over questions of interpretation between departmental administrators and the government's legal advisers extended to the drafting of new statutes.[186] Amendments that contemplated new expenditures could also be thwarted by treasury controls.[187] And, finally, there was no assurance that new legislation would prevail where old legislation had been treated dismissively by the courts.

For these reasons, and probably because of a shift in the political winds, administrators became increasingly reluctant to embark upon legislative campaigns, and their political masters increasingly restrained such activity.[188] Where they could enact regulations or improvise their own quasi-legislation by the imaginative use of existing statutes, they did so. Where new or amending legislation was clearly needed, it was often limited to the specific situation at hand: 'we provided a plaster for the wound, but we do not make it larger than the wound.'[189] This attitude represented a retreat from the early Benthamite legislative ideal of comprehensive and formal specification.[190] But it was a tactical retreat only. Comprehensiveness and specificity flourished in the regulations, rules, and practices developed under the protective umbrella of general enabling legislation.[191] What parliament could not or would not enact, what judges could not or would not read into legislation, might be provided by commissioners and inspectors themselves, through subordinate law-making and the daily routine of administration.

This brings us, ultimately, to the task of clarifying the emerging relationship between administrative law and the general legal system. Even Thomas, an administrative historian highly sympathetic to the new Victorian bureaucracy,[192] sees the early experience of the factory inspectorate as a rejection of legal values: 'The arbitrary functions with which these servants of the Executive had been invested were admittedly indefensible on any grounds of constitutional propriety.'[193] The 'freedom to experiment,' which was needed in this relatively unprecedented venture in central administration, would not have resulted 'had a system of administrative regulation been incorporated in the statute.' However, says Thomas, 'the Inspectors did not abuse this freedom.'

Yet there is a difficulty with Thomas's formulation of the issues. To define the functions of the inspectors as 'arbitary,' to characterize them as constitutionally improper, is to accept too readily what is, after all, only one of several competing views of legality and propriety. Thomas's view raises two problems. First, it casts into doubt the constitutionality of a scheme which, whatever its shortcomings, was sanctioned by parliament. This opens up the difficult issue of whether properly enacted legislation can be said to be unconstitutional, an issue that can hardly be addressed in the present context.[194] Second, it equates 'arbitary powers' with 'full freedom to experiment' and impliedly contrasts these with legality.[195] This view raises directly the relationship between law and administration. How did it happen that although the inspectors' powers were arbitrary they were not abused, even though (as Thomas perhaps wrongly suggests) the inspectors 'did not fail to take full advantage' of them?[196] The answer may be that the constraints on abuse were found not in constitutional or common-law rules external to the administration, but in norms developed internally.

Some hint of this position is found in the suggestion that administrators were 'not unfriendly to the old conception of law as custom,' a conception explored in earlier chapters.[197] Administrative law is the pattern of rules that emerges from the hybrid and complementary processes of administration, the issuance of rules and regulations, the glosses developed by informal discussion and formal adjudication, and the distillation of understandings into circulars and manuals and statements of policy and practice.[198]

Parris, who describes the emergence of an administrative law of railway regulation very much in these terms, also observes that '[b]ecause this body of administrative law grew up in such a way, its existence was little known. "The new laws were not lawyer's law; lawyers did not study them." Hence even today the nineteenth century origins of modern administrative law are not generally recognised.'[199] Is this an accurate judgment, or does Parris too easily attribute Dicey's later, peculiar views to lawyers of the mid-nineteenth century?

Lawyers helped to draft and implement the new administrative law; they obviously resisted its implementation in various courts on behalf of clients;

and they recognized that practice before tribunals was an increasingly important source of legal business. As early as 1846 the law officers had been served with notice that they were dealing with a new creature, an 'administrative Board,' which was different from a court.[200] And lawyers wrote, and presumably read, a spate of books dealing with the new regulatory legislation.[201] A royal commission on legal education recommended in 1846 that legal scholars study administrative law.[202] Even leading judges such as Baron Pollock were prepared to concede the emergence of 'what may be almost now called a new branch of the law.'[203]

'Administrative law' in this context was gradually coming to be understood as more than the statutes themselves and the glosses given them by the courts. It was increasingly acknowledged that internally generated rules and practices had legal significance. Judges, for example, were invited to consider administrative practice as an aid to interpreting the legislation,[204] and authors of legal texts sometimes noted both the 'elaborate reports' of inspectors and circulars requiring specific protective measures.[205] Here we see at least the beginnings of a recognition that English administrative law might indeed exist. If it is wrong to imagine, as Parris reminds us, that 'administration could be reduced to law,' it is equally wrong, as he also shows, to ignore the emergence of 'law' within the administration.[206]

CONCLUSION

We have seen that during the mid-nineteenth century there emerged in England what can only be called 'administrative law,' a system (or series of systems) that largely originated within the administration, encompassed its distinctive techniques of legislation and adjudication and its legal values, advanced its purposes, and regulated its activities. What does the emergence of administrative law imply for our general understanding of the English legal system?

We might begin by exploring the issue of whether administrative law was or was not part of the legal system. Such exploration would involve a great deal of aimless trekking between two distant landmarks at opposite points of the compass. One of these we might call legal formalism. Those attracted to it would perhaps say that whatever aspects of administrative law reside in or are expressly contemplated by a governing statute (as interpreted by a court of competent jurisdiction) are part of the legal system; all else is mere administration. In the opposite direction is a position we might identify as socio-legal. Its adherents would be prepared to place a wide range of phenomena – including administrative law – within the legal system, so long as they performed law-like functions, such as defining norms of conduct and securing compliance with them.

The business of such an inquiry is the 'true nature' of law, a subject we must continue to skirt if we are to press on to any historical conclusions. But whether administrative law is in theory within or outside the legal system, we can at least make one important factual observation. In the areas addressed by the regulatory regimes of mid-century, the law of parliament and the courts was not the most immediate, effective, or proximate legal reality: not for the administration, not for its clientele, not for those whose conduct was being regulated. That reality was administrative law in the broadest sense.

We have already made similar observations in other contexts. The local lay justices whose administrative functions were progressively assumed by agencies of central and local government administered highly distinctive systems of local law, partly because of the earlier proliferation of local statutes, partly because of their wide discretionary powers. Ordinary claims in tort and especially in contract were frequently adjudicated not in common-law courts but in local courts of ancient or modern provenance also typically exercising broad discretionary powers, usually without the participation of legally trained advocates or judges, and often quite self-consciously reluctant to follow common-law procedure or doctrine. A significant number of commercial disputes found their way into private tribunals, which were largely or wholly beyond the reach of the common-law courts and which tended to apply trade custom. And custom rather than common law provided both the norms of decision and the procedures in the surviving manor, forest, or stannary courts.

Does the cumulative effect of such observations bear in some way upon the development of administrative law and help to explain its place within, or its relationship to, the legal system?

It is tempting to conclude that the existence of what can fairly be called legal pluralism provided a hospitable climate, a legitimating precedent, for administrative law. It is indeed the case that there was in England a centuries-old practice of creating special courts for special purposes, to operate with special procedural and substantive norms within a special constituency. But it does not follow that the practice can be shown to have directly influenced the growth of administrative law. Before leaping to such a conclusion we would have to show that such a practice was understood to exist and that it was influential at various moments when the new systems of administrative law were being designed, debated, and implemented.

As to contemporary consciousness of pluralism, the evidence is equivocal. People knew, of course, of the wayward Welsh and their courts, of the tin miners with their arcane and archaic laws and privileges, of the ancient borough courts and the merchants with their curious penchant for trade custom and arbitration. But there was precious little sympathy for any of these, at least in legal circles or, as things turned out, in parliament. Still less was there an appreciation that these disparate groups and their laws formed an integral part of the English legal system and lent it its distinctive pluralistic character. On the contrary, they tended to be viewed as undesirable anomolies to be eliminated in the great integrative enterprise of law reform which culminated in the judicature commissions of the 1870s. That reforming enterprise, it will be recalled, suppressed courts of local and special jurisdiction, sought to draw arbitration into the orbit of the common law, and forestalled the establishment of tribunals of commerce. And parallel developments preserved the purity of adjudication against proposals to link it with conciliation, sought to minimize the role of discretion and enhance that of principled adjudication, and held out as an ideal (unattained in practice) the integration and rationalization of substantive law in the form of coherent, complete, and universal legal codes.

In the light of these tendencies, it is difficult to conclude that administrative law was part of the prevailing legal centralism. On the contrary, its architects created ways and means of making and applying law that relied heavily on conciliation, expanded the role of discretion, diminished that of formal adjudication, and unleashed a proliferation of rules which, by virtue of their source and purpose, were specific to a given activity or industry.

If the new administrative law was obviously not following current legal fashion, did it consciously respond to older pluralist precedents? Almost surely not. Unlike law (or perhaps like law, depending upon one's convictions), history does not obey precedents. It responds to and is in fact the outcome of social forces. The new administrative law in its various manifestations was shaped by economic power, social consciousness, and political ideology, by the limiting factors of parsimony in government and traditions of decentralized authority, by the liberating factors of new legal and scientific technologies, by factors that were sometimes trivial and circumstantial, sometimes of profound and abiding significance – but that were almost always extrinsic to law itself.

Almost always, but not always. At least two indigenous legal influences were at work in the growth and development of administrative law. The first was the hostile influence of the legal profession, an influence largely stimulated by self-interest and rooted in an ideology of self-importance. Yet even here there was a countervailing current: the new administrative regimes began to generate their own special constituency within the legal profession, comprising those who conceived regulatory policies, drafted statutes and administered them, and those who practised administrative law. A second indigenous influence was the capacity of the new legal technology to stimulate its own further growth and development. In technique if not in fundamental policy matters, the new regimes built upon the lessons of experience. The state of the art advanced considerably between 1830 and 1870.

To return to our hypothesis: if administrative law was not consciously constructed on an acceptance of legal pluralism, did it none the less have the effect of promoting greater pluralism within the legal system? At one level the answer is certainly affirmative. If legal pluralism implies a diversity of normative systems emanating from a variety of sources, engaging different audiences and actors by procedures and processes which are not all derived from a single prototype, then administrative law contributed greatly to the general pluralist character of English law.

At another level, it must be asked whether a pluralism based on administrative structure, technique, and personnel actually altered the social impact and significance of law. This question will be addressed more fully in the next chapter. To anticipate, we may note that the new administrative law did purport to revise social reality for workers, emigrants, consumers, railway travellers, and indigents. We do not have to take each claim of benign intentions at face value or assume their total success in order to conclude that some changes were brought about by them, or at least ratified by them.

Between 1830 and 1870 there was some increase in popular power, some acceptance of the state's responsibility for social welfare, some shift in the geographic locus of social control and in the intellectual perception of how and to what ends it might be exercised. A hundred years on, many feel that we have not come far enough (and others, no doubt, that we have gone too far). That is not the business of this book; but at least we can say that the expansion of legal pluralism, which was associated with the advent of administrative law, also coincided with some expansion of pluralism in the distribution of political, social, and economic power. Whether this tentative conclusion rests upon false consciousness is a point to which we will ultimately return.

Finally, even if we are able to detect the expansion of pluralism in the legal system (and perhaps in the socio-political system) associated with the rise of administrative law, there is one area where pluralism seems hardly to have registered. Only at the margins, where particular individuals were implicated in administrative law, did the legal profession's view of the nature of law broaden perceptibly. On the contrary, the legal profession was in many ways more closely identified with the centralist paradigm of law at the end of the period than at the beginning. The significance of that fact will be examined in the next chapter.

6

Making Change: The English Legal System, 1830–1870

Any standard history of English law will duly record the extent of the changes that occurred during the middle decades of the nineteenth century. The superior courts were reorganized; their procedures and pleadings simplified; their doctrines (then or soon after) made somewhat more systematic; and their relationship to other legal institutions more clearly defined. Most of the old local courts were abolished and a new system of county courts was introduced. Parliament was 'reformed' in 1832, and gradually, sometimes grudgingly, came to terms with a broadened franchise, the secret ballot, the party system, ministerial responsibility, and other now-familiar indicia of democracy. The civil service learned salutary lessons about neutrality, accountability, and professionalism. Statutory draftsmanship, commercial conveyancing, and legal scholarship progressed apace.

These developments, so far as they go, present the picture of an increasingly orderly legal universe, of a legal system whose institutions were more coherently related, whose rules were more clearly articulated, whose capacity for purposeful action was enhanced, whose tendency was more centripetal than centrifugal. But how far did they go? Let us revisit the evidence. This study has not been directly concerned with the formal rules or institutions of law – common law and equity, the superior courts and, after 1846, the county courts. Its focus has been upon 'special' law and 'special' tribunals, both formal and informal, and only upon some of those. Generalizations about the relative importance of each must therefore remain tentative.

To be sure, we have some suggestive evidence. We have seen that in 1830 more than 300,000 claims were brought in 'special' courts and only 90,000 in Westminster. By 1846, the 'special' courts dealt with about 400,0000 claims, while complaints abounded in the ranks of the legal profession concerning the paucity of litigation in the superior courts. We have seen also that arbitration attracted increasing attention from both businessmen and lawyers after 1850 while commercial litigation was, by contemporary accounts, conspicuous by its absence from the courts. We know that important decisions affecting the economic and physical shape of the country were being taken by such bodies as the Railway and Inclosure Commissions and the General Board of Health, that those decisions reached the superior courts but rarely and for the limited purpose of review, and that miners and factory workers, emigrants and consumers increasingly resided within a protective regulatory regime in which the significant figures were administrators rather than judges.[1]

But for several reasons these facts and impressions do not provide a firm basis for either quantitative or qualitative judgments. Numbers are lacking for many important matters. How many arbitrations? How many orders to fence machinery? How many magistrates' judgments? And we lack a basis upon which to compare the numbers we do have. Do we equate a claim for twenty shillings in a court of requests with a claim for twenty pounds in a county court or a claim for two hundred pounds in Queen's Bench? Does it matter that the smallest claim is likely to have been recovered with more speed and less expense than the largest? Or that the largest may have represented a tiny fraction of a value of a rich man's landholdings while the smallest may have been the cost to a poor man of feeding his family for several weeks? What is equal to what?

The ability to judge the importance of formal law is not simply a matter of identifying, counting, and attributing the correct weight to 'decisions.' A 'decision' deals with pathology, with the occasional violation of a rule, not with the creation and widespread observance of the rule. Were relationships between commercial enterprises, between employers and employed, between buyers and sellers actually defined by statute and common-law rule, or by custom or contract, by values slowly internalized as the result of moral suasion, self-interest, and the nagging nuisance of inspection, or by social and economic forces transcending 'rules' of any sort? When we focus on the creation of rules and the causes of conforming behaviour, our task becomes more difficult, but at the same time more significant. Now we are comparing the living law with the law in books even though, at a distance of a hundred years or more, we are singularly ill-equipped to observe the very phenomenon we wish to explore.

Still, we can make some intelligent guesses. We know today that rules are not always what they seem. Discretion, fact-finding, and analytical and interpretative techniques can generate either false analogies or illusory differences, thus creating exceptions to rules or subtly extending them. We are only too well aware of the gap between enacted law (or judicial precedent, or administrative rulings) and the law in action. We are sensitive, finally, to the effect of material circumstances on access to law, and to the problem this presents for making law a presence in the lives of most of us. So we at least treat sceptically all claims that in the mid-nineteenth century the legal system responded to a central, organizing intelligence, and served a single, defined set of values.

But making due allowance for a deficit of facts and for difficulties of interpretation, there are things we can say about law in the nineteenth century. It was complex, contradictory, and ephermeral – not simple, integrated, and authoritatively established. Important decisions were made by people who were not judges, responding to rules not made by parliament, using structures and procedures not derived from or effectively subject to those of the formal legal system. People often ordered their affairs indifferent to and ignorant of that system, consciously or unconsciously responding to local custom, to business convention, to administrative expectations.

Whether we address the number of moving parts in the legal system, the variety and complexity of normative systems, the range of talents and tactics and techniques of dispute resolution and social control employed, or the sources from which all these emanated and the interests they were designed to advance – whichever of these is an appropriate measure of pluralism – our judgment will probably be the same. Between 1830 and 1870, the English legal system underwent far-reaching changes. But it likely was no less pluralistic at the end of the period than at the beginning.

To identify a strain of pluralism in English law persisting into and through the nineteenth century is to be disrespectful of the conventional wisdom.[2] Most historical accounts ignore, misperceive, or undervalue evidence of pluralism, and tend to focus upon the formal achievement of centralism within the legal system.

It will be recalled that Holdsworth attributed to early nineteenth-century central courts a virtual monopoly of adjudication, shared only with local magistrates.[3] In a similar vein, Atiyah's important book on contract law in the nineteenth century neither mentions courts of requests, where so many consumer disputes were decided, nor discusses the use of arbitration, to which much important commercial litigation was remitted by the parties or by the judges themselves.[4] And of course Dicey believed that the hegemony of the 'ordinary courts' and 'ordinary law' was unchallenged until after 1870, when the new 'collectivist' regime and its tribunals began to appear in alleged defiance of constitutional tradition.[5]

In the light of these views, which either assume or project a centralist image of English law, we must ask ourselves how and why this triumph of form over fact occurred. The dynamic between pluralism and centralism, between events and their formal characterization, will be explored in several contexts: a discussion of the general impact of social change upon the legal system, an assessment of certain specific forces at work within the legal system itself, and speculation about technical and ideological influences that may have reinforced the paradigm of legal centralism.

EXPLAINING CHANGE

We cannot proceed far along the way toward an understanding of the influences that shaped English law without reminding ourselves that 'law' has several very different meanings. In a generic sense, law is social technique: it is a process of ording relationships and resolving disputes by reference to norms and according to procedures that are agreed or accepted as appropriate, valid, or 'legitimate.' But to English lawyers of the nineteenth century (or today) 'law' had a much more restricted, formal meaning which emphasized their own distinctive and exclusive experience: the use of state law as a foundation for conveyancing and for the conduct of litigation, especially before professionally qualified judges.

There is yet another pertinent meaning of 'law.' As we sometimes encounter it in the scholarly literature, 'law' is not simply technique but ideology. An ideology, of course, is a world view, a system of beliefs, a statement of principles that purports to guide its adherents in their conduct and rally them to a common cause while presenting them to others in a particular light. In the case of Victorian England, we can refer to an ideology of legalism: a belief that things ought to be done according to 'law' in the formal sense, as it was understood by lawyers.[6]

With these three meanings of law in mind, we can begin the difficult task of exploring law's relationship to the state, society, and the economy.

We can postulate different versions of this relationship as it relates to formal law. First, we might assert that social events have legal causes – for example, that English banking laws facilitated commercial transactions and thus created a favourable climate for industrial investment and development. Or, to the contrary, we might believe that legal events have social causes – for example, that a restrictive interpretation of regulatory legislation resulted from the class sympathies of judges. Or we might imagine that legal change is evoked by a zeitgeist, is a response to a 'felt need,' social consciousness, or public opinion, or is merely the specific manifestation of a general tendency toward 'progress' – for example, that public derision or increasing professional sophistication led to the abolition of the old writs and ancient rules of pleading.

In each case there seems to be a plausible connection between the legal development and its assumed cause. But the examples can each be reinterpreted in light of another theory with no risk of losing plausibility. Indeed, a fourth theory might equally encompass all of them. If we were to look at law – at the system of formal rules – at any given moment in 1830 or 1850 or 1870, we would see serious discrepancies between law and social and economic behaviour. Law seemed to require people to do things they did not do, and people did things under apparent compulsion of rules that were not found in formal law or mandated, even contemplated, by it. Moreover, a great deal of law seemed not to be intended to be obeyed – law of times past that had grown obsolete but remained formally valid, and law of the period whose language was obscure or whose sanctions were clearly inadequate to intimidate. On balance, it is hard to deny that much formal law seemed to have no connection at all with the general social and economic environment.[7]

Here we find ourselves, then, unable to subscribe to a single overarching theory of historical causation, yet unwilling to accept that formal law is not only independent of but virtually irrelevant to its social context. This Luddite treatment of historiographic technique is not a protest against all forms of interpretation, however. It is rather a plea for modesty of scale in any enterprise that seeks to link great social, economic, or intellectual movements with relatively minor changes in formal law.

Fewer problems are encountered when we attempt to explain the development of law as social technique. Thus defined, law exists as a feature of social and economic relationships rather than externally to them; the search for the causes of law is more narrowly confined. Law in the form of custom, of patterns of interaction and expectation, may exist at any given moment, but is always in the process of changing in response to changes in its context. It is possible for law formally created by a deliberate legislative or contractual act to become part of the social technique of law. However, the test of whether law exists and what its content is at a given moment is a matter for empirical enquiry: law is not law simply because it possesses certain formal characteristics, but rather because it functions in a particular way.

This analysis of law as social technique can be illustrated by the case of administrative law, extensively canvassed in earlier chapters. Administrative law was treated neither as the statutory framework of regulation per se nor as the formal law of judicial review. Rather, it encompassed all operational aspects of the administrative regime, however informal, however remote from the model of law familiar to lawyers, so long as they were indeed operational. Thus, circular letters, technical manuals, and patterns of enforcement were considered law not because they could be fancifully analogized to formal legislation or common law, but because they helped to secure compliance with statutory policies.

It will already be clear that when we speak of law in the formal lawyers' sense we are evoking the centralist paradigm of law. But reference to law as social technique obviously draws upon the pluralist paradigm. The two, then, are liable to yield very different conclusions about how, in the period from 1830 to 1870, the state, society, and the economy related to 'law.'

So far we have not considered the connection between legalism, the ideology of law, and legal change. On the one hand, legalism invited both lawyers and laymen to respect and obey law because it was law; on the other, it asserted that the formal qualities of law were themselves to be valued because of their capacity to promote the interests of men and the state, of society and economy.

Legalism proposed a model of behaviour drawn from the formal system and sought to secure conformity to it. It accomplished both of these objectives – for example, by disparaging overt attempts to depart from the formal model as 'unconstitutional,' by treating departures as a ground for judicial review that delegitimated the offending social technique, and by seeking to ensure that those who participated in law as social technique were either themselves lawyers or under the close control of legal advisers. Familiar episodes epitomize each tactic: arbitrators were denounced for their tendency to decide cases in derogation of 'law'; the factory inspectors and the Railway Commission were harassed in judicial review proceedings; and the courts of requests were manoeuvred first into the control of legal assessors and then out of the hands of lay judges altogether.

We will next try to establish the relevance of these definitions of law, and the paradigms in which they were rooted, to specific changes in law. At some point, it seems, the influence of large historical forces attenuates, the credibility of historiographic explanation declines, and law in its particular aspects (if not in general) comes to be shaped more by proximate than by remote causes. Examples come readily to mind.

Urban growth, population movements, and changes in transport and trade patterns following the industrial revolution generated pressures for the replacement of the old local courts by a new national system of minor courts. Towns grew beyond the ancient boundaries that had defined the jurisdiction of borough, hundred, or manor courts; trade became increasingly regional, national, and international rather than merely local; idiosyncratic and limited jurisdictions held few charms for law reformers intent upon 'rationalizing' the justice system. Hence, we might say, the necessity for the new county court system: debtors could no longer escape by moving across invisible jurisdictional boundaries; a seller could now sue a distant buyer with relative ease; and uniform national legal standards facilitated the growth of a national economy.

But does 'necessity' explain everything? Why did Brougham, as lord chancellor and head of the expansionist central legal system, originally emphasize arbitration and conciliation in his proposals for a new system of district courts? Why was the county court system in its first incarnation, from 1846 to 1850, quite inhospitable to lawyers, and how were changes in it brought about? Why were businessmen, who were most vitally interested in 'the more easy recovery of small debts and demands,' heard from so infrequently in the extended debates over the creation of the county courts?

In the critical translations from general ideas to specific legislative language, and from that language to operational reality, we can no longer hear the voice of 'necessity.' Instead, we recognize the cultivated accents of Brougham and his implacable parliamentary and judicial foes, the well-modulated professional advocacy of the common-law commissioners dissecting provincial courts, the self-interested clamour of legal editorialists, local élites, and 'low attorneys,' the relatively hushed tones of parliamentary draftsmen and officials, and the busy hum of several hundred new judges, registrars, and clerks.

Let us consider a second example. The literature leaves a strong impression that the Victorian 'discovery' of the social costs of industrialization led to several important meliorative measures, including the factories acts, and that experience with those and other acts produced in due course now-familiar strategies of inspection and enforcement. We must also contend with interpretations of the same events that attribute the enactment of factories legislation to programs of social pacification and control, to internecine rivalry among contending groups of employers, and to mystificatory diversions by those who wished to escape regulation altogether.

But only occasionally do we catch a glimpse of the specific emerging

from the general. We 'know,' for example that employers formed a powerful lobby to resist an attempt to force them to fence factory machinery; Bartrip demonstrates how that lobby worked, what reactions it engendered,
and to what extent it succeeded.[8] He shows us how the manufacturers
pressed for a provision requiring arbitration of a disputed order to instal
fencing, but he also reveals how the inspectors, having failed to prevent the
enactment of such a provision, were none the less ultimately able to neutral-
ize it. The overall significance of the episode is no doubt open to diverse
interpretations. We will pay special attention to the way in which the inspectors, a small, relatively obscure, and politically weak group, came to influence the course of events that directly involved themselves as primary actors.

A third example will suffice to make the point. Our investigation of commercial disputes in the nineteenth century suggests that arbitration came to
enjoy greater and greater recognition and support within the legal system,
but that at the same time it was drawn closer and closer to it. By 1889, with
the enactment of the Arbitration Act, the process was complete: promises to
arbitrate and arbitrators' awards were legally enforceable; arbitrators and
parties alike enjoyed a variety of needed powers and protections; and a new
jurisdiction to require arbitrators to state a case ensured judicial control and
the observance of legal principles. The autonomy of commercial law, we
might say, was surrendered to the hegemony of the legal system. (Or, we
might say, the legal system placed itself at the disposal of commercial interests and their self-made law.)

But notice: although a critical technical aspect of this process was the acquisition by the courts of uninhibited power to compel arbitrators to state a
case, we do not know where this power came from. It was not in the proposals that emanated from the business community, not in the original
parliamentary bill, not in Hansard, not in the legal press. Did it come from
its sponsor at the last moment after second reading? From a law officer consulted on some other matter of interpretation or draftsmanship? From a
well-connected lawyer seeking to advance legal orthodoxy or professional
economic opportunities? Perhaps more diligent research will someday provide the answer. Now it is enough to understand that at a crucial juncture
significant influence was wielded by someone who was very close to events.

What shall we conclude? No case is being made for a want-of-a-nail
theory of history, nor it is proposed that individuals have the capacity to
decide the fate of nations, of classes, or even of legislative proposals.
Rather, a modest conclusion seems warranted by our examples: it is possible
to identify professional influences as a separate and distinct factor in the

calculus of events. In this context the term 'professional' is meant to encompass both legal professionals and administrators. Although neither group was or is homogeneous, both did possess certain common characteristics that might explain their influence on the development of Victorian law.[9]

The first such characteristic was knowledge or skill, the essential distinguishing feature of all professional elements. Lawyers 'knew' legal doctrine, procedure and history, draftsmanship, advocacy, and analytical techniques; administrators 'knew' the blue books, which so often gave rise to reforming legislation, details of scientific and technical developments that might alleviate presumed social evils, and the practical bureaucratic techniques by which government might accomplish its purposes. No matter that the 'knowledge' was often superficial, the 'facts' misleading or wrong, or the techniques primitive. The professionals were convinced they 'knew,' acted as if they 'knew,' gradually did in fact come to 'know,' and, most important, persuaded others that they 'knew.' Thus we find Chadwick and his colleagues in one parliamentary inquiry after another and in one administrative role after another, and we find the law officers and other prominent lawyers called in again and again to draft legislation, to interpret it, and to redraft and reinterpret it.

The knowledge base of these professional groups in turn generated a value system or ideology that tended to emphasize the centrality of their own contribution to human progress and the well-being of the nation. If it was not always overtly expressed, we can none the less detect the presence of ideology in the manic activities of the Poor Law commissioners and the jeremiads of the mines inspectors no less than in the self-laudation of legal writers or the oracular pronouncements of Her Majesty's judges.

It must be stressed that there is more here than self-interest masked by self-delusion. There seems little doubt that most lawyers believed in the superior qualities of British justice or that commissioners, inspectors, and other officials genuinely wished to preserve the lives of emigrants or the morals of women factory workers. Indeed, this combination of knowledge and authentic concern provided professional groups with the means of influencing decisions about policy, especially at the level of detailed design and implementation. The author of a parliamentary blue book or the secretary to a regulatory commission was strategically located: he might define the problem, deploy the facts and arguments, propose the solutions, polish the recommendations, interpret language to correspondents, help to draft statutes and supplementary legislation, and perhaps to some extent influence the selection of other senior and subordinate administrators. Which of these he could do and to what extent obviously depended on political circumstances, personalities, patronage decisions and the like. The point is that his influence derived from what he 'knew' and from the moral force of his own commitment.

Lawyers operated in somewhat analogous fashion, although generally their direct influence was more episodic. A law officer rendering an opinion would not expect – would not tolerate – disobedience by an administrator; a lawyer–critic of proposed reform legislation would often mobilize the irresistible force of alleged constitutional principles; a lawyer drafting a code of commercial law would not hesitate to pronounce ex cathedra the rules that would best suit businessmen. What gave cogency to such peremptory statements was the notion that lawyers knew what the law said and how the legal system operated, and that they were using this knowledge in good faith and for the public's benefit.

These, then, were men of influence in the context of public debate and decision-making. The more nearly a particular aspect of a problem touched the territory bounded by their knowledge and moral claims, the more influence they exercised. The convergence of knowledge, concern, and influence is seen most clearly in reforms of the legal system itself. Lawyers who dominated enquiries into the system's operation from the 1830s to the 1870s, recommended the abolition of the communal courts, spurned the use of conciliation, brought higher costs and the right of appeal to the county courts, refused to countenance tribunals of commerce, and ultimately constructed the grand formal edifice of the merged superior courts in the 1870s. Lawyers shunted railway regulation into Common Pleas in 1854, demolished the privative clause of the Railway and Canal Commission in 1873, and ultimately harassed that body into a state of virtual paralysis. And lawyers' skill and devotion as advocates, draftsmen, and tacticians won or lost important battles over key interpretations of other regulatory statutes.

All of these things, as the record shows, professionals did, but of course they did not do them alone. They acted with or through political allies in parliament, in the cabinet, and in the press. They co-operated with each other and with various influential groups and individuals, to whom they were linked by common membership of the National Association for the Advancement of Social Science, by participation in law-reform and other special interest groups, by social, intellectual, or familial ties, or simply by professional relationships. Their influence, then, must be understood as attributable not merely to their own views and activities but to their place in a network of groups and individuals.

It is important to recall the context within which this rather unsurprising observation is made. I have suggested that the members of two professional groups – lawyers and administrators – were able to influence specific legal manifestations of general socio-historical developments. But I have not argued that these groups influenced the legal system in isolation from each other, or to the exclusion of influences emanating from other groups. Still less have I argued that the legal system was, in effect, deliberately designed at a 'conference' attended by delegates from all groups in society.

The role and influence of professional and other groups can perhaps be analogized to the emergence of human settlements on a legal landscape whose basic elements were determined by the movement of socio-economic forces far below the surface, crudely shaped by the glacial events of industrial change, and made fertile by political wind and weather. It is foolish to pretend that man can simply ignore nature, or that lawyers or administrators or businessmen or other local worthies could have engrafted on the legal system any general or particular feature they wished. But it is equally foolish to deny entirely that such persons had a capacity for choice and that the cumulative consequences of exercising choice affected the legal system overall. This extended metaphor is more than a literary conceit. It closely parallels the analysis of several social anthropologists and historians who have attempted to trace the interaction of state law with 'semi-autonomous social fields,' 'law communities,' or 'legal subsystems' – social organizations which themselves generate forms of 'law.' This parallel will be explored after we have canvassed their views.

LAW AND ADMINISTRATION AS SOCIAL CONTEXTS

In his integrative and insightful essay, Galanter draws together several strands of historical, social, and anthropological research that have 'entailed recurrent rediscovery that law in modern society is plural rather than monolithic, that it is private as well as public in character and that the national (public, official) legal system is often a secondary rather than a primary locus of regulation.'[10] He demonstrates how private and public law exist along a spectrum of possibilities rather than as complete dichotomies, how they influence each other, and how each resides to some extent 'in the shadow' of the other. He emphasizes that 'the survival and proliferation of indigenous law' is linked to 'the immense profusion and variety of "semi-autonomous social fields" existing within a single society.'[11] Weber's identification of such 'law communities' has been mentioned earlier. They also are the predicate of Fuller's argument that law is generated by 'interactional expectancy' based upon social settings where the participants' moves fall within a predictable pattern,[12] and they reappear in numerous recent studies to which Galanter frequently refers.

How do these 'semi-autonomous social fields,' which Galanter also describes as 'a multitude of associations and networks ... a world of loosely-joined and partly overlapping partial or fragmentary communities,' actually generate their own law and influence the legal system of the state? Moore, who coined the unwieldy term 'semi-autonomous social field,' gives us the most detailed account.[13] A 'field,' Moore tells us, is defined not by its formal organization, but by 'a processual characteristic, the fact that it can generate rules and coerce or induce compliance to them.'[14] Such fields do not exist in total isolation. They are set 'in a larger social matrix which can, and does, affect and invade' them, and they are linked in a complex chain with other fields. Hence, they are 'semi-autonomous.'

Since fields become manifest by their very performance of the tasks of social ordering, it is important to observe them at work. Although 'a tremendous body of rules ... envelop any social field, only some are significant ... the rest are ... in the background.' The participants in the field may respond to rules which are indigenous to it, to rules emanating from other social fields, or to those of the state, but it is the processes of selection and securing compliance that ultimately dictate what will be the 'law' within the field.

Acknowledging that 'no social field in a modern state can be totally autonomous from a legal point of view,' Moore contends that absolute domination of the field by the state is almost equally difficult to conceive. Thus, the effectiveness of a state legal system is in part a function of the willingness of those who populate a social field either to ignore state law or to lend support to it. Moreover, a mark of the strength of a social field is its ability to enlist the coercive forces of government to help it enforce its own law.

Does this brief account of Moore's thesis advance our understanding of legal pluralism in Victorian England?[15] In certain obvious respects the notion of a social field does help to locate developments in civil justice and in commercial law within a larger theoretical frame. One can readily identify village communities, perhaps even small pre-industrial towns, as social fields or networks of social fields with considerable capacity to generate and enforce indigenous law and to resist, embrace, or adapt state law. As the pressure from state law became more intense, and as the fields' force diminished with the attenuation of local social and economic ties, these capacities declined.[16]

Similarly, economic sectors that were formally organized into exchanges or trade associations or loosely bound together by informal patterns of dealing reinforced by personal relationships and shared interests were strong social fields. They generated rules by adopting formal trading codes, standard-form contracts, and 'customs of the trade,' and enforced them by expulsion from an exchange, suspension of a course of dealing, withholding of trade courtesies, and, on occasion, formal adjudication by a domestic tribunal, arbitrator, or judge. As a relatively powerful social field or series of social fields, business groups were often able to ignore or resist state law, enforce it selectively, or even secure its formal revision to suit their own purposes. But the strength of the group was a function of its cohesion: as interests and roles within the groups diverged, the force of the field flickered. A sharp decline in the market or the introduction of new means of communication and transport might intensify competition and prompt appeals to state law and the abandonment of group norms. Conversely, a denser concentration of firms, perhaps prompted by new requirements for capital, might create conditions more favourable to indigenous law.

Do we do violence to the notion of the semi-autonomous social field when we apply the same analysis to the legal profession and especially to administrative regimes? Both of these present challenging issues of interpretation. The legal profession is the more easily understood as a social field. Beyond the obvious affinities of a common professional affiliation, culture, economic interests, and frequent interaction at a professional and social level, lawyers intended to share a core of technical knowledge and a common ideology. It is true that numerous subgroupings emerged within the social field of the legal profession. Barristers and solicitors had some things in common, but their interests and activities diverged at many points. So too with leading counsel and the many barristers who migrated to business, administrative, and political careers; so too with solicitors who served commercial clients and those who became involved in managing great estates or advocacy in the lower courts. This multiplicity of linked social fields also helps to explain the peculiar capacity of the legal profession to generate internal law, which influenced – and often became – the law of the state.

Consider the key positions occupied by lawyers. Judges generated common law, pronounced authoritatively upon the meaning of statutes, instructed local justices and administrative officials in the proper performance of their duties, and influenced the direction of legal change by speaking, writing, and serving on committees or as members of the House of Lords. Barristers were also strategically located. They served in cabinet and as members of parliament; as law officers they drafted new statutes, advised government on the legality of proposed action under existing legislation, and issued interpretative opinions for the guidance of magistrates and administrators. Their impact on the development of policy, and especially its expression in institutional form, was obviously great. Even when conducting legal proceedings on behalf of government, barristers had the opportunity to influence policy by the opinions offered before or after the litigation and by their imaginative defence of administrative initiative or their virtual repudiation of it in argument. Barristers, moreover, served as administrators, advisers, and counsel to railways, local authorities, stock exchanges, and financial interests, and as officers and directors of firms. They sat as judges in minor courts and as tribunal members. And they spoke and wrote about both the technical aspects and the public-policy implications of new regulatory legislation. Solicitors and attorneys served in a variety of roles, often very close to the point at which administrative policies were implemented – as members of, or clerks to, local authorities and local courts, as advisers to business, as estate stewards and managers, as conveyancers of land and other forms of property, as parliamentary lobbyists for railway and other interests, and as spokesmen for clients in dealings with the inspectorates and commissions. They were also active contributors to political debate, commissions of inquiry, and the literature of the law.

Thus, we see lawyers everywhere. They helped to shape basic public policies, to translate these into legislative form and ultimately practical reality, and to resist both enactment and implementation of policies. To repeat: the legal profession cannot be regarded as homogeneous in most respects – political philosophy, economic interest, social background, clientele, daily tasks, or even all intellectual skills. But does the very fact of its ubiquitous presence not suggest that the whole was somehow greater than the sum of its parts? Were there perhaps connections between 'all' lawyers that were as powerful as the particular characteristics that divided them? Were these connections in some way distinctively 'professional,' and different from those that bound lawyers to their clients, political allies, neighbours, or social circle?

It is not easy to identify the connections that would enable us to treat lawyers themselves as a social field. As a tentative hypothesis, however, we may explore the notion that legalism – the notion of law as ideology – performed this function. Victorian lawyers seem generally to have had a relatively fixed notion of law as a formal system, a conception that such a system ought to work in its familiar mode (albeit with greater efficiency), and the conviction that the functioning of the formal system was indispensable to national purposes. This ideology of legalism had adjectival rather than substantive content. Its impact therefore was greatest in defining lawyers' attitudes toward the legal system as such, toward the relationship of laymen and other actors to the system, and toward state action affecting the system. When this powerful social field, energized by its ideology, projected its indigenous law, it was able to influence the law of other social fields, and even of the state, especially in adjectival matters.

We will return shortly to a further exploration of lawyers' conception of law, legal procedure, and values. First, however, we must try to detect the presence of another social field, that of administration. The administrators shared at least one basic attribute with the lawyers: the group was not homogeneous. Chadwick, Treemeheare, and Mackworth were all very different people, and each of them was different again from the sinecurists, time-servers, patronage appointees, and retired warriors who filled so many positions in the public service before (and no doubt to some extent after) the Northcote–Trevelyan reforms.

The inspectors, commissioners, and senior departmental officers, however, seem to have had certain affinities with each other. Like lawyers, these administrators tended to share certain notions about the proper role of the administration, procedural habits, and convictions concerning their own 'mission' even when they were divided on substantive issues and philosophies of government. For example, it seems to have been widely understood that the administration's aim should be to advance the policy of parliament, however imperfectly expressed. Many administrative bodies had to confront problems of securing compliance with a large new body of rules in the absence of adequate staff or powers. They 'solved' these problems by the familiar inventions already described: requirements for keeping records and submitting reports; attempts to persuade those being regulated to comply by means of instruction and negotiation; occasional inspection, periodic auditing of returns, and specification of detailed standards for compliance; and the securing of compliance by threat and promise, persuasion and patient exhortation, rather than by recourse to penal sanctions. And very commonly encountered was an outspoken conviction concerning the moral imperatives of the policy being pursued.

Like the legal profession, then, the administrators tended to generate adjectival law for themselves. But unlike the legal profession, they also often produced their own substantive law, which derived from state law only in the most formal sense. Sometimes they were expressly mandated to make subordinate legislation; sometimes they did so in particular cases in the course of exercising adjudicative and regulatory powers conferred by statute. But the actual content of this law of the administration did not derive directly from statute; instead, it was the indigenous law of the social field.

Was the social field that yielded substantive administrative law congruent with that which produced adjectival law? Studies cited in earlier chapters seem to show that the content of administrative law was indeed influenced by many groups and individuals other than the administrators. Mine owners, for example, clearly dictated the contents of 'special rules' for safe operation; engineering experts and railway owners had much to say about the codified 'requirements' for new lines and equipment. We can identify, then, a social field populated not only by administrators but also by those being regulated and by knowledgeable experts, and we can see that the law emerging from this field sometimes exhibited little connection with the governing statute beyond the fact that it did not overtly contravene it. In a sense, we are witnessing a phenomenon contemplated by Moore: a social field that adopted state law as its own and gave it force and effect while mediating it through a domestic system of values and enforcement techniques.

Finally, like the legal profession, members of the new administrative élite were active at a number of crucially important locations. They had close ties to the political process at each stage of the development of legislative policy. Indeed, they were often active in groups that had agitated originally for legislation to prevent some social evil, participated in public inquiries into its existence, and helped to draft and secure the enactment of the very statute they were administering. By means of annual reports and other public appeals – including writing for newspapers, addressing meetings, and publishing circulars, pamphlets, or books – the administrators were able to influence other political actors. They worked with the law officers, instructed or co-operated with counsel, and corresponded with local officials, magistrates, and magnates. And they were often a conduit between the technical and scientific communities and business interests; they transmitted knowledge and promoted the use of the latest inventions in so far as they contributed to the safety of workers, consumers, or the travelling public. We should hardly wonder, then, at the capacity of administrators to create their own law or to secure adherence to it within (and occasionally beyond) the permeable boundaries fixed by state law.

Both lawyers and administrators thus seem to have functioned as carriers of techniques and of attitudes and values, disseminating them among the many groups with which they were involved. At the same time they were responsible for cross-pollenization, and apparently carried back to their familiar legal tasks and administrative settings the techniques, attitudes, and values of other social fields, including national political networks, business organizations, technical experts, local élites, and communal groups. In so doing, lawyers and administrators were able to transform state law in some respects and to use it in an effort to deflect or dominate the internal law generated by each other and by other social fields.

If some of these complex and contradictory processes had the effect of suppressing aspects of pluralism, others had the effect of stimulating it. This helps to explain the change in the nature of pluralism during the period. But why should the very existence of pluralism in any form have attracted so little attention from contemporary and subsequent legal observers? The answer to that question holds important consequences for our understanding of administrative law.

LAW, IDEOLOGY, AND ADMINISTRATION

We have seen how law was used as the basis of an ideology of legalism, how that ideology became in effect the internal law of the legal profession, and how its projection affected the law of the state and of other law communities or social fields. We will now retrace our steps a little in order to focus on the connection between legal ideology and administrative law.

To document fully law's emergence as ideology in Victorian England is too ambitious a project for the present context, although the important developments did not escape Weber's notice, and some contemporary scholars have now signed on for the task.[17] As it happens, however, the period from 1830 to 1870 is neatly framed by two statements of persisting significance; these will serve to remind us of the essentials.

At the beginning of the period, Austin proposed his well-known definition of law as the command of the sovereign.[18] In that relatively simple notion, we see implied a requirement of obedience to law elicited by both respect for the sovereign and fear of his sanctions; an assimilation of legal functionaries to the prestige and central social significance of the sovereign; and the assumption that law cannot be generated by sources other than the sovereign (or the sovereign's delegates, the judges and parliament). Each of these implications serves to define the subordinate relationship of laymen both to law and to those who create, dispense, administer, or know law.

By the end of the period, we are approaching the moment when Dicey restated an idea that had had currency throughout the century – the idea of the rule of law.[19] Given Dicey's insistence that 'law' meant the 'ordinary law' administered by the 'ordinary courts,' we can immediately perceive the persistence of the very notions implicit in the Austinian definition of law: it is 'law' that rules rather than men, so that law appropriates the very authority of the sovereign and binds even him; lawyers and especially judges, as the human agencies through which law is made manifest, are therefore entitled to derivative deference;[20] since only 'ordinary' law and courts fall within the principle, 'non-ordinary' law and legal institutions are unworthy of equivalent deference if they are not altogether in conflict with the rule of law;[21] and since, as Dicey also urged, judge-made law is more 'ordinary' than legislation, the highest prestige within legal circles attaches to those most closely identified with it, especially judges.[22]

Exegesis on two well-known texts, of course, does not conclusively prove that the legal profession embraced and promoted a particular ideology of law; still less does it show that non-lawyers subscribed to it. But when we rehearse – yet again, and briefly – the events of 1830 to 1870, the existence and power of legalism as an ideology of law seem to be verified.

Lawyers did gain (so far as the state could confer it) formal pre-eminence in the whole field of adjudication by suppressing the courts of local and special jurisdiction, maintaining or extending curial supervision of arbitration and administrative tribunals, and fending off tribunals of commerce. Lawyers came to dominate legislative draftsmanship and made significant forays into private rule-making by preparing standard-form contracts. Lawyers infiltrated the administration, parliament, and business circles, often gaining influence and commanding deference as advisers on law when they did not serve as principals. And they did all of these things, we must remember, by asserting ancient privileges (or, in the case of solicitors, recently acknowledged prerogatives) and by relying on arcane knowledge not yet derived from organized study, systematic scholarship, or scientific methodology.

Indeed, so completely did legalism come to dominate thinking about law that it rendered other manifestations of law virtually invisible to contemporary observers. This was the special fate of administrative law. The standard legalist account of administrative law noted its emergence only from about 1870 onward, treated it as an encroachment on the traditional jurisdiction of the courts, attributed its presence to a rising tide of collectivism, and asserted that the courts were able to keep this juridical aberration in check.[23]

But we now know that between 1830 and 1870, or, more precisely, between the Factory Act of 1833 and the Railway and Canal Commission Act of 1873, almost the entire repertoire of modern administrative techniques, and objections to them, had developed. Moreover, the superior courts never did have much to do with the business of regulation. As the experience of mine and factory accidents shows, the ordinary original civil or criminal jurisdictions of the courts had no relevance to matters that came to be the concern of the administration. Except for atypical instances, such as the experiment with railway regulation by the Court of Common Pleas from 1854, the new regulatory regimes therefore did not impinge upon the historic jurisdiction of the courts. The real rivals of the administration were not the senior judges of the superior courts but the local lay magistrates. It was upon their jurisdiction, exercised so often obstructively, perversely, and even dishonestly, that the administration encroached. And even here 'encroachment' hardly seems the right word. The magistrates, to a large extent, were given ultimate power to impose sanctions, but could not or would not exercise it. In the end, as we have seen, the administration did not so much encroach as circumvent.

Arguments about the collectivist impulse in Victorian administrative law have been treated elsewhere in this text. The issue is pertinent here only in so far as it provides an insight into the real political and instrumental motives of legalists in emphasizing that access to judicial review was constitutionally inevitable. And as for judicial review, although sometimes hurtful and occasionally profoundly demoralizing, it was sporadic, encapsulated by privative clauses and corrective legislation, and ultimately, therefore, probably of marginal significance.

These, then, are some of the implications of legalism. Are we to conclude that these implications are the unintended, even unsuspected, consequences of an ideology of law that coincidentally placed a premium upon the special knowledge and exclusive functions of lawyers? Are we to set aside any notion that by adopting and advancing this ideology lawyers came to possess a negotiable asset of great value – the gift of legitimacy?

Again, the case of administrative law is instructive. From one perspective, the regulatory and social welfare statutes we have examined can only be defined as formal state law. They were, after all, the sovereign's command; they were 'ordinary' law in the sense that they were enacted in the ordinary way. In principle, they could easily have been encompassed within even the limited lawyers' ideology of law. But they patently were not regarded as 'legitimate,' they did not secure the willing adherence of those to whom they were directed, and they often could not even elicit technical legal virtuosity in draftsmanship, advocacy, or interpretation.

As we have seen, much of the litany of complaint against the new administrative regimes was directed toward their departure from accepted models of law-making and adjudication. These models embodied a worldview, beliefs, and principles: 'ordinary law' (essentially common law) was the only real law worthy of respect, and those who assisted in its rites, who practised it and dispensed it in the courts, were entitled to respect as well. The factory and mines inspectorates, the railway commissioners, and the General Board of Health were an affront both to 'ordinary law' and to lawyers: in the new world of administrative tribunals and departments, judges and lawyers (in their conventional roles) were largely superfluous, their special skills and knowledge irrelevant, their status as expositors of the sovereign's command and as executors of the rule of law devalued.

However, the indictment of the administration was not often framed in terms of injury to lawyers; what was stressed was the insult to law itself. In this subtle shift – also witnessed in connection with disputes over local courts, arbitration, mediation, and commercial tribunals – we see the ultimate function of law as ideology. Legalism enabled lawyers to defend their interests without being seen to do so; and it also enabled them, as the authentic spokesmen for law, to advance the interests of powerful groups of potential patrons threatened by the new administrative regimes. Legalism, then, was negotiable: in the marketplace of ideas, it was available to those who could use and afford it.

Let us now square the circle. Law as ideology, law as lawyers' technique: we have already encountered both in the paradigm of legal centralism. Lawyers, we might say, came to believe in legal centralism because it was in their interest to do so, but also because this notion of law suited the interests of large and powerful client groups in their struggle against state intervention. The logic of legal centralism likewise appealed to lawyers in the context of local justice systems; here, client groups had relatively little to gain but equally little to lose, and the county courts were quickly made safe for law.

When lawyers' techniques and ideology were found unacceptable to important commercial interests, accomodations were found. The ideology of law was vindicated at a symbolic level by the rejection of commercial tribunals and the courts' capture of arbitration. But at a practical level, lawyers worked out a modus vivendi with businessmen, acquiescing in their efforts to escape legal centralism through the use of de facto autonomous domestic tribunals and standard-form contracts and, at a later period, striving to reassure them that formal legal developments such as judicial decisions, codification of statutes, and the creation of the Commercial Court were undertaken in their interest.

The existence of the legal profession as a social field (or series of social fields) was reinforced by the ideology of legalism. This, in turn, enhanced the profession's ability to influence the enactment of law, especially in matters addressed by its ideology, and to effect accommodations between the law of the state and the interests of important client groups.

PLUS C'EST LA MÊME CHOSE?

While we have devoted considerable attention to the ideology of legalism, the limited nature of the claims implied by this analysis must again be stressed. The legal profession and its ideology, techniques, and influence were not in any sense the hinge upon which the state, the economy and society turned in Victorian England. In fact, they may have been largely irrelevant to most important developments, save for this: they did influence the way we came to perceive the legal system, an influence that was manifest especially in the design of formal structures of law and in the conduct of formal legal discourse.

Moreover, even the emergence of legal centralism as a dominating image of law did not, in the end, rest only upon the self-serving attitudes and activities of lawyers. In an era when intellectuals often sought to propound universal principles, when political, commercial, and industrial power tended to consolidate, when changes in transport and communications challenged local, particular, and anomalous arrangements in every sphere, the growth of legal centralism is not surprising. Nor was law the only sphere of intellectual or social activity in which theory was at odds with observable reality. That reality, we must again remind ourselves, was pluralism, not centralism.

7

Postscript: Legal Pluralism and Administrative Law in Contemporary Perspective

SOME QUESTIONS FROM THE PAST

We have seen William Hutton distributing 'peace and justice ... with pleasure,' Acton Ayrton and his colleagues striving to bring to the aid of a reclusive legal system 'the sagacity and experience of commercial men,' and Herbert Mackworth, driven by his 'sacred duty' to his miserable miners, making the bricks of a new regulatory regime without the straw of sanctions. But what have they to do with us?

The answer to this question depends in part upon whom we mean by 'us.' For general social historians, the lessons learned from these figures and the experiences they symbolically represent are relatively limited. Essentially, they are a reminder that the volatility and diversity of social, economic, and political life in the 'reform' period following the industrial revolution were replicated even in the staid world of law. For legal historians, their testimony is somewhat more important. It shows that legal centralism was essentially a Victorian artifact, that we are not very far removed if at all from the days when English law was demonstrably pluralistic, and that prescriptive claims about the legal system based upon our supposed legal-constitutional traditions must therefore be re-examined. For most lawyers, to ask what Hutton, Ayrton, or Mackworth have to do with 'us' is to ask what lay people have to do with law. The conventional answer is that they do not produce it, they consume it. Our three symbolic figures thus have little to do with lawyers because they have little to do with 'law' as lawyers define it.

But if we set aside social and legal history and the lawyer's limited perspective, we are still left with important questions that derive from the experiences of Hutton, Ayrton, and Mackworth. They, after all, were none of them lawyers, yet each was involved in an important manifestation of law as seen from a pluralist perspective. Are there not Huttons, Ayrtons, and Mackworths – lay judges and commercial arbiters and administrators – with us still? Cannot our own legal system, then, be described as pluralistic? If so, what is the relationship of the whole to the parts, and specifically of administrative law to the general legal system? How does pluralism speak to the function of law in contemporary society? And by what criteria might we evaluate proposals to enhance either the centralist or the pluralist character of our legal system?

CENTRALISM AND PLURALISM:
AN AGENDA FOR ANALYSIS

These questions from the past continue to assert urgent claims on our attention. Centralist or pluralist assumptions, often not made explicit, lie beneath many contemporary legal policy proposals and intellectual controversies. A much fuller articulation of these assumptions is need if we are to see clearly and judge wisely.

On the one hand, legal centralist tendencies are apparent in England, Canada, the United States, and elsewhere. These tendencies emphasize the hegemony of formal state law and the crucial position of professional actors within the legal system. For example, an emphasis on judicially defined fundamental rights was manifest in the judicial activism of the United States Supreme Court from the 1950s through the 1970s. Civil libertarians, blacks, women, poor people, anti-war protesters, consumers, and environmentalists all looked to the courts to transform politics and society. Their opponents urged judicial restraint and warned of the incapacity of law to change hearts and minds and marketplace behaviour. Recently, positions have begun to shift. Those who spurned judicial activism have begun to discover its charms, while those who embraced it seek solace elsewhere, disappointed by backsliding in the jurisprudence of rights and by the persistence of many of the problems it addressed.

If constitutional adjudication is moving into partial eclipse in the United States, it still shines brightly elsewhere. Canada has just adopted its Charter of Rights and Freedoms, which gives judges unprecedented opportunities to make law, and presumably to effect 'reforms,' in many spheres of public policy; the European Community has now had two decades of similar experience under its Convention on Human Rights and Fundamental Freedoms; and the United Kingdom continues to flirt with the notion of a domestic bill of rights.

Bills or charters of rights are, in a sense, the ultimate expression of legal centralism. All law, all political behaviour, all economic and social policy is ultimately to be measured against a single fixed constitutional standard whose interpretation depends upon professional advocacy and formal adjudication. But they are not the only manifestations of legal centralism.

The line between public-law litigation and political action as techniques of public-policy formation in the United States is in imminent danger of disappearing.[1] Legislative preclusion of judicial review of administrative action in Canada has been swept aside; judicial restraint now rests on no more than a self-denying ordinance.[2] And even in the post-Denning era, it remains to be seen whether judicial modesty will ever again attract a respectable following in England.[3]

Nor is legal centralism confined to the public sector. Ingenious tort actions, new notions of property, the extension of contractual doctrines and remedies, and the legal enfranchisement of wives and children in all three countries bespeak a naïve belief in the capacity of law – and of judges and lawyers – to rectify imbalances of power without recourse to politics and to sort out the debris of personal misfortune and fractured relationships by sifting them through a mesh of legal doctrines.

We see, in short, aggressive promotion of the centralist paradigm of law by an odd assortment of advocates: jurisprudes devoted to taking rights seriously; the legal profession (its historic enthusiasm bolstered by its recent embrace of Keynesian strategies in its own labour market); citizen groups which, lacking economic or electoral strength, seek compensatory legal power; business groups hoping that law will hobble state intervention in the economy; intellectuals despairing of politics and idealists despairing of social action; high technologists, low opportunists, and middling minds with an instinct for the quick and easy. All of these are convinced that the answer to their concerns lies with the formal legal system, with laws and lawyers and courts. They have either tacitly accepted centralist assumptions about the legal system, or they wish to bring about changes in it which will validate those assumptions.

But centralism is not the only important tendency in law today. In institutional design, legal discourse, and scientific inquiry the paradigm of pluralism is also much in evidence. It serves both to describe the facts of legal life and as a practical and principled program for change.

The 'discovery' of legal pluralism by social scientists is a relatively recent event involving three separate developments in legal thought. First, efforts have been made to describe patterns of social behaviour in our own contemporary society as well as in other places and at other times. These efforts have yielded rather similar revelations about the creation of, adherence to, and enforcement of normative systems that lack the characteristics of the state legal system familiar in Western industralized societies.[4] And these revelations have in turn underscored the contingent and problematic nature of all formal legal systems, including our own. No less important is a second empirical perspective which has shown that our own formal legal system did not function as we thought it did. Research into the actual causes and effects of law has falsified many of the claims of legal centralism.[5] Third, exploration of law's ideological function has enabled us to reflect upon the extent to which legal centralism itself is more than an inaccurate representation of social reality. We may now see it as a form of special pleading, as a technique for the projection of particular values and the vindication of particular interests.[6]

Given the disconcerting, even destructive, qualities of each of these assaults upon legal centralism, we can understand the strength of legal pluralism. As a paradigm of law it can accommodate many different systems; it can freely acknowledge the widest range of influences playing upon each; and it can demote state law from its position of pre-eminence and presumed legitimacy without denying that it too functions in the world of affairs and of ideas. The pluralist perspective also enables us to understand the pertinence of nineteenth-century English legal history to the contemporary experience of the United States, Canada or, for that matter, England itself. But legal pluralism, like legal centralism, is a program as well as a paradigm. And like legal centralism, pluralism may be advocated in aid of very different social perspectives. A brief sketch of contemporary pluralism and a mention of its friends reveals this lack of coherence.

First, as in the nineteenth century, we may identify residual traces of an older communal pluralism. These are typically found in ethnic or religious communities, and represent efforts by those communities to uphold established values – above all, the value of preserving the community itself.[7] While less obvious examples may be found 'imbricated' (in E.P. Thompson's phrase) in neighbourhoods, workplaces, and other contemporary social or economic relationships,[8] the future of communal pluralism in a world of dissolving communities is not promising. None the less, those who genuinely seek a revival of community life often propose as well measures that will encourage the development of communal legal systems.

Second, we see the persistence of the very state-sponsored pluralism whose origins were explored in our account of early administrative law. In their interventionist posture, governments in the United Kingdom, Canada, and the United States have had to create boards, commissions, and tribunals to regulate the economy, promote health and safety measures, resolve group conflicts, and ensure the preservation of culture, resources, amenities, and social equity. In their protective stance, governments have also established family and juvenile courts and other special civil and criminal courts. In all of these cases states have deliberately decided that the norms, procedures, personnel, or costs of the central legal system will not permit it to do what has to be done. New ideas of social policy engender new institutional forms. In the nineteenth century as in the twentieth, in law as in architecture, form is made to follow function.[9]

Third, commercial pluralism is said to be widespread and desirable today, just as it was a century ago. While it is difficult to estimate their number or relative significance, many civil disputes are submitted to arbitration, either by prior agreement or in preference to imminent litigation.[10] Much of this arbitration occurs in organized exchanges or between major contracting or interacting parties in such industries as insurance, sports and entertainment, construction, and shipping. At this level, we can imagine a degree of mutual interest and parity of economic power between the parties, so that it is reasonable to read arbitration outcomes as a projection of their relationships and expectations. But submissions to arbitration are sometimes buried in the small print of form contracts, sometimes forced upon unknowledgeable or powerless consumers. In this context, arbitration may become merely a projection of initial disparities of power, and have the effect of forcing consumers to settle for even less than formal law would give them. Similar pluralist possibilities, good and bad, exist within organizations such as professions, universities, and labour unions.

A fourth and more recent development is the professional promotion of informalism. Various proposals, often emanating from the bench or bar or from experts in court administration, urge the 'diversion' of disputes from the formal legal system to newly created dispute-resolving mechanisms, usually employing mediation or informal arbitration, usually operating in the shadow of the formal system, but sometimes mobilizing community resources and non-legal personnel. While these proposals often nod at the need to democratize justice and to make law a more flexible instrument of social ordering, they tend to emphasize three related propositions: justice is costly; a cheaper way must be found to handle minor claims; and the formal system must be reserved for the efficient handling of 'imporant' disputes. Typically, little attention is paid in such proposals to the deliberate substitution of 'informal' norms for those of formal law, or to the possibility that doing so might result in differing qualities of justice for persons of large and little means.[11]

Fifth, there is a form of pluralism that can be described as circumstantial. It can result from informal adaptation of established legal procedures to accommodate local circumstances – as, for example, the use of pre-hearing procedures to promote settlements or of adjournments to encourage minor offenders to placate their victims by acts of contrition or compensation. Or it may emerge from changes in normative and decision-making systems within corporate structures as they strive to fend off formal law by becoming more equitable and orderly.[12] Or it may be seen in such varied contexts as the ombudsman activities of newspapers, radio, and television programs and off-the-record dispute processing by police, administrative officials, and neighbourhood social networks. In each of these contexts, the potential for social 'good' may be discovered after a period of informal experimentation, and efforts can be made to generalize and institutionalize what was previously specific and circumstantial.

Finally, there is a strain of ideological pluralism that stretches from right to left without, so far, expressing itself in intermediate social reality. In one incarnation, this pluralism would represent a restoration of personal autonomy, 'privatization' of yet another government function, justice following in the wake of economic regulation, education, and welfare.[13] In the other, it would symbolize an attack upon the exclusive control of legitimacy and coercion now enjoyed by the state apparatus of monopoly capitalism.[14]

It is now clear that in speaking of pluralism we have been addressing a number of very different notions current among very different constituencies. These constituencies, moreover, are devoted not to pluralism in and for itself, but to specific ideological perspectives and forms of social ordering which cannot be accomplished through existing formal legal arrangements. Is it appropriate to try to capture all of them within a single paradigm of legal pluralism? What, after all, do they share? Not attachment to particular institutional, adjectival or substantive features; not political ideology or social circumstance; not even the same intensity of commitment to a distinctive legal regime.

Yet three themes do recur in these different visions of pluralism. First, there is a sense of estrangement from the existing general regime of state law, courts, and lawyers. Second, there is an attachment, conscious of implicit, to a special system of law directed to a limited range of purposes and persons, with a limited range of powers, and with at least partial autonomy from the general legal system. Third, there is a resulting need to define the relationship between the general and special legal systems.

We have seen how the first and second of these themes are influenced by peculiar experiences and perspectives. But the third theme is one that largely transcends context. It raises, in effect, an issue of basic principle: can a modern state constitute its legal system so as to give form and substance to legal pluralism, in the same way that present systems seek to make real the paradigm of legal centralism?

To pose the question in this way is admittedly to assume away its most problematic aspects: what sort of state would wish to, or be prepared to, embark upon such a course of action? To what end? In aid of whom? But our focus is now upon constitutional architecture, not deep socio-political structures: whatever the nature of those deep structures, it is difficult to imagine that certain architectural conventions can be ignored in any formally constituted house of law.

When the pluralist state seeks to define itself in relation to its constituent elements, it is in a sense retracing the well-worn path of federalism. To return to an earlier metaphor, it is possible to see the pluralist state as a federation of Alsatias, of law communities, of semi-autonomous social fields. But the metaphor must not be overextended. Pluralism is not federalism.

Unlike the units of political federations with which we are familiar, the components of such a pluralist state would lack defined geographic boundaries, fixed or ascertainable populations, uniformity (or close similarity) of responsibilities and powers, and even, at any given moment, a verifiable existence. Thus, unless the pluralist state is to be completely self-effacing – in which case it would be neither 'modern' nor a state – it must adopt criteria of some sort for identifying or 'recognizing' its components, a process whereby recognition is accorded them, and a definition of the consequences of recognition. These are issues most federations need address only rarely; but in a pluralist state they would be a matter of almost daily concern. [15]

However, some closely related issues are dealt with by most federations. Rules exist that delimit the jurisdictional competence of each component, tell us whether that competence is exclusive or shared with other components and the 'federal' entity itself, and identify group or individual rights immune from all intrusion. Because individuals would be able to move from component to component, participate simultaneously in two or more components, or interact with individuals from other components, rights of mobility and conflicts of laws rules would be needed as well. And, because in a pluralist state, even state instrumentalities would enjoy a degree of autonomy, some attention would have to be paid to problems of devolution and accountability.

It would be easy enough to draw up an even longer agenda for what we can metaphorically describe as the constituent assembly of a pluralist state, but there is no need to do so. The analysis has already proceeded far enough to permit us to see what we have done. At the beginning of this chapter we moved from historical analysis to speculation concerning our own legal system. Now we are edging toward utopian fantasy – the drafting of imaginary constitutions for ideal states. Yet, like so many utopias, ours is no more than extrapolation – perhaps even less, a mirror image – of the world in which we now live. We set about to create the new world of pluralism, but we had to take as our point of departure many of the premises of centralism.

What, after all, does the very notion of a constitution imply? It assumes that law can be made certain while all else is contingent; that formal structure can be imposed on social process; that individuals, institutions, and groups do not themselves generate legitimacy, they borrow it on stiff terms from the central bank of the state legal order.

Perhaps this brief attempt to reconstruct legality along pluralist lines suffers from a simple deficit of imagination. I am, it appears in the end, a lawyer whose short leash of experience will not allow him to stray very far from existing examples of states that have either federal or plural legal systems. Yet perhaps the fact that the exercise so soon revealed its limits is also a reminder that we cannot reconstitute law without reconstituting the state itself. And finally, perhaps we have learned that it will not be possible to move from paradigm to prescription, from reality to rule. In such a transition we necessarily leave behind much that is alive and organic, complex and problematic, specific and unstated – much that is genuinely 'plural' in pluralism.

There is no doubt some truth in each of these explanations for my inability to propose a radical vision of legal pluralism as it might exist in a modern state. At the same time, it does not follow that the centralist paradigm would survive a pluralist critique unscathed. To demonstrate this point, I offer a pluralist critique of administrative law. In so doing, I must make clear two underlying premises. First, much of what I will say about administrative law will not apply to other manifestations of pluralism. Second, while I will speak generically of 'administrative law,' I fully appreciate that the term acquires real meaning only when it is located within specific contexts of time and place, of institutional function and social reality. The mid-nineteenth century is not the late twentieth; England is not Canada or the United States; adjudication is not rule-making or enforcement; business markets are not labour markets, and welfare benefits are not television licences. These limitations understood, how might we view administrative law from a pluralist perspective?

ALSATIA REVISITED: THE CASE OF ADMINISTRATIVE LAW

What are our concerns about administrative law today? We want to be assured that the vast machinery of administration which is characteristic of all modern governments is performing its appointed tasks effectively. We are anxious that, in so doing, it should be appropriately respectful of the rights of both those whom it is meant to protect and those whom it is meant to protect against. We are therefore preoccupied with institutional design – discretion, natural justice, remedial powers – and with institutional relationships – judicial review, legislative oversight, and ombudsmanship. These issues are themselves important, but to some extent they serve as proxies for a two-hundred-year-old political controversy: should the invisible hand of the market or the visible hand of the state determine the course of our lives?[16]

Administrative law, after all, is the vehicle of state intervention, not of private action. There is therefore a risk – indeed, a probability – that, like war, administrative law will be seen as 'nothing more than the continuation of politics by other means.' If so, it will command no more respect than the political positions it serves.[17] During the depression of the 1930s, during wartime, during the perturbations of the 1960s, state intervention to stimulate the economy, hasten victory, and redistribute wealth and power led to a considerable expansion of the administration and to widespread support for administrative law. During the 1950s and 1970s, renewed faith in the miracles of private enterprise and a passion for deregulation (both largely unfulfilled) coincided with an erosion of confidence in administrative law. The correlation is crude, the trends conjectural, but students of administrative law will perhaps concede that this analysis is to some extent an accurate one.[18]

Yet administrative law cannot be reduced to the political policies it seeks to advance. In so far as it can be seen as a system (or series of systems) of social ordering, administrative law can also fairly claim to be 'the continuation of law by other means.' To the extent that this claim is accepted, administrative law may be able to command the same respect that law itself enjoys, a respect that somehow transcends that accorded the persons, policies, or procedures equated with 'law' in a particular situation.[19]

Hence the potential importance to administrative law of legal pluralism. It is a legitimating device, the means by which administrative law transcends politics and becomes law.

Of course, those who abominate the welfare state or reject all forms of regulatory intervention in the marketplace will not be so easily pacified. For them – and Dicey was of this persuasion – administrative law can never be law. But those who believe that we will continue to enjoy a mixed economy and that we cannot escape from (if we cannot quite afford) a generation of commitments to adequate social services must come to terms with administrative law as law. In order to do so, they will have to abandon the view that it is merely 'ordinary' law writ small, that it derives from and must imitate and conform to ordinary law. Administrative law can only be understood as law if we accept that it has distinctive characteristics, generally related to those of ordinary law but demanding evaluation in their own terms.

As we turn to that task of evaluation, we must remember that administrative law seeks to combine legitimacy with distinctiveness. With legitimacy comes responsibility, and with distinctiveness comes accountability. It is not enough to argue that administrative law is, or must be, different. It is also necessary to establish why and how it should be different and with what results.

At the threshold of this exercise, we must also remind ourselves that administrative law emerged in response to a series of judgments that the norms, institutions, and procedures of the formal legal system were unsuitable for the performance of particular social tasks. These judgments, made by governments left, right, and centre in the nineteenth century and the twentieth, were not arrived at lightly. For the most part, governments in the United Kingdom and other Western democracies have been both respectful of traditional legal institutions and loath to embark upon intrusive or extensive programs of regulation or social assistance. That they embarked upon such programs at all, and that the administration and its law were their chosen instruments, shows that to be elected, governments must be seen to be effective in dealing with real or perceived evils and in seizing important opportunities. For administrative law, therefore, effectiveness has been the touchstone of legitimacy.

It is not surprising, then, that one of the important criticisms of modern administrative law has been that the promise of effectiveness has not been kept.[20] It is often argued that regulatory agencies established to control powerful interests are captured by them and used by them to impose upon the public. Similarly, welfare bureaucracies that were intended to relieve the plight of the poor are accused of creating further dependency and engendering abuse.[21] Such criticisms are made sometimes with vindictive glee by those who were opposed to the administrative enterprise from the beginning, sometimes with disillusionment by those whose unrealistically high hopes could never have been realized. Even less partisan observers may be inclined to agree with these criticisms. There is, however, less unanimity about the extent to which blame for these serious failures is properly assigned to the administrative process itself.

The process, of course, does not exist in isolation from a number of other forces. If a regulatory regime has been captured, it may be because the political authorities have failed to appoint administrators genuinely committed to its success or to give them necessary political support, staff, and powers. If a welfare bureaucracy has failed to enhance the dignity and well-being of its clientele, it may be because of our tendency to perceive poverty as a social misdemeanour and to assign spending for its relief and very low priority.

Curiously, this line of criticism, which emphasizes the failures of administrative law, is paralleled by one that proceeds from precisely the opposite premise. Administrative law is criticized not because it has failed but because it has succeeded. In their desire to be effective, it is said, administrators are prepared to issue detailed edicts concerning every aspect of economic activity and to trample upon the rights of those being regulated. Nor does the administration necessarily trample with heavy boots. Its ultimate power is often the power to obstruct, which is exercised through a variety of discretion-based devices against which there is no defence: paper-burden, foot-dragging, obfuscation, 'scowl and growl.' While a determined victim might resist a particular episode of administrative imposition, he must ultimately succumb, if not from fear of sanctions then because he must deal with the administration on future occasions. And, it is said, the cost of compliance with regulatory programs has overtaxed the management structure and undermined the competitive position of many businesses.[22]

Here again we run the risk of confusing administration with the policies it expresses. Can we reduce the toll of industrial accidents, correct certain gross disparities of market power, or curb the sale of adulterated food without using administrative law? The historical evidence tells us we cannot. If administrative law is to be used for such purposes, can it be used in ways that are no less effective but more efficient and more respectful of the interests of those being regulated? On occasion, yes; who would deny it? But these charges of excessive administrative intrusion seem to speak only to marginal transaction costs, not to the basic compliance costs which are the real grounds for complaint.

Thus, we have two lines of criticism of administrative law: it does not effectively achieve its stated objectives, or it achieves them too effectively and with too great a sacrifice of other interests. Their combined effect is to leave administrative law in considerable disrepute, with few friends and many powerful and articulate enemies. But why should administrative law, as a system, attract the hostility that is generated largely by the policies it serves or is attributable to atypical instances of inefficiency or overreaching?

The contrast between the position of 'ordinary' law and that of administrative law is instructive on this point. The 'ordinary courts' and 'ordinary law' have shown themselves to be ineffective in dealing, for example, with crime, pollution, industrial conflict, accidents, and family disputes. They have shown themselves, as E.P. Thompson and others argue, all too effective in the protection of certain property rights and the suppression of others. How is it, then, that ordinary courts should continue to attract support and respect and should even acquire new constitutional and civil-liberties responsibilities, or that Thompson himself should describe law as 'an unqualified human good'?[23] The answer is surely embedded in our culture, in our very notion of what 'law' is, in the dominant legal centralist paradigm.

Our willingness to forgive in 'real,' 'ordinary,' or lawyers' law what we regard as unacceptable in administrative law is in itself of great significance. The law of the state and of the centralist paradigm can survive the attacks of its critics, can indeed convert its critics into admirers (as it did Thompson), because it has an existence that transcends the particular context. It can detach itself from the results it achieves and the purposes it serves and command respect simply because it is 'law'. This administrative law has not been able to do, any more than the informal private systems that populate the pluralist paradigm of law. Those private systems have no meaning, command no loyalty, lead no existence beyond the life of a particular trade, community, or relationship. So too with administrative law: it is what it does. The doctrine of ultra vires, it seems, applies to both the legal powers and the legitimacy of the administration.

If we have correctly identified the differences between administrative and 'ordinary' law, we may next consider various proposals that seek to cure the ills of administrative law by a massive injection of ordinary law. Such proposals are centralist in nature. They envisage that the law of courts and legislatures and constitutions will be imposed *ab extra*, that administrative law will be assimilated to the general legal system, and that imposition and assimilation are effective and appropriate strategies for the legitimation of administrative law. (They are to be distinguished, however, from proposals that contemplate the emergence of an internal law of administration; this latter approach, pluralist in its assumptions, is dealt with below.)

Those who wish to reinforce particular regulatory or welfare regimes sometimes contend that 'ordinary' law can rescue administrative law from its present disrepute. Administrative agencies might be recaptured by the public if procedures for public participation were mandated by constitution or statute and enforced by the courts. The debilitating effects of welfare administration might be diminished if claimants were accorded legally enforceable rights rather than discretionary entitlement and were guaranteed formal adjudication rather than palmed off with informal disposition.[24] Similar but perhaps less ingenuous proposals are also advanced by those who fear effective administrative action. Require notice of proposed regulation-making, they urge; eliminate discretion; give us formal hearings and full rights of appeal. This will curb administrative abuse. These centralist strategies are not new. As the historical record shows, they are as old as administrative law itself. And as the record also shows, they offer little to those who hope to stimulate the administration, but rather more to those who hope to sedate it.

Judges, even today's judges, have often displayed antipathy or insensitivity toward regulatory and social welfare schemes. The delays and costs and technicalities involved in adversary hearings, appeals, and other legal proceedings become a new factor in the calculus of 'rights,' a factor that tends to favour those with time and money and access to the best lawyers. Nor, as it turns out, do judicial review or appeal always operate effectively *in terrorem* to ensure administrative compliance with legislative policy or fair procedures. The doctrine is too incoherent, the outcomes too random, the very object of review too elusive and ill-defined to support any credible assessment of the net results of judicial intervention.[25]

But most important, ordinary legal attitudes, procedures, and remedies seldom address the defects they are meant to correct. The appeal to ordinary law does not add a penny to the total welfare budget, but it may divert some part of that limited budget from the benefits account to administration and litigation. A constitutional or statutory requirement of notice prior to regulation-making will not alter the attitude of a regulator who has been captured, but it may speed his capitulation in the face of a well-financed frontal assault by the big battalions of industry. On the other hand, the requirement of trial-type hearings and full-scale appeals may well have, from the point of view of a regulated industry, the desired effect of discouraging all but the most determined administrator by forcing him to focus his scarce resources on a relatively small number of cases so clear that they are likely to survive even judicial scrutiny. The public's interest in attaining regulatory objectives is, in the end, not likely to be served by appeals to ordinary law.

It is not surprising that ordinary law does not greatly assist us. We can hardly expect much from a system now largely designed and administered by a relatively homogeneous group of lawyers, whose expertise seldom extends beyond legal doctrine, whose ideology tends toward conservatism, and whose experience largely consists in dealing with isolated cases in an adversarial context. The difficulty with the solutions offered by ordinary law is that they indeed tend, for these reasons, to be so ordinary.

If ordinary law will not do the job, what will? In truth, there are two kinds of jobs to be done, and each requires a different approach.

First, there are the political jobs. If, as has been suggested, regulatory capture results from a collapse of political will, then governments must be forced to confront their responsibility for appointing administrators who are not resolute, or for failing to revive their flagging morale. If welfare budgest are insufficient to meet the need, governments should make bold to acknowledge this fact by overt policy statements which the voters can judge. If regulation is thought to cost society more than it is worth, let government deregulate, if it dares to. These are not tasks for either administrators or judges.

Second, there are the more limited jobs of ensuring the effectiveness and integrity of administration in each specific instance where it is mandated by the political process. Quality control, as we have come to understand in the context of industrial production, is more than a matter of careful inspection after the fact; it must be 'engineered in' from the beginning and accepted as a cardinal commitment by everyone involved in the productive process. So too with administration. Accepting the need to check administrative behaviour from time to time (although not necessarily by means of conventional judicial review), the best prospects for improving the quality of administration reside in the initial design of structures and procedures and in the genuine commitment of administrators to high standards of performance.

Methods of selecting, training, and motivating administrators are beyond the scope of this analysis. But the importance of motivation, especially, is brought home to us when we recall how the resourcefulness and prodigious energy of the early Victorian administrators were fuelled by moral commitment. If today we cannot always rekindle administrative fervour, we can at least appeal to administrative pride of craft. Craft is what is needed if we are to meet the challenges of institutional design and operation.

Our study of institutional design again draws upon the basic insights of legal pluralism. When we considered informal systems of law and dispute settlement, we saw how their distinctive qualities might emerge in response to the needs, beliefs, and internal dynamics of the constituencies they serve. In one situation, mediation as a means of preserving amicable relations may be preferred; in another, ritualized adjudication may be selected as a means of dramatizing group values; in a third, informal group consensus may both create and enforce norms. These arrangements emerge, survive, and subside as they serve the needs of the group or fail to respond to changes within it.

In the more deliberately structured context of administrative law, institutional design should also reflect the special qualities of the specific activity being addressed. The need for speedy decisions must be weighed against the complexity of the problem and the potential for harm involved in a wrong decision. Structures that make hundreds of thousands of decisions cannot be carbon copies of those that make only a few. Forms of intervention may vary depending upon whether ongoing relationships are being created or adjusted or whether the parties encounter each other only once. Methods of proof must respond to the mix of adjudicative, legislative and scientific facts. The promulgation of rules cannot be treated like the disposition of complaints. In short, specialization is the key to effectiveness; administrative structures tend to be unique; pluralism within pluralism is almost inevitable.[26]

This is not to deny that lessons learned in one context can frequently be adapted to another. As our historical study showed, the state of the administrative art evolved through several decades of experimentation. Moreover, even the formal system sometimes borrows from the informal and administrative systems, which thus function as institutional laboratories. To refer again to historical experience, the parties were permitted to testify in courts of requests and county courts before they were allowed to do so in the common-law courts. Contemporary examples of this practice include the use of mediation in matrimonial disputes and of relatively complicated consent orders in certain kinds of corporate litigation, both devices that were first used outside the regular courts.

There are risks in all of this, however. Idiosyncracy in design is not necessarily purposeful and effective. It may simply reflect anachronism, in the case of informal systems, or miscalculation, in the case of the administration. Or it may represent something more sinister. Private systems may evolve which protect the interests of a dominant group of insiders, disregarding those of outsiders or less powerful group members. Public systems may be deliberately designed to ensure that regulation remains relatively innocuous, giving symbolic solace to the public but no provocation to powerful interests.[27] And there is the risk most frequently mentioned although less frequently encountered: the risk that fairness wil be sacrificed, deliberately or in an unthinking excess of zeal, to efficiency.

Each of these risks is real enough, but do they cumulatively justify insistence upon conformity by all types of bodies to the single model of adversarial adjudication typically associated with the courts? This is not an argument which, baldly stated, attracts much support; even Dicey rejected it. None the less, in a number of respects we have retained an attachment to the court model, embedded as it is in the legal centralist paradigm which continues to dominate our thinking about administrative law.[28]

Consider some important examples. Legislation in many jurisdictions requires standard, courtlike procedures for the exercise of statutory powers of decision by all administrative tribunals and the presence on those tribunals of a legally trained presiding officer who can, presumably, give a passable imitation of a judge. Courts reviewing the activities of administrative and domestic bodies conclusively presume that the legislature intended them to roughly approximate, or even slavishly duplicate, courtlike behaviour, to act 'fairly' or 'judicially.' Legal critics, disconcerted by the unfamiliar fact-finding techniques of the administration, harass them into the more familiar adversary–adjudicative mould. Concerned reformers, seeking to facilitate public participation and enhance administrative responsiveness, return atavistically to the judicial trial for both symbolism and substance. Finally, even in the absence of such external legal compulsions, the virtues of adversarial adjudication are sufficiently widely advertised that they are sometimes adopted in private domestic contexts, where they need not be.

What are the effects of this continuing infatuation with adversarial adjudication in administrative law? Interests, issues, events are redefined in terms that make them amenable to trial techniques. The public interest becomes a 'party,' confronting an opponent equal in status, and standing equally at arm's length from the administrative decision-maker; the decision-maker becomes passive and neutral rather than proactive and purposeful. Achieving general compliance with legislative policy is replaced as an administrative priority by the disposition of single cases. Persuasive patterns of conduct are dissolved into isolated instances so they can be subjected to conventional proof or disproof.[29]

In any given situation, of course, courtlike procedures could be the right answer. But as the experience of the courts themselves shows, it is by no means always so. Pluralism's importance for administrative law is its ability to liberate us from the constraints of a single institutional design. It permits us to consider other designs on their merits and without the stigma of contravening 'law.'

Still, our ultimate choice will have to be measured by some standard external to the particular system. The appalling state of the superior courts in the nineteenth century shows us, if nothing else how dangerous it is to leave the design of a system entirely in the hands of people immersed in it on a daily basis. And not even the most devoted admirer of twentieth-century bureaucracies and informal systems would argue that they are beyond reproach or improvement. The case for judging the administration by some external standard becomes even more compelling when we focus on questions of operation rather than design. There are obviously minimum standards below which no system can be allowed to fall. Gross inefficiency, corruption, infidelity to its own norms, and antipathy or partiality based upon illicit considerations: none of these is acceptable.

Yet even here problems lurk. What is illicit to some may be licit to others. The pluralism of the legal system reaches back to the pluralism of society itself.[30] But at least pluralism presents a broader range of choices than does the traditional legal model, and forces us to think about what the essence of, say, procedural 'fairness' really is, apart from the meaning grafted onto it by lawyers and judges.

We have so far treated pluralism as if it were largely a matter of form, of procedure, of institutional design. But it is more. Pluralism relates to the very substantive norms by which conduct is moulded and by which disputes are resolved and decisions made. We have already made note of the origin of these norms in work, in communal custom, and in patterns of administration. To this list should be added, especially in the case of administrative law, precedential reasoning by both boards and courts, and legislation, both parliamentary and subordinate. The link between the sources and the content of norms in administrative law must now be explored.

All administrative activity has its roots in a statute. Why then should we be at pains to stress the importance of other normative sources for administrative action? The answer is that normative language in regulatory statutes is often vague and uninformative: 'hear and determine,' 'may in its discretion approve,' 'public convenience and necessity.' The reasons are altogether understandable. The government may lack technical knowledge of the evil at which the legislation is aimed and thus may be hesitant to commit itself to possibly inappropriate standards. The situation may be a rapidly changing one, and the operative norms may require constant revision. There may be a desire to facilitate compromise, to change conduct through education, or to allow those being regulated to participate in the formation of norms; none of these arrangements is facilitated by precise normative language. As a result there is ample opportunity – often, indeed, a compelling necessity – for the administration itself to give meaningful specificity to such statutes.[31] New norms are constantly being created by decisions, rulings, regulations, interpretative bulletins, policy statements, and patterns of enforcement. All of these, it is true, claim a particular statute as their progenitor and must, upon challenge, be able to trace legal lines of descent; but the links are often more historical than operational. Legal challenge is, of course, not the only (or necessarily even the most effective) form of challenge. The government is ultimately accountable for administrative behaviour through the political process. But that process will usually focus on a limited number of matters that are of special importance or offer special potential for embarrassment by the press, the opposition, or some interested segment of the public.

In the light of the attenuated and sporadic influence of external law and politics on the substantive specifics of administration, what does give them shape and direction? To a significant extent, these substantive norms derive from what the administration conceives to be its mandate – its reformulation and adumbration of the statutory standard – tempered by such bureaucratic considerations as practicality, internal consistency, and a desire to preserve internal autonomy. It is therefore not simply new policy determinations by parliament but the preponderant influence of the administration itself that often gives a distinctive character to the norms of administrative law systems. This internal influence is preponderant; it is not exclusive. External law and politics do enter somewhat into administrative calculation: legal forms must be found that will survive judicial scrutiny; political defences must be maintained. When these minimum conditions are met, however, the administration in fact if not in theory enjoys considerable autonomy in the creation of norms.

The processes by which the administration makes its internal law are not very different from those we encounter in the formal legal system. Administrative norms may be created by word or by deed, by the promulgation of a rule or by the making of a decision or by doing both simultaneously. But both processes are liable to attract criticism. If the administration makes a decision, it may be criticized for arbitrariness, since that decision is not clearly referable to any standard precise enough to make it predictable. If the administration promulgates a rule, especially one that is specific and detailed, it may be criticized for lack of flexibility, since it has narrowed the range of its own future options or, as the courts sometimes put it, fettered its own discretion. One is almost tempted to say that only when the administrative process produces a reasoned decision that derives from a rule and helps to create a new rule will it escape censure – in other words, when it adheres to the style of the common law. Sometimes, of course, it moves even more dramatically away from the common-law model when it acts informally to secure complying conduct. And here, although informal disposition is by far the most common fate of controversies ostensibly governed by ordinary law, the administration is attacked most vigorously.

When we compare administrative law with the formal legal system, we see that the latter also confronts the problems of vagueness, of normative ambiguity and even internal contradiction, if anything to an even higher degree than the administration. The same tendencies in legislative draftsmanship can be seen in many statutes that judges must interpret and apply, and the common law is replete with norms such as 'reasonable,' 'probable,' 'justifiable,' and 'wrongful.' Yet we no longer pretend that our legal system comprises a coherent body of principles harmoniously blending the legislation of five centuries and the common law of ten. We accept that our legal system is not fashioned anew in each age, and that the influences playing upon all parts of the system are not necessarily consistent at any given moment. We know that institutional relics of an earlier time coexist with contemporary structures and the prototypes of future developments. Even legal structures of the same era are seen to sit in uneasy juxtaposition, reflecting the power, style, and expectations of their respective architects and clienteles. Most important, we have altered our understanding of the way in which legal decisions are made. We now know that we are able to choose from among legal rules that offer different guides to conduct and different outcomes to disputes; we accept that we must make such choices openly and for reasons we can justify.

To be sure, when the formal legal system is faced with the need to dispose of a particular controversy, it does so with relative ease. Forum-shopping is inhibited by more stringent jurisdictional controls; conflicting lines of cases are reconciled by the creation of a new rule; statutory language is given priority over common law or interpreted so as to avoid incompatibility. Order and integration are achieved, if not permanently throughout the system then briefly in a part of it.

This process is no doubt made easier by the centralist forms of discourse our legal system conventionally employs: every legal problem can have only one authoritative answer; like cases will be treated alike; parliament is sovereign; judges apply law, they do not make it; lower-court judges will obey interpretations of the law provided by higher-court judges. These conventional assumptions may bear little resemblance to life in the real world; they are indeed being rendered increasingly problematic by developments in legal scholarship, in public perception, and even within the formal system – for example, by the constitutional entrenchment of basic rights. But so far, at least, they continue to serve, especially for professional participants in the system, as justifying explanations for most legal decisions. No doubt stated or unstated bureaucratic considerations also operate within the formal legal system as they do within the administration. Some controversies are de minimis; some consequences are too extreme to accept although they would flow from the literal application of a rule; some decisions are doubtless tempered by the desire to immunize the courts from public criticism. In short, issues faced by the courts in creating norms do not differ greatly from those confronted by the administration. Both seem to be more deeply implicated in a paradigm of pluralism than has generally been conceded.

This suggestion of certain affinities between administrative law and the general, formal legal system brings us back to the problem with which, in a sense, we have been preoccupied throughout. What is the appropriate relationship between these two systems or, indeed, between state law and all other particularistic systems? Do we see in the ability of the state system to harmonize, or at least tolerate, its own diverse institutions and contradictory normative regimes some hope for the formal acceptance of administrative law itself as a distinct and autonomous regime?[32] If so, does this hope extend to other informal regimes?

The need for accommodation, for reconciliation, of different legal systems flows from the fact that we live simultaneously in several contexts. We may live in a neighbourhood, belong to a religious or ethnic community, work in a trade or profession, buy or sell goods in an organized market, and function as producers or consumers under an administrative–regulatory regime. In general, we may be prepared to be governed by the legal norms of each of these contexts. But individuals at particular moments may abjure loyalty to such norms and wish to rely upon their rights under general law.

These appeals to different legal systems might become manifest in several ways. A person who is involved in some informal legal system might decline to submit to its norms or its dispute-settling procedures. A party to conventional civil litigation might rely upon a claim or a defence that originates in a special legal regime. Or, most significant for present purposes, administrative action might be brought into an ordinary court for review. In each case, the question is whether and to what extent the norms of the special regime should be vindicated. If those who are involved in it can simply exit as they please, the reliance interests of others, the survival of the group, or the effectiveness of the regulatory regime will be jeopardized. If they cannot exit, they may be denied rights available to other citizens. If 'ordinary' courts try to enforce the norms of the special regime, they may misconstrue them; if they do not, they may subvert them. If administrative action is reviewed, the autonomy and integrity of the regime may be compromised; if not, it may overreach itself.

We have now arrived at the crucial dilemma of legal pluralism: neither complete deference nor complete indifference to other legal regimes can be expected among the components of a pluralistic legal system. What is needed is a mediating principle. But what principle? And by whom interpreted?

In a general and analogical sense, the concept of jurisdiction functioned as a mediating principle in administrative law, as it had earlier served in relation to local and special courts. So long as a body was competent to deal with a matter, it could, if authorized to do so, apply its distinctive law. (This principle did not touch matters that came directly to some other forum; there, the tendency was to apply the law of the forum, or at least to give it primacy over other systems that might arguably apply.) Yet jurisdiction is no longer available as a mediating principle. Its decline and fall is a cautionary, or at least a diverting, tale. That tale begins, for our purposes, in the first half of the nineteenth century. During this period, according to deSmith, a reaction set in against an earlier tendency of English judges 'to treat nearly all an inferior court's findings as touching its jurisdiction. This reaction made it possible to construct a coherent theory of jurisdiction which, *had it but prevailed*, would have seriously limited the scope of judicial review ... in administrative law.'[33] 'Had it but prevailed': but it did not.

Ignoring, for present purposes, several fluctuations in the judicial view of 'jurisdiction' over the next century, we need speak only of its recent history. We may be witnesses to its ultimate triumph, to the Viking funeral of jurisdiction. In 1952, the Court of Appeal rediscovered its long-lost power to quash decisions for 'error of law on the face of the record.'[34] In effect, this development allowed more extensive review while apparently leaving the notion of jurisdiction unaltered and, arguably, unnecessary. But the same divine winds that revived error of law soon filled the sails of jurisdiction; by 1969, it was launched on what seems in retrospect to have been its final journey. Judicially overladen with what formerly had been regarded as merely banal errors of law,[35] jurisdiction could no longer perform any analytical functions. Now it was fit only to be set alight for a ceremonial voyage, bearing the last remains of administrative autonomy. And so, by 1979, English judges no longer stirred the cold ashes of 'jurisdiction'; their right to review had become virtually unlimited. Attention shifted to a liturgical dispute over whether this unlimited review should be conducted in the idiom of jurisdiction or merely that of legal error.[36]

The story of jurisdiction in Canada is hardly more edifying. As I have recounted elsewhere,[37] the Supreme Court of Canada, in a brief period of ten or fifteen years, moved from virtually unlimited judicial review under the rubric of jurisdiction to virtually no review at all, and back again, without troubling to rationalize its own precedents. Its most recent decision holds out no promise of rationalization at an early date:

[N]othing said in this case can be taken to establish any general principle ... No doubt there will be required on occasion some refinement of the proper limits of jurisdictional review where an administrative tribunal, when responding to questions of fact, must construe and apply its constitutive authority ... Nothing herein determined should be read as bearing on such considerations.[38]

Exit jurisdiction, confusedly.

This is not the context in which to parse precedents or to reconstruct the historic circumstances of leading cases. Whether jurisdiction has ceased to have any functional significance because it was always ill-defined and vague, or because judges ignored its clear limits as they strove to reach desired results, is by the by. It is sufficient that we know that courts are now likely to require compliance with their own law and, at least if they are convinced that egregious legal error exists, are unlikely to respect contractual or statutory restraints on review.

Neither in theory nor in fact, then, is there any assurance that the distinctive norms of administrative law, or of other elements of our pluralistic legal system, will be respected. And since the ordinary courts are able to impose ordinary law on all disputants that come before them, they may effectively disrupt or suppress other special legal systems. In practice, it is true, ordinary courts may never be given the chance to do so; people may choose not to invoke their aid, or may be unable to do so as a practical matter. And when the courts' aid is invoked, they may overtly or tacitly support other systems by finding they are consistent with the law of the courts, or that they should prevail notwithstanding any inconsistency because it was the manifest intention of the parties or the legislature that they should do so. None the less, the last word belongs to the ordinary courts.

The demise of jurisdiction as a mediating principle did not occur only in the formal discourse of post-war English and Canadian courts. Jurisdiction can also be viewed as a metaphor that once revealed some tolerance of pluralism within the legal culture and the legal system. In this metaphorical sense, as we have seen, its decline began in the middle decades of the nineteenth century. By the late decades of the twentieth, the evocative power of the metaphor had clearly waned. Pluralism is no longer what governments expect: in their choice of procedures and personnel they stipulate more and more frequently for legalism. Pluralism is no longer what citizens seem to want: they have taken to demanding legal rights and judicial procedures. And these changing expectations and desires are encouraged today, as they were in the nineteenth century, both by legal professionals and by partisans of every stripe and hue, who see some tactical advantage to their cause in embracing formal legality.

Thus, administrative law, whose relative autonomy we earlier explored, can be seen to flourish only in the cracks and fissures of ordinary law. It remains visible and distinctive not because a viable principle of jurisdiction protects it, not because any theory of pluralism accords it formal constitutional recognition, but only because the practical means do not exist to suppress, transform, or entirely assimilate it to the formal legal system. It follows that if we are to reinforce administrative law and other distinctive systems, we will have to address both the fundamental legal terms of their existence and the institutional arrangements through which those terms are enforced.

What is needed is a principle that recognizes both the constitutional necessity that all parts of the system comply with certain fundamental values, and the practical necessity that those values be expressed in quite different ways. Derived from such a principle would be a rule of comity ensuring mutual respect by each part of the others. Adoption of such a principle would accord pluralism the recognition in the realm of formal law appropriate to its existence in the world of affairs.

The ordinary courts are unlikely to adopt any such principle of their own volition, although there is nothing to prevent them from doing so. After all, in times past common-law judges accepted in principle the autonomy of equity. Today, they are prepared to respect the decisions of competent foreign courts and to give effect to foreign law. But in domestic matters, they now seem firmly wedded to the notion that 'inferior' special courts – especially administrative tribunals – must adhere to the ordinary law of 'superior' courts of general jurisdiction.

If the ordinary courts will not accede voluntarily to legal pluralism, will the 'mediating principle' on which it rests necessarily be lost? Explicit adoption of the principle by constitutional amendment is a second possibility, and is even more unlikely. But a third option is that courts of general jurisdiction will cease to function as self-interested arbiters in the demarcation of the limits between their own concerns and those of other legal regimes. To whom, then, might one apply to stay the king's writ at the boundaries of Alsatia?

The notion that administrative legality should be adjudicated by a special body established for the purpose is not a new one. It is well-accepted in French law,[39] has recently been acted upon in the establishment of the Australian federal Administrative Appeals Tribunal,[40] received grudging recognition in the early 1970s in Canadian legislation creating federal and provincial courts with primary (not exclusive) administrative law functions,[41] and remains a project of some academic commentators in the United Kingdom.[42] The premise of each of these arrangements or projects, occasionally explicit but often not, is that to an extent administrative law must be understood and responded to in its own terms rather than subsumed within a general and undifferentiated notion of law. This premise extends sometimes only to matters of procedure, sometimes to context and subject matter, sometimes to the entire intellectual structure of administrative law. The extent of autonomy and specialization manifest in the reviewing tribunal defines the extent of recognition of the distinctiveness of administrative law. By emphasizing the need for a new structure for review, then, it may be possible to bring about a change in the assumptions of review.

We must now remind ourselves of the reason such a change is necessary. We have explored the close linkages between economic activity or social relationships and special law. The tacit nature of such law, its internal logic, the many distinctive techniques of declaring law and deciding disputes: all these factors serve valid and important social purposes, but they may not be understood or appreciated by reviewing judges of the ordinary courts. If they merely do what they are best suited by training and ideology to do – apply ordinary law – they may be contributing to the destruction of pluralism and of the public policies and private values it institutionally expresses.

And, we must now ask, is pluralism a good in itself, like law, so that its destruction is necessarily undesirable? It is, in a limited way. Like the content of ordinary law, the expressions of pluralism may be humane or oppressive and may succeed or fail in what they seek to achieve. But pluralism itself is desirable, like law, for several reasons.

We have already seen that it performs social tasks for which formal law may be unsuited, both in accommodating and reconciling group interests and in making effective through administrative action public policies that have been democratically determined. However, in so doing, pluralism creates a potential contradiction. On the one hand, the strengthening of private groups helps them to act autonomously, thus promoting the dispersal of power more widely throughout our society. On the other, the growth of administrative law, which pluralism also promotes, helps to concentrate power in the hands of the state. Whether either or both of these tendencies is desirable in particular circumstances depends upon one's ideological preferences. But the two tendencies each represent important strengths in a political democracy. Ironically, it is their convergence rather than their divergence that has attracted criticism, partly jurisprudential, partly political.

First, there is a concern that pluralism undermines the rule of law. This is clearly true in the sense that it helps to legitimate administrative law, which was anathema to Dicey, whose peculiar views of the rule of law have had such influence. But, it is said, in a broader sense pluralism also undercuts the generality and autonomy of the idea of law, upon which depend its appeal to higher order principles of justice and its strength as a bulwark against arbitrary government action.[43] Second, there is a concern that the legitimation of law-making by private groups and administrative bodies promotes corporatism. The strengthening of the state and of interest groups, it is feared, will be accomplished by the sacrifice of individual freedom.[44]

The weight to be accorded to those concerns is difficult to assess. Their most problematic element is that they juxtapose an idealized version of formal law with the worst imaginable version of pluralism. Why not reverse these assumptions? After all, we have seen in our historical evidence lawyers and judges who did not hesitate to subvert the law for personal gain or from class bias, and administrators whose moral presence and humane concerns were exemplary. We have heard of regular courts whose procedures had atrophied, whose costs were bloated, whose capacity to deliver justice or defend liberty had virtually ceased to exist. And alongside these we have glimpsed communal institutions and administrative bodies that offered most Englishmen the only justice they would ever receive.

Perhaps things are different now. Perhaps the daily deeds of Hutton and Mackworth and the arbitrators Ayrton sought to transform into a new species of commercial judge were less worthy of our admiration than those who coined ringing phrases like 'the rule of law.' Perhaps the twentieth-century successors of Hutton and Mackworth and Ayrton have revealed the same human and institutional weaknesses as judges and lawyers of the nineteenth century. Perhaps, therefore, we should turn our backs on the historical evidence we have examined and place our trust in ordinary law as we imagined we had always done. Perhaps not. Perhaps it is preferable, at least pending the perfection of human character, to accept that intelligence and integrity are found with equal frequency among judges and senior administrators. Each may have particular experience or knowledge; each may have access to a particular dispute-settling mechanism; each may command particular loyalties. The most we can hope to do is to use what is 'particular' where it can be most useful.

Yet, paradoxically, even though the particular is indisputably important, it contains the seeds of its own destruction. For example, knowledge of the norms of the state legal system and the ability to use them to solve problems are largely confined to those with legal training, although other highly trained groups, such as the police, may master some part of them. Some informal systems likewise depend upon priests or arbitrators for authoritative exposition of their special norms, although others develop and apply their own law through the active participation and consensus of an entire 'law community.' Administrative law too has a number of specialists who act as decision-makers and advocates, sometimes in competition with each other – trade union officials, lawyers, consultants, accountants, engineers, and tribunal members.

A similar relationship tends to exist, therefore, between knowledge and experts in the various systems. Knowledge becomes complex, sometimes arcane. Ordinary people can seldom deal with it, and it becomes the exclusive property of specialists and professionals. As they become more and more adept in the manipulation of norms, the complexity of those norms increases, and they become even less accessible to ordinary people. Finally, in partial explanation of the failures of administrative law mentioned earlier, an affinity develops among the experts based upon their shared knowledge, regardless of whether they are expected to be decision-makers or advocates.

Ironically, this affinity, which may work against achieving the purposes of the regulatory scheme, may simply be yet another example of what was earlier called imbricated law. Norms of acceptable behaviour may emerge among adversaries who confront each other regularly in negotiations or before a tribunal, and their demeanour toward the tribunal may also come to be defined by patterns of familiar responses to typical situations. What reliance will be placed on technicalities, what face-saving arrangements will be provided for losers, what degree of departure from the norms of the system will be tolerated as inconsequential, and what mitigating circumstances will earn the favourable exercise of discretion? As answers are provided to these questions, norms emerge that may significantly affect substantive outcomes in particular cases, but are likely to be known only to experts or insiders. Indeed, they are unlikely to emerge in the absence of such experts, or if they do, they are unlikely to be available to someone whose involvement in the regulatory regime is limited to a single episode.

This phenomenon is not dependent upon the articulation of a complex body of special law. The characteristic vagueness of many administrative statutes poses a special difficulty for non-expert outsiders. They are unaware of the patterns of administrative activity that provide a basis for predicting future behaviour, and they have no rules to which they can appeal to confound the conspiracy of the experts. Moreover, although imbricated law, by contrast, tends to be specific, with rules implicit in each task or transaction, the outsider is again at a great disadvantage. Because he is an outsider, he is not only ignorant but, by definition, ineligible for instruction or assistance, at least until he becomes a member of the group, perhaps by initiation or apprenticeship.

Thus, to create norms, to win recognition and legitimacy for them, to embed them within a well-designed institutional structure, is not necessarily to ensure that they become law – 'the rules by which persons in society order their conduct.' How to make norms into law in this sense is the secret of good administration. Beside this secret other issues pale into relative insignificance.

What, then, is the future of Alsatia? It is difficult to speak of the prospects for administrative law, or pluralism in general, without becoming platitudinous. But this much seems clear. If administrative law does not serve social purposes that attract widespread support and at least acquiescence from those being regulated, it will not likely be effective. To an extent, therefore, its first task must be to nail its colours to a moral mast, to identify the purposes that justify its own existence. Second, if administrative law cannot define itself affirmatively, if it is only what 'real' law says it is, then it will not achieve any independent legitimacy in the eyes of those who are associated with it as officials or as 'clients.' Third, if administrative law lacks social purpose and legitimacy, it may become (may have already become, in some cases) the chosen occupation of mediocre and indifferent individuals, while those with talent and commitment work in opposition to it. Finally, without purpose, without legitimacy, without talent and zeal, administrative law cannot become effective. If it is not effective, it has no future. It will be at most, in Kipling's phrase, 'such boastings as the Gentiles use, or lesser breeds without the law.'

Notes

1 PARADIGMS OF LAW

1 Gordon 'Historicism in Legal Scholarship'
2 Galanter 'Justice in Many Rooms'
3 Evan 'Public and Private Legal Systems' 166
4 *Law of the Constitution* 188ff
5 Dicey 'Introduction to the Second Edition' *Law and Public Opinion*
6 I have examined Dicey's works and influence at some length in 'Rethinking Administrative Law'; the following comments are developed in greater detail there.
7 See, for example, Pigeon 'Pourquoi un Controle Judiciaire des Organismes Administratifs'; see also *Martineau & Butters* v *Matsqui Institution* (1977) 74 DLR (3d) 1 (SCC) per Pigeon J at 7.
8 See, for example, Denning 'The Rule of Law in the Welfare State' 30ff.
9 See, for example, *Report of the Committee on Administrative Tribunals and Public Inquiries (Franks Report)* and *First Report of the Royal Commission Inquiry into Civil Rights (McRuer Report)*.
10 Wade 'Administrative Tribunals and Administrative Justice'; Taylor 'The Appearance of Justice'
11 See, for example, Foulkes *Introduction to Administrative Law* 6–8; Garner *Administrative Law* 17–19; and Grey 'The Ideology of Administrative Law.'
12 Dicey ultimately conceded that 'it becomes almost inevitable that jurisdiction [to adjudicate] should be given to a department of the Government or to officials,' although he insisted that 'such a transference of authority saps the foundation of [the] rule of law': 'The Development of Administrative Law in England' 150.
13 *Law of the Constitution* 369–72

14 Ibid. 188; Hewart *The New Despotism* 37
15 A good example is *Cooper* v *Wandsworth Board of Works* (1863) 143 ER 414
(CP). In that case, a local authority demolished a house that had been
constructed without giving notice to the authority, which would have
permitted inspection of its sanitary facilities. The court regarded demolition
as a 'punishment' for the failure of notice, and concluded that the authority
ought to have afforded the owner a hearing prior to ordering demolition.
Byles J relied on an early seventeenth-century case, *Dr. Bentley's Case*, in
order to 'establish that, although there are no positive words in a statute
requiring that the party shall be heard, yet the justice of the common law
will supply the omission of the legislature': 143 ER at 40. *Cooper* v
Wandsworth is frequently cited today. As a result, despite enormous changes
in the relationship of courts, parliament, and the executive, in the
appropriate scope of state action, and in the technology of legal
draftsmanship a four-hundred-year-old case lives on.
16 Indeed, the *Franks Report* explicitly sought to assimilate administrative
tribunals to the judicial arm of government rather than the executive arm (at
9).
17 It is true that Henderson *Foundations of English Administrative Law* traces
the development of judicial review back to attempts to control the sewer
commissioners in the seventeenth century. However, by far the most
common invocation of prerogative writs was to review decisions of local
justices.
18 *Crévier* v *A-G Quebec* (1982) 127 DLR (3d) 1 (SCC). It is important to note
that at least two attempts to make such guarantees explicit were rebuffed
during the recent adoption of the Canadian Charter of Rights and Freedoms.
The first was the proposal of the Canadian Bar Association to confer a
specific right to judicial review; the second was a Progressive Conservative
effort to extend constitutional guarantees to the protection of property,
which was explicitly rejected by New Democratic Party spokesmen on the
ground that it would enhance judicial intervention into governmental
regulatory activity: see [1981] 43 Hansard 56, 44 Hansard 27.
19 See, for example, Abel *The Politics of Informal Justice*; Hooker *Legal
Pluralism*; Engel 'Legal Pluralism in an American Community'; and Moore
'Law and Social Change.'
20 See, for example, Evan 'Public and Private Legal Systems'; Abel *The Politics
of Informal Justice; Special Issue on Dispute Processing and Civil Litigation*;
Fitzpatrick 'Law, Plurality and Underdevelopment'; Fuller 'Human
Interaction and the Law'; Kidder 'Toward an Integrated Theory of Imposed
Law'; and Moore *Law as Process.*

21 Friedman 'Law and Social Change' 350
22 Rheinstein *Max Weber on Law in Economy and Society* 301–3
23 Ibid. at 231
24 Friedman 'Legal Culture and Social Development' 43
25 Sugarman has made two particularly important contributions. See 'Legality, Ideology and the State' and 'Theory and Practice in Law and History.'

2   CIVIL JUSTICE IN ENGLAND 1830–1850

1 See appendix 1 'Note on Sources.'
2 Holdsworth *History of English Law* 1: 188
3 Atiyah *The Rise and Fall of Freedom of Contract*
4 Manchester *A Modern Legal History of England and Wales* 111–25 and 150–60 provides a recent and more accurate description. See also Abel-Smith and Stevens *Lawyers and the Courts* 12ff.
5 However, recent scholarship suggests that cases were disposed of with little delay once they were ready for trial: see Danzig *The Capability Problem* 92.
6 Parkes *The State of the Court of Requests* 5. Parkes's experience corroborates the later estimate of Snagge *Evolution of the County Court* 8, to the effect that an action for £20 could not be tried for less than £80.
7 In 1826–8, King's Bench judges awarded £836,343 to plaintiffs, but taxed costs in their favour of £1,205,000 – exclusive of counsel fees: Francis 'The Structure of Judicial Administration' 35 n. 68.
8 Parkes *The State of the Court of Requests* 5
9 Snagge *Evolution of the County Court* 8. If anything, the numbers declined after the enactment of the County Courts Act, 1846. In 1851, for example, it was estimated that only 84,860 cases were commenced in all the superior courts; see Liverpool Chamber of Commerce *Report of the Special Committee on Mercantile Law Reform* 1852, 21. Snagge's evaluation of the relation between the costs of litigation and the amount being sued for also seems accurate. For example, the average amount of verdicts in 'the great commercial and agricultural county of Lancaster' was less than £15; see 'Railway Tribunals' 418.
10 *Fourth Report of the Royal Commission on Practice and Proceedings of the Courts of Common Law* 1831–2 (239) xxv, 104.
11 Holdsworth *History of English Law* 1: chap. 2, and 14: 182
12 Goebel 'King's Law and Local Custom' 417
13 Dawson *A History of Lay Judges* chap. 4
14 Holdsworth *History of English Law* 1: 65
15 This categorization deliberately ignores the various methods by which courts

were originally established or their mandates renewed: custom or prescription; legislation; and franchise, charter, or prerogative grant. There is no consistent pattern. By the eighteenth century, however, legislation was the only method by which new tribunals were created (aside from consensual bodies such as arbitration tribunals). An elaborate taxonomy of 'inferior courts of common law,' 'courts of bankruptcy and insolvency,' 'courts of special or local jurisdiction' 'ecclesiastical and maritime courts,' and courts 'whose jurisdiction had been transferred, abolished or become obsolete,' as well as criminal courts of 'local, private or special jurisdiction' is set out in Maugham *Outlines of the Jurisdiction of all the Courts in England and Wales.*

16 Holdsworth *History of English Law* 1: 109; Archer *The Queen's Courts* 145; Walker *The Courts of Law* 153–5

17 See, for example, *Rules and Orders in the Court of the County of Durham*; Evans *The Practice of the Court of Common Pleas*; Oldnall *The Practice of the Court of Great Sessions.*

18 'Recollections of a Deceased Welch Judge': In my time ... the whole appearance of the Court was different from an English court; the habits of the people, and even their dress, were distinct; and then in most cases the witnesses could not talk English' (46).

19 *First Report of the Royal Commission on Practice and Proceedings of the Courts of Common Law* 1829 (46) IX; An Act for the more effectual Administration of Justice in England and Wales (1830) 11 Geo. IV and 1 Wm. IV, c 70 s 14

20 See, for example, Brougham 'State of the Courts of Common Law' Hansard 18 (1828) 146ff; and *First Report ... on the Courts of Common Law* 38.

21 See, for example, evidence of Messrs Minshall and Sabine, Atty's, favouring suppression of the Welsh courts: '[A] considerable number of Ancient Britons [are opposed] because they do not like to see the ancient institutions of their country changed, and made like English ones': *First Report ... on the Courts of Common Law* appendix E 393.

22 See, for example, evidence of D.S. Davies, Barr. and chairman of Quarter Sessions, County of Cardigan: '[J]ustice is administered cheaply and at the suitors' own doors': *First Report ... on the Courts of Common Law* appendix E 383. The abolition of the Welsh courts in 1830 meant that all claims of over 40s had to be sued for at Westminster, a 'considerable hardship on Welsh suitors': Odgers 'Changes in Procedure and in the Law of Evidence' 231.

23 See, for example, *Minute of the Manchester Chamber of Commerce* 25 June 1834, resolving that the Lancaster Court of Common Pleas was 'remarkable

for its dispatch and economy [and] well-adapted to the exigencies of a mercantile and maritime County,' although endorsing 'assimilation as nearly as circumstances would permit' to the Westminster courts, with which it should enjoy concurrent jurisdiction: Minute Book, Feb. 1833–Dec. 1834 155–6.

24 The Courts Act, Stat. 1971, c 23, s 41

25 Holdsworth *History of English Law* 1: 64; Cross 'The Old English Local Courts'; and see Thompson 'The Development of the Anglo-American Judicial System' 395.

26 Of the 44 local courts in which more than 1,000 claims were instituted in 1830, only 14 were county courts, and only two of the 13 local courts in which more than 5,000 claims were issued were county courts: *Fourth Report ... on the Courts of Common Law* appendix I, part V.

27 9 & 10 Vict. c 95

28 It will be suggested infra that the true antecedents of the new county courts were the courts of requests.

29 These courts were 'inferior courts of record' distinguished from the superior courts primarily by their geographically limited jurisdiction. See Brandon *The Mayor's Court of the City of London*; Moseley *The Law of Inferior Courts* esp. part 2, chap. 5; Cole 'The Ancient Tolzey and Pie Poudre Courts of Bristol'; Peel *Jurisdiction and Practice of the Court of Passage*. For the report of increased activity, see 'Local Courts of Record.' The following figures offer some indication:

	1830	1870
Bristol Tolzey Court	486	349
Liverpool Court of Passage	1,917	2,653
Lord Mayor's Court of London	679	14,944
Hundred of Salford Court of Record		
(includes Court Baron for the Manor of Manchester)	1,654	7,490

(Sources: *Fourth Report ... on the Courts of Common Law* appendix I, part V; Judicial Statistics (1870); *Accounts and Papers, 1871* (chap. 422) LXVII 17ff)

30 Walker *The Courts of Law* states at 158 that the Bristol Tolzey Court was at that time (1970) 'still very much alive,' and that 1,391 writs were issued in the Liverpool Court of Passage in 1968.

31 See, for example, pamphlet addressed to the Working Men of Birmingham entitled 'Injustice, Oppression, and Cruelty,' itemizing serious complaints against the Hundred Court of Hemlingford, the County Court of Warwick,

and the Borough and Corporation Court of Record; and *Report of a Meeting Relative to the Abuses of the Hundred and Borough Courts*. Numerous complaints were also made to the common-law commissioners about specific inferior courts of record, for example, the Peverel Court of Nottinghamshire and Derbyshire: evidence of J.W. Lee, *Fifth Report of the Royal Commission on Practice and Proceedings of the Courts of Common Law* 1833 (247) XXII, appendix A 149A. Legal literature also contained unflattering references to these courts; see, for example, 'Letter to the Editor' (1832): 'It too often happens, in the superior courts, that the costs exceed the importance of the matter litigated; but in the Salford [Hundred] Court that is invariably the case.' See also Brandon *The Mayor's Court of the City of London*.

32 See generally Moseley *The Law of Inferior Courts for the Recovery of Debts* part 2, chap. 4. See, for example, at a later period, *Cox v Mayor of London* (1867), 2 LR E. & I. App. Cas. 239 (HL), where the House of Lords rejected a claim that the Lord Mayor's Court had acquired by custom a power of 'foreign attachment,' or jurisdiction based on the mere presence of the defendant's goods. See Brandon *The Mayor's Court of the City of London*.

33 Municipal Corporations Act (1835) 5 & 6 Wm. IV, c 76, s 118; Better Administration of Justice Act (1836) 6 & 7 Wm. IV, c 105, s 9

34 Municipal Corporations Act, supra, note 33, s 118. The local courts of record were given jurisdiction in cases up to £20 not only in debt but also in trespass to goods and ejectment between landlord and tenant (but not in cases involving title to property).

35 Borough Courts Act (1839) 2 & 3 Vict., c 27, s 1

36 Ibid. s 3

37 Section 14 of the County Courts Act, 1846, supra, note 27, permitted but did not compel the surrender of the right to hold various manor, feudal, and franchise courts; presumably those courts established by statute continued until the statute was repealed.

38 Rheinstein *Max Weber on Law in Economy and Society*, chap. 5

39 Pollock and Maitland *History of English Law* 2d ed. XXX (emphasis added)

40 See ibid. 458–75.

41 Thompson *Whigs and Hunters* at 36ff

42 Lewis *The Stannaries* chap. 4; and Trevithick Society *Laws of the Stannaries of Cornwall*

43 Goebel 'King's Law and Local Custom' remarks: 'So accustomed are we to focus our attention upon the expansion of the "King's law" that we have closed our eyes to the fact that at the outset of the seventeenth century, local custom and local courts were still an immensely important part of the law

administration in England ... [T]he law of England was something greater and more multiform than that of the courts of Westminster' (417). For developments in the eighteenth century, see Webb and Webb *The Manor and the Borough* chaps. 1 and 2.

44 The *Fifth Report ... on the Courts of Common Law* points out that the jurisdiction of the old local courts was based on the assumption that real property rather than commercial wealth was the primary subject of litigation; hence the linkage between local courts and local law (17). While this suggestion was perhaps at one time accurate in relation to manor courts, it was obviously inapplicable to the courts of requests, which dealt only with monetary claims and had no jurisdiction to decide disputes involving title to property.

45 Royal Commission on Assizes and Quarter Sessions, *Report*: '[I]f they were seen to meet some real and important need locally, we did not wish to recommend their abolition without being sure that the system which we proposed would fulfill such need wherever it might exist' (115). But '... [a]s these courts are practically moribund, we leave it to the Government to decide whether formal termination of their existence is worthwhile' (123).

46 Dawson *A History of Lay Judges*

47 Webb and Webb *The Manor and the Borough* suggest that lawyers did appear in some exceptional cases (17).

48 Webb and Webb *The Manor and the Borough* chap. 1 'The Lord's Court,' esp. 18–19

49 One of the most detailed accounts of customary law is contained in a study of its trans-Atlantic migration: see Allen *In English Ways*.

50 Spring *The English Landed Estate* mentions that most estates used a barrister or solicitor as 'agent' (though not necessarily as manorial steward) during the nineteenth century (58–9).

51 Dawson *A History of Lay Judges*

52 Abel-Smith and Stevens *Lawyers and the Courts* 12–13

53 Thompson 'The Grid of Inheritance' 329; and see Perkin *Origins of English Society* 125–7.

54 Brougham 'State of the Courts of Common Law' 171–2

55 See, for example, 'Copyhold Enfranchisement' and 'The Common Law of Kent.'

56 See, for example, Browne *The Law of Usages and Customs* chaps. 2 and 3, and generally Spring 'Landowners, Lawyers and Land Law Reform.'

57 See, for example, XII Court Leet Records of the Manor of Manchester (1832–46), which show the court leet, inter alia, electing municipal officers, inspectors, and constables and providing for their salaries (94ff), requiring

the abatement of nuisances, and amercing butchers for the possession of diseased meat, householders for accumulating night soil, and the owners of several cotton factories for discharging smoke and soot (169ff). (Amercement rendered wrongdoers liable to fine unless the wrongs were abated.) The Court Baron of the Manor of Manchester continued to function throughout the period, hearing mostly tort cases (about 430 claims were brought in 1830): Evidence of S. Kay, Solicitor, *Fifth Report ... on the Courts of Common Law* appendix B at 2.

58 This was a busy court; 11,083 claims were issued in 1830, and approximately 16,000 in 1835 and 1840. About 250 claims were issued on each date sampled in 1830, 1835, and 1840, mostly for goods sold and delivered (67–88 per cent), for money lent, promissory notes, etc. (5–23 per cent), and for rent and lodging (3–8 per cent). However, between 25 and 50 per cent of all claims were made by plaintiffs with multiple claims, more than 20 per cent of which were sometimes issued simultaneously; in 1835 and 1840, about one-third of all multiple claims were for medical attention or for ale and alcoholic beverages: Court Baron of the Manor of Sheffield, Proceedings Books. The court baron was converted de facto into a court of requests but continued to be known by its former names; An Act to Regulate the Proceedings of the Court Baron of the Manor of Sheffield (1808) 48 Geo. III, c 103.

59 Lewis *The Stannaries*; Tregoning *The Laws of the Stannaries*; Wordsworth *Joint Stock Companies* chap. 5; Bainbridge *The Law of Mines and Minerals*; Holdsworth *History of English Law* 1: 151ff

60 The court was reorganized by the Stannaries Act (1836) 6 & 7 Wm. IV, c 106. Upon abolition the business of the stannary court was transferred to the county court by 59 & 60 Vict., c 45. For a description of local support for retention, see *Second Report of the Royal Commission on the Judicature* 1872 (631) XX, vol. 2, part 2, 471ff.

61 In that year a statute (1 & 2 Wm. IV, c 12) authorized the apointment of a commission to ascertain the Boundaries of the Forest of Dean, to explore the rights and privileges claimed by 'the Free Miners of the Hundred of Saint Briavels,' to inquire into 'the Constitution, Powers, Jurisdiction and Practice of a Court called the Mine Law Court,' and to define certain interests in quarries and in the taking of timber.

62 *Fourth Report of the Dean Forest Commissioners* 1835 (610) XXXVI, 10. The customs, and the decline of the old Mine Court that enforced them, are traced in the earlier reports of the commission. See also Nisbet 'History of the Forest of Dean' 455ff; and Hart *The Free Miners* 144ff, 319ff.

63 Hart *The Free Miners* at 319. It must also be recorded that the fate of the

Court of St Briavels was not dissimilar to that of the manor courts of Sheffield and Manchester. In 1830, it was functioning as a local civil court, theoretically of unlimited jurisdiction but in practice limited to claims under £10; it disposed of over 400 ordinary contract cases in that year, albeit in a manner that was criticized by the commissioners, who recommended it be converted into a court of requests: *First Report of the Dean Forest Commissioners*, 1835 (283) XXXVI, 3.

64 Ibid. at 144; Bainbridge, *The Law of Mines and Minerals*; Tapping *Treatise on the High Peak Act* and *Treatise on the Derbyshire Act*

65 See, for example, High Peak Mining Customs and Mineral Courts Act (1851) 14 & 15 Vict., c 94; Derbyshire Mining Customs and Mineral Court Act (1852) 15 & 16 Vict. c 163.

66 Tapping *Treatise on the Derbyshire Act* VI

67 Thompson *Whigs and Hunters*

68 Holdsworth *History of English Law* 1: 94, 99–100

69 Ibid. at 104

70 Thompson *Whigs and Hunters* at 36ff

71 The Wild Creatures and Forest Laws Act, Stat. 1971, c 47, s 1, 'abrogates' forest law, although it preserves any rights of common originating in it.

72 See Hart *Verderers and Speech-Court of the Forest of Dean*, where reference is made to legislation establishing (or confirming) the powers of the verderers: Dean Forest (Encroachments) Act (1844) 7 Vict., c 13; Dean Forest (Amendment) Act (1861) 24 & 25 Vict., c 40. Hart also mentions that the verderers refused to hear lawyers (at 70).

73 Thomspon *Whigs and Hunters*

74 Ibid. at 261

75 Thompson 'The Moral Economy of the English Crowd'; compare Brewer and Styles *An Ungovernable People.*

76 Thompson *The Making of the English Working Class* 64ff

77 Ibid. 73, note 2

78 Ibid. 64

79 Thompson *Whigs and Hunters* 241. Hart *The Free Miners* gives a similar account of the breakdown of customary mining law (319ff).

80 Thompson *Whigs and Hunters* 39–40

81 Dawson *A History of Lay Judges* chap. 5

82 Quoted in Dicey *Law of the Constitution* 186

83 See, for example, Diamond 'The Rule of Law versus the Order of Custom'; Fitzpatrick 'Law, Plurality and Underdevelopment'; and Kidder 'Toward an Integrated Theory of Imposed Law.'

84 Browne *The Law of Usages and Customs*

85 The phrase is borrowed from Nelson *Dispute and Conflict Resolution*
86 Courts of requests: Blackheath (5,146), Liverpool (21,334), Manchester (10,364), City of London (9,678), Tower Hamlets (28,624), Southwark (16,655), Birmingham (7,926), Halifax (22,864), Sheffield (11,518), Bristol (7,495). County courts: Lancashire (7,524), Ossulston (28,251). Court Baron: Pontefract (5,171); *Fourth Report ... on the Courts of Common Law* appendix I, part V. The Sheffield court of requests was 'derivative from the ancient Court Baron of Sheffield': ibid. 306.
87 Ibid. 186; evidence of G. Offor and J.G. Hammuck, *Fifth Report ... on the Courts of Common Law* appendix B, 43
88 A'Beckett 'Objections to the County Courts Bill' 313
89 'Old Local Courts' 122. The development of the courts of requests is traced in Winder 'Courts of Requests' and in Slatter 'Norwich's Lost Court.'
90 Winder 'Courts of Requests' 387.
91 A fairly standard act was the London Court of Requests Act (1800) 39 & 40 Geo. III, c 104.
92 Ibid. s 5. Winder 'Courts of Requests' 375 mentions that such courts as Blackheath, Loughborough, and Hinckly, created in the early 1830s, possessed similar powers. However, the subsequent Exeter Court of Requests Act (1841) 4 & 5 Vict., c 73, s 24, required the court to decide cases 'according to the laws and statutes'.
93 Winder 'Courts of Requests' 375, 381, 388
94 The following seems to represent a consensus on what various parts of the population earned in the 1830s (per week): farm labourers, 10s; navvies, dockworkers, 20s; unskilled factory workers, 18s; skilled factory workers, 20-30s; skilled artisans, 25-30s; clerks and teachers, 20-25s; lower middle class, 60-75s; 'comfortable' middle class, 120s. Sources: Harrison *The Early Victorians* chaps. 2 and 4; Mathias *The First Industrial Nation* chap. 6; Perkin *Origins of English Society* chap. 5; Thompson *The Making of the English Working Class* chaps. 8 and 9.
95 Jones *Before Rebecca* chap. 6; and Williams *The Merthyr Rising* (both recount the antipathy of working people to the court of requests, and the burning during a riot, which ultimately focused on other grievances, of both the court and the home of its clerk). Thompson *The Making of the English Working Class* states that Hutton, author of an early book on courts of requests, was mobbed in Birmingham in 1791 because he 'had earned particular unpopularity' as a commissioner of that court (79-80). However, Thompson also acknowledges that the mob had identified Hutton as sympathetic to the French Revolution. In fact, Hutton purchased his safety by buying 329 gallons of ale at a nearby tavern, and survived to become

known as 'the English Franklin': *Dictionary of National Biography* 10: 362. His work on the court of requests is discussed infra.

96 Evidence of J. Pym, *Fifth Report ... on the Courts of Common Law* appendix A, 109a. The witness stated that of '20,000 heads of families employed in the cotton trade in Manchester ... not 500 of them pay ready money for their household necessaries,' that they pay just enough to preserve their credit and, exhausted by hard work and poor diet, when Saturday comes, 'they fly to the ale-house to recruit their wasted spirits.'

97 Harrison *The Early Victorians* 68–9. Hutton *Courts of Requests* makes the same point much more modestly, pointing out that the giving of credit is made possible by the existence of an easy method of recovery (22) and that part of his court's caseload was indeed 'debts due from the lower class' (25).

98 Supra, note 58

99 See, for example, the evidence of A. Galloway in the *Reports of Minutes of Evidence from the Select Committee on Artisans and Machinery* 1824 (51) v, 28: 'I have been obliged to pay two guineas to a man who was not worth 12s. and such men invariably made me pay at that rate through the court of requests ... for they invariably give verdicts against the employers where no agreement has been; they have always allowed the men to be judges of their own value, if there was no special agreement to the contrary.' Fragmentary records from the Isle of Wight court of requests in the very early 1800s record claims by seamen for wages. I am indebted for these references to Stewart Anderson, Hereford College, Oxford. Hutton *Courts of Requests* mentions several claims for wages and for sick benefits by workmen.

100 I have made a preliminary analysis of the Bristol records and of several other sources in 'Without the Law'.

101 See, for example, Harrison *The Early Victorians* 23–4.

102 'Events of the Quarter' 481

103 Supra, note 58; a similar pattern can be seen in the Bristol court of conscience and requests.

104 Hutton *Courts of Requests* case xxv; confirmed by the Small Debts Act (1845) 8 & 9 Vict., c 127, s 1, and An Act to Regulate Courts for the Recovery of Small Debts (1786) 26 Geo. iii, c 38, ss 1, 2; Bankruptcy Act (1844) 7 & 8 Vict., c 96, s 57.

105 For example, Parkes *The State of the Court of Requests* records the formation of a committee of reform-minded commissioners (judges) of the Birmingham Court of Requests to investigate 'the present inefficient and corrupt state' of the court, including the method of appointing of commissioners and other officials, its administration, cash accounts, fees and jurisdiction, and the state of the debtors' prison (1). But while cataloguing

'the crying evils of this abominable court' (7), Parkes did 'admit, in the most unqualified manner, that the court does accomplish extensive ends of justice, notwithstanding its defects' (2). Even a bitterly hostile 'victim' of the same court was prepared to concede that 'a Court for the speedy recovery of small debts' was necessary: see Jenkinson, untitled pamphlet, 1827. I am obliged to Dr A. Manchester of the University of Birmingham for copies of these pamphlets.

106 *Fifth Report ... on the Courts of Common Law* 5, 6
107 'The County Courts Chronicle' 6
108 Especially the Small Debts Act, 1845, supra, note 104. The state of the art was also enhanced by specific local statutes passed after 1833: see generally Winder 'Courts of Requests' 381ff.
109 D.D. K[eane] 'The Small Debts Act' 194
110 Winder 'Courts of Requests' 375
111 A synopsis of ninety-nine of his cases is found in Hutton *Courts of Requests.*
112 Ibid. VIII
113 Ibid. 198
114 See, for example, case XXXIX, where Hutton distinguishes authority attributed to Lord Mansfield, Lord Loughborough, and Blackstone by showing that the application of the alleged rule in particular circumstances would produce 'an absurdity beneath Lord Mansfield' (198).
115 Evidence of G. Offor and J.G. Hammuck, *Fifth Report ... on the Courts of Common Law* appendix B, 43. This was one of the busiest courts in the county; it disposed of almost 30,000 cases in 1830.
116 For example, the London Court of Requests Act, s 9, allowed infants to be sued for debts contracted for 'necessarys,' and permitted infant servants to sue for their wages.
117 Hutton *Courts of Requests* 120
118 Atiyah *The Rise and Fall of Freedom of Contract*
119 Ferguson 'The Horwitz Thesis' does not directly test Atiyah's thesis. However, his careful longitudinal analysis of English commercial-law judgments detects no obvious trends in the nature of judicial discourse during the nineteenth century.
120 Hutton *Courts of Requests* 6
121 *Fifth Report ... on the Courts of Common Law* 11
122 Hutton's book appears to be the only actual record of the reasons for decision of a court of requests. So far as can be established, reasons were not published in any series of reports. Even newspaper accounts of proceedings and decisions are virtually nonexistent.
123 See, for example, Hutton *Courts of Requests* case LXVIII: 'The vouchers

produced by both [parties] throw some light upon the subject, but our perfect knowledge of your characters throws more' (268–9); case XXV: peremptory dismissal of servant girl held wrongful because of failure to observe custom that one warning would be given (140); case XXX: 'We do right in ordering the payment of a just debt, we do wrong in breaking the act. We shall abide by the consequences, common justice is in our favour' (165).

124 See Hutton *Courts of Requests*. The court of requests tries to 'put a period to the contest by as gentle a decision as the case will bear, to prevent further mischief ... [and] to leave both parties contented' (16).

125 According to Snagge *Evolution of the County Court*, one-third of the writs issued in the superior courts in 1830 were for £20 or less, and one-third for £20–£50; however, a case could not actually be tried at a cost of less than £80–£100 (8).

126 Winder 'Courts of Requests' mentions at 375–6 that commissioners typically were aldermen, mayors, etc. However, in the London court of requests, for example, the commissioners were two aldermen and twenty other inhabitants (with appropriate property qualifications); 39 & 40 Geo. III, c 104, s 2; and see Phillips 'The Black County Magistracy.'

127 'Property, Authority and the Criminal Law' in Hay et al. *Albion's Fatal Tree* 17; see also Webb and Webb *The Parish and the County* 319–64; and Perkin *Origins of English Society* at 40–2.

128 Hay 'Property, Authority and the Criminal Law' at 62

129 Thompson *The Making of the English Working Class* chap. 14

130 See, for example, the description of the magistracy in several industrial communities in the mid-nineteenth century in Perkin *Origins of English Society* at 398–9. Compare Webb and Webb *The Parish and the County* at 575–85.

131 Quoted in Winder 'Courts of Requests' at 370

132 The 'Hackney Map case' involved an allegation that commissioners of the court of requests for Tower Hamlets, elected from Hackney, 'Attended Expressly ... to protect the interests of those who sent them there' against the plaintiff; evidence of Thomas Starling, *Fifth Report ... on the Courts of Common Law* appendix B, 20. The charge seems to have been entirely without substance: evidence of G. Offor and J.G. Hammuck, 42ff.

133 'Injustice, Oppresion, and Cruelty' 1

134 See, for example, 'Letter to the Editor,' proposing that the 'legitimate business' of the Salford Hundred Court (a court of record) 'might be conveniently transacted in a Court of Requests.'

135 See, for example, 'Railway Tribunals.'

136 'Foreword to a Discussion of Current Developments in Administrative Law.'
137 Thompson *Whigs and Hunters* at 261 and *The Grid of Inheritance*. A
striking example was the 'ancient constitution' of the Crowley Iron Works in
the eighteenth century. This private legal code, amended frequently and
administered by a court of arbitration and other internally established bodies,
in effect governed the life of Crowley workers both as employees and as
residents of the Crowley estates. 'The Crowley Kingdom obtained its own
laws as the laws of England gave up trying to control industrial
relationships': Harding *A Social History of English Law* 327. See also
Mathias *The First Industrial Nation* 153–4; and Thompson *The Making of
the English Working Class* chaps. 8 and 9, esp. 328ff.
138 Compare Hart's explanation of the breakdown of the miners' court of St
Briavels: the difficulty of resolving disputes with 'foreigners' with large
capital capable of developing larger workings than were contemplated by
customary law, and the problem of acquiring surface rights for the
installation of new machinery needed for working deep deposits of coal: *The
Free Miners* 319ff.
139 But they did linger in some communities, apparently; see Administration of
Justice Act (1977) c 38, schedule 4, part II.
140 See Hutton *Courts of Requests* case IV, at 85.
141 In Manchester, an atypical case, the Court Leet of the Manor of Manchester
had evolved into a virtual municipal government, until purchased by the
Town Council in 1846 for £200,000. See Webb and Webb *The Manor and
the Borough* 99ff.
142 Even so, Hutton himself was mobbed in 1791, albeit for reasons that are
somewhat obscure: supra, note 95.
143 Hutton *Courts of Requests* 11, 374; supra, note 86
144 Hutton *Courts of Requests* 13. 26 Geo. III, c 38, s 8, established a minimum
property qualification for commissioners of courts of requests of ownership
of real property of an annual value of £20, or of personal property of £500.
145 See generally Briggs *Victorian Cities*.
146 5 & 6 Wm. IV, c 76
147 See Parkes *The State of the Courts of Requests*; see supra, note 100.
148 See Phillips 'The Black Country Magistracy' 166ff, and Foster 'The
Lancashire County Magistracy.'
149 Modern commentators on 'informal justice' and 'delegalization' have
suggested that ruling élites may be willing to stand aside from minor arenas
of dispute-settling in order to focus their influence in areas more directly
pertinent to their own interests and in order to save expense: see, for
example, Santos 'Law and Community' and Abel 'The Contradictions of
Informal Justice.'

150 Hutton *Courts of Requests* 10–11 had already noted this difficulty forty years earlier.
151 Considerable evidence of such a problem in the important centres of Manchester and Liverpool was given to the Commission on Provincial Courts; even the Lancashire county court was some fifty to sixty miles away.
152 Even during the 1830s and 1840s, some forty-nine local statutes were passed to establish or extend the jurisdiction of courts of requests: Winder 'Courts of Requests' 381.
153 Supra, note 61
154 Thompson 'The Grid of Inheritance' 329–31
155 Goebel 'King's Law and Local Custom' 417
156 Indeed, Goebel himself refrains from making such anachronistic judgments: ibid. 420–1.
157 Hutton *Courts of Requests* 9
158 Evidence of James Fenton *Fifth Report ... on the Courts of Common Law* appendix A, 76a.
159 Ibid. 151a
160 Evidence of John Gould Lee, ibid., at 150a
161 Evidence of Thomas Allright, ibid., 81a.
162 Brougham 'State of the Courts of Common Law' 19
163 Snagge *Evolution of the County Court* 10
164 *Fifth Report ... on the Courts of Common Law* 11
165 Supra, note 27
166 *Fifth Report ... on the Courts of Common Law* 12
167 Ibid. 11
168 Ibid.
169 Ibid. 20, 21
170 Atiyah *From Principles to Pragmatism*
171 Hutton *Courts of Requests*
172 'Small Debts Act: A Letter to the Editor.' The author himself feared 'that every case will be determined according to the impulse of the judge and without regard to any established rule of law or equity.'
173 Hutton *Courts of Requests* 13
174 Supra, note 132; *Fifth Report ... on the Courts of Common Law* 12
175 Winder *The State of the Court of Requests* 381
176 But see the Exeter Court of Requests Act, 1841, supra, note 92, s 24, directing the court to decide cases 'according to the laws and statutes.'
177 Supra, note 104, s 72
178 Small Debts Act, 1845, supra, note 104, ss 9, 11
179 Supra, notes 33–6, and see generally Moseley *The Law of Inferior Courts.*
180 For example, the Small Debts Act, 1845, gave legally trained judges of courts

of requests power to secure examination of a judgment debtor on his assets, and to order payment of the debt in instalments, both enforceable by a power of commital (ss 1, 4). Where the court had a legally trained judge, its jurisdiction might be extended geographically in amounts up to £20 and in subject-matter to include all debts and demands, by order-in-council rather than by statute (s 9). In addition, courts were authorized to levy a special 'poundage' fee on claimants to be used to provide courthouses and court offices and for other court expenses (s 17).

181 'Old Local Courts'
182 Winder 'Courts of Requests' 391
183 'Letters to the Lord Chancellor (from A Barrister)' 147
184 Snagge *Evolution of the County Court* 10.
185 However, a county court judge could refer matters to arbitration: 9 & 10 Vict. s 77.
186 Snagge makes the additional point that the efficiency of the new county court promoted out-of-court settlements (14).
187 'Extract of a Letter from Lord Brougham to the Earl of Radnor' 181. See also *Law Mag. & Law Rev.* 16 (1863) 181 at 182.
188 7 *Sol. J.* 7 (1863) 637. See also 'Chambers of Conciliation.' However, one correspondent at least was prepared to embrace conciliation, provided it was undertaken by solicitors and attorneys rather than judges: 'such courts would increase professional business to a considerable extent': 'Letter' *Sol. J. & Rep.* 7 (1863) 662.
189 Hutton *Courts of Requests* at 35–6 states that attorneys were used in Birmingham, but never counsel, although barristers did have a right of audience. In Bristol, they were allowed only when a party was 'infirm or incapacitated, or unable from some sufficient cause' to attend personally: evidence of the board of directors of the Chamber of Commerce, Bristol, *Fifth Report ... on the Courts of Common Law* appendix A, 100a.
190 For example, only six attorneys were licensed to practise in the Palace Court, a fairly busy court in which fifteen writs were issued and four cases tried, on average, each week: evidence of B.E. Willoughby, ibid. appendix B, 5.
191 Keane 'The Small Debts Act' 242; evidence of Sir John Cross, *Fifth Report ... on the Courts of Common Law* appendix B, 11. However, the former exclusion of lawyers may have been a relatively late development; it occurred in the very busy Tower Hamlets court of requests only in 1832: see evidence of George Offor and J.G. Hammuck, ibid. 43.
192 Evidence of J.W. Lee, ibid., appendix A, at 149a; 'Local Courts' 1845–6.
193 'Local Courts' 1846. Not all those who advocated legal representation were similarly motivated. One witness appearing before the Commission on

Provincial Courts urged that the 'Government appoint an attorney with a salary in each Court, to assist the very poor who cannot defend themselves': evidence of W. Beale, *Fifth Report ... on the Courts of Common Law* appendix A, at 82a.

194 County Courts Act, 1846, supra, note 27, s 91; Keane 'The Small Debts Act' 255

195 Snagge *Evolution of the County Court* 23

196 Lawyers were permitted to appear in proceedings involving over 40s, and their fees were limited to 10s in any action under £5, and to 15s in other cases. Party-and-party costs were taxable only where more than £5 was recovered: Keane 'The Small Debts Act' 241-2; County Courts Act, 1846, supra, note 27, s 91.

197 'County Courts' (1847) 1. Compare Keane 'The Small Debts Act': 'The legal profession, in all its sections, will sustain a large diminution of emoluments ...' (255). And see 'The Prospects of the Bar.'

198 County Courts Extension Act (1850) 13 & 14 Vict. c 61, s 6

199 A'Beckett 'Objections to the County Court Bill' 332. Compare 'Letters to the Lord Chancellor' 146-7.

200 'Letters to the Lord Chancellor'

201 'The Judgeships of the Courts of Requests'

202 'County Courts' (1847) 3

203 'Revival of the Law Courts'; Compare 'The Prospects of the Bar.'

204 I have read all of the published decisions of the superior courts for 1830. This source of information is subject to two obvious weaknesses. First, it is not clear that all cases decided by those courts in 1830 would have been reported, especially those confined to factual issues that collaterally involved issues also triable in the local or special courts. Second, the activity of the superior courts is contrasted with that of other courts for the same year. Actual review of 1830 local court decisions would require scrutiny of superior court decisions in later years; in view of the uncertain time delays (especially where collateral review is involved) this exercise was not undertaken. However, since what is being assessed is the relative order of magnitude of original and review decisions, it is unlikely that these two weaknesses produce any serious distortion.

205 Common rights: *Codling* v *Johnson* (1830) 8 LJOS 68 (KB); *Doe d. Sweeting* v *Wellard & Griffiths* (1830) 8 LJOS 79 (KB); *Maxwell* v *Martin* (1830) 8 LJOS 174 (CP); disputes involving tithes, access to chapel, etc.: *Maddison* v *Nuttall* (1830) 8 LJ Rep. 27 (CP); *Shepherd* v *Bishop of Chester* (1830), 8 LJOS 141 (CP); *Lediard* v *Anstie* (1830) 148 ER 1297 (Exch. Ch. in Eq.); *Beck* v *Bree* (1830) 148 ER 1410 (Exch. of Pleas); *Denchfield* v *Strong* (1830) 5 ER 48 (HL);

use of customary weights and measures: *Watts* v *Friend* (1830) 8 LJOS 181 (KB); liability to market toll: *Stamford* v *Pawlett* (1830) 148 ER 1334 (Exch. of Pleas)

206 *Bingham* v *Woodgate* (1830) 8 LJOS 46 (Ch.)

207 *Richards* v *Bassett* (1830) 8 LJOS 289 (KB)

208 *King* v *Scriveners' Company* (1830) 8 LJOS 199 (KB)

209 *King* v *Wilson* (1830) 8 LJOS 101 (KB)

210 *In Matter of Sutton* (1830) 8 LJOS 7 (KB), and *Davis* v *Jones* (1830) 8 LJOS 88 (KB)

211 *Wright* v *Nuttall* (1830) 8 LJOS 188 (KB); *Smith* v *Hurrell* (1830) 8 LJOS 198 (KB); *Copland* v *Jacobs* (1830) 8 LJOS 321 (KB); *Rothery* v *Munnings* (1830) 8 LJOS 386 (KB); *Harris* v *Widdowson* (1830) 8 LJOS 122 (CP); but compare *Andrews* v *Phillips* (1830) 8 LJOS 122 (CP).

212 *Hall* v *Tayler* (1830) 8 LJOS 180 (KB); *Furnish* v *Swan* (1830) 8 LJOS 224 (KB); *Clarke* v *Denton* (1830) 8 LJOS 333 (KB); *Godley* v *Marsden* (1830) 8 LJOS 138 (CP)

213 See, for example, London Court of Requests Act, 1800, s 12; and see note 211.

214 London Court of Requests Act, 1800, s 5; compare Cirencester Court of Requests Act (1792) 32 Geo. III, c 77, s 29: 'No proceeding [in the court of requests] shall or may be removed into any Superior Court, but ... judgments, decrees and proceedings of the said court, shall be final and conclusive to all intents and purposes.'

215 Keane *Courts of Requests* asserts that prohibition lay for 'some act done in some cause dependent in an inferior court, either contrary to the general law of the land, or manifestly out of the jurisdiction of such court' where the jurisdictional error appeared on the face of the proceedings (114–15). However, he cites no cases of review on the merits of decisions of courts of requests, even where the error alleged was an error of law.

216 See, for example, evidence of Sir John Cross, *Fifth Report ... on the Courts of Common Law* appendix B, 11.

217 Supra, note 104 s 21

218 Keane 'The Small Debts Act' 240. This was accomplished by s 3, making the new county courts courts of record.

219 See, for example, 'County Courts' 2. However, as a court of record, the county court was subject to the inherent reviewing jurisdiction of the superior courts, somewhat modified by ss 90 and 108.

220 County Courts Extension Act, 1850, supra, note 198, ss 14–6; appeals were made available 'in point of law or upon the admission or rejection of any evidence'; recourse to prerogative writ review was precluded.

221 This is a slight exaggeration. The County Courts Act, 1846, supra, note 27, ss 5 and 14, permitted the survival of some old local courts, the last of which were only brought within the county court system or abolished in the 1970s by the Courts Act (1971) c 23, ss 41, 42, and 43 and the Administration of Justice Act (1977) c 38, s 23.
222 'County Courts'; 'The Law and the Lawyers'
223 Danzig *The Capability Problem*
224 Jackson *The Machinery of Justice in England* 351
225 'Tribunals of Commerce' 1040
226 Sir Richard Bethell, quoted in 'The Juridical Society'
227 'The National Association for the Promotion of Social Science' at 168
228 *Second Report ... on the Judicature* 18–19
229 *Law of the Constitution* chap. 4
230 Judicature Act (1873) 36 & 37 Vict., c 66
231 Rheinstein *Max Weber on Law and Economy* 352
232 For example, the anomalous retention of the Liverpool Court of Passage and the Lord Mayor's Court of the City of London, down to modern times: see supra, note 221.
233 The 'owners of property and principal inhabitants' of Wales – 'many of them non-residents, connected with iron works,' according to a Welsh MP – favoured abolition of the Welsh judicature. See evidence of the Magistrates of the County of Glamorganshire, and of John Jones, MP, contra, *First Report ... on the Courts of Common Law* appendix E 386, 391. With an astonishing lack fo self-consciousness, a local barrister and landowner testified: 'I effected by my own endeavours ... important improvements in Trythin, where Welsh was then almost the only language understood by ordinary farmers ... I indicted the inhabitants for not repairing the roads .... A few English tenants were introduced ... extensive mines of coals and iron were worked with advantage to the proprietors and owners ... The district is now more populous and prosperous, and there is scarcely a Welshman around who does not speak English': Evidence of John Denton, Barrister, appendix E, 460–1.

3   COMMERCIAL RELATIONSHIPS

1 Holdsworth *History of English Law* 14: 182 et seq.
2 Landes 'The Structure of Enterprise'
3 Ferguson 'Legal Ideology and Commercial Interests'
4 See generally ibid. 187–96; Murray 'Arbitration in the Anglo-Saxon and Early Norman Periods'; Holdsworth *History of English Law* 14: 187ff;

Parker *History and Development of Commercial Arbitration*; Wolaver 'Historical Background of Commercial Arbitration'; Sayre 'Development of Commercial Arbitration Law.'

5 For an insightful review of the current literature on the relationship between law and the economy, see Sugarman 'Theory and Practice in Law and History.' A classic account is found in Rheinstein *Max Weber on Law in Economy and Society* chap. 5.

6 Holdsworth *History of English Law* 1: 526 et seq. and vol. 5: 102 et seq.

7 For the text of one collection of rules of the law merchant see Teetor 'England's Earliest Treatise on the Law Merchant.'

8 Holdsworth *History of English Law* 1: 569

9 In fact the courts of piepoudre, courts of the staple, and courts of the clerks of the markets were only formally abolished by the Administration of Justice Act, 1977, c 38, s 23(1), schedule 4, part I. The Tolzey Court of Bristol and the Bristol Court of Pie Powder, discussed as being 'still very much alive' in 1970 (see Walker *The Courts of Law* 158) were abolished by the Courts Act, 1971, c 23, s 43(1).

10 See generally Sanborn *Origins of English Maritime and Commercial Law* 325 et seq.; Holdsworth *History of English Law* 5: 102 et seq. and 8: 99 et seq.; and Sutherland 'The Law Merchant in England.'

11 Holdsworth *History of English Law* 5: 136

12 Ibid. 137–40

13 Ibid. 140–3. However, even in the seventeenth century 'the bulk of mercantile legal business was still carried on by customary arbitration without any legal sanction': Sutherland 'The Law Merchant in England' 164.

14 Holdsworth *History of English Law* 5: 143–8; Parker *History and Development of Commercial Arbitration* 10; Macassey 'International Commercial Arbitration' 519; Burdick 'Contributions of the Law Merchant' 44

15 See, for example, Sale of Goods Act (1893) 56 & 57 Vict., c 71; Bills of Exchange Act (1882) 45 & 46 Vict., c 61, consolidating (1878) 41 & 42 Vict., c 13, (1855) 18 & 19 Vict., c 67; Factors Act (1889) 52 & 53 Vict., c 45, consolidating (1877) 40 & 41 Vict., c 39, (1842) 5 & 6 Vict., c 39, (1825) 6 Geo. IV., c 94, (1823) 4 Geo. IV., c 83. The American literature suggests that during the nineteenth century private practitioners 'invented' a number of devices that facilitated credit transactions and the emergence of sophisticated corporate organization. See, for example, Hurst *The Growth of American Law* 333 et seq. In England (where little major research into the activities of nineteenth-century lawyers appears to have been undertaken until recently), solicitors seem to have been relatively less active, sharing responsibility for commercial 'invention' with banks and accountants, inter alia. See Abel-

Smith and Stevens, *Lawyers and the Courts* 58; and compare Spring *The English Landed Estate* chap. 3. However, this view may underestimate the inventive contribution of English lawyers and judges in the commercial area; see Sugarman 'Capitalism and Company Law' and Duman *The English and Colonial Bars*.

16 Holdsworth *History of English Law* 12: 464 et seq., esp. 526-8; and see MacKinnon 'Origins of Commercial Law' 40.

17 Danzig *The Capability Problem* 94-5

18 Ferguson 'Adjudication of Commercial Disputes' 144-5

19 'Railway Tribunals' 418. It was also estimated that 'at no sittings, even in Guildhall, are there more than three or four cases with more than £1000 in dispute.'

20 '[Mercantile Law] is a system of sudden and comparatively modern growth, having been begun, matured and perfected within the limits of the last half-century': 'Mercantile Law' 48.

21 Ibid. 47

22 'The Principles and Law of Banking' 84-5

23 Liverpool Chamber of Commerce *Report of the Special Committee on Mercantile Law Reform* 15

24 'Tribunals of Commerce – Natural Procedure' (1851-2) 96

25 Ilersic and Liddle *Parliament of Commerce* 83

26 Liverpool Chamber of Commerce *Report of the Special Committee on Mercantile Law Reform*

27 Bristol Chamber of Commerce *Printed Minutes* 1866-71 (1866) 9; Beresford *The Leeds Chamber of Commerce* 46-7; 'Legal Topics of the Week 517, and 'Mercantile Tribunals' 524-5; *Proceedings of the Manchester Chamber of Commerce 1849-1858* (1852) 242; (1854) 374; Manchester Commercial Association *Minutes of the Board of Directors 1845-58*, 13 Mar. 1857 (ms); and *Proceedings of the Manchester Chamber of Commerce 1858-1867* (1858?) 639-40, 705-12

28 Ilersic and Liddle *Parliament of Commerce* 84

29 'A Tribunal of Commerce' 477

30 'Report of the Society for Promoting the Amendment of the Law' 107-8; and see 'Tribunals of Commerce' 1857-8 and 1864-5.

31 Mr Fox Turner (apparently a solicitor) in *Proceedings of the Manchester Chamber of Commerce 1858-67* 706, 710

32 *Report from the Select Committee on Tribunals of Commerce* 1858 (413) XVI; *Report from the Select Committee on Tribunals of Commerce* 1871 (409) XII

33 *Third Report of the Royal Commission on the Judicature* 1874 (957) XXIV, 8

34 Ibid. 7

35 *First Report of the Royal Commission on the Judicature* 1868-9 (4130) xxv

36 Evidence, *Third Report ... on the Judicature* appendix, 2-6

37 For example, Liverpool Corn Trade, ibid. 2-3; Liverpool General Brokers' Association, ibid. 3-4; Stock Exchange, ibid. 5-6

38 Ibid. 8-12, 28-33

39 For example, Baron Bramwell reluctantly favoured a tribunal that would have jurisdiction only with the consent of the parties, and that would be established only on an experimental basis in London, despite the fact that 'advocates of such Tribunals are ... in a minority of numbers, and ... the weight of reasoning and of authority is against them': ibid. 106. And see 'A Judge on Tribunals of Commerce' 1. However, he concurred in the *Report* as a commissioner, although his proposal was rejected.

40 *Third Report ... on the Judicature* 8

41 *First Report ... on the Judicature* 13

42 Colman *Matthew's Practice of the Commercial Court* 5

43 Separate reasons, *Second Report of the Royal Commission on the Judicature* 1872 (631) xx, 23-4. A lawyer, Liberal MP, and first commissioner of works and public buildings, Acton S. Ayrton was a member of the parliamentary committees of 1858 and 1871; the latter recommended the establishment of tribunals of commerce.

44 *Third Report ... on the Judicature* 10

45 Ibid. 11

46 Ibid. Lord Penzance, dissenting, 11

47 Ibid. Acton S. Ayrton, 10; see also Sir Sydney Waterlow to the same effect, 11.

48 This device was belatedly adopted for the Admiralty Division by the Judicature Amendment Act (1891) 54 & 55 Vict., c 53, s 3, and for the whole of the Supreme Court by the Supreme Court of Judicature (Consolidation) Act (1925) 15 & 16 Geo. v, c 49, s 98(1).

49 Ilersic and Liddle refer to a bill introduced in 1877: *Parliament of Commerce* 85; and see (1881) 71 LT 358, and (1889-90) 88 LT 377, 393.

50 The triggering event has been variously identified as a particularly horrendous judicial performance by Mr Justice Lawrance (described in F.D. MacKinnon 'The Origin of the Commercial Court' or a letter to *The Times* (London) by a judge drawing attention to the fact that the courts seldom heard commercial cases, and that businessmen preferred arbitration, with all its defects, to litigation (see Colman *Matthew's Practice of the Commercial Court* 5-6).

51 Colman *Matthew's Practice of the Commercial Court* 6-8

52 Ibid. 7 et seq.
53 Ibid. chaps. 3 and 7–13, and appendix C
54 Parker *History and Development of Commercial Arbitration* 23
55 H.G.M. 'The Commercial Court and Arbitration'
56 Colman *Matthew's Practice of the Commercial Court* 22, 23
57 Macassey 'International Commercial Arbitration' 518
58 Wolaver 'Historical Background of Commercial Arbitration' 137–8
59 Parker *History and Development of Commercial Arbitration* 9
60 Arbitration under compulsion of statute was known early in the nineteenth century, and became especially common in the 1840s. It is dealt with in chap. 4, infra.
61 Abel-Smith and Stevens *Lawyers and the Courts* suggest that by mid-century the obvious preference of the 'agricultural, mechanical and trading classes' for arbitration amounted to a 'revolt of the whole nation against the constitutional administrators of the law' (39). However, the quoted language is found in an article in (1844) 3 LT 211 describing a boycott of the Irish courts organized by the 'Loyal National Repeal Association' in protest against certain British proposals for self-government. The statistics are impressive – arbitration tribunals were established in 104 localities; returns from 33 of them show that 1,345 cases were decided in two months, and in only twelve cases were awards not obeyed – but they describe only a very specific situation.
62 For example, Crump 'The Leeds Woollen Industry' examines the papers of several leading manufacturers and mentions disputes and litigation, but makes no reference to arbitration; Marriner *Rathbones of Liverpool 1845–73* mentions that disputes with overseas agents might be submitted 'to some indifferent person such as a mutual friend,' but in context suggests that this was a relatively rare event; scores of other business histories and records were searched, and no mention of litigation or arbitration – or even unresolved disputes – was found (64).
63 See appendix 1, 'Notes on Primary Sources,' arbitration and domestic adjudication.
64 Thompson *Whigs and Hunters* 261
65 Ferguson 'Adjudication of Commercial Disputes' 148–50
66 For an insightful analysis see ibid., and by the same author 'Commercial Dispute Settlement.'
67 Bowden *Industrial Society in England* 164ff; Checkland *The Rise of Industrial Society* 106; and see chapter 4 infra, 'Self-regulation by domestic tribunals.'
68 *Third Report … on the Judicature* appendix, at 2

69 Ibid. 118
70 Supra, note 61
71 Liverpool Chamber of Commerce *Report of the Special Committee on Mercantile Law Reform* 22ff. The same reports states that the chambers of Glasgow, Hull, and Belfast, like that of Liverpool, 'are all uniform in their testimony of the rarity of the calls for the exercise of this function' (22).
72 Ibid. 22, 25
73 For example, the chambers of commerce of Birmingham (*Half-yearly Report*, 25 Jan. 1866, *Birmingham Chamber of Commerce Reports 1865–87*), Bristol (Bristol Chamber of Commerce *Printed Minutes* 1858, 42) and Leeds (Beresford *The Leeds Chamber of Commerce* 49)
74 See, for example, 'Tribunals of Arbitration' (Manchester): Manson 'London Chamber of Arbitration'; and Murray 'Commercial Arbitration' (London).
75 'Arbitration Court of Wakefield Law Society'
76 Manson 'London Chamber of Arbitration'
77 Much of the statutory history in this section was taken from a memorandum prepared for Mr Justice Michael Mustill of the English High Court by Mark Hapgood, in June 1979. Mr Justice Mustill kindly provided me with a copy of that memorandum, and I am indebted to him and to Mr Hapgood.
78 Arbitration Act (1698) 9 & 10 Wm. III, c 15
79 See, for example, Watson *The Law of Arbitration and Awards* 2.
80 *Second Report of the Royal Commission on the Practice and Proceedings of the Courts of Common Law* 1830 (123) XI, 25–7
81 Common Law Procedure Act (1854) 17 & 18 Vict., c 125, ss 3, 6
82 Law Amendment Act (1833) 3 & 4 Wm. IV, c 42, ss 39–41
83 Common Law Procedure Act, 1854, supra, note 81, s 17. The County Courts Act (1846) 9 & 10 Vict., c 95, s 77, enabled judges to remit disputes to arbitration, the award being 'binding and effectual to all intents as if given by the judge.' Compulsory refernce powers were given to the superior courts only by the Judicature Act (1873) 36 & 37 Vict., c 66, ss 56–9.
84 Common Law Procedure Act, 1854, supra, note 81, s 11
85 Ibid. ss 12–14
86 'The Laws of Arbitration'
87 'Juries versus Arbitrators' 43
88 'Arbitration and Compromise' and 'Arbitration' 176
89 'Local Courts of Record' 223
90 'Arbitration and Compromise' 260
91 Holdsworth *History of English Law* 5: 130, 136, 139, 152
92 Ibid. 14: 187 *et seq.*; and compare Parker *History and Development of Commercial Arbitration* 12ff.
93 (1609) 77 ER 595 (CP)

94 Taeusch 'Extrajudicial Settlement of Controversies' at 152; Cohen *Commercial Arbitration and the Law* chaps. 8–11
95 Wolaver 'Historical Background of Commercial Arbitration' 139; Sayre 'Development of Commercial Arbitration Law' 603
96 Holdsworth *History of English Law* 14: 182–3. Holdsworth also describes the attack by Coke and the common-law judges on the jurisdiction of the Admiralty court as 'unscrupulous': see vol. 1, 558.
97 *Dr. Bonham's Case* (1609) 77 ER 638, 646 (CP), and see Plucknett 'Bonham's Case and Judicial Review.'
98 *History and Development of Commercial Arbitration* 15
99 Ibid. 13
100 Horwitz *Transformation of American Law* 154–5
101 Views on this point differ. See supra, note 15.
102 See, for example, Aiken 'New Netherlands Arbitration'; and Jones 'Three Centuries of Commercial Arbitration.'
103 Jones 'Historical Development of Commercial Arbitration'; and Mentschikoff 'Commercial Arbitration' 854 et seq. Horwitz *Transformation of American Law* states that by the late 1830s 'an increasingly self-conscious legal profession had succeeded in suffocating alternative forms of dispute settlement' (154). See also Harrington 'Delegalization Reform Movements.
104 Wolaver 'Historical Background of Commercial Arbitration' 144
105 Ferguson 'Adjudication of Commercial Disputes' 150, n 48, citing O. Prausnitz 'The Standardization of Commercial Contracts in English and Continental Law' (1937)
106 Ibid. 145.
107 Common Law Procedure Act, 1854, supra, note 81, s 17
108 Watson *The Law of Arbitration and Awards* 154
109 Supra, note 78, s 2
110 Parker *The History and Development of Commercial Arbitration* 15, 18
111 Russell *The Power and Duty of an Arbitrator* 1st ed. 113–5, 7th ed. 119–20: '[D]isregarding special exceptions, there is abundant authority for laying down a general rule that an arbitrator, like every other judge, is bound by the rules of law, and that it is beyond his authority to award anything contrary to law ... although a mere mistake in law ... is rarely fatal to the award ... It has been said by judges of great celebrity that under a general reference of all matters in difference the arbitrator is not confined within the rules of law and equity, that he has greater latitude than the courts of law in order to do complete justice between the parties, and that he may take all moral questions into consideration in forming his judgment.' See also 1st ed. 629, 7th ed. 652. Russell's ambivalence persisted even after the enactment of the Arbitration Act, 1889.

112 The *Annual Practice 1883-4* states: 'An award which is good on the face of it, will not be sent back to the arbitrator on the ground that he has made a mistake of law, unless he admits the mistake' (82). For cases (both purely consensual and under judicial auspices) where the court refused to set aside an award for mistake of law, see *Ching* v *Ching* (1801) 31 ER 1052 (Ch.); *Chace* v *Westmore* (1811) 104 ER 408 (KB); *Wohlenberg* v *Lageman* (1815) 128 ER 1031 (CP); *Steff* v *Andrews* (1816) 56 ER 237 (Ch.); *Richardson* v *Nourse & Christian* (1819) 106 ER 648 (KB); *Goodman* v *Sayers* (1820) 22 RR 112 (Ch.); *Price* v *Jones* (1828) 148 ER 855 (Ex.); *Henty* v *Rally* (1841) 4 Jur. 1091 (Ex.); *Hagger* v *Baker* (1845) 153 ER 367 (Ex.); *Saunders* v *Damer* (1850) 16 LT 153 (Ex.); *Re Simpson & Hornsby* (1868) 17 LTR 17 (Bail Ct); *Kirk & Randall* v *East and West India Dock Co.* (1886) 55 LTR 245 (CA); unless illegality (or miscalculation) is clear on the face of the award: *Cramp* v *Symons* (1882) 130 ER 43 (CP); *In re Hall* (1841) 10 LJCP 210 (CP); *Hutchinson* v *Shepperton* (1849) 13 QB 955 (KB).

113 *Mason* v *Wallis* (1829) 8 LJOS 109 (KB); *Leggett* v *Finlay* (1829) 8 LJOS 52 (CP)

114 *Middleton* v *Frost,* (1830) 8 LJOS 249 (KB); *Hayllar* v *Ellis,* (1829) 8 LJOS 1 (CP); *Ashworth* v *Heathcote* (1830) 8 LJ 206 (CP)

115 *Tucker* v *Chelsea Water Works* (1830) 8 LJOS 195 (KB)

116 *Skee* v *Coxon* (1830) 8 LJOS 224 (KB); *Green* v *Pole* (1830) 8 LJOS 149 (CP)

117 *Chichester* v *M'Intire* (1830) 5 ER 28 (HL)

118 *The Law of Arbitration and Awards* 161-9

119 *Little, Roberts & Mitchell* v *Newton* (1840) 133 ER 627 (CP); *Ex p. Michie* (1840) 9 LJ (NS) 23 (Bkrptcy)

120 *De Rossi* v *Polhill* (1840) 9 LJ (NS) 334 (CP); *Lambert & Curling* v *Hutchinson* (1841) 133 ER 991 (CP)

121 *Taylor* v *Shuttleworth* (1840) 9 LJ (NS) 138 (CP); *Wood* v *Hotham* (1839) 9 LJ (NS) 3 (Ex. of Pleas); *Wilson* v *Thorpe* (1840) 9 LJ (NS) 232 (Ex. of Pleas); *Bird* v *Penrice* (1840) 9 LJ (NS) 257 (Ex. of Pleas); *Brooke* v *Mitchell* (1840) 9 LJ (NS) 269 (Ex. of Pleas); *Hill et al.* v *White et al.* (1839) 133 ER 9, 10 (CP) (2 cases); *Brown* v *Watson* (1839) 133 ER 46 (CP); *In matter of Hare, Milne & Haswell* (1839) 133 ER 62 (CP): *Hobdell* v *Miller* (1840) 133 ER 115 (CP); *Bignall* v *Gale* (1841) 133 ER 786, 980 (CP); *Arbitration of Cockburn* v *Newton* (1841) 133 ER 1007 (CP); *Wynn* v *Wynn* (1841) 133 ER 642 (CP); *Hawksworth* v *Bramall* (1840) 41 ER 377 (Ch.); *Hobbs* v *Ferrars* (1840) 4 Jurist 825 (Ex.); *Henty* v *Rally* (1840) 4 Jurist 1091 (Ex.).

122 *Fisher* v *Pyne* (1840) 133 ER 334 (CP).

123 *Seecombe* v *Babb* (1840) 9 LJ (NS) 65 (Ex. of Pleas); *Arbitration of Salkeld, Slater & Harrison, assignees of Stringer* (1840) 113 ER 1005 (QB); *France & Hill* v *White & Williams* (1839) 133 ER 13 (CP); *Waller* v *Lacy* (1840) 133 ER

245 (CP); *Arbitration of Hall and Hinds* (1841) 133 ER 987 (CP); *Fenton v Dimes* (1840) 9 LJ (NS) 297 (QB).

124 'The Law of Arbitration' (1849)

125 Liverpool Chamber of Commerce *Report of the Special Committee on Mercantile Law Reform* 23

126 Supra, note 81

127 Arbitration supported on procedural grounds: *Reference betw. Marsack & Webber* (1860) 29 LJ (NS) 109 (QB); *Whaley v Laing* (1860) 29 LJ (NS) 313 (Ex.); *Rogers v Kearns* (1860) 29 LJ (NS) 328 (Ex.); *Lipscomb v Palmer* (1860) 3 LT (NS) 265 (Ch.); *Dodd v Platt* (1859) 6 Jurist (NS) 631 (CP); arbitration successfully attacked on procedural grounds: *Reference betw. European & American Steam-Shipping Co. & Croskey & Co.* (1860) 29 LJ (NS) 155 (CP); *Horton v Sayer* (1859) 29 LJ (NS) 28 (Ex.); *Carter v Burial Board of Tonge* (1860) 29 LJ (NS) 293 (Ex.); *Crookey v European & American Steam-Shipping Co.* (1860) 2 LT (NS) 566 (Ch.)

128 *Proctor v Williamson* (1860) 29 LJ (NS) 157 (CP); *Hawkins v Rigby* (1860) 29 LJ (NS) 278 (CP); *Whitmore v Smith* (1860) 29 LJ (NS) 402 (Ex.); *Thompson v Bowyer* (1860) 3 LT (NS) 276 (CP); *Wigans v Cook* (1860) 6 Jurist (NS) 72 (CP)

129 *Jones v Jones* (1860) 29 LJ (NS) 151 (CP); *Ex parte Wyld* (1860) 3 LT (NS) 794 (Ch.); *Bennett v Watson* (1860) 29 LJ (NS) 357 (Ex.)

130 The reports for 1830, 1840, and 1860 do not cover identical periods, and we have no indication of unreported cases.

131 The information available is too scant and sketchy to permit meaningful distinctions to be drawn among the three types of arbitration identified earlier. However, there seems to be no litigation in these particular years originating in the domestic adjudication systems of exchanges or similar milieux; a significant number of cases apparently originated in arbitration conducted under judicial auspices.

132 The County Courts Act, s 77, supra, note 83, simplified this procedure by empowering a judge 'if he thinks fit' to 'set aside any such award' made on a compulsory reference by him to an arbitrator.

133 5 & 6 Wm. IV, c 76, 5 & 6 Vict., c 98; the growth of statutory arbitration is described in the next chapter.

134 7 & 8 Vict., c 93

135 See, for example, Russell *The Power and Duty of an Arbitrator* 1st ed.

136 Section 5: 'It shall be lawful for the arbitrator … if he shall think fit, and if it is not provided to the contrary, to state his award … in the form of a special case for the opinion of the court.'

137 52 & 53 Vict., c 49, s 19. The Rules of the Supreme Court, 1883 (as amended), order LIX, rule 3, also provided that 'where a compulsory

reference to arbitration has been ordered, any party to such reference may appeal from the award or certificate of the arbitrator or referee upon any question of law ...' (quoted in Russell *The Power and Duty of an Arbitrator* 7th ed., 801). Cohn *'Commercial Arbitration and the Rule of Law'* observes that no evidence in the legislative history of the Arbitration Act, 1889, suggests a deliberate intention existed to require arbitrators to decide cases according to law, although this was the result of the legislation (19). Lord Bramwell's original bill, introduced in 1884 on behalf of the London Chamber of Commerce, retained the permissive language of the 1854 statute, which enabled but did not compel an arbitrator to state a case; see 'The Law of Arbitrations' (1884) 'The Arbitration Bill' (1884). This bill was ultimately withdrawn in favour of another which became the act of 1889 (335 Hansard 1219, 6 May 1889), but the debates provide no explanation for the enlargement of the court's power to require a case to be stated; this provision was not part of the original bill, but was added by a subcommittee. It attracted no contemporaneous comment, although it was described in passing as a 'new and very useful power, which seems to be founded on Order XXV, r. 4, of the Rules of the Supreme Court, 1883 'Arbitrations Bill (1888-89) 413.

138 Cohn 'Commercial Arbitration and the Rule of Law' 8
139 (1856) 10 ER 1121
140 Ibid. 1133 (Coleridge J)
141 Ibid. 1138
142 (1856) 25 LJ Ex. (NS) 308 at 313
143 (1922) 2 KB 478 (CA)
144 Ibid. 491
145 Ibid. 484
146 Ibid. 488 (emphasis added).
147 'Alsatia': a London district near the wharves, from Temple to the Fleet; 'This was the refuge of every sort of criminal. For many years it was a sanctuary giving immunity from arrest, and although this privilege was abolished in 1697, it remained the home of footpads and murderers, highwaymen, debtors and prostitutes': Barker and Jackson *London* 181.
148 'The Arbitration Bill' (1854) 50
149 Ferguson 'Commercial Dispute Settlement' 20
150 Wolaver 'Historical Background of Commercial Arbitration' 144
151 'Arbitration and Compromise' 176
152 Ibid. 176
153 'Legal Topics of the Week' 517
154 Atiyah *The Rise and Fall of Freedom of Contract* esp. 345ff and 388ff

155 Ibid. chaps. 10–13
156 Unger *Law in Modern Society* 73–4
157 Isaacs 'Two Views of Commercial Arbitration'
158 Sirefman 'In Search of a Theory of Arbitration' 30
159 Carlston 'Theory of the Arbitration Process' 631
160 Ibid. 650
161 *Law of the Constitution* 146
162 Mentschikoff 'The Significance of Arbitration' 708
163 Mentschikoff 'Commercial Arbitration' 846, 868
164 'Commercial Arbitration' (1967–8) 1238
165 Bonn 'Nonlegalistic Adjudication' 563
166 Mentschikoff 'The Significance of Arbitration' 709–10
167 See, for example, Kronstein 'Business Arbitration'; Kronstein 'Arbitration is Power'; 'Judicial Supervision of Commercial Arbitration'; 'Commercial Arbitration' 1229–30.
168 Ellenbogen 'English Arbitration Practice' 677
169 Cohn 'Commercial Arbitration and the Rule of Law' 3
170 Ellenbogen 'English Arbitration Practice' 659, 677
171 Evidence of C.W. Cookworthy Hutton, Sheriff of London and Middlesex, *Third Report ... on the Judicature* appendix, 154
172 'Mercantile Tribunals' 525; compare Beresford *The Leeds Chamber of Commerce* 48–9.
173 'Mercantile Tribunals' 525. Liverpool Chamber of Commerce *Report of the Special Committee on Mercantile Law Reform* 18
174 'Tribunals of Commerce' (1889–90) 379
175 Liverpool Chamber of Commerce, *Report of the Special Committee on Mercantile Law Reform* 32
176 'Legal Topics of the Week' 517
177 Ibid.
178 'Tribunals of Commerce' (1857–8)
179 For example, conveyancers were able to transfer 'use rights' on occasion to facilitate the commercial exploitation of certain resources: see Thompson 'The Grid of Inheritance'; 'agreed' litigation was proposed in order to obtain the interpretation of a superior court of certain provisions of the Factories Act, 1844.
180 Sugarman 'Legality, Ideology and the State' 215
181 These theories, which he characterized as the 'determinist view' and the 'consensus view,' are adumbrated by Sugarman 'Theory and Practice in Law and History,' as is the much more complex view he described as 'experiential.' Sugarman offers extensive references to the literature. Other

important contributions include Kidder 'An Integrated Theory of Imposed Law' and Abel *The Politics of Informal Justice*.
182 See esp. Moore 'Law and Social Change' and Moore *Law as Process*; Galanter 'Justice in Many Rooms.'
183 *Society and Legal Change* 130
184 Ibid. 8
185 See esp. Kidder 'An Integrated Theory of Imposed Law' 297.
186 'Human Interaction and the Law' 9
187 Ibid. 13
188 Ibid. 24

4 THE NEW ADMINISTRATIVE TECHNOLOGY

 1 Dicey *The Law of the Constitution* 203
 2 Dicey *Law and Public Opinion*. His celebrated acknowledgment of 'The Development of Administrative Law in England' contributes to the confusion in so far as it also ignores developments in the mid-nineteenth century.
 3 Dicey *The Privy Council* 109
 4 See, for example, Neuhauser 'Privy Council Regulation of Trade.'
 5 Holdsworth *History of English Law* 10 165ff, 195ff, and 256–332
 6 Ibid. 256
 7 Its lingering presence even at the beginning of the nineteenth century is recorded in Thompson 'The Moral Economy of the English Crowd.'
 8 Holdsworth *History of English Law* 10: 256
 9 Webb and Webb *The Parish and the County* VI
10 Exceptions included such bodies as the commissioners of sewers and various turnpike trusts: see Holdsworth *History of English Law* 10: 195 and Parris *Constitutional Bureaucracy* 18.
11 Watson *The Reign of George III* 45, quoted in Abel-Smith and Stevens *Lawyers and the Courts* 9
12 See, for example, Roberts *Origins of the British Welfare State* 12ff; Parris *Constitutional Bureaucray* esp. chap. 1.
13 The legal-intellectual history of the period is chronicled in Atiyah *The Rise and Fall of Freedom of Contract*.
14 Harding *A Social History of English Law* 325–6
15 Checkland *The Rise of Industrial Society* 329
16 Mathias *The First Industrial Nation* 32
17 Parris *Constitutional Bureaucracy* 160ff
18 Webb and Webb *The Parish and the County* 557
19 The reference to 'cleansing' is more than metaphorical. A concern for public-

health standards appears to have been a consistent and central theme of legislation from the 1830s onward, and a special preoccupation of Edwin Chadwick, the quintessential Benthamite reformer who played a key role in the enactment of the Factory Act, the new Poor Law, and especially public health legislation until the mid-1850s. See generally Roberts *Origins of the British Welfare State* 35ff.

20 See generally Checkland *The Rise of Industrial Society*; Mathias *The First Industrial Nation*; Perkin *Origins of Modern English Society*; Thompson *The Making of the English Working Class*; Harrison *Early Victorian Britain*; Osborne *The Silent Revolution*.

21 Roberts *Origins of the British Welfare State* 101

22 Perkin *Origins of Modern English Society* 319–39; Fraser *Evolution of the British Welfare State* esp. chap. 5 'Laissez Faire and State Intervention in the Mid-nineteenth Century'

23 For a study of Bentham's views on administration, see Hume *Bentham and Bureaucracy*; for a more general assessment of his influence, see Taylor *Laissez-Faire and State Intervention* esp. chap. 5 'Bentham, Laissez-Faire and Interventionism.'

24 Roberts *Origins of the British Welfare State* 101

25 See, for example, Carson 'Conventionalisation of Early Factory Crime'; Bartrip and Fenn 'A Reassessment'; and Carson 'Early Factory Inspectors.'

26 Marvel 'Factory Regulation'

27 Donajgrodzki ' "Social Police" and the Bureaucratic Elite' 52

28 See, for example, MacDonagh 'The Nineteenth Century Revolution in Government'; Fraser *Evolution of the British Welfare State* 113–14

29 However, some figures, such as Chadwick, were ubiquitous, and some, such as Treemeheare (an early mines inspector) and Chadwick himself, did perceive linkages among the various new programs of social melioration and control: see Donajgrodzki ' "Social Police" and the Bureaucratic Elite.'

30 See esp. Taylor *Laissez Faire and State Intervention* chap. 6 'Interventionism and Laissez Faire in Practice.'

31 Thomas 'Origins of Administrative Centralisation' 215

32 Roberts *Origins of the British Welfare State* 12–13

33 Ibid., 8. The peculiar picture of the court leet, an ancient manorial institution, trying to cope with the pollution and filth of Manchester in the mid-nineteenth century is sketched in chap. 2, supra.

34 Roberts *Origins of the British Welfare State* 11

35 The public departments of government as of 1833 are described in ibid., 14–16; see also Chester *The English Administrative System*.

36 Parris *Constitutional Bureaucracy* esp. 40ff

37 Ibid., 24, 106–7. Of course 'trivial' is a matter of perception. Thompson *The Making of the English Working Class* records that members of the London Corresponding Society (including a fourteen-year-old boy) were charged with treason in 1794 and interrogated by members of the privy council – including the prime minister, the home secretary, and even the lord chancellor (19ff).

38 See Roberts *Origins of the British Welfare State* 8ff; Webb and Webb *The Parish and the County* book 2, chap. 4.

39 Perkin *Origins of Modern English Society* 40–1, 435–6; Thompson *English Landed Society* 287–8; Thomas *Early Factory Legislation* 117; McCord 'The Government of Tyneside'; Phillips 'The Black Country Magistracy.'

40 Roberts *Origins of the British Welfare State* records that 'in 1833 the Central Courts gave judgments in sixty cases concerning the duties of magistrates and parishes. But sixty cases count very little against 15,500 parishes, 5,000 justices, and innumerable local commissioners, and suggest that the courts – notoriously slow, cumbersome, and costly – posed little threat to irresponsible local officials' (17).

41 See esp. Thomas *Early Factory Legislation*. The Factories Act, 1833, is discussed infra.

42 See Finer *Sir Edwin Chadwick*.

43 See Roberts *Origins of the British Welfare State* 33ff; Webb and Webb *English Poor Law History Part II*. The Poor Law, 1834, is discussed infra.

44 Webb and Webb *The Manor and the Borough* chap. 11

45 See Roberts *Origins of the British Welfare State* 22ff.

46 I have speculated at length on this point: see Arthurs 'Rethinking Administrative Law.'

47 Parris *Constitutional Bureaucracy* 258–66, and see infra.

48 Sugarman 'The Legal Boundaries of Liberty'

49 Perkin *Origins of Modern English Society* 107ff; Checkland *The Rise of Industrial Society* 106; for a slightly earlier period, see Bowden *Industrial Society in England* 164ff.

50 Harding *A Social History of English Law* 327; and compare Thompson 'Time, Work and Industrial Capitalism' 82ff. It has been suggested that the early industrial experience of 'rational adaptation of means to ends [and] ... the more efficient use of resources' helped to lay a foundation for rational-bureaucratic government; see Hume *Bentham and Bureaucracy* 45ff.

51 Keyser *Transactions on the Stock Exchange* 21. And see the rules of the stock exchange, reproduced in Melsheimer and Laurence *Law and Customs of the London Stock Exchange* appendix, 125ff. Morgan and Thomas *The Stock Exchange* date the first rule book of the exchange from 1812 (61–2). Duguid *Story of the Stock Exchange* suggests that regulations were passed

and enforced ten years earlier, but only codified in 1812 (95). Poley and Gould *History, Law, and Practice of the Stock Exchange* suggest that even prior to 1802 'there were rules and regulations in existence drawn up by a committee, and the relationship of broker and jobber seems to have been determined by this body' (25).

52 See Thomas *Provincial Stock Exchanges* 97.

53 Keyser *Transactions on the Stock Exchange* refers to 'the vast increase of business, alike in the Courts of Law and Equity, which has resulted of late years from transactions concerned with the Stock Exchange' (VI).

54 Melsheimer and Laurence *Law and Customs of the London Stock Exchange* 72

55 Ibid., appendix, rule 52

56 'The Stock Exchange is not an Alsatia; the Queen's laws are paramount there ...' per James LJ, in *Ex parte Saffery* (1876) 4 Ch.D. 555 at 561, quoted in Melsheimer and Laurence *Law and Customs of the London Stock Exchange* 73. See also chap. 3 supra.

57 Melsheimer and Laurence *Law and Customs of the London Stock Exchange* 74ff and 83ff

58 Keyser *Transactions on the Stock Exchange* 263ff

59 Cooper and Cridlan *Law and Procedure of the Stock Exchange* 29–32

60 See Gibb *Lloyds of London*.

61 Holdsworth *History of English Law* 13: 330ff. See also Mathias *The Brewing Industry in England* 236–7; Birch *The British Iron and Steel Industry* 115; Mathias *The First Industrial Nation* 389. And see generally chap. 3 supra.

62 Ellison *The Cotton Trade of Great Britain, Part II*

63 Ibid. 272

64 Ibid. 273

65 Ibid. 274–5

66 *Report of the Select Committee on the State of the Coal Trade* 1836 (522) XI, 4–8; compare Mathias *The Brewing Industry in England* (beer); Flinn *Readings in Economic and Social History* 222ff (iron); Chaloner 'William Furnival' (salt).

67 See Mathias *The First Industrial Nation* 38–9, 294–5; Checkland *The Rise of Industrial Society* 342ff.

68 Perkin *Origins of Modern English Society* 120

69 The leading exception to this generalization is, of course, the bar. See Manchester *A Modern Legal History of England and Wales* 50ff. See also Martin *Law Relating to Medical Practice* chap. 1; Walker *The English Legal System* 211–3, 224–6; Forbes and Watson *Legal Aspects of Dental Practice* 15–23; Dale and Appelbe *Pharmacy Law and Ethics* 120–5.

70 For example, a royal commission appointed in 1877 to 'inquire into the origin, objects, present constitution, customs and usages' of the exchange generally endorsed the concept of self-regulation. However, it sought public scrutiny of broker licensing and the issuance of prospectuses and also recommended that the exchange should be incorporated under statute or royal charter, and that its bylaws should be subject to approval by the president of the Board of Trade or some other public authority. Objections to this 'intrusion' on the autonomy of the exchange stressed that it had imposed a higher standard of conduct on traders than did the general law. These arguments apparently prevailed; the commission's recommendations were not implemented. See Duguid *Story of the Stock Exchange* chap. 16.

71 Factories Act (1844) 7 & 8 Vict., c 15, s 43; Coal Mines Inspection Act (1855) 18 & 19 Vict., c 108, s 5 (adequacy of safety arrangements)

72 Act Concerning Masters and Workmen (1824) 5 Geo. IV, c 96 (arbitration of wages, hours, and quality of work by justice or arbitrator)

73 Evans *The Contentious Tithe* 53

74 Companies Clauses Consolidation Act (1845) 8 & 9 Vict., c 16, ss 128–34

75 Lands Clauses Consolidation Act (1845) 8 & 9 Vict., c 18, ss 21–37, 63–8

76 Railways Clauses Consolidation Act (1845) 8 & 9 Vict., c 20, ss 44, 126–37

77 Public Health Act (1848) 11 & 12 Vict., c 63, ss 123–8, as amended by the Local Government Act (1858) 21 & 22 Vict., c 98

78 Act to provide for the Conveyance of the Mails by Railways (1838) 1 & 2 Vict. c 98, s 16, as amended by 36 & 37 Vict., c 48, s 19

79 Railway and Canal Traffic Act (1854) 17 & 18 Vict., c 31; Railways Companies Arbitration Act (1859) 22 & 23 Vict., c 59; Regulation of Railways Act (1873) 36 & 37 Vict., c 48, s 8; Board of Trade Arbitrations Act (1874) 37 & 38 Vict., c 40, part II

80 For example, in the Companies Clauses Consolidation Act, 1845, ss 128–34; Lands Clauses Consolidation Act, 1845, ss 21–37; and the Railway Clauses Consolidation Act, 1845, ss 126–37.

81 Russell *The Power and Duty of an Arbitrator* 5th ed. gives examples of submissions relating to drainage (730), canal building (731) and railway construction (748–58), awards relating to injurious affection in sewer construction (796–9) and canal building (800–1, 806–13), and compulsory purchase of land for a railway (813–6). In other cases, for example, agreements to arbitrate were enforced by a court (*Caledonian Ry.* v *Greenock & Wemyss Bay Ry.* (1874) 1–2 LR Sc. & Div. 347) and by the railway commissioners (*Torbay & Brixham Ry.* v *South Devon Ry.* (1876) 2 Nev. & Mac. 391); and the railway commissioners themselves arbitrated casues pursuant to arbitration clauses in inter-railway agreements in one case

by reason of the failure of an arbitrator to render an award (*Carmarthen & Cardigan Ry.* v *Central Wales & Carmarthen Junction Ry.* (1874) 2 Nev. & Mac. 23), in the other by reason of their statutory substitution for consensual arbitrators (*Stokes Bay Ry.* v *London & S.W. Ry.* (1875) 2 Nev. & Mac. 143). These examples do not appear to be unusual.

82 Holdsworth *History of English Law* 5: 338–9 refers to 'bitterness [in] the relations of employers and workmen which was fatal to any attempt to make use of the machinery of arbitration.'

83 Coal Mines Inspection Act, 1855, supra, note 71, s 5

84 See *Reports of the Inspector of Coal Mines* reports of Joseph Dickinson, inspector, until 1856, for Lancashire, Cheshire and the North Wales District, and then for North and East Lancashire, 1857 (hereafter Dickinson) 27; report of Herbert Mackworth, inspector for Southern District, 1856 (hereafter Mackworth) 96, 117, and 124, and report of William Alexander, inspector for Western District of Scotland, 1856 (hereafter Alexander) 163.

85 Bartrip *Safety at Work* 40–4, and MacDonagh 'Delegated Legislation' 40–1

86 See generally Paulus *The Search for Pure Food* and Carson 'Early Factory Legislation.'

87 3 & 4 Wm. IV, c 103

88 An Act for the Preservation of the Health and Morals of Apprentices (1802) 42 Geo. III, c 73, amended by (1819) 59 Geo. III, c 66; (1819) 60 Geo. III, 1 Geo. IV, c 5 (no relevant amendments); (1825) 6 Geo. IV, c 63; (1829) 10 Geo. IV, c 51; re-enacted (1831) 1 & 2 Wm. IV, c 39.

89 Holdsworth *History of English Law* 13: 338

90 See, for example, Thomas 'Origins of Administrative Centralisation' and Thomas *Early Factory Legislation*; Parris *Constitutional Bureaucracy* 166; Carson 'Early Factory Legislation' 114; Hutchin and Harrison *History of Factory Legislation*; and Djang *Factory Inspection in Great Britain.*

91 The act of 1802, supra, note 88, ss 13 and 15, provided for fines of 40s to £5, with imprisonment of up to two months for non-payment.

92 The act of 1819, s 7, increased the fines from £10 to £20; the act of 1825, s 8, imposed a cumulative limit of £100 for offences committed on the same day; the act of 1831, s 21, removed this limit; the act of 1825, s 10, disqualified any justice who was the proprietor or master, or the father or son of any proprietor or master, of any factory or mill from hearing prosecutions. The act of 1831, s 10, also disqualified brothers, and s 14, provided for the appointment of other magistrates if all those in a locality were disqualified. The act of 1825, s 11, gave magistrates power to compel testimony, the act of 1831, s 18, created a presumption of illegal operation if a mill was shown to be working outside designated hours, shifting the onus

of disproof to the accused. The act of 1829, s 1, and the act of 1831, ss 15 and 16, facilitated service. The act of 1825, s 13, and the act of 1831, s 19, prohibited appeals. The act of 1831, s 12, restricted the technical defences available.

93 Supra, note 88, s 9.
94 Ibid. s 14, amended by the act of 1825, s 9. By the act of 1831, s 9, parents and guardians were made liable to punishment for false register entries.
95 Act of 1802, s 10
96 The act of 1831 repealed all earlier legislation, and did not re-enact the original provisions for visitors and for their powers.
97 Carson 'Early Factory Legislation' 121ff and 129ff, and see the exchange between Carson and Bartrip and Fenn, supra, note 25.
98 Thomas *Origins of Administrative Centralisation* 235
99 Supra, note 87, ss 17–18
100 Ibid. s 31
101 Ibid. ss 32–4, 38, 41
102 Ibid. s 42. The only right of appeal was against a conviction for forging the register.
103 Thomas 'Origins of Administrative Centralisation' 227–8
104 Factories Act, 1884, supra, note 71, s 2
105 Thomas *Early Factory Legislation* 116ff
106 See ibid. 129–33, 241–3, and 305; and see Bartrip *Safety at Work* 22–5.
107 See Bartrip and Fenn 'A Reassessment' 179ff.
108 Thomas *Early Factory Legislation* 118ff; Bartrip and Fenn 'A Reassessment' 181
109 Carson 'Early Factory Legislation' suggests that the larger manufacturers may have been more willing to comply than small firms, partly out of altruistic conviction, partly out of desire to suppress the competition of the small firms and, it is suggested, partly because their size and profit margins allowed them to organize themselves in conformity with the law (118ff). However, Thomas 'Origins of Administrative Centralisation' suggests that 'gentle methods were calculated only to encourage defiance of the law' (223).
110 Thomas 'Origins of Administrative Centralisation' 226–7
111 Thomas *Early Factory Legislation* chaps. 7, 9, 15, and 16
112 Supra, note 71, s 2
113 Ibid. ss 19–21
114 See generally Thomas *Early Factory Legislation* chaps. 14 and 18.
115 For example, by restoring the disqualification of biased magistrates, s 71; by the stipulation of presumptions and prima facie evidence, ss 52–3; and by expanded powers of inspection, s 3 (supra, note 71).

116 Ibid. s 43
117 See 'Statutory Arbitration,' supra, and Djang *Factory Inspection* 153
118 Factory and Workshop Act (1891) 54 & 55 Vict., c 75, s 8, and schedule I.
119 Factory and Workshop Act (1878) 41 & 42 Vict., c 16, s 81. In addition, by the Factory and Workshop Act (1895) 58 & 59 Vict., c 37, provision was made for courts of summary jurisdiction to prohibit the use of dangerous machinery or premises.
120 Supra, note 71, s 60
121 This was the subject of a restrictive opinion by the law officers; see Thomas *Early Factory Legislation* 241-3.
122 See, for example, Thomas *Early Factory Legislation* 244; compare Roberts *Origins of the British Welfare State* chap. 9.
123 See Roberts *Origins of the British Welfare State* 293; Tapping *The Factory Acts* VI-VII; Bartrip *Safety at Work* esp. 35ff.
124 See generally Roberts *Origins of the British Welfare State* 293-300.
125 *The Search for Pure Food* 32-4, 122-30
126 Roberts *Origins of the British Welfare State* 287-93; Thomas *Early Factory Legislation* chaps. 9, 15-18
127 Bartrip *Safety at Work* 51
128 Paulus *The Search for Pure Food* 120-2
129 Compare Carson 'Early Factory Legislation.'
130 Boyd *Coal Mines Inspection* chap. 2
131 5 & 6 Vict., c 99; See MacDonagh 'Coal Mines Regulation'
132 The hortatory tactics of the first (and for eight years, the only) mines inspector, H.S. Treemeheare, and recounted in MacDonagh, 'Coal Mines Regulation' and Donajgrodzki ' "Social Police" and the Bureaucratic Elite.'
133 13 & 14 Vict., c 100
134 Ibid. ss 2, 8
135 *Reports of the Inspectors of Coal Mines* report of Charles Morton, inspector, until 1856, for the Counties of York, Derby, Nottingham, and Leicester and then for Yorkshire, 1853 (hereafter Morton) 43; Morton (1854) 68; Morton (1855) 60
136 Morton (1855) 60
137 Morton (1856) records the holding of a coroner's jury that a worker engaged in sinking a new shaft was not employed in a coal mine (60).
138 Morton (1854) 68. But see contra, *Reports of the Inspectors of Coal Mines*, reports of Thomas Wynne, inspector for the counties of Stafford, Worcester and Salop (hereafter Wynne), (1854) 98, 106; and Wynne (1855) 93.
139 Dickinson (1854) 24
140 Morton (1855) 64, 68

141 Morton (1854) 71
142 *Reports of the Inspectors of Coal Mines*, report of Mathias Dunn, inspector for the counties of Durham, Northumberland and Cumberland (hereafter Dunn), (1854) 8; Mackworth (Dec. 1854) 119; Mackworth (1857) 92
143 Morton (1855) 60
144 Dickinson (1854) 24; Dickinson (1855) 18–19. There was some similar experience with test case litigation under the Factories Act; see Bartrip *Safety at Work* 12–13.
145 Mackworth (1854) 128
146 Dec. 1854, 112ff
147 Morton (1854) 68; Mackworth (1855) 123; *Reports of the Inspectors of Coal Mines*, report of Henry G. Longridge, inspector for South Staffordshire and East Worcestershire (1858) 102
148 Morton (1854) 68, 69
149 Mackworth (Dec. 1854) 118
150 Ibid. 117
151 See, for example, Dunn (1854) 8; Morton (1853) 56; Mackworth (Dec. 1854) 119; Morton (1854) 74ff.
152 Mackworth (1855) 116ff
153 Boyd *Coal Mines Inspection* 132
154 Supra, note 71, s 5
155 Ibid. s 7
156 Dickinson (1856) n.p.; Dickinson (1857) n.p.; Dickinson (1858) 43–4; Morton (1856) 57–61; Morton (1857) 158ff; Wynne (1856) 77; *Reports of the Inspectors of Coal Mines*, report of Thomas Evans, inspector for South Wales (1856) 144; *Reports of the Inspectors of Coal Mines*, report of J. Hedley, inspector for Derby, Nottingham, Leicester, and Warwick (hereafter Hedley) (1856) 70.
157 Wynne (1856) records two payments of £10 to widows to avoid prosecution (77). Dickinson (1858) states that a fine of £10 was paid at the direction of the secretary of state to a widow (44). And Morton (1860) similarly mentions that a £20 fine was paid over to a widow (6).
158 Dickinson (1857) 27
159 By the end of the 1850s fines were increasing to a range of £10 to £35; Morton (1858) 8–9; and in one case of repeated offences, up to £70: Morton (1860) 5–6.
160 Hedley (1858) 64. Morton (1856) records the settlement of two civil actions, for £15 and £100 respectively, in which owners were sued for negligence in hiring managers who did not 'exercise ordinary caution and skill' (60).
161 For example, the Cymmer explosion, 114 killed: judge directed acquittal of

manager, foreman, and three firemen on charge of manslaughter: Mackworth (1856) 142; the Lundhill Colliery explosion, 189 killed: owners acquitted by jury of criminal negligence despite lax discipline and non-observance of special rules: 'the jury do not attach blame to the proprietors ... who were not cognizant of the loose discipline and misconduct': Morton (1857) 155.

162 Mackworth (1857) 92ff and appendix

163 Morton (1856) states that he settled over three hundred special rules without recourse to arbitration which, he laments, was 'likely to be ... unproductive of substantial and beneficial results' (64-5).

164 *Reports of the Inspectors of Coal Mines*, report of Peter Higson, inspector for West Lancashire and North Wales (hereafter Higson) (1857) 43

165 Morton (1858) 9

166 Dickinson (1855) 42-8; Dickinson (1856) 30; Morton (1854) 89

167 Mackworth (1855) 119

168 Morton (1856) 61; *Reports of the Inspectors of Coal Mines*, report of Robert Williams, inspector for the Eastern District of Scotland (1856) n.p.

169 Morton (1856) 64; Morton (1858) 9

170 For example, Morton (1856) recounts that after the mine owners disregarded his earlier advice concerning the need for special rules, 'I was ... compelled, after this second fatal occurrence, to institute legal proceedings against them for their contumacy.' A fine of £9 was levied, for wilful negligence, for failure to establish and publish special rules, and for non-compliance with general rules (57-8).

171 Mackworth (1855) states that he could visit any given mine only once in several years (122).

172 Hedley (1858) 66; Morton (1858) 10

173 Mackworth (1857) 92

174 Mines Regulation and Inspection Act (1860) 23 & 24 Vict., c 151

175 25 & 26 Vict., c 79, ss 3, 6

176 Act of 1850, supra, note 133, s 3; Act of 1860, supra, note 174, s 21

177 Act of 1850, supra, note 133, ss 5 and 6; Act of 1860, supra, note 174, ss 19 and 20

178 Act of 1855, supra, note 71, ss 5, 6, and 7

179 Act of 1855, ibid. s 11; Act of 1860, supra, note 174, s 22

180 MacDonagh 'Coal Mines Regulation' 81-4

181 Djang *Factory Inspection in Great Britain* states this only began to occur late in the nineteenth century (108). Roberts *Origins of the British Welfare State* suggests co-operation occurred much earlier (300ff).

182 Paulus *The Search for Pure Food* 117ff

183 See, for example, Parris *Constitutional Bureaucracy* 180ff; Roberts *Origins of the British Welfare State* chaps. 7 and 8.

184 See, for example, Simon *English Sanitary Institutions* chap. 10 re role of Edwin Chadwick, secretary to the Poor Law commissioners, in promoting public health legislation; and Perkin *Origin of Modern English Society* 328–39.

185 See, for example, Roberts *Origins of the British Welfare State* 70–85 and 95ff.

186 On this point Carson and Bartrip and Fenn seem agreed; see supra, note 25 'A Reassessment' 185, 187; see also Roberts *Origins of the British Welfare State* chaps. 5 and 6.

187 Mackworth (1855) 123

188 Higson (1858) 46

189 Actually, beginning with the Factories Act (1831) 1 & 2 Wm. iv, c 39, ss 12, 19, opportunities for appeal or review – for 'legal' correction – of magistrates' decisions were systematically diminished or abolished. Similar immunity attached to inspectors' decisions under the Factories Act, 1833, supra, note 87, s 42 (except in the case of prosecutions for forgery). See also Factories Act, 1844, supra, note 71, s 69, and Act to Prohibit the Employment of Women and Girls in Mines (1842) 5 & 6 Vict., c 99, ss 21–2. However, these provisions were not carried forward in subsequent legislation.

190 Mitchell 'The Ombudsman Fallacy' 26–7

191 Thomas *Origins of Administrative Centralisation* 223ff

192 Palmerston, as home secretary, was particularly active in directing the inspectorate, negotiating the terms of new legislation (over their objection), and dealing with its political consequences; see Bartrip, *Safety at Work* and see also Thomas 'Origins of Administrative Centralisation' 224–30; and *Early Factory Legislation* 255–8.

193 They did, however, retain some degree of autonomy within their respective jurisdictions; see Roberts *Origins of the British Welfare State* 234.

194 The passage was neither easy nor without cost in terms of restraints on zealous officials eager to protect the public. See, for example, Bartrip *Safety at Work*; Clark 'Statesmen in Disguise' 311ff.

195 MacDonagh 'Delegated Legislation' 37ff

196 MacDonagh 'Coal Mines Regulation' 69–70; Simon *English Sanitary Institutions*; Parris *Government and the Railways* chap. 6

197 Of course, the requirement that a new device be installed would have differential effects on businesses, depending on the existing state of their own equipment and their financial capacity. See Bartrip *Safety at Work*; Marvel 'Factory Regulation.'

198 See, for example, MacDonagh 'Delegated Legislation' at 42; Bartrip and Fenn 'A Reassessment' 183.
199 Carson 'Conventionalisation of Early Factory Crime'
200 An analysis of the backgrounds, attitudes, and careers of the inspectors from 1833 to 1854 is found in Roberts *Origins of the British Welfare State* 152–85.
201 Willson 'Ministries and Boards'
202 Roberts *Origins of the British Welfare State* 14–22
203 Maugham *Jurisdiction of all the Courts* 91–3; Henderson *English Administrative* Law 28ff
204 Henderson *English Administrative Law* 99ff
205 See Holdsworth *History of English Law* 11: 453–7.
206 See generally Mathias *The First Industrial Nation* 60–2; Perkin *Origins of Modern English Society* 125–7; Spring 'Landowners, Lawyers and Land Law Reform.'
207 Inclosure Act (1836) 6 & 7 Wm. IV, c 115, s 3
208 Ibid. s 5
209 Inclosure Act (1845) 8 & 9 Vict., c 118, s 1
210 Ibid. ss 9, 10, 25, and 27
211 Ibid. ss 27, 30, 31, 32, and 33
212 Ibid. s 166
213 Ibid. s 56
214 Ibid. s 60
215 'Commissions, Commissioners and the Bar' 120
216 Willson 'Ministries and Boards' 50–1
217 4 & 5 Wm. IV, c 76
218 For references to protests by working people and their Radical allies, see Thompson *The Making of the English Working Class* 295–6, 334–5. For a Tory attack on the act as a 'cold-blooded edict' which imposed 'hardship and injustice' see 'On the Laws for the Relief of the Poor' 16
219 See, for example, an editorial complaint in a self-styled Tory journal that the Poor Law commissioners 'are becoming the rulers of every parish in the Kingdom': 'Fourth Annual Report of the Poor Law Commissioners' 110, and more generally, Gutchen 'Local Improvements.'
220 Supra, note 217, s 15
221 Public Health Act, 1848, supra, note 77, s 8, and see generally Simon *English Sanitary Institutions*.
222 Act of 1834, supra, note 217 ss 26, 38
223 For example, the City of London was urged to create a single, unified Poor Law Union: *Minutes of the Poor Law Commissioners* (hereafter PLC), 3 Jan. 1837.

224 Webb and Webb *English Poor Law History Part II* 113ff
225 PLC 4 Jan. 1837
226 *Minutes of the General Board of Health* (hereafter GBH), 22 Nov. 1848
227 Act of 1834, supra, note 217, ss 15–18. See generally Roberts *Origins of the British Welfare State* 109ff.
228 See Webb and Webb *English Poor Law History Part II* 202–3.
229 GBH, 13 Mar., 29 Mar. 1849; *Minutes of the Railway Department of the Board of Trade* (hereafter RDBT), 16 Feb. 1853
230 RDBT, 16 Aug. 1844
231 Ibid. 17 Oct. 1844
232 Parris *Government and the Railways* 182ff
233 Act of 1834, supra, note 217, ss 2, 12; Webb and Webb, *English Poor Law History Part II* 206ff
234 Simon *English Sanitary Institutions* 208–9
235 RDBT, 21 Mar. 1853, 14 Aug. 1844
236 GBH 28 Feb. 1849
237 RDBT, 16 Dec. 1844, GBH 6 June 1849
238 GBH, 21 Dec. 1848, RDBT 19 and 25 Jan. 1853
239 Act of 1834, supra, note 217, s 15
240 RDBT, 16 Oct. 1844.
241 PLC 7–27 Jan. 1837
242 GBH, 16 Feb., 18, 25, and 28 Apr. 1849
243 Ibid. 7 Feb., 18 and 25 Apr. 1849
244 RDBT, 16 and 27 Aug., 3 and 21 Sept. 1844
245 Ibid. 5 and 10 Oct. 1844
246 Ibid. 19 and 24 Jan. 1843
247 Ibid. 17 Sept. 1844, 19 Jan. 1853
248 Ibid. 3, Sept. 1844, 27 Aug. 1844, 16 and 17 Oct. 1844
249 Ibid. 21 Sept. 1844
250 Ibid. 18 and 21 Sept. 1844; 21 Mar. 1853
251 This statement is less true of the Poor Law commissioners who were often intransigent and unyielding in their insistence upon compliance with their detailed instructions for the administration of indoor relief. But even they tended in practice to prefer persuasion and accommodation, at least as an initial tactic.
252 For example, the Poor Law Amendment Act, 1834, supra, note 217, authorized justices of the peace to visit workhouses to ensure that all regulations and orders of the commissioners were 'duly observed and obeyed' (s 43); disobedience of regulations and orders or other contempt was punishable (s 98); and the commissioners had the right to summon violators before justices of the peace (s 101).

253 GBH, 21 Dec. 1848; PLC, 24 Jan. 1837. The Board of Health armed its inspectors with an extensive legal opinion, to be shown to local authorities, suggesting that non-compliance with its requirements, if death resulted, might lead to charges of homicide and prosecution for violation of public health legislation: GBH, 14 Feb. 1849.

254 GBH, 12 Dec. 1848

255 PLC, 3 and 10 Jan. 1837

256 Ibid., 10 Jan. 1837

257 Act of 1834, supra, note 217, ss 52, 89. The effect of these provisions appears to have been to expose guardians to personal liability for violation of the rules of the commission: PLC, 24 Jan. 1837.

258 Supra, note 230, and accompanying text. A similar device was used by the emigration commissioners: see MacDonagh 'Delegated Legislation' 43.

259 RDBT, 27 Aug. 1844. An inspector recommended that, because of engineering defects, an Irish railway should be permitted to operate only as a single line with a single engine. The commission entered into negotiations with the railway in order to work out terms upon which it might be permitted to operate in order to enable it to open on the occasion of a visit by the Queen to Dublin: RDBT, 1 July 1853.

260 Ibid. 9 Dec. 1844

261 Ibid. 20 Aug. 1844

262 Ibid. 27 Aug. 1844

263 Ibid. 16 Sept. 1844

264 'Railway Legislation, Board of Trade' 354; 'The New Railway Board'

265 'The New Railway Board'

266 Webb and Webb, *English Poor Law History Part II*. They were not alone in holding this view. See, for example, Roberts *Origins of the British Welfare State* 133ff; Parris *Constitutional Bureaucracy* 90-1; Carr *Concerning English Administrative Law* 11-12; Chester *The English Administrative System* at 275ff; Clark 'Statesmen in Disguise' 29-30.

267 Act of 1834, supra, note 217, s 10

268 10 & 11 Vict., c 109

269 Simon *English Sanitary Institutions* chap. 11

270 See generally, Mathias *The First Industrial Nation* chap. 10 for the economic significance of railway development, and see Parris *Government and the Railways* chap. 1 on the resulting need for government action.

271 Railways Regulation Act (1840) 3 & 4 Vict., c 97, s 1, as amended by the Railways Regulation Act (1842) 5 & 6 Vict., c 55 and the Railways Regulation Act (1844) 7 & 8 Vict., c 85. See generally Parris *Government and the Railways* chap. 2 and Cleveland-Stevens *English Railways* chap. 3.

272 See Roberts *Origins of the British Welfare State* 64-5; Parris *Constitutional*

Bureaucracy 92; Smith *The Board of Trade* chap. 6; Parris *Government and the Railways* chap. 3.

273 Commissioners of Railways Act (1846) 9 & 10 Vict., c 105. See Cleveland-Stevens *English Railways* chap. 6; Parris *Government and the Railways* chap. 4.

274 Commissioners of Railways Repeal Act (1851) 14 & 15 Vict., c 64

275 See generally Willson 'Ministries and Boards'; Roberts *Origins of the British Welfare State* 118ff

276 Railway and Canal Traffic Act, 1854, supra, note 79, s 3

277 'Railway Accidents and Their Prevention' 129

278 Regulation of Railways Act, 1873, supra, note 79, s 4. The history of attempts to regulate the railways is set forth in *Report from the Joint Select Committee of the House of Lords and the House of Commons on Railway Companies Amalgamation* 1872 (364) XIII, part 1.

279 Act of 1873, supra, note 79, s 11, 'reenacting' and 'clarifying' the Railway and Canal Traffic Act, 1854

280 Supra, note 79, ss 8, 9, 10, 11, 16, and 19

281 Neville and MacNamara (Nev. & Mac.) *Reports of the Railway Commissioners* vols. 1 and 2; Cleveland-Stevens *English Railways* provides confirmatory statistics at 269-70.

282 Cleveland-Stevens *English Railways* 190.

283 Ibid. 195

284 Mr Chichester Fortescue, president of the Board of Trade (1873) 214 Hansard (3d ser.) 235 (first reading). The speaker also referred (235-6) to the prediction of Lord Campbell in 1853 that the judges of the Court of Common Pleas would not be able to administer the original act as well as a lay tribunal. Lord Campbell (a 'great and eminent Judge') had 'confessed he was wholly unacquainted with railway management; he knew not how to determine what was a reasonable fare, what was undue delay, etc.'

285 Mr Chichester Fortescue, ibid. 1056 (second reading)

286 Act of 1873, note 79, ss 4 and 5

287 Ibid. ss 21, 23, and 25. Under the 1854 act, s 3, the judges had also been explicitly authorized 'by such engineers, barristers, or other persons as they shall think proper [to make] all such inquiries as may be deemed necessary.' These powers, apparently, were not exercised (see supra, note 284) despite experience under earlier legislation when officials of the Railway Department of the Board of Trade were used as assessors by the courts on technical matters: see Parris *Government and the Railways* 151.

288 Act of 1873, supra, note 79, s 27

289 The Regulation of Railways Act, 1873, anticipated by some fourteen years

the American Interstate Commerce Act, 1887, which established the Interstate Commerce Commission, with broadly similar functions. The design of the ICC, often referred to as the first of the independent regulatory agencies (see, for example, Davis *Administrative Law Treatise* 1: 34–5), was apparently only indirectly influenced by the British experience with the Railway Commission. However, various state agencies antedating the ICC had been created with knowledge of the British model. See Schwartz *American Administrative Law* 11–12. Many of the provisions of the Railway Regulation Act closely resemble those that have become common in Canadian legislation establishing such commissions.

290 Hadley *Railroad Transportation* 173, quoted in Schwartz *American Administrative Law* 12; to the same effect see Cleveland-Stevens *English Railways* chap. 10.

291 Parris *Constitutional Bureaucracy* 190

292 Carr *Concerning English Administrative Law* 8

5   THE EMERGENCE OF ADMINSTRATIVE LAW

1 Rheinstein *Max Weber on Law in Economy and Society* 22

2 Parris *Constitutional Bureaucracy* 166

3 Ibid. 161

4 Carr *English Administrative Law* 8

5 MacDonagh *Early Victorian Government* 6

6 See Finer *Sir Edwin Chadwick*, and generally Parris *Constitutional Bureaucracy* 178ff; Roberts *Origins of the British Welfare State*, chaps. 7 and 8; and the discussion of the inspectorates, chap. 4, supra.

7 See, for example, Boyd *Coal Mines Inspection* 40 and 49ff, for a description of the role of Lord Ashley in securing enactment of mine safety legislation, and see generally Henriques *Before the Welfare State* 246ff.

8 See, for example, the rapid repudiation by the government of Gladstone's early attempt to secure effective regulation of the railways; Parris *Government and the Railways* 53ff, and Cleveland-Stevens *English Railways* chap. 3.

9 'On the Laws for the Relief of the Poor' 8

10 'Fourth Annual Report of the Poor Law Commissioners' 110

11 'Railway Legislation, Board of Trade' 354; 'Railway Tribunals' 420

12 Roberts *Origins of the British Welfare State*, chap. 3

13 Carr *English Administrative Law* 11

14 Parris *Government and the Railways* chap. 3

15 As early as 1839, solicitors were said to be receiving fees of £10,000 to

£15,000 for appearances in connection with railway bills: 'On the Employment and Charges of Attornies and see 'The New Tribunals for Railway and Other Private Bills.'

16 At a slightly later period, it has been estimated, no less than one-fifth of the members of the House of Commons and one-tenth of the Lords were 'Chairmen, Directors, Engineers or Constructors of Railways ... not taking into account the far larger proportion who, without being officeholders, are proprietors or shareholders and otherwise interested in Railways': Moore *Handbook of Railway Law* XVI.

17 'The Machinery of Private Bills' 306 and 309. There is no hint of irony here, although the legislation referred to was a Welsh Turnpike Act.

18 Compare the insistence by mines inspectors that special safety rules should be drafted in plain language.

19 For example, following the unsuccessful prosecution in *Ryder* v *Mills*, infra, note 172, attempts by the prosecutor and 'four QC's' to redraft the Factories Act ended in deadlock: Thomas *Early Factory Legislation* 316

20 Poor Law Amendment Act (1834) 4 & 5 Wm. IV, c 76, s 15; Factories Act (1833) 3 & 4 Wm. IV, c 103, s 18; Factories Act (1844) 7 & 8 Vict., c 15, s 6

21 MacDonagh, 'Delegated Legislation' 34

22 See, for example, Thomas *Early Factory Legislation* 116; chap. 4, supra, note 226 and accompanying text.

23 Compliance with the requirements was necessary in order to induce the inspectors to exercise their discretionary power to certify the completion of new railway lines. See Parris *Government and the Railways* 182ff. A similar 'quasi-legislative' code was developed by the education inspectors: see Parris *Constitutional Bureaucracy* 194–5.

24 For example, the Coal Mines Inspection Act (1855) 18 & 19 Vict., c 108, s 5, Mines Regulation and Inspection Act (1860) 23 & 24 Vict., c 151, s 13, and Regulation of Railways Act (1873) 36 & 37 Vict., c 48, s 29

25 Webb and Webb *English Poor Law History Part II* 202ff

26 Compare Parris *Constitutional Bureaucracy* at 18: 'Once parliament felt confident in its control of the executive, it showed itself ready to delegate powers to ministers.'

27 For example, an extensive memorandum adopted by the Poor Law commissioners to establish their own internal procedures was found by an opinion of the law officers to involve an illegal delegation of powers; the requirements laid down by the law officers would have stultified the work of the commissioners: *Case respecting the mode observed by the Poor Law Commissioners for transacting their business*, Law Officers' Opinions, Treasury Solicitors' Department, opinion 50/46 (1846).

28 See, for example, Thomas *Early Factory Legislation* 303.
29 See Roberts *Origins of the British Welfare State* 295ff.
30 See MacDonagh 'Delegated Legislation' 43.
31 See Bartrip *Safety at Work* 45.
32 Atiyah *The Rise and Fall of Freedom of Contract*
33 MacDonagh 'Delegated Legislation'
34 Ibid. 42–3
35 MacDonagh 'Delegated Legislation' states that on certain technical matters, the opinion of an immigration officer was 'little better than that of a layman' (42). MacDonagh 'Coal Mines Regulation' reports that the mines inspectorate suffered constant turnover, and no doubt diminished effectiveness, owing to poor pay (and, one might speculate, extreme frustration) (42). And Simon *English Sanitary Institutions* recounts that the General Board of Health initially had no medical member (208).
36 Bartrip *Safety at Work* records such an attack on the knowledge of the inspectors, two of whom then had over twenty years' experience in their positions (49).
37 See, for example, Henriques *Before the Welfare State* chaps. 6 and 7; Simon *English Sanitary Institutions* and Briggs *Victorian Cities* 214–17 for controversies concerning the linkages between proper sanitation and the control of disease, and the most effective techniques of draining sewage.
38 MacDonagh 'Delegated Legislation' 35
39 Greg *The Factory Question* 129–30, quoted in Thomas 'Origins of Administrative Centralisation' 220
40 See MacDonagh 'Revolution in Government' 58ff.
41 Roberts *Origins of the British Welfare State* 294; Mitchell 'Causes and Effects'
42 Lederman 'Independence of the Judiciary'
43 Holdsworth *History of English Law* 14: 180–204
44 Roberts *Origins of the British Welfare State* 113–14
45 Act of 1833, supra, note 20, s 34
46 Roberts *Origins of the British Welfare State* 114
47 See, for example, MacDonagh 'Delegated Legislation' 71.
48 See, for example, Factories Act, 1844, supra, note 20, s 7; Public Health Act (1848) 11 & 12 Vict., c 63, ss 123–8, s 129; Coal Mines Inspection Act, 1855, supra, note 24, s 11; and Poor Law Amendment Act, 1834, supra, note 20, s 98.
49 For example, Oats, *Factory Acts* 141–5, notes f and g lists a large number of cases broadening the scope of review under the Factories Act, 1833, notwithstanding an apparently restrictive privative clause.

50 Dicey *The Privy Council* 109

51 See, for example, Paulus *The Search for Pure Food* at 123–4; Carson 'Early Factory Legislation' 130ff; Thomas *Early Factory Legislation* 116ff; Boyd *Coal Mines Inspection* 107–8, and supra, chap. 4, notes 150 and 151 and accompanying text.

52 Thomas *Early Factory Legislation* shows that between 1833 and 1836, convictions under the Factories Act were secured in 458 cases; in 345 cases (75 per cent) the fine was 20s., the minimum permitted (118). Paulus *The Search for Pure Food* shows that between 1872 and 1874, only 276 convictions were secured under the Food and Drink Act; the fines averaged less than £2, excluding costs (34). The level of fines under the Coal Mines Inspection Act (recorded supra, chap. 4, at notes 158 and 159 and accompanying text) was somewhat higher, but still very low relative to the serious consequences of the violations.

53 See Mines Regulation and Inspection Act, 1860, supra, note 24, as amended by 25 & 26 Vict., c 79, s 6; Factory and Workshop Act (1878) 41 & 42 Vict., c 15, s 81; Parris *Government and the Railways* chap. 6; Prouty, *Transformation of the Board of Trade* 62; and Parris *Constitutional Bureaucracy* 198–9.

54 See Coal Mines Inspection Act, 1855, supra, note 24, s 7; Regulation of Railways Act of 1873, supra, note 24, s 26; Factories Act of 1844, supra, note 20, s 60; and Prouty *Transformation of the Board of Trade*.

55 Law Officers' Opinions, supra, note 27, opinion 50/46, 20–1.

56 See, for example, the attack on the procedures of the Railway Commission, supra, note 11.

57 See, for example, Bartrip *Safety at Work* 28.

58 MacDonagh 'Government Growth' 252

59 Ibid.

60 Bartrip *Safety at Work* 23, 24; Thomas *Early Factory Legislation* 139, 303.

61 *Legal Opinions and Instructions on the Factories Acts, 3 & 4 Wm. IV, c 103 (1833) (as revised), 7 Vict., c 15* (1844) 'Opinion re section 13' 13 Feb. 1845 (n.p.)

62 For example, one opponent of factory legislation attacked the inspectors on the grounds that their 'will is law without appeal,' that they can 'convict on view,' and that they possess the power of a 'Pacha of Three Tails': see Greg *The Factory Question*, one supporter of factory legislation none the less attacked 'the exercise of arbitrary and unconstitutional power' by the inspectors: see Thomas 'Origins of Administrative Centralisation.'

63 Thomas 'Origins of Administrative Centralisation' 227–8

64 Bartrip *Safety at Work*, 40ff, shows how the introduction of a requirement

for arbitration was used by factory owners as part of a deliberate campaign to inhibit the enforcement of fencing requirements for machinery.

65 Holdsworth *History of English Law* 10: 256
66 See, for example, Factories Act (1831) 1 & 2 Wm. IV, c 39, s 19; Factories Act, 1833, supra, note 20, s 42; Act to Prohibit the Employment of Women and Girls in Mines (1842) 5 & 6 Vict., c 99, ss 21-2.
67 'The State of the Profession' 160
68 'Commissions, Commissioners and the Bar' 120, 140
69 Railway and Canal Traffic Act (1854) 17 & 18 Vict., c 31, s 3
70 See, for example, the exchange between Carson and Bartrip and Fenn, supra, chap. 4, note 24
71 Bartrip and Fenn, 'A Reassessment' 179
72 See generally Galanter 'Justice in Many Rooms.' Galanter speaks of both 'bargaining and regulation "in the shadow of the law" ' (2ff) and 'the law in the shadow of indigenous ordering' (17ff). Historical references include Sugarman 'Theory and Practice in Law and History' and Ferguson 'Commercial Dispute Settlement' as to civil justice; and Hay 'Property, Authority and Criminal Law' and Brewer and Styles *An Ungovernable People* as to criminal justice.
73 Hume *Bentham and Bureaucracy* 82
74 Thomas 'Origins of Administrative Centralisation' 218-19
75 Parris *Constitutional Bureaucracy* 188
76 Ibid. 221-2
77 Carr *English Administrative Law* 5
78 Monroe *Intolerable Inquisition?* 9-12
79 Factories Acts (1825) 6 Geo. IV, c 63, s 13; 1831, supra, note 66, s 19; 1833, supra, note 20, s 42; 1844, supra, note 20, ss 69-70
80 Act of 1842, supra, note 66, ss 21-2; however, this provision was not re-enacted by the Coal Mines Inspection Act (1850) 13 & 14 Vict., c 100, or by further amending legislation in 1855 or 1860, supra, note 24, or (1862) 25 & 26 Vict., c 79.
81 Supra, note 20, ss 101, 103
82 Inclosure Act (1845) 8 & 9 Vict., c 118, ss 56, 60, s 166
83 'The State of the Profession' 160-1
84 Cited in Oats, *Factory Acts* 141-5, notes f and g
85 20 & 21 Vict., c 43, ss 2, 6. Perusal of vols. 1-5 of the *Law Times* (NS), covering the period to 1862 reveals no appellate cases dealing with either the Factory Act or mine safety legislation.
86 Parris *Constitutional Bureaucracy* 221-2
87 MacDonagh 'Government Growth' 252, 254

88 Supra, chap. 4, note 209, and accompanying text
89 Supra, chap. 4, note 151, and accompanying text
90 *Legal Opinions and Instructions on the Factory Acts* 'Opinions,' 9 June 1848, 22 June 1848
91 Supra, note 80
92 Railway and Canal Traffic Act, 1854, supra, note 69, s 3
93 Mr Chichester Fortescue, (1873) 215 Hansard 591 (committee stage)
94 Ibid. 591–2
95 Ibid. 592
96 Ibid. Mr Childers
97 Ibid. 592–3
98 Ibid. Mr Chichester Fortescue
99 Regulation of Railways Act, 1873, supra, note 24, s 26
100 Ibid.
101 *London, Chatham & Dover Ry.* v *South-Eastern Ry.* (1877) 3 Nev. & Mac. 79 (QB) (prohibition granted)
102 Cleveland-Stevens *English Railways* 270
103 Railway and Canal Traffic Act (1888) 51 & 52 Vict., c 25, s 17(1)(2)(4)(6)
104 Ibid., s 4
105 See, for example, Roberts *Origins of the British Welfare State* Parris *Government and the Railways* chap. 6; Paulus *The Search for Pure Food* 38; Spring *The English Landed Estate* 164.
106 'Commissions, Commissioners and the Bar' 121
107 Paulus *The Search for Pure Food* 126–7
108 De Smith *Judicial Review* referred in his second edition to English administrative law as 'an asymmetrical hotchpotch' (4), a position from which he and his editor, J. Evans, retreated somewhat in later editions. Without opening up for debate the effect of very recent trends, it does not necessarily follow that the apparent rationalization of doctrine has the effect of achieving consistency of result in its application in specific cases.
109 However, as de Smith points out (ibid. 85), 'Ultra vires' first achieved general usage 'to denote excess of legal authority by independent statutory bodies ... in the middle years of the nineteenth century,' and older lines of cases were used to 'supply the omission of the legislature' by reading a requirement of natural justice into modern regulatory legislation beginning with *Cooper* v *Wandsworth Board of Works* (1863) 14 CB (NS) 180, 194 (ibid. 141). De Smith accepts that the basic concepts emerged much earlier, however.
110 Holdsworth *History of English Law* 10: 251
111 Rheinstein *Max Weber on Law in Economy and Society* 9

112 *The Law of the Constitution* 188
113 I have examined Dicey's writings on this point critically and at some length in 'Rethinking Administrative Law.'
114 Dicey did not define the term 'ordinary courts,' but the context makes it clear that he was referring to the superior courts; see 'Rethinking Administrative Law.' He does suggest, however, that 'the judges ... are influenced by the feelings of magistrates' (ibid. 413).
115 For example, the factory inspectors adopted a general code in 1836: Thomas 'Origins of Administrative Centralisation' 226–7; and the railway inspectors promulgated their requirements in 1858: Parris *Government and the Railways* 182ff. The Poor Law Commission was a somewhat different case. In order to avoid the political controversy engendered by producing a general code for parliamentary scrutiny, the commission adopted the expedient of issuing thousands of 'special orders' in identical terms to local authorities; Webb and Webb *English Poor Law History Part II*.
116 This the emigration officers did even when parliament deliberately decided to leave them with open-ended discretion; see note 30 and accompanying text.
117 For example, in June 1836, the factory inspectors advertised the fact that they were about to embark upon a campaign of strict enforcement of the education provisions of the Factories Act, and followed this up with a circular letter to all manufacturers; see Thomas *Early Factory Legislation* at 116. The Poor Law commissioners not only made extensive use of circulars, but authorized an assistant commissioner to write (for a fee) a lengthy and lively account of the administration of the law for publication in an influential journal; see Brundage *The New Poor Law* 98–9. The ability of factory inspectors to issue instructions to factory owners was greatly curtailed by the interposition, after 1837, of the law officers as the authoritative expositors of the legislation; Thomas 'Origins of Administrative Centralisation' 227. The Poor Law Commission and the General Board of Health frequently advised on the legality of proposed behaviour and of conduct that violated relevant legislation; see supra, chap. 4, notes 226–7 and accompanying text, and, generally, Roberts *Origins of the British Welfare State* 216–17.
118 See generally Roberts 272–7 and chap. 3. Webb and Webb's claim that this attitude of singlemindedness characterized the Poor Law Commission (*English Poor Law History Part II* 153ff) is challenged by more recent research; see, for example, Brundage *The New Poor Law* chap. 5 and esp. 182–3, and Dunkley 'The "Hungry Forties." ' The example of public-health legislation seems equally controversial; see Henriques *Before the Welfare State* 144ff, and see contra Gutchen 'Local Improvements and Centralization.'

119 See Brundage *The New Poor Law* and Dunkley 'The "Hungry Forties" ';
compare Simon *English Sanitary Institutions.*

120 See generally Prouty *Transformation of the Board of Trade*, chap. 3; Parris
Government and the Railways chaps. 5 and 6. A specific illustration was the
Coal Mines Inspection Act, 1855, supra, note 24, s 5, which first introduced
the notion that each mine was to adopt special rules, subject to
administrative approval; and see Paulus *The Search for Pure Food*
'Postscript'; Carson 'Early Factory Legislation'; Boyd *Coal Mines Inspection*
chap. 6; and Bartrip *Safety at Work.*

121 For example, initial faults were found in the design of the factory
inspectorate (MacDonagh *Early Victorian Government* 51–4). As to
inadequate staffing and financing, see Henriques *Before the Welfare State*
106 (factory inspectors), and MacDonagh *Early Victorian Government* (mines
inspectors); the Poor Law commissioners seem to have been somewhat better
supported; see Brundage *The New Poor Law* 81ff. A lack of technical
expertise was a particular problem in both public health and mines
inspection: MacDonagh *Early Victorian Government* 85, 141ff; Henriques
Before the Welfare State chap. 6.

122 An example of excessive (not to say oppressive) 'rationality' and 'uniformity'
is provided by the Poor Law Commission's stipulation of the daily diet for
workhouse inhabitants; see Oastler *The Fleet Papers* 191–2, quoted in Evans
Social Policy 66.

123 MacDonagh *Early Victorian Government* 8. See generally Hume *Bentham
and Bureaucracy*; Fraser *Evolution of the British Welfare State* chap. 5.

124 this is not to imply that political support and judicial deference would
automatically follow in the wake of administrative legality; see Bartrip *Safety
at Work.*

125 Webb and Webb *The Parish and the County* 550ff

126 *The Law of the Constitution* 193

127 Thomas *Early Factory Legislation* 117; see Boyd *Coal Mines Inspection* 26,
and chap. 4, supra, re prosecutions for manslaughter resulting from mine
accidents.

128 Beginning with the Act to Prohibit the Employment of Women and Girls in
Mines, 1842, supra, note 66, s 22, regulatory statutes often stated that
convictions would not be quashed for 'defect of form'; see, for example,
Factories Act, 1844, supra, note 20, s 69. In the *Reports of the Inspectors of
Coal Mines*, Thomas Wynne, mines inspector for Staffordshire,
Worcestershire, and Shropshire, in his report for the year ending 31 Dec.
1856, recorded that a stipendiary magistrate three times adopted a perverse
view of the mine safety legislation, despite the contrary opinion of 'eminent

counsel' (78). Wynne concluded: 'Under these circumstances it is useless taking any further proceedings in this court unless I am sure of other magistrates being on the bench, who will take a common sense view of the Act of Parliament.' A more egregious example was the ruling that an employer who worked a large number of children in contravention of the limitations of the Factories Act, 1833, committed only a single offence; see Henriques *Before the Welfare State* 104. See also note 52, supra.

129 See Thomas *Early Factory Legislation* 138; Paulus *The Search for Pure Food* 123ff.

130 Thomas *Early Factory Legislation* 75ff, 107–8; compare Parris *Government and the Railways* 34; Henriques *Before the Welfare State* 105; MacDonagh *Early Victorian Government* 82; Thomas 'Origins of Administrative Centralisation' 228–9; Simon *English Sanitary Institutions* 208–9; MacDonagh *Early Victorian Government* 89.

131 Factories Act, 1825, supra, note 79, s 10; disqualification broadened by Factories Act, 1831, supra, note 66, s 10: omitted from Factories Act, 1833, supra, note 20; restored in broad form by Factories Act, 1844, ibid., s 71. Coal Mines Inspection Acts, 1850, supra, note 80, and 1855, supra, note 24 contain no disqualification; introduced by Mines Regulation and Inspection Act, 1860, supra, note 24, s 22.

132 See, for example, Thomas *Early Factory Legislation* 117ff; and Bartrip *Safety at Work* 25–5. Particularly flagrant examples of such behaviour are found in the *Reports of the Inspectors of Coal Mines*; see supra, chap. 4, note 162 and accompanying text. Inspector Mackworth, for example, reported that a bench of magistrates deliberately postponed the hearing of charges until a limitation period had intervened: report for the year ending 31 Dec. 1856, 114.

133 Donajgrodzki ' "Social Police".' Inspector Mackworth spoke of his duty as being 'of too sacred a character' to permit him to misrepresent conditions in the mines: supra, chap. 4 note 187 and accompanying text.

134 See, for example, Simon *English Sanitary Institutions* 231ff for an account of Chadwick's role in engendering hostility toward, and ultimately the destruction of, the Board of Health. Other 'zealots' are described in Parris *Constitutional Bureaucracy* 139–40, 202; and see more generally Roberts *Origins of the British Welfare State* chap. 4.

135 MacDonagh 'Revolution in Government' proposes a five-step model of legislative developments (55ff), which has been challenged by, inter alia, Bartrip *Safety at Work* at 55ff, and Fraser *Evolution of the British Welfare State* at 102ff.

136 For example, the Factories Act, 1833, and the Poor Law, 1834

137 Clark 'Statesmen in Disguise' 38
138 Thomas *Early Factory Legislation* 251–3
139 Bartrip *Safety at Work*
140 Clark 'Statesmen in Disguise' 22
141 Parris *Constitutional Bureaucracy* 93–100; compare Thomas *Early Factory Legislation* 256–8; Clark 'Statesmen in Disguise'; Chester *The English Administrative System* 311ff
142 Parris *Constitutional Bureaucracy* 84–93; Chester *The English Administrative System* 120ff, 275ff; Willson 'Ministries and Boards.' The Railway and Canal Commission of 1873 (not discussed by Willson) was something of an exception to this trend.
143 Apart from their role as the 'extra-legal' government, the justices often were MPs and were certainly closely identified with party politics. See generally Webb and Webb *The Parish and the County* chap. 2; Thompson *The Making of the English Working Class*.
144 Phillips 'The Black Country Magistracy' shows how during this period coal and iron masters increased their dominance of the bench from zero per cent in 1835 to over 50 per cent in 1860 (166ff). The effects on the enforcement of mines safety legislation have been shown. Similarly, Paulus *The Search for Pure Food* suggests: 'The literature available leaves no doubt that, *had* magistrates been *willing* to use the maximum provisions of the law available to them, food adulteration would have disappeared as a "social problem" much sooner than it actually did. Instead, fifty years were needed to bring gross abuses under control' (124).
145 MacDonagh *Early Victorian Government* shows how the recruitment of the new commissioners, inspectors, assistant commissioners, and other officials 'did nothing to improve the old civil establishments. The inspectorates ... were concentrated in the novel fields of state activity. The core of the civil service was untouched' (201). Elsewhere he refers to 'a general undifferentiated mass of drones and mediocrity' (200). See McCord 'Government of Tyneside' for an account of the positive contribution of the magistracy in one area.
146 For example, in the leading case of *Dimes* v *Proprietors of Grand Junction Canal* (1852) 3 HLC 759, a decision of the vice-chancellor was set aside because of his financial interest in the litigant canal company. Coupled with the necessity of special legislation to disqualify justices of the peace with financial or personal interests in matters to be tried by them, discussed supra, it is clear why the administration had to develop its own standards of propriety.

147 *Constitutional Bureaucracy* chap. 5
148 Ibid. 143
149 *Origins of the Welfare State* 153, 162
150 Ibid. 148
151 Ibid. 160-1
152 'Commissions, Commissioners, and the Bar' 136
153 Henriques *Before the Welfare State* 251-2
154 Trilling *The Opposing Self* 214, quoted in Spring *The English Landed Estate* 56
155 Hume *Bentham and Bureaucracy* 40ff
156 See Edwards *The Law Officers of the Crown* chaps. 7 and 8; and Roberts *Origins of the British Welfare State* 299.
157 MacDonagh 'Revolution in Government' 62. Weber traces the attitudes of English lawyers to legislation to their predominantly guild-controlled, practical, and non-conceptual education; Rheinstein *Max Weber on Law in Economy and Society* 202ff.
158 *Case Respecting the Construction of the Factories Act, 7 Vict., c 15*, Law Officers Opinions, supra, note 27, opinion 35 / 46 (14 May 1846). This opinion was contrary to the magistrates' decisions in two successful prosecutions at Bradford.
159 *Legal Opinions and Instructions on the Factories Acts*, supra, note 61, 'Opinion,' 2 Jan. 1857
160 *Further Case respecting the application of the Factories Act to Rope Works*, Law Officers Opinions, supra, note 27, opinion 52 / 45 (19 Nov. 1845)
161 Thomas 'Origins of Administrative Centralisation' 227; and *Early Factory Legislation* 243
162 *Early Factory Legislation* 252-3
163 *Legal Opinions* supra, note 61 (undated opinion, c 1848)
164 For example, the General Board of Health, at its first meeting adopted a lengthy statement of its powers under two statutes, with an exegisis on the statutory language; supra, chap. 4, note 226. On another occasion, it circulated 'a sound exposition of the common law responsibilities in respect of neglects involving injury to health and life,' prepared by a London coroner: *Minutes of the General Board of Health* 14 Feb. 1849. However, the board was attacked on the ground, inter alia, that it had no 'legal mind' among its members: [1849] *Magistrate* 240.
165 See, for example, Thomas *Early Factory Legislation* 241-3, 305.
166 Nonet *Administrative Justice*
167 See, for example, Thomas *Early Factory Legislation* 137, 244, 245-6, 303;

Parris *Government and the Railways* 151.

168 *Early Factory Legislation* 241–3; Parris *Constitutional Bureaucracy* 172–9

169 Compare Atiyah 'From Principles to Pragmatism.' He suggests that 1875 marked the high tide of 'principle' and the lowest ebb of 'discretion' within the English legal system.

170 See generally Thomas *Early Factory Legislation* 108–9; Roberts *Origins of the British Welfare State* 22ff, 273ff; Bartrip *Safety at Work*; compare Brebner 'Laissez Faire' and Parris *Constitutional Bureaucracy* chap. 10.

171 See Paulus *The Search for Pure Food* 123ff; see also Parris *Government and the Railways* 151, 165ff, for a case where a key judicial interpretation sustained a long-standing administrative practice.

172 *Ryder* v *Mills* (1850) 19 LJMC (pt. 2) 82 (Exch.), reproduced in Thomas *Early Factory Legislation* appendix 20

173 Ibid. 424

174 Quoted in Parris *Constitutional Bureaucracy* 188

175 Thomas *Early Factory Legislation* 316

176 Roberts *Origins of the British Welfare State* 299

177 Cleveland-Stevens *English Railways* 270

178 Roberts *Origins of the British Welfare State* 108

179 Ibid. 109

180 Cleveland-Stevens *English Railways* 195; Parris *Government and the Railways* 163ff

181 Roberts *Origins of the British Welfare State* 299. Roberts records that Horner, one of the factory inspectors, had lost ten or eleven prosecutions on the 'relay' system even before the decision in *Ryder* v *Mills*. He does mention, however, that two other inspectors 'were favoured by magistrates who felt that the relay was illegal' (298, note 52).

182 Bartrip *Safety at Work* 12–3; cf supra, chap. 4, notes 142–4 and accompanying text.

183 *The Search for Pure Food* 73

184 See, for example, Prouty *Transformation of the Board of Trade* 93 (Thomas Farrer, revision of shipping legislation); Paulus *The Search for Pure Food* 54–5, 57 (Sir John Simon, adulteration legislation); Parris *Constitutional Bureaucracy* 180, and Roberts *Origins of the British Welfare State* 226 (Leonard Horner, factory and ten-hour-day legislation); Finer *Sir Edwin Chadwick* (Chadwick, factory act, poor law, public-health legislation, etc.); Parris *Constitutional Bureaucracy* 215–17 (Robert Low, passenger acts.)

185 See, for example, Carson 'Early Factory Legislation'; Boyd, 'Coal Mines Inspection chaps. 5 and 6; Simon *English Sanitary Institutions* chap. 10; Perkin *Origins of Modern English Society* 319ff; Parris *Government and the*

Railways chap. 3; Paulus *The Search for Pure Food* 69–74.
186 See, for example, Parris *Constitutional Bureaucracy* 176–6.
187 Ibid. chap. 8
188 Ibid. 187. For example, the government simply curtailed publication and distribution of the reports of the outspoken mines inspectors in 1858: supra, chap. 4, note 189.
189 G.C. Lewis to Lord Russell, 4 Mar. 1851, quoted in Parris *Constitutional Bureaucracy* 184
190 See Hume *Bentham and Bureaucracy.*
191 Parris *Constitutional Bureaucracy* suggests that in the long run administrative powers may have been expanded in an attempt to offset adverse judicial treatment (188).
192 'Origins of Administrative Centralisation' 235
193 *Early Factory Legislation* 145
194 See Arthurs 'Rethinking Administrative Law' 16–17.
195 Compare Parris *Constitutional Bureaucracy* where he suggests that 'administrative action may precede legislation, as well as follow it,' and that 'within the limits ... of what the law said he must *not* do' the administrator was 'expected to suggest the course which ... was most conducive to the general welfare' (211–12).
196 *Early Factory Legislation* 145. However, Thomas overstates. For example, as noted, under Home Office direction the inspectors ceased to exercise their adjudicative functions in 1837, thus leaving enforcement entirely in the hands of an unsympathetic magistracy.
197 Sisson *Spirit of British Administration* 72, quoted in Parris *Constitutional Bureaucracy* 183
198 Compare Fuller 'Human Interaction and the Law' 20ff.
199 Parris *Government and the Railways* 210
200 Supra, note 55, and accompanying text
201 See, for example, Tapping (1855) and Oats (1862) on the Factories Acts; Lumley (1840), Palmer (1844), and Parker (1849) on the Poor Laws; Lawes (1849) and Lumley (1859) on the Public Health Acts; Hodges (1847) and Walford (1845) on railways; Tapping (1861) and Rogers (1964) on mines inspection, inter alia.
202 Abel-Smith and Stevens *Lawyers and the Courts* 69
203 *Holmes* v *Clarke* (1860) 3 LTR (NS) 675 at 677 (Ex.)
204 For example, *Ryder* v *Mills* supra, note 172, argument of the attorney-general 90–1
205 For example, Tapping *The Factories Acts* 16, note a, and 44–6, note s
206 *Constitutional Bureaucracy* 211

6 MAKING CHANGE

1 For a dismal account of the courts' inability to deal with analogous problems see McLaren 'Nuisance Law.'
2 Some other writers have recently urged similar conclusions based on historical evidence, for example, Manchester *Legal History of England and Wales*, or on theoretical grounds, for example, Evan 'Public and Private Legal Systems' esp. in his preface.
3 Holdsworth *History of English Law* 1: 188
4 Atiyah *The Rise and Fall of Freedom of Contract*
5 Dicey 'Introduction to the Second Edition' *Law and Public Opinion*
6 See generally Shklar *Legalism*; in the following passages, I borrow Shklar's general notion but do not purport to rely on her analysis.
7 See generally Watson *Society and Legal Change.*
8 Bartrip *Safety at Work*
9 In the following discussion of lawyers, much general information had been derived from Duman *The English and Colonial Bars* and Cocks *Foundation of the Modern Bar.* Information concerning administrators derives principally from Roberts *Origins of the British Welfare State.* For general background on professionalism in the nineteenth century, see Elliott *Sociology of the Professions* esp. chap. 2, and Larson *The Rise of Professionalism.* Because my allusions are impressionistic, specific citations are usually omitted.
10 Galanter 'Justice in Many Rooms' 20
11 Ibid. 22. Galanter himself acknowledges the risk of generalization based upon research largely concerned with the legal system of America in the twentieth century (2).
12 Fuller 'Human Interaction and the Law'
13 Moore 'Law and Social Change'
14 Ibid. 722 passim
15 For a fuller account see Moore *Law as Process* esp. his introduction.
16 Valuable discussions on this point are found in Kidder 'An Integrated Theory of Imposed Law' and Fitzpatrick 'Law, Plurality and Underdevelopment.'
17 Weber pointed to the close connections between legalism and legitimacy, detected the special quality of legalism as it was espoused by England's lawyers and manifested by her legal system, demonstrated the connections between that legalism and the interests of powerful economic and social interests, and showed how it could not easily be reconciled with the requirements of bureaucratic justice. For two insightful contemporary attempts to document law's emergence as ideology, see Sugarman 'Theory and Practice' and esp. 'Legality, Ideology and the State.'

18 Austin *Lectures on Jurisprudence* (1832)
19 Dicey *Introduction to the Study of the Law of the Constitution Part II* (1885)
20 Despairing of the possibility of comprehending constitutional law through the eyes of historians ('antiquarians') or political theorists ('these ... are not inquiries which will ever be debated in the law courts'), Dicey advised his students that 'the true law of the constitution is to be gathered from the sources whence we collect the law of England in respect to any other topic': ibid., 15, 20–1, 34.
21 *Law and Public Opinion* at XLIII; *Introduction to the Study of the Law of the Constitution* chap. 12. As Cocks has observed, Dicey '... was a wonderful source of consolation for the barrister. With immense sincerity and lucid arguments of apparent simplicity he seemed to show that the Bar could, as it were, "have its cake and eat it." It could preserve its traditional hold over administration, and could go far beyond this and play a vital role in public affairs': Cocks *Foundations of the Modern Bar* 208.
22 'Reverence ... for the supremacy of law is seen in its very best aspect when we recognize it as being in England at once the cause and the effect of reverence for our judges': *Introduction to the Study of the Law of the Constitution* 395
23 Dicey *Law and Public Opinion* 64; Hewart *The New Despotism*; Holdsworth *History of English Law* 14: 203; and Dicey 'Development of Administrative Law in England'

7   POSTSCRIPT

1 See, for example, Chayes 'The Role of the Judge'
2 See Crévier v *A.G. Quebec* (1982) 127 DLR (3d) 1 (SCC); and see comments by Arthurs 'Protection Against Judicial Review' and Mullan 'Canada's Administrative Appeal Tribunals.'
3 See Young 'A System of Administrative Law?'
4 This literature is extensively reviewed in Galanter 'Justice in Many Rooms.'
5 A typical display of research perspectives is found in the 'Special Issue on Dispute Processing and Civil Litigation' of the *Law and Society Review*.
6 See, for example, Santos 'Law and Community.'
7 Auerbach *Justice Without Law* chaps. 2 and 3
8 Compare Selznick *Law, Society and Industrial Justice.*
9 An integrative essay on recent theoretical interpretations of these developments is found in Teubner 'Substantive and Reflexive Elements in Modern Law.'
10 See, for example, Milner 'Settling Disputes'; Ferguson 'Adjudication of

Commercial Disputes'; Horrocks 'Alternatives to the Courts in Canada'; and see Auerbach *Justice Without Law* chap. 4.

11 Auerbach *Justice Without Law* chap. 5

12 See, for example, Macauley *Law and the Balance of Power*; Ross *Settled Out of Court*.

13 The idea is explored in what the authors term a 'non-normative' fashion in Landes and Posner 'Adjudication as a Private Good' and for discussion see 'Symposium.'

14 For an insightful study of the relationship between Marxist and pluralist perceptions of law, see Fitzpatrick 'Marxism and Legal Pluralism.'

15 Hooker *Legal Pluralism* is the best available account of formal relationships between the components of plural legal systems. In his preface, Hooker raises the possibility that his account may have some pertinence in non-colonial, modern contexts.

16 See generally Freedman *Crisis and Legitimacy* 31ff.

17 Jaffe 'The Illusion of Ideal Administration'

18 Freedman *Crisis and Legitimacy* refers to and documents the 'recurrent sense of crisis' in American administrative law.

19 A number of authors, writing from very different perspectives, have focused on the legitimating functions of administrative law; see, for example, Freedman *Crisis and Legitimacy* chaps. 10, 20; Nonet *Administrative Justice*; Prosser 'Towards a Critical Theory of Public Law'; Rabin 'Administrative Law in Transition.'

20 An early and influential example of this perspective was Jaffe 'The Effective Limits of the Administrative Process.'

21 The criticisms are captured in Freedman *Crisis and Legitimacy* esp. chaps. 4 and 5; see also the seminal works of Reich 'The New Property' and Cahn and Cahn 'The War on Poverty.'

22 See, for example, Stewart 'Regulation, Innovation and Administrative Law.'

23 Thompson *Whigs and Hunters* 266

24 Among the many works that sensibly examine this perspective – and its limits – in the context of administrative law are Jowell *Law and Bureaucracy*; Wexler 'Discretion'; and Nonet *Administrative Justice*.

25 See, for example, McAuslan 'Administrative Law, Consumption and Judicial Policy.'

26 Interesting explorations of the possibilities of purposeful pluralism include Jowell 'Legal Control of Administrative Discretion'; Diver 'Policymaking Paradigms'; Brooks 'The Legalization of Planning'

27 Edelman *The Symbolic Uses of Politics*.

28 See, for example, Willis 'The McRuer Report'; McAuslan 'Administrative

Law and Administrative Theory'; Verkuil 'The Emerging Concept of Administrative Procedure'; and esp. Prosser 'Towards a Critical Theory of Public Law.'

29 McAuslan 'Administrative Law, Consumption and Judicial Policy'; Laughlin 'Procedural Fairness'

30 Compare Prosser 'Towards a Critical Theory of Public Law.'

31 Nonet *Administrative Justice*; Jowell *Law and Bureaucracy*

32 For a vigorous dissent from the notion of autonomous administrative law see Harlow ' "Public" and "Private" Law.'

33 Evans *De Smith's Judicial Review* 110 (emphasis added)

34 *R.* v *Northumberland Compensation Appeal Tribunal* [1952] 1 KB 338 (CA). Evans *De Smith's Judicial Review* suggests that the particular error of law in question might have been treated instead as a jurisdictional error (121, note 63).

35 *Anisminic* v *Foreign Compensation Commission* [1969] 2 AC 147

36 *Pearlman* v *Harrow School Keepers* [1979] 3 QB 56 (CA), but see *South East Asia Brick* v *Non-metallic Mineral Products Manufacturing Employees Union* [1981] AC 363 (PC) and *Re Racal Communications* [1981] AC 374.

37 Arthurs 'Protection Against Judicial Review'

38 *CLRB* v *Halifax Longshoremen's Association* (1983) 144 DLR (3d) 1 at 10 (SCC)

39 Bermann 'Judicial Review in French Administrative Law'

40 Whitmore *Australian Administrative Law* chap. 10

41 Mullan 'The Federal Court Act' and Mullan 'Reform of Judicial Review'

42 Parris *Constitutional Bureaucracy* 312–14; Mitchell 'Causes and Effects'; Robson 'Justice and Administrative Law Reconsidered'

43 See, for example, Unger *Law in Modern Society* 53 passim, where he stresses that a legal order is characterized by 'an attachment to the aims of generality in legislation and of uniformity in adjudication.'

44 See generally Winkler 'Law, State and Economy'; Daintith 'Public Law and Economic Policy'; Jowell 'The Limits of Law in Urban Planning.' The issue is not a new one; the charge of 'corporatism' was bandied about almost half a century ago. See Fuchs 'Anglo-American Administrative Law Theory' 550–1.

Bibliography

NOTES ON PRIMARY SOURCES

Although secondary sources, both contemporary and modern, were consulted extensively, the diffuse nature of the phenomena studied made it necessary to sample primary sources relating to local courts, arbitration, and administrative jurisdictions. This note is intended to convey some sense of the sampling process.

Local Court Records
The most active local courts were the courts of requests, which were not courts of record and did not form part of the national judicial system. Accordingly, some fragmentary records of courts of requests are found in the Public Record Office, but only in a few instances where they were apparently treated as part of the records of a county court, which succeeded to their jurisdiction after 1846. Searches were also made (largely without success) in local and county records offices in Birmingham, Bristol, Leeds, Liverpool, Manchester, Norwich, Preston, and Sheffield in an effort to find local court records, especially those of courts of requests.

These searches produced only one extensive and useful set of records, the journals of the Bristol Courts of Requests and Conscience (Bristol Records Office) which identify litigants by class or occupation, and which disclose the cause of action and the amount involved. A sampling of these journals yielded an analysis of cases for January, April, and September 1830 (300 cases) and for certain weeks in those same months for 1835 (220 cases) and 1840 (260 cases). Somewhat similar journals are extant for the Sheffield Court of Requests (formerly the Court Baron of the Manor of Sheffield, found in the Sheffield Central Library), but these lacked any descriptive material concerning litigants. Sampling of these records for 1 or 2 July

1830, 1835, and 1840 involved 58, 130, and 83 claims respectively. My findings based on these analyses are reported in chapter 2 and in greater detail in ' "*Without the Law*": *Local Courts in Nineteenth Century England.*'

Apart from these two sets of records (and a few others of limited value), what we know of courts of requests and other local courts must be deduced from other sources. Most important is the evidence given to the common-law commissioners in 1831–3, and found in appendices to their fourth and fifth reports (cited infra). This evidence includes a list of all inferior courts operating in England in 1830–1, showing their provenance, jurisdiction, and caseload, as well as conventional oral and written testimony from lawyers, judges, litigants, and other interested citizens.

Contemporary literary evidence is found in two books on courts of requests, especially that of William Hutton (1787, reprinted 1840), in legal journals, and occasionally in general and local histories, parliamentary papers, and archival collections of pamphlets.

Arbitration and Domestic Adjudication
Arbitration in the nineteenth century arose in one of several contexts: before statutory arbitrators, under judicial auspices by rule of court (with or without the parties' consent), and before ad hoc consensual arbitrators. Awards of the first two types are readily accessible in law reports or court records. However, the fact that such awards are likely to be influenced by the administrative or judicial regimes from which they emanate makes them less interesting as evidence of legal pluralism.

On the other hand, purely consensual ad hoc arbitration not conducted under judicial auspices is more likely to reflect the parties' own distinctive needs and expectations, norms, and procedures. Put negatively, the parties may have chosen to arbitrate precisely because they wished not to be governed by the formal legal system. However, awards of this type are extremely difficult to find. They are not 'public records' both because they are private (hence not to be found in 'public' court records or other official depositories) and because they were often ephemeral, unsupported by pleadings or written evidence, and sometimes rendered orally (hence not to be found in any 'records,' public or private).

However, a few written awards rendered by ad hoc consensual arbitrators have survived. Some such awards dealt with property interests, or similar matters, which necessitated their preservation; these were located in collections of miscellaneous legal documents in local records offices, particularly in collections of solicitors' files. Some related to business disputes, including partnership disputes, and were located in firm records on deposit in university archives or elsewhere. Through random samplings of the records of a number of firms, reading correspondence files and other documents covering periods of several weeks at a time, some twenty awards were located, together with a few letters agreeing to submit disputes to arbitration, or arranging for the hearing.

These awards are analysed in chapter 3. Because they are so few in number and scattered so broadly across the nineteenth century and among various disputants, analysis based on these awards is advanced with extreme diffidence. However, in light of the frequent reference to arbitration in the periodical literature, it is important to try to reconstruct the phenomenon to which reference is made.

Finally, the secondary literature contains extensive reference to the existence, size, and function of domestic systems of adjudication in commodity, shipping, and stock exchanges. These references form the basis of observations concerning such systems.

Administrative Regimes
The records of the new administrative regimes of the 1830s, 1840s, and 1850s have been examined minutely by many other authors, although generally with a view to giving an account of a particular administrative department, such as the Poor Law Commission. Since my purpose was to get a sense of the development of administrative technology in general, I sampled the records of several bodies merely to see how they performed their functions.

Thus, I have consulted a limited range of primary sources: minutes and reports of the Poor Law commissioners (1830s), the General Board of Health (1840s), the Railway Commission and the Railway Department of the Board of Trade (1840s and 1850s), the Mines Inspectors (1850s), and the opinions of the law officers (1840s); detailed citations are found below. All of these are available in the Public Record Office, Kew. A particular interest in the Railway and Canal Commission, which in 1873 succeeded to the railway jurisdiction of the Court of Common Pleas, led to me to examine the law reports containing decisions of both bodies.

These investigations apart, I have largely relied on secondary sources for accounts of administrative behaviour.

BOOKS AND THESES

Abel, Richard L., ed *The Politics of Informal Justice* (New York, Academic Press 1982)
Abel-Smith, Brian, and Robert Stevens *Lawyers and the Courts: A Sociological Study of the English Legal System 1750–1965* (London, Heinemann 1967)

Allen, David G. *In English Ways* (Chapel Hill, University of North Carolina Press 1981)

Annual Practice, 1883–84 (London, Maxwell and Sweet 1884)

Archer, Peter *The Queen's Courts* 2d ed. (Middlesex, Penguin 1963)

Atiyah, P.S. *From Principles to Pragmatism: Changes in the Function of the Judicial Process and the Law* (Oxford, Clarendon Press 1978)

– *The Rise and Fall of Freedom of Contract* (Oxford, Clarendon Press 1979)

Auerbach, Jerold S. *Justice Without Law?* (New York, Oxford University Press 1983)

Austin, John *Lectures on Jurisprudence* (London, John Murray 1913, reissued 1977)

Bainbridge, William *A Treatise on the Law of Mines and Minerals* (London, Butterworths 1841)

Barker, Felix, and Peter Jackson *London – 2,000 Years of a City and Its People* (London, Cassell 1974)

Bartrip, Peter *Safety at Work: The Factory Inspectorate in the Fencing Controversy, 1833–1857* (Oxford, Centre for Sociolegal Studies 1979)

Beresford, M.W. *The Leeds Chambers of Commerce* (Leeds, Leeds Incorporated Chamber of Commerce 1951)

Birch, Alan *The Economic History of the British Iron and Steel Industry 1784–1879* (London, Frank Cass 1967)

Bowden, Witt *Industrial Society in England towards the End of the Eighteenth Century* 2d ed. (London, Frank Cass 1965)

Boyd, R.N. *Coal Mines Inspection: Its History and Results* (London, W.H. Allen 1879)

Brandon, Woodthorpe *Notes of Practice of the Mayor's Court of the City of London, in Ordinary Actions* (London, Butterworths 1864)

Brewer, John, and John Styles *An Ungovernable People: The English and Their Law in the Seventeenth and Eighteenth Centuries* (New Brunswick, NJ, Rutgers University Press 1980)

Briggs, Asa *Victorian Cities* (Harmondsworth, Penguin 1968)

Browne, J.H. Balfour *The Law of Usages and Customs* (London, Stevens and Haynes 1875)

Brundage, Anthony *The Making of the New Poor Law: The Politics of Inquiry, Enactment and Implementation, 1832–39* (New Brunswick, NJ, Rutgers University Press 1978)

Carr, Sir Cecil Thomas *Concerning English Administrative Law* (New York, Columbia University Press 1941)

Checkland, S.G. *The Rise of Industrial Society in England 1815–1885* (London, Longmans, Green 1964)

Chester, Sir Norman *The English Administrative System 1780–1870* (Oxford, Clarendon Press 1980)

Cleveland-Stevens, Edward *English Railways: Their Development and Their Relation to the State* (London, George Routledge and Sons 1915)

Cocks, Raymond *Foundations of the Modern Bar* (London, Sweet and Maxwell 1983)

Cohen, Julius Henry *Commercial Arbitration and the Law* (London, D. Appleton 1918)

Colman, Anthony D. *Matthew's Practice of the Commercial Court* 2d ed. (London, Butterworths 1967)

Cooper, Geoffrey, and Richard J. Cridlan *Law and Procedure of the Stock Exchange* (London, Butterworths 1971)

Dale, J.R., and G.E. Appelbe *Pharmacy Law and Ethics* (London, Pharmaceutical Press 1976)

Danzig, Richard *The Capability Problem in Contract Law: Further Readings in Well-Known Cases* (Mineola, Foundation Press 1978)

Davis, Kenneth Culp *Administrative Law Treatise* (St Paul, West 1958)

Dawson, John P. *A History of Lay Judges* (Cambridge, Harvard University Press 1960)

de Smith, S.A. *Judicial Review of Administrative Action* 2d ed. (London, Stevens and Sons 1968)

Denning, Lord Alfred *The Changing Law* (London, Stevens and Sons 1953)

Dicey, Albert Venn *The Privy Council* (London, Macmillan 1860, reissued 1887)

– *Lectures on the Relation Between Law and Public Opinion in England During the Nineteenth Century* 2d ed. (London, Macmillan 1914)

– *Introduction to the Study of the Law of the Constitution* 10th ed. (London, Macmillan 1965)

Dictionary of National Biography ed. Sidney Lee (London, Smith, Elder 1908)

Djang, T.K. *Factory Inspection in Great Britain* (London, George Allen and Unwin 1942)

Duguid, Charles *The Story of the Stock Exchange: Its History and Position* (London, Grant Richards 1901)

Duman, D. *The English and Colonial Bars in the Nineteenth Century* (Beckenham, Croom, Helm 1983)

Edelman, Murray *The Symbolic Uses of Politics* (Urbana, University of Illinois Press 1964)

Edwards, J.Ll.J. *The Law Officers of the Crown: A Study of the Offices of Attorney-General and Solicitor-General of England with an Account of the Office of the Director of Public Prosecutions of England* (London, Sweet and Maxwell 1964)

Elliott, Philip *The Sociology of the Professions* (London, Macmillan 1972)

Ellison, Thomas *The Cotton Trade of Great Britain, Part II: History of the Liverpool Cotton Market and of the Cotton Brokers' Association* (London, Frank Cass 1886, reissued 1968)

Evan, W.M., ed *Law and Sociology: Exploratory Essays* (New York, Free Press 1962)

Evans, Eric J. *The Contentious Tithe: The Tithe Problem and English Agriculture, 1750–1850* (London, Routledge and Kegan Paul 1976)

- *Social Policy 1830–1914: Individualism, Collectivism and the Origins of the Welfare State* (London, Routledge and Kegan Paul 1978)

Evans, J. *The Practice of the Court of Common Pleas for the County Palatine of Lancaster* (np. 1813)

Evans, J.M. ed. *DeSmith, Judicial Review of Administrative Action* 4th ed (London, Stevens and Sons 1980)

Finer, S.E. *The Life and Times of Sir Edwin Chadwick* (London, Methuen 1952)

Flinn, M.W., *Readings in Economic and Social History* (London, Macmillan 1964)

Forbes, G., and A.A. Watson *Legal Aspects of Dental Practice* (Bristol, John Wright and Sons 1975)

Foster, D. 'The Changing Social and Political Composition of the Lancashire County Magistracy, 1821–51' (PHD thesis, University of Lancaster 1971)

Foulkes, David *Introduction to Administrative Law* 3d ed. (London, Butterworths 1972)

Fraser, Derek *The Evolution of the British Welfare State* (London, Macmillan 1973)

Freedman, James O. *Crisis and Legitimacy: The Administrative Process and American Government* (Cambridge, Cambridge University Press 1978)

Garner, John F. *Administrative Law* 3d ed. (London, Butterworths 1970)

Gibb, D.E.W. *Lloyds of London: A Study in Individualism* (London, Macmillan 1957)

Goody, J., J. Thirsk, and E.P. Thompson *Family and Inheritance – Rural Society in Western Europe 1200–1800* (Cambridge, Cambridge University Press 1976)

Greg, Robert Hyde *The Factory Question* (London, J. Ridgway and Sons 1837)

Hadley, Arthur Twining *Railroad Transportation: Its History and Its Laws* (London, G.P. Putnam's Sons 1885)

Harding, Alan *A Social History of English Law* (Baltimore, Penguin 1966)

Harrison, J.F.C. *The Early Victorians 1832–1851* (London, Weidenfeld and Nicolson 1971)

Hart, Cyril E. *The Verderers and Speech-Court of the Forest of Dean* (Gloucester, John Bellows 1950)

– *The Free Miners* (Gloucester, British Publishing 1953)

Hay, Douglas, P. Linbaugh, and E.P. Thompson eds. *Albion's Fatal Tree: Crime & Society in Eighteenth Century England* (New York, Pantheon Books 1975)

Henderson, Edith G. *Foundations of English Administrative Law: Certiorari and Mandamus in the Seventeenth Century* (Cambridge, Harvard University Press 1963)

Henriques, Ursula R.Q. *Before the Welfare State: Social Administration in Early Industrial Britain* (London, Longman, 1979)

Heuston, R.F.V. *Essays in Constitutional Law* 2d ed. (London: Stevens and Sons 1964)

Hewart, Lord *The New Despotism* (London, Ernest Benn 1929, reissued 1945)

Hodges, William *The Law Relating to Railways and Railway Companies* (London, Sweet 1847)

Holdsworth, Sir William *History of English Law* 16 vols (London, Methuen and Boston, Little, Brown 1923–66)

Hooker, M.B. *Legal Pluralism: An Introduction to Colonial and Neo-colonial Laws* (London, Oxford University Press 1975)

Horwitz, Morton J. *The Transformation of American Law, 1780–1860* (Cambridge, Harvard University Press 1977)

Hume, L.J. *Bentham and Bureaucracy* (Cambridge, Cambridge University Press 1981)

Hurst, James Willard *The Growth of American Law: The Law Makers* (Boston, Little, Brown 1950)

Hutchins, B.L., and A. Harrison *A History of Factory Legislation* 2d ed. (London, King and Son 1911)

Hutton, William *Courts of Requests: Their Nature, Utility and Powers* Birmingham, Pearson and Rollason 1787)

Ilersic, A.R., and P.F.B. Liddle *Parliament of Commerce* (London, Newman Neame 1960)

Injustice, Oppression and Cruelty: Local Courts for the Recovery of Small Debts and Extortionate and Ruinous Costs (Birmingham, 1846) Birmingham Public Library

Jackson, R.M. *The Machinery of Justice in England* 5th ed. (Cambridge, Cambridge University Press 1967)

Jones, David J.V. *Before Rebecca – Popular Protests in Wales 1793–1835* (London, Allen Lane 1973)

Jowell, Jeffrey L. *Law and Bureaucracy* (Port Washington, NY, Kennikut Press 1975)

Keane, D.D. *Courts of Requests* 3d ed. (London, Shaw and Sons 1845)

Keyser, Henry *The Law Relating to Transactions on the Stock Exchange* (London, Butterworths 1850)

Larson, M.S. *The Rise of Professionalism, A Sociological Analysis* (Berkeley, University of California Press 1977)

Law Officers' Opinions, 1843-48 (Public Record Office, Treasury Solicitors' Department)

Lawes, Edward *The Act for Promoting the Public Health* (London, Shaw and Sons 1851)

Legal Opinions and Instructions on the Factories Acts 3 & 4 Will IV c 103 (1833) (as revised) 7 Vict., c 15 (1844) (Public Record Office, Ministry of Labour)

Lewis, George Randall *The Stannaries: A Study of the English Tin Miner* (Cambridge, Harvard University Press 1907)

Lumley, William Golden *An Abridgement of the Cases upon the Subject of the Poor Law* (London, C. Knight 1840)

- *The New Sanitary Laws* (London, Shaw and Sons 1859)

Macaulay, Stewart *Law and the Balance of Power: The Automobile Manufacturers and Their Dealers* (New York, Russell Stage Foundation 1966)

MacDonagh, Oliver *Early Victorian Government, 1830-70* (London, Weidenfeld and Nicolson 1977)

Manchester, A.H. *A Modern Legal History of England and Wales 1750-1950* (London, Butterworths 1980)

Marriner, Sheila *Rathbones of Liverpool 1845-73* (Liverpool, Liverpool University Press 1961)

Martin, C.R.A. *The Law Relating to Medical Practice* (London, Pitman and Sons 1973)

Mathias, Peter *The Brewing Industry in England 1700-1830* (Cambridge, Cambridge University Press 1959)

- *The First Industrial Nation: An Economic History of Britain 1700-1914* (London, Methuen 1969)

Maugham, Robert *Outlines of the Jurisdiction of all the Courts in England and Wales* (np. 1838)

Melsheimer, Rudolf E., and Walter Laurence *The Law and Customs of the London Stock Exchange* (London, Sweet 1879)

Monroe, Hubert *Intolerable Inquisition? Reflections on the Law of Tax* (London, Stevens and Sons 1981)

Moore, Arthur *A Handbook of Railway Law* (London, W.H. Smith and Son 1859)

Moore, S.F. *Law as Process* (London, Routledge and Kegan Paul 1978)

Morgan, E. Victor, and W.A. Thomas *The Stock Exchange: Its History and Functions* 2d ed. (London, Elek Books 1969)

Moseley, Joseph *The Law of Inferior Courts for the Recovery of Debts* (London, Stevens Norton 1845)

Nelson, William E. *Dispute and Conflict Resolution in Plymouth County, Massachusetts, 1725-1825* (Chapel Hill, University of North Carolina Press 1981)

Nonet, Philippe *Administrative Justice: Advocacy and Change in a Government Agency* (New York, Russell Sage Foundation 1969)

Oastler, Richard *The Fleet Papers; being letters to Thomas Thornhill, esq. of Riddlesworth in the County of Norfolk; from Richard Oastler his prisoner in the Fleet* (London, Pavey 1841)

Oats, Henry Carne, ed. *The Factory Acts* (London, Stevens and Haynes 1862)

Oldnall, William Russell *The Practice of the Court of Great Sessions on the Carmarthen Circuit* (London, Butterworths 1814)

Osborne, J.W. *The Silent Revolution* (New York, Scribners 1970)

Palmer, William *Principles of the Legal Provision for the Relief of the Poor* (London, Butterworths 1844)

Parker, Henry Walter *A Digest of the Law Relating to the Relief of the Poor* (London, Knight 1849)

Parker of Waddington, Lord *The History and Development of Commercial Arbitration: Recent Developments in the Supervisory Powers of the Courts Over Inferior Tribunals* (Jerusalem, Magnes Press, Hebrew University 1959)

Parkes, J. *The State of the Court of Requests and the Public Office of Birmingham* (Birmingham, Beilby, Knott and Beilby 1828)

Parris, Henry *Government and the Railways in Nineteenth-Century Britain* (London, Routledge and Kegan Paul 1965)

- *Constitutional Bureaucracy: The Development of British Central Administration Since the Eighteenth Century* (London, George Allen and Unwin 1969)

Paulus, Ingeborg *The Search for Pure Food: A Sociology of Legislation in Britain* (London, Martin Robertson 1974)

Peel, W., ed *Jurisdiction and Practice of the Court of Passage of the City of Liverpool* (Liverpool, H. Young and Sons 1909)

Perkin, Harold *The Origins of Modern English Society, 1780-1880* (Toronto, University of Toronto Press 1969)

Poley, A.P. and F.H. Carruthers Gould *The History, Law and Practice of the Stock Exchange* (London, Pitman 1920)

Pollock, Sir Frederick and William Maitland *The History of English Law Before the Time of Edward I* ed S.F.C. Milsom (Cambridge, Cambridge University Press 1898, reissued 1968)

Prouty, Roger *The Transformation of the Board of Trade, 1830-1855: A Study of Administrative Reorganization in the Heyday of Laissez Faire* (London, Heinemann 1957)

Rheinstein, M. *Max Weber on Law in Economy and Society* (Cambridge, Harvard University Press 1954)

Roberts, David *Victorian Origins of the British Welfare State* (Hamden, Ct, Archon Books 1960, reissued 1969)

Robson, Peter, and Paul Watchman, eds. *Justice, Lord Denning and the Constitution* (Aldershot, Gower 1981)

Rogers, Arundel *The Law Relating to Mines, Minerals & Quarries in Great Britain and Ireland; with a Summary of the Law of Foreign States, and practical directions for obtaining government grants to work foreign mines* (London, Stevens and Haynes 1864)

Ross, H. Laurence *Settled Out of Court: The Social Process of Insurance Claims Adjustment* (Chicago, Aldine 1970)

Rules and Orders in the Court of the County of Durham (n.p. 1775)

Russell, Francis *A Treatise on the Power and Duty of an Arbitrator, and the Law of Submissions and Awards* 1st ed. (London, William Benning 1849); 5th ed. (London, Stevens and Sons 1878); 7th ed. (London, Stevens and Sons 1891)

Sanborn, Frederic Rockwell *Origins of the Early English Maritime and Commercial Law* (London, The Century Co. 1930)

Schwartz, Bernard *An Introduction to American Administrative Law* 2d ed. (London, Pitman 1962)

Selznick, Philip *Law, Society and Industrial Justice* (New York, Russell Sage 1969)

Shklar, Judith *Legalism* (Cambridge, Harvard University Press 1964)

Simon, Sir John *English Sanitary Institutions, Reviewed in their Course of Development, and in Some of Their Political and Social Relations* (London, Johnson 1890, reprinted 1970)

Sisson, C.H. *The Spirit of British Administration, and Some European Comparisons* (London: Faber and Faber 1959)

Smith, Sir Hubert Llewellyn *The Board of Trade* (London, Putnam's Sons 1928)

Snagge, Thomas William *The Evolution of the County Court* (London, W. Clowes and Sons 1904)

Spring, David *The English Landed Estate in the Nineteenth Century: Its Administration* (Baltimore, Johns Hopkins University Press 1963)

Tapping, Thomas *A Treatise on the High Peak Mineral Customs and Mineral Court Act, 1851* (London, Shaw and Sons 1851)

- *A Treatise on the Derbyshire Mining Customs and Mineral Court Act, 1852* (London, Shaw and Sons 1854)

- *The Factory Acts* (London, Shaw and Sons 1855)

- *An Exposition of the Statutes (5 & 6 Vict., c 99 & 23 & 24 Vict., c 151), passed for the regulation of ore-mines, collieries and ironstone mines* (London, Stevens 1861)

Taylor, Arthur J. *Laissez-Faire and State Intervention in Nineteenth Century Britain* (London, Macmillan 1972)

Thomas, Maurice Walton *The Early Factory Legislation: A Study in Legislative and Administrative Evolution* (Westport, Ct, Greenwood Press 1970)

Thomas, W.A. *The Provincial Stock Exchanges* (London, Frank Cass 1973)

Thompson, E.P. *The Making of the English Working Class* 2d ed. (Harmondswoth, Penguin 1968)

- *Whigs and Hunters, The Origin of the Black Act* (New York, Pantheon Books 1975)

Thompson, F.M.L. *English Landed Society in the Nineteenth Century* (London, Routledge and Kegan Paul 1963)

Tregoning, J. *The Laws of the Stannaries of Cornwall* (London, Longman, Hurst 1808)

Trevithick Society *Laws of the Stannaries of Cornwall* ed Robert B. Pennington (Cornwall, Headland Printing Co. 1974)

Trilling, Lionel *The Opposing Self: Nine Essays in Criticism* (New York, Viking Press 1955)

Unger, Roberto Mangabeira *Law in Modern Society* (New York, Free Press 1976)

Walford, Frederick *A Summary of the Law of Railways* (London, Blenkarn 1845)

Walker, Peter N. *The Courts of Law: A Guide to Their History and Working* (Newton Abbot, David and Charles 1970)

Walker, R.J. *The English Legal System* 4th ed. (London, Butterworths 1976)

Watson, A. *Society and Legal Change* (Edinburgh, Scottish Academic Press 1977)

Watson, J. Steven *The Reign of George III 1760–1815* (Oxford, Clarendon Press 1960)

Watson, William Henry *The Law of Arbitration and Awards* (London, Sweet, Maxwell and Stevens 1825)

Webb, Beatrice, and Sidney Webb *English Local Government from the Revolution to the Municipal Corporations Act: The Parish and the County* (London, Longmans, Green 1906)

- *English Local Government from the Revolution to the Municipal Corporations Act: The Manor and the Borough* (London, Longmans, Green 1908)

- *English Poor Law History Part II: The Last Hundred Years* (London, Longmans, Green 1929)

Whitmore H. *Principles of Administrative Law* 5th ed. (Sydney, The Law Book Company 1980)

Williams, Gwyn A. *The Merthyr Rising* (London, Croom Helm 1978)

Wordsworth, Charles *The Law of Joint Stock Companies* 3d ed. (London, Saunders and Benning 1842)

ARTICLES AND ESSAYS

Abel, Richard L. 'The Contradictions of Informal Justice' in *The Politics of Informal Justice* ed Richard L. Abel (New York, Academic Press 1982)

A'Beckett, Gilbert Abbott 'Objections to the County Court Bill now before Parliament' *Law Magazine* 25 (1841) 310

Aiken, John R. 'New Netherlands Arbitration in the Seventeenth Century' Arbitration Journal 29 (1974) 145

'Arbitration' *Law Times* 47 (1869) 175

'Arbitration and Compromise' *Law Times* 41 (1865-6)

'The Arbitration Bill' *Law Times* 23 (1854) 50

'The Arbitration Bill' *Law Times* 77 (1884) 419

'Arbitration Bill' *Law Times* 86 (1888-9) 412

'Arbitration Court of the Wakefield Incorporated Law Society' *Law Times* 87 (1889) 292

Arthurs, H.W. 'Alternatives to the Formal Justice System: Reminiscing about the Future' in Canadian Institute for the Administration of Justice *The Cost of Justice* (Toronto, Carswell 1980)

- 'Protection Against Judicial Review' in Canadian Institute for the Administration of Justice *Judicial Review of Administrative Rulings* (Cowansville, PQ, Blais 1983)

- 'Rethinking Administrative Law: A Slightly Dicey Business' *Osgoode Hall Law Journal* 17 (1979) 1

- ' "Without the Law": Courts of Local and Special Jurisdiction in Nineteenth Century England' in *Proceedings of the Sixth British Legal History Conference* (forthcoming)

Bartrip, P.W.J., and P.T. Fenn 'The Conventionalisation of Factory Crime - A Reassessment' *International Journal of Sociology of Law* 8 (1980) 175

Bermann, George A. 'The Scope of Judicial Review in French Administrative Law' *Columbia Journal of Transnational Law* 16 (1977) 195

'A Bill to Establish Tribunals of Commerce' *Law Times* 88 (1889-90) 377

Bonn, Robert L. 'The Predictability of Nonlegalistic Adjudication' *Law and Society Review* 6 (1971-2) 563

Brebner, J. Bartlet 'Laissez Faire and State Intervention in Nineteenth-Century Britain' *Journal of Economic History* 8 supp. VIII (1948) 59

Brooks, Richard O. 'The Legalization of Planning within the Growth of the Administrative State' *Administrative Law Review* 31 (1979) 67

Burdick, Francis Marion 'Contributions of the Law Merchant to the Common Law' in American Association of Law Schools *Select Essays in Anglo-American Legal History* vol. 3 (Boston, Little, Brown 1909)

Carlston, Kenneth S. 'Theory of the Arbitration Process' *Law and Contemporary Problems* 17 (1952) 631

Carson, W.G. 'The Conventionalisation of Early Factory Crime' *International Journal of Sociology of Law* 7 (1979) 37

- 'Early Factory Inspectors and the Viable Class Society – A Rejoinder' *International Journal of Sociology of Law* 8 (1980) 187

- a 'Symbolic and Instrumental Dimensions of Early Factory Legislation: A Case Study in the Social Origins of Criminal Law' in *Crime, Criminology and Public Policy: Essays in Honour of Sir Leon Radzinowics* ed R. Hood (London, Heinemann 1974)

Chaloner W.H. 'William Furnival, H.E. Falk and the Salt Chamber of Commerce, 1815–1889' *Historical Society of Lancashire and Cheshire* 112 (1961) 121

'Chambers of Conciliation' *Solicitor's Journal and Reporter* (1863) 653

Chayes, A. 'The Role of the Judge in Public Law Adjudication' *Harvard Law Review* 89 (1976) 1281

Clark, W. 'Statesmen in Disguise: Reflexions on the History of the Neutrality of the Civil Service' *Historial Journal* 2 (1959) 19

Cohn, E.J. 'Commercial Arbitration and the Rule of Law – A Comparative Study' *University of Toronto Law Journal* 4 (1941–2) 1

Cole, Sanford D. 'The Ancient Tolzey and Pie Poudre Courts of Bristol' *Transactions of Bristol and Gloucestershire Arch. Society* 28 (1905–6) 3

'Commercial Arbitration: Expanding the Judicial Role' *Minnesota Law Review* 52 (1967–8) 1218

'Commissions, Commissioners and the Bar,' *Law Magazine* new series 18 (1853) 117

'County Courts,' *Law Times* 16 (1850–1) 157

'The County Courts Chronicle' quoted in 'County Courts' *Law Magazine* new series 7 (1847) 1

Cross, Arthur Lyon 'The Old English Local Courts and the Movement for Their Reform' *Michigan Law Review* 30 (1931–2) 369

Crump, W.B. 'The Leeds Woollen Industry, 1780–1820' Thoresby Society 36 (1931)

Daintith, Terence 'Public Law and Economic Policy' Journal of Business Law (1974) 9

Denning, Lord Alfred 'The Rule of Law in the Welfare State' in *The Changing Law* (London, Stevens 1953)

Diamond, Stanley 'The Rule of Law versus the Order of Custom' *The Rule of Law* ed R.P. Wolff (New York, Simon & Schuster 1971)

Dicey, A.V. 'The Development of Administrative Law in England' *Law Quarterly Review* 31 (1915) 148

Diver, Colin S. 'Policymaking Paradigms in Administrative Law' *Harvard Law Review* 95 (1981) 393

Donajgrodzki, A.P. ' "Social Police" and the Bureaucratic Elite: A Vision of Order in the Age of Reform' in *Social Control in Nineteenth Century Britain* ed A.P. Donajgrodzki (London, Croom Helm 1977)

Dunkley, Peter 'The "Hungry Forties" and the New Poor Law: A Case Study' *Historical Journal* 17 (1974) 329

Engel, David M. 'Legal Pluralism in an American Community: Perspectives on a Civil Trial Court' *American Bar Foundation Research Journal* (1980) 425

Eisenberg, Melvin Aron 'Private Ordering Through Negotiation: Dispute-Settlement and Rulemaking' *Harvard Law Review* 89 (1975-6) 637

Ellenbogen, G. 'English Arbitration Practice' *Law and Contemporary Problems* 17 (1952) 656

Evan, William M. 'Public and Private Legal Systems' in *Law and Sociology: Exploratory Essays* ed W.M. Evan (New York, Free Press 1962)

'Events of the Quarter' *Law Magazine* 19 (1838) 478

'Extract of a Letter from Lord Brougham to the Earl of Radnor' *Law Magazine and Law Review* 10 (1860-1) 176

Ferguson, Robert 'Legal Ideology and Commercial Interests' *British Journal of Law and Society* 4 (1977) 18

- 'Commercial Dispute Settlement and the Legal System' (unpublished ms, 1980)

- 'The Adjudication of Commercial Disputes and the Legal System in Modern England' *British Journal of Law and Society* 7 (1980) 141

- 'The Horwitz Thesis and Common Law Discourse in England' *Oxford Journal of Legal Studies* 3 (1983) 34

Fitzpatrick, Peter 'Law, Plurality and Underdevelopment' in *Legality, Ideology and the State* ed. D. Sugarman (New York, Academic Press 1982)

- 'Marxism and Legal Pluralism' *Australian Journal of Law and Society* 1 (1983)

'Fourth Annual Report of the Poor Law Commissioners' *Monthly Law Magazine* 4 (1839) 109

Francis, Clinton W. 'The Structure of Judicial Administration and the Development of Contract Law in Seventeenth Century England' *Columbia Law Review* 83 (1983) 35

Frankfurter, Felix 'Foreword to a Discussion of Current Developments in Administrative Law' Yale Law Journal 47 (1937-8) 515

Friedman 'Legal Culture and Social Development' *Law and Society Review* 4 (1969) 29

- 'Law and Social Change in an Urban Environment' *Osgoode Hall Law Journal* 8 (1970) 347

Fuchs, Ralph F. 'Concepts and Policies in Anglo-American Administrative Law Theory' *Yale Law Journal* 47 (1937-8) 538

Fuller, Lon C. 'Human Interaction and the Law' *American Journal of Jurisprudence* 14 (1969) 1

Galanter, Marc 'Justice in Many Rooms: Courts, Private Ordering and Indigenous Law' *Journal of Legal Pluralism* 19 (1981) 1

Goebel, Julius 'King's Law and Local Custom in Seventeenth Century New England' *Columbia Law Review* 31 (1931) 416

Gordon, Robert W. 'Historicism in Legal Scholarship' *Yale Law Journal* 90 (1981) 1017

Grey, Julius H. 'The Ideology of Administrative Law' *Manitoba Law Journal* 13 (1983) 35

Grossman, Joel B., and David M. Trubek, eds. 'Special Issue on Dispute Processing and Civil Litigation' *Law and Society Review* 15 (1980–1) 391

Gutchen, Roberts M. 'Local Improvements and Centralization in Nineteenth-Century England' *Historical Journal* 4 (1961) 85

H.G.M. 'The Commercial Court and Arbitration' *Solicitor's Journal* 107 (1963) 143

Harlow, Carol ' "Public" and "Private" Law: Definition without Distinction' *Modern Law Review* 49 (1980) 241

Harrington, Christine B. 'Delegalization Reform Movements: A Historical Analysis, in *The Politics of Informal Justice* ed R. Abel (New York, Academic Press 1981)

Hay, Douglas 'Property, Authority and the Criminal Law' in *Albion's Fatal Tree: Crime and Society in Eighteenth Century England* ed Douglas Hay (New York, Pantheon Books 1975)

Horrocks, Russell L. 'Alternatives to the Courts in Canada' *Alberta Law Review* 20 (1982) 326

Isaacs, Nathan 'Two Views of Commercial Arbitration' Harvard Law Review 40 (1926–7) 929

Jaffe, Louis L. 'The Effective Limits of the Administrative Process: A Re-evaluation' *Harvard Law Review* 67 (1953–4) 1105

– 'The Illusion of the Ideal Administration' *Harvard Law Review* 86 (1972–3) 1183

Jones, Sabra A. 'Historical Development of Commercial Arbitration in the United States' *Minnesota Law Review* 12 (1927–8) 240

Jones, William Catron 'Three Centuries of Commercial Arbitration in New York: A Brief Survey' *Washington University Law Quarterly* (1956) 193

Jowell, Jeffrey 'The Legal Control of Administrative Discretion' *Public Law* (1973) 178

– 'The Limits of Law in Urban Planning' *Current Legal Problems* 30 (1977) 63

'A Judge on Tribunals of Commerce' *Chamber of Commerce Chronicle* (1 June 1874) 1

'The Judgeship of the Courts of Requests,' *Law Times* 5 (1845) 46

'Judicial Supervision of Commercial Arbitration' *Georgetown Law Journal* 53 (1964–5) 1079

'The Juridical Society' *Law Magazine and Law Review* 3 (1857) 1

'Juries Versus Arbitrators' *Law Times* 41 (1865–6) 42

Keane, D.D. 'The Small Debts Act' *Law Magazine* 36 (1846) 189

Kidder, Robert L. 'Toward an Integrated Theory of Imposed Law' in *The Imposition of Law* ed B.E. Harrell-Bond and S.B. Burman (New York, Academic Press 1979)

Kronstein, Heinrich 'Business Arbitration – Instrument of Private Government' *Yale Law Journal* 54 (1944–5) 36

– 'Arbitration Is Power' *New York University Law Review* 38 (1963) 661

Landes, D. 'The Structure of Enterprise in the Nineteenth Century – The Cases of Britain and Germany' *Rapport du XIe Congrès Internationale de Sciences Historiques* (1960) 107

Landes, William M. and Richard A. Posner 'Adjudication as a Private Good' *Journal of Legal Studies* 8 (1979) 235

– eds. 'Symposium: Private Alternatives to the Judicial Process' *Journal of Legal Studies* 8 (1979) 231

Laughlin, Martin 'Procedural Fairness: A Study of the Crisis in Administrative Law Theory' *University of Toronto Law Journal* 28 (1978) 215

'The Law and the Lawyers' *Law Times* 22 (1853–4)

'The Law of Arbitration' *Law Review* 10 (1849) 225

'The Law of Arbitrations. Arbitration Bill' *Law Times* 77 (1884) 295, 307

'The Laws of Arbitration' *Law Times* 48 (1869–70) 449

Lederman, W.R. 'The Independence of the Judiciary' *Canadian Bar Review* 34 (1956) 769

'Legal Topics of the Week' *Law Times* 40 (1864–5) 517

Letter *Solicitor's Journal and Reporter* 7 (1863) 662

Letter *Law Magazine and Law Review* 16 (1863) 181

Letter to the Editor *Legal Observer* 4 (1832) 377

'Letters to the Lord Chancellor (from a Barrister)' *Legal Observer* 1 (1830–1) 145

'Local Courts' *Law Times* 6 (1845–6) 385

'Local Courts' *Law Times* 7 (1846) 195

'Local Courts of Record' *Law Magazine and Law Review* 18 (1864) 219

Macassey, Sir Lynden 'International Commercial Arbitration – Its Origin, Development and Importance' *American Bar Association Journal* 24 (1938) 518

McAuslan, Patrick 'Administrative Law and Administrative Theory: The Dismal Performance of Administrative Lawyers' *Cambrian Law Review* 9 (1978) 40

- 'Administrative Law, Collective Consumption and Judicial Policy' *Modern Law Review* 46 (1983) 1

McCord, N. 'The Government of Tyneside 1800–1850' *Transactions of the Royal Historical Society* 5th ser 20 (1969) 5

MacDonagh, Oliver 'Delegated Legislation and Administrative Discretions in the 1850's: A Particular Study' *Victorian Studies* 2 (1958) 29

- 'The Nineteenth Century Revolution in Government: A Reappraisal' *Historical Journal* 1 (1958) 52

- 'Coal Mines Regulation: The First Decade, 1842–1852' in *Ideas and Institutions of Victorian England* ed R. Robson (London, Bell and Sons 1967)

'The Machinery of Private Bills' *Law Magazine* 36 (1846) 300

MacKinnon, F.D. 'Origins of Commercial Law' *Law Quarterly Review* 52 (1936) 30

- 'The Origin of the Commercial Court' *Law Quarterly Review* 60 (1944) 324

McLaren, John P.S. 'Nuisance Law and the Industrial Revolution – Some Lessons from Social History' *Oxford Journal of Legal Studies* 3 (1983) 155

Manson, Edward 'The City of London Chamber of Arbitration' *Law Quarterly Review* 9 (1893) 86

Marvel, Howard P. 'Factory Regulation: A Reinterpretation of Early English Experience' *Journal of Law and Economics* 20 (1977) 379

Mentschikoff, Soia 'The Significance of Arbitration – A Preliminary Inquiry' Law and Contemporary Problems 17 (1952) 698

- 'Commercial Arbitration' *Columbia Law Review* 61 (1961) 846

'Mercantile Law' *Law Magazine* 1 (1828–9) 45

'Mercantile Tribunals' *Law Times* 40 (1864–5) 524

Milner, Alan 'Settling Disputes: The Changing Face of English Law' *McGill University Law Journal* 20 (1974) 521

Mitchell, J.D.B. 'The Causes and Effects of the Absence of a System of Public Law in the United Kingdom' *Public Law* (1965) 65

- 'The Ombudsman Fallacy' *Public Law* (1962) 24

Moore, Sally Falk 'Law and Social Change: The Semi-Autonomous Social Field as an Appropriate Subject of Study' *Law and Society Review* 7 (1973) 719

Mullan, David J. 'The Federal Court Act – A Misguided Attempt at Administrative Law Reform *University of Toronto Law Journal* 23 (1973) 14

- 'Reform of Judicial Review of Administrative Action – The Ontario Way' *Osgoode Hall Law Journal* 12 (1974) 125

- 'The Constitutional Position of Canada's Administrative Appeal Tribunals' *Ottawa Law Review* 14 (1982) 239

Murray, Daniel E. 'Arbitration in the Anglo-Saxon and Early Norman Periods' *Arbitration Journal* 16 NS (1961) 193

Murray, Kenric B. 'Commercial Arbitration' *Law Times* 78 (1884–5) 15

'The National Association for the Promotion of Social Science (Meeting in Liverpool, 1858)' *Law Magazine and Law Review* 6 (1858–9) 117

Neuhauser, Paul M. 'Privy Council Regulation of Trade under James I' *Iowa Law Review* 50 (1964–5) 1032

'The New Railway Board' *Law Review* 5 (1846–7) 359

'The New Tribunals for Railway and other Private Bills' *Law Review* 5 (1846–7) 53

Nisbet, John 'The History of the Forest of Dean in Gloucestershire' *English Historical Review* 21 (1906) 445

Odgers, W. Blake 'Changes in Procedure and in the Law of Evidence' in *A Century of Law Reform: Twelve Lectures on the Changes in the Law of England During the Nineteenth Century: Delivered at the Request of the Council of Legal Education* (London, Macmillan 1901)

'Old Local Courts' *Legal Observer* 1 (1830–1) 121

'On the Employment and Charges of Attornies' *Monthly Law Magazine* 4 (1839) 54

'On the Laws for the Relief of the Poor' *Monthly Law Magazine* 2 (1838) 1

Phillips, David 'The Black Country Magistracy 1835–60' *Midland History* 3 1975–6) 161

Pigeon 'Pourquoi un Controle Judiciaire des Organismes Administratifs' in Canadian Institute for the Administration of Justice *Judicial Review of Administrative Rulings* (Cowansville, PQ, Blais 1983)

Plucknett, Theodore F.T. 'Bonhams's Case and Judicial Review' *Harvard Law Review* 40 (1926–7) 30

'The Principles and Law of Banking' *Law Magazine and Law Review* 7 (1859) 84

'The Prospects of the Bar' *Law Magazine* new series 15 (1851) 276

Prosser T. 'Towards a Critical Theory of Public Law' *British Journal of Law and Society* 9 (1982) 1

Rabin, Robert L. 'Administrative Law in Transition: A Discipline in Search of an Organizing Principle' *Northwestern University Law Review* 72 (1977–8) 120

'Railway Accidents and Their Prevention' *Law Magazine and Law Review* 8 (1859–60) 113

'Railway Legislation. Board of Trade' *Law Review* 2 (1845) 1

'Railway Tribunals' *Law Review* 3 (1846) 415

'Recollections of a Deceased Welch Judge' *Law Review* 4 (1846) 46

Reich, Charles A. 'The New Property' *Yale Law Journal* 73 (1964) 733

'Report of the Society for Promoting the Amendment of the Law' *Law Review* 20 (1854) 101

'Review, The Common Law of Kent, or the Customs of Gavelkind' *Law Magazine and Law Review* 6 (1858–9) 333

'Review, Copyhold Enfranchisement' *Law Magazine and Law Review* 6 (1858–9) 274

'Revival of the Law Courts' *Law Times* 14 (1849–50) 558

Robson, William 'Justice and Administrative Law Reconsidered' *Current Legal Problems* 32 (1979) 107

Santos, Boaventura De Sousa 'The Law of the Oppressed: The Construction and Reproduction of Legality in Pasargada' *Law and Society Review* 12 (1977–8) 5

– 'Law and Community: The Changing Nature of State Power in Late Capitalism' *International Journal of Sociology of Law* 8 (1980) 379

Sayre, Paul L. 'Development of Commercial Arbitration Law' *Yale Law Journal* 37 (1927–8) 595

Sirefman, Josef P. 'In Search of a Theory of Arbitration' *Arbitration Journal* 15 (1960) 27

Slatter, Michele 'Norwich's Lost Court' in *Proceedings of the Sixth British Legal History Conference* (forthcoming)

'Small Debts Act: A Letter to the Editor' *Law Times* 7 (1846) 379

Spring, Eileen 'Landowners, Lawyers and Land Law Reform in Nineteenth-Century England' *American Journal of Legal History* 21 (1977) 40

'The State of the Profession' *Law Review* 10 (1849) 148

Stewart, Richard B. 'Regulation, Innovation, and Administrative Law: A Conceptual Framework' *California Law Review* 69 (1981) 1256

Sugarman, David 'Capitalism and Company Law: The British Companies Acts 1825–1856 as Imposed Law' in *The Imposition of Law* ed B.E. Harrell-Bond and S. Burman (New York, Academic Press 1979)

– 'Theory and Practice in Law and History: A Prologue to the Study of the Relationship between Law and Economy from a Socio-historical Perspective' in *Law, State and Society* ed Bob Fryer, Alan Hunt, Doreen McBarnet, and Bert Moorhouse (London, Croom Helm 1981)

– 'Legality, Ideology and the State in England, 1750–1914' in *Legality, Ideology and the State* ed D. Sugarman (New York, Academic Press 1982)

– 'The Legal Boundaries of Liberty: Dicey, Liberalism and Legal Science' *Modern Law Review* 46 (1983)

'Summary' *Law Times* 3 (1844) 211

Sutherland, L. Stuart 'The Law Merchant in England in the Seventeenth and Eighteenth Centuries' *Transactions of the Royal Historical Society* 17 (1934) 149

Taeusch, Carl F. 'Extrajudicial Settlement of Controversies – The Business Man's Opinion: Trial at Law v. Nonjudicial Settlement' *University of Pennsylvania Law Review* 83 (1934–5) 147

Taylor, Martin R. 'The Appearance of Justice: A Sober Second Look at Statutory Tribunals, Despotism, and the Rule in *R.* v *Sussex Justices*' in

Proceedings, Administrative Law Conference (Vancouver, University of British Columbia 1979)

Tedeschi, G. 'Custom and Modern Law' *University of Western Ontario Law Review* 15 (1976) 1

Teetor, Paul R. 'England's Earliest Treatise on the Law Merchant' *American Journal of Legal History* 6 (1962) 178

Teubner, G. 'Substantive and Reflexive Elements in Modern Law' *Law and Society Review* 17 (1983) 239

Thomas, Maurice Walton 'The Origins of Administrative Centralisation' *Current Legal Problems* 3 (1950) 214

Thompson, E.P. 'Time, Work and Industrial Capitalism' *Past and Present* 38 (1967) 56

– 'The Moral Economy of the English Crowd' *Past and Present* 50 (1971) 76

Thompson, George Jarvis 'The Development of the Anglo-American Judicial System' *Cornell Law Quarterly* 17 (1931–2) 9

'A Tribunal of Commerce' *Law Times* 16 (1850–1) 477

'Tribunals of Arbitration' *Law Times* 71 (1881) 358

'Tribunals of Commerce' *Solicitor's Journal and Reporter* 2 (1857–8) 498, 966

'Tribunals of Commerce' *Solicitor's Journal and Reporter* 9 (1865) 1040

'Tribunals of Commerce' *Law Times* 88 (1889–90) 377

'Tribunals of Commerce – Natural Procedure' *Law Review* 15 (1851–2) 93

Untitled *Magistrate* (1849) 240

Untitled *Solicitor's Journal and Reporter* 7 (1863) 637

Verkuil, Paul A. 'The Emerging Concept of Administrative Procedure' *Columbia Law Review* 78 (1978) 258

Wade, H.W.R. 'Administrative Tribunals and Administrative Justice' *Australian Law Journal* 55 (1981) 374

Wexler, Steve 'Discretion: The Unacknowledged Side of Law' *University of Toronto Law Journal* 25 (1975) 120

Willis, John 'The McRuer Report: Lawyers' Values and Civil Servants' Values' *University of Toronto Law* Journal 18 (1968) 351

Willson, F.M.G. 'Ministries and Boards: Some Aspects of Administrative Development since 1832' *Public Administration* 33 (1955) 43

Winder, W.H.D. 'The Courts of Requests' *Law Quarterly Review* 52 (1936) 369

Winkler, J.T. 'Law, State and Economy: The Industry Act 1975 in Context' *British Journal of Law and Society* 2 (1975) 103

Wolaver, Earl S. 'The Historical Background of Commercial Arbitration' *University of Pennsylvania Law Review* 83 (1934–5) 132

MINUTES, REPORTS, AND PROCEEDINGS

Birmingham Chamber of Commerce 'Half-yearly Report, Jan. 25, 1866' in *Birmingham Chamber of Commerce Reports* 1865–87 (Birmingham Central Library)

Bristol Chamber of Commerce *Printed Minutes* 1858, 1866–71

Report of the Committee on Administrative Tribunals and Enquiries (Franks Committee) Cmd. 218 (1957)

Court Baron of the Manor of Sheffield *Proceeding Books* 1830, 1835, 1840 (Sheffield Central Library)

Court Leet Records of the Manor of Manchester vol. 12 (1832–46) (Manchester, Blacklock 1890)

Courts of Conscience and Requests of Bristol *Journals* 1830, 1835, 1840 (Bristol Records Office)

First Report of the Dean Forest Commissioners 1835 (283) XXXVI

Fourth Report of the Dean Forest Commissioners 1835 (610) XXXVI

General Board of Health *Minutes* Nov. 1848–June 1849 (Public Records Office MH 5 / 1)

Reports of the Inspectors of Coal Mines 1854–60 (Public Records Office, POWE 7 / 1 and 7 / 2)

Report of the Joint Select Committee of the House of Lords and the House of Commons on Railway Companies Amalgamation 1872 (364) XIII

Judicial Statistics (1870) *Accounts & Papers* 1871 (442) LXVII

Liverpool Chamber of Commerce *Report of the Special Committee on Mercantile Law Reform & Tribunals of Commerce* (London, Effingham Wilson, Royal Exchange 1852)

Manchester Chamber of Commerce *Minute Book* Feb. 1833–Dec. 1834 (Manchester Public Library)

– *Proceedings* 1849–58, 1858–67

Manchester Commercial Association *Minutes of the Board of Directors* 1845–58 (Manchester Public Library)

Neville and McNamara *A Collection of the Cases Decided under the 2nd Sect. of The Railway and Canal Traffic Act, 1854, and Reports of Cases Decided by the Railway Commissioners under the Regulation of Railways Act, 1873* vol. 1 (London, Henry Sweet 1874)

– *Reports of Cases Decided by the Railway Commissioners under the Regulation of Railways Act, 1873 and the Board of Trade Arbitrations Act, 1874* vol. 2 (London, Henry Sweet 1876)

First Report of the Royal Commission Inquiry into Civil Rights (McRuer Report)

(Toronto, Queen's Printer 1968)

Poor Law Commissioners *Minutes* Jan. 1837 (Public Records Office, MH 1 / 9)

Railway Department of the Board of Trade *Minutes* 14 Aug.–1 Nov. 1844;
Dec. 1844; 1 Jan.–13 Mar. 1853; 1 July 1853–31 Dec. 1855 (Public Records
Office, MT 13 / 1, 13 / 2, 13 / 19, 13 / 20)

*Report of a Meeting Relative to the Abuses of the Hundred and Borough Courts,
1852* (Birmingham Public Library)

Report of the Royal Commission on Assizes and Quarter Sessions (Beeching
Report) Cmnd. 4153 (1966–9)

First Report of the Royal Commission on the Judicature 1868–69 [4130]

Second Report of the Royal Commission on the Judicature 1872 [631] XX

Third Report of the Royal Commission on the Judicature 1874 [957] XXIV

*First Report of the Royal Commission on the Practice and Proceedings of the
Courts of Common Law* 1829 (46) IX

*Second Report of the Royal Commission on the Practice and Proceedings of the
Courts of Common Law* 1830 (123) IX

*Fourth Report of the Royal Commission on the Practice and Proceedings of the
Courts of Common Law* 1831–2 (239) XXV

Fifth Report on the Practice and Proceedings of the Courts of Common Law
1833 (247) XXII

Select Committee on Artisans and Machinery *Reports of Minutes of Evidence*
1824 (51) V

Report of the Select Committee on the State of the Coal Trade 1836 (522) XI

Report of the Select Committee on Tribunals of Commerce 1858 (413) XVI

Report of the Select Committee on Tribunals of Commerce 1871 (409) XII

STATUTES

Arbitration and Commercial Law

Act Concerning Masters and Workmen (Act to consolidate and amend the Laws
relative to the Arbitration of Disputes between Masters and Workmen) (1824) 5
Geo. IV, c 96

Act to enable Barristers appointed to arbitrate between Counties and Boroughs
to submit a Special Case to the Superior Courts (1844) 7 & 8 Vict., c 93

Arbitration Act (Act for determining Differences by Arbitration) (1698) 9 & 10
Wm. III, c 15

Arbitration Act (1889) 52 & 53 Vict., c 49

Bills of Exchange Act (1878) 41 & 42 Vict., c 13

Bills of Exchange Act (1882) 45 & 46 Vict., c 61

Board of Trade Arbitrations Act (1874) 37 & 38 Vict., c 40

Companies Clauses Consolidation Act (1845) 8 & 9 Vict., c 16
Factors Act (1823) 4 Geo. IV, c 83
Factors Act (1825) 6 Geo. IV, c 94
Factors Act (1842) 5 & 6 Vict., c 39
Factors Act (1877) 40 & 41 Vict., c 39
Factors Act (1889) 52 & 53 Vict., c 45
Lands Clauses Consolidation Act (1845) 8 & 9 Vict., c 18
Railways Clauses Consolidation Act (1845) 8 & 9 Vict., c 20
Railways Companies Arbitration Act (1859) 22 & 23 Vict., c 59
Sale of Goods Act (1893) 56 & 57 Vict., c 71
Summary Procedure on Bills of Exchange Act (1855) 18 & 19 Vict., c 67

Courts
Act for ascertaining the Boundaries of the Forest of Dean, and for inquiring into
    the Rights and Privileges claimed by Free Miners of the Hundred of Saint
    Briavels and for other Purposes (1831) 1 & 2 Wm. IV, c 12
Act for regulating the Proceedings in the Courts Baron of the Manors of
    Sheffield and Ecclefall, in the County of York (1808) 48 Geo. III, c 103
Act for the more effectual Administration of Justice in England and Wales (1830)
    11 Geo. IV and 1 Wm. IV, c 70
Act to amend the laws concerning Prisons (1842) 5 & 6 Vict., c 98
Act to Regulate Courts for the Recovery of Small Debts (Act for Regulating the
    Time of the Imprisonment of Debtors imprisoned by Process from Courts
    instituted for the Recovery of Small Debts) (1786) 26 Geo. III, c 38
Administration of Justice Act (1977) c 38
Bankruptcy Act (Act to amend the law of Insolvency, Bankruptcy and Execution)
    (1844) 7 & 8 Vict., c 96
Better Administration of Justice Act (Act for the better Administration of Justice
    in certain Boroughs) (1836) 6 & 7 Wm. IV, c 105
Borough Courts Act (Act for regulating the Proceedings in the Borough Courts
    of England and Wales) (1839) 2 & 3 Vict., c 27
Cirencester Court of Requests Act (1792) 32 Geo. III, c 77
Common Law Procedure Act (1854) 17 & 18 Vict., c 125
County Courts Act (Act for the more easy Recovery of Small Debts and
    Demands in England) (1846) 9 & 10 Vict., c 95
County Courts Extension Act (Act to extend the Act for the more easy Recovery
    of Small Debts and Demands in England) (1850) 13 & 14 Vict., c 61
Courts Act (1971) c 23
Derbyshire Mining Customs and Mineral Courts Act (1852) 15 & 16 Vict., c 163
Exeter Court of Requests Act (Act for the more easy and speedy Recovery of

Small Debts within the City and County of Exeter) (1841) 4 & 5 Vict., c 123
High Peak Mining Customs and Mineral Courts Act (1851) 14 & 15 Vict., c 94
Law Amendment Act (Act for the further Amendment of the Law and the better Advancement of Justice) (1833) 3 & 4 Wm. IV, c 42
London Court of Requests Act (1800) 39 & 40 Geo. III, c 104
Small Debts Act (Act for the better securing the Payment of Small Debts) (1845) 8 & 9 Vict., c 127
Stannaries Act (Act to make Provisions for the better and more expeditious Administration of Justice in the Stannaries of Cornwall, and for enlarging the Jurisdiction and Improving the Practice and Proceedings in the Courts of the said Stannaries) (1836) 6 & 7 Wm. IV, c 106
Stannaries Court (Abolition) Act (1896) 59 & 60 Vict., c 45
Summary Proceedings Act (Act to improve the Administration of the law so far as respects summary Proceedings before Justices of the Peace) (1857) 20 & 21 Vict., c 43
Supreme Court of Judicature Act (1873) 36 & 37 Vict., c 66
Supreme Court of Judicature Act (1891) 54 & 55 Vict., c 53
Supreme Court of Judicature (Consolidation) Act (1925) 15 & 16 Geo. V, c 49
Wild Creatures and Forest Laws Act (1971) c 47

Regulation and Administrative Law
An Act to provide for the Conveyance of the Mails by Railways (1838) 1 & 2 Vict., c 98
Coal Mines Act (Act to prohibit the Employment of Women and Girls in Mines and Collieries, to regulate the Employment of Boys, and to make other provisions relating to persons working therein) (1842) 5 & 6 Vict., c 99
Coal Mines Inspection Act (Act for Inspection of Coal Mines in Great Britain) (1850) 13 & 14 Vict., c 100
Coal Mines Inspection Act (Act to amend the law for the Inspection of Coal Mines in Great Britain) (1855) 18 & 19 Vict., c 108
Coal Mines Inspection Act (Act to amend the law relating to coal mines) (1862) 25 & 26 Vict., c 79
Commissioners of Railways Act (Act for constituting Commissioners of Railways) (1846) 9 & 10 Vict., c 105
Commissioners of Railways Repeal Act (Act to repeal the Act for constituting Commissioners of Railways) (1851) 14 & 15 Vict., c 64
Factories Act (Act for the Preservation of the Health and Morals of Apprentices and others employed in Cotton and other Mills and Cotton and other Factories) (1802) 42 Geo. III, c 73
Factories Act (Act to amend an Act of the last Session of Parliament, to make

further Provision for the Regulation of Cotton Mills and Factories, and for the Preservation of the Health of Young Persons employed therein) (1819) 60 Geo. III & 1 Geo. IV, c 5

Factories Act (Act to amend the law relating to the Employment of children in Cotton Mills and Factories) (1829) 10 Geo. IV, c 51

Factories Act (Act to amend the laws relating to Labour in Factories) (1844) 7 & 8 Vict., c 15

Factories Act (Act to make further Provisions for the Regulation of Cotton Mills and Factories, and for the better Preservation of the Health of young Persons employed therein) (1819) 59 Geo. III, c 66

Factories Act (Act to make further Provisions for the Regulation of Cotton Mills and Factories, and for the better Preservation of the Health of young persons employed therein) (1825) 6 Geo IV, c 63

Factories Act (Act to repeal the laws relating to Apprentices and other young persons employed in Cotton Factories and in Cotton Mills, and to make further Provisions in lieu thereof) (1831) 1 & 2 Wm. IV, c 39

Factories Act (Act to regulate the Labour of children and young persons in the Mills and Factories of the United Kingdom) (1833) 3 & 4 Wm. IV, c 103

Factory and Workshop Act (1878) 41 & 42 Vict., c 16

Factory and Workshop Act (1891) 54 & 55 Vict., c 75

Factory and Workshop Act (1895) 58 & 59 Vict., c 37

Inclosure Act (Act for facilitating the Inclosure of Open and Arable Fields in England and Wales) (1836) 6 & 7 Wm. IV, c 115

Inclosure Act (1845) 8 & 9 Vict., c 118

Local Government Act (1858) 21 & 22 Vict., c 98

Municipal Corporations Act (Act to provide for the Regulation of Municipal Corporations in England and Wales) (1835) 5 & 6 Wm. IV, c 76

Poor Law Amendment Act (Act for the Amendment and better Administration of the laws relating to the Poor in England and Wales) (1834) 4 & 5 Wm. IV, c 76

Poor Law Board Act (Act for the Administration of the laws for Relief of the Poor in England) (1847) 10 & 11 Vict., c 109

Public Health Act (1848) 11 & 12 Vict., c 63

Railway and Canal Traffic Act (1854) 17 & 18 Vict., c 31

Railway and Canal Traffic Act (1888) 51 & 52 Vict., c 25

Railways Regulations Act (Act for regulating Railways) (1840) 3 & 4 Vict., c 97

Railways Regulation Act (Act for the better Regulation of Railways, and for the Conveyance of Troops) (1842) 5 & 6 Vict., c 55

Railways Regulation Act (Act to attach certain Conditions to the Construction of future Railways authorized or to be authorized by an Act of the present or succeeding Sessions of Parliament; and for other Purposes in relation to Railways) (1844) 7 & 8 Vict., c 85

Regulation and Inspection of Mines Act (1860) 23 & 24 Vict., c 151

Regulation of Railways Act (1873) 36 & 37 Vict., c 48

Index